"*Planting Design* begins with a compr‍ theories which explain why people have nature. Dr. Mooney then distills this resea‍rch into practical design principles that help us understand how our aesthetic preferences are formed through spatial structure, pattern, color and light. This book validated many of the intuitive decisions I made over years of practice—it will be an interesting read as well as a source of inspiration for both the novice garden designer and the seasoned landscape architect."
—*Andrea Cochran, Andrea Cochran Landscape Architecture*

Planting Design

Landscape designers have long understood the use of plants to provide beauty, aesthetic pleasure and visual stimulation while supporting a broad range of functional goals. However, the potential for plants in the landscape to elicit human involvement and provide mental stimulation and restoration is much less well understood.

This book meshes the art of planting design with an understanding of how humans respond to natural environments. Beginning with an understanding of human needs, preferences and responses to landscape, the author interprets the ways in which an understanding of the human–environment interaction can inform planting design. Many of the principles and techniques that may be used in planting design are beautifully illustrated in full colour with examples by leading landscape architects and designers from the United Kingdom, Europe, North America and Asia, including:

- Andrea Cochran, Andrea Cochran Landscape Architecture, San Francisco, CA
- Design Workshop Inc.
- Richard Hartlage, Land Morphology, Seattle, WA
- Shunmyo Masuno, Japan Landscape Consultants Ltd., Yokohama
- Piet Oudolf, Hummelo, The Netherlands
- Melody Redekop, Vancouver
- Christine Ten Eyck, Ten Eyck Landscape Architects Inc., Austin, TX
- Kongjian Yu, Turenscape Ltd., Beijing.

The book stimulates thought, provides new direction and assists the reader to find their own unique design voice. Because there are many valid processes and intentions for landscape design, the book is not intended to be overly prescriptive. Rather than presenting a strict design method and accompanying set of rules, *Planting Design* provides information, insight and inspiration as a basis for developing the individual designer's own expression in this most challenging of art forms.

Patrick Mooney is an award-winning landscape architect who teaches at the University of British Columbia. He writes, lectures and consults in the areas of restorative landscapes, planting design and multi-functional urban landscapes that support biodiversity.

Planting Design
Connecting People and Place

Patrick Mooney

With collaborations by
Andrea Cochran, Andrea Cochran Landscape
 Architecture, San Francisco, CA
Design Workshop Inc.
Richard Hartlage, Land Morphology,
 Seattle, WA
Shunmyo Masuno, Japan Landscape
 Consultants Ltd., Yokohama
Piet Oudolf, Hummelo, The Netherlands
Melody Redekop, Vancouver
Christine Ten Eyck, Ten Eyck Landscape
 Architects Inc., Austin, TX
Kongjian Yu, Turenscape Ltd., Beijing

Routledge
Taylor & Francis Group

LONDON AND NEW YORK

First published 2020
by Routledge
2 Park Square, Milton Park, Abingdon, Oxon OX14 4RN

and by Routledge
52 Vanderbilt Avenue, New York, NY 10017

Routledge is an imprint of the Taylor & Francis Group, an informa business

© 2020 Patrick Mooney

The right of Patrick Mooney to be identified as author of this work has been asserted by him in accordance with sections 77 and 78 of the Copyright, Designs and Patents Act 1988.

All rights reserved. No part of this book may be reprinted or reproduced or utilised in any form or by any electronic, mechanical, or other means, now known or hereafter invented, including photocopying and recording, or in any information storage or retrieval system, without permission in writing from the publishers.

Trademark notice: Product or corporate names may be trademarks or registered trademarks, and are used only for identification and explanation without intent to infringe.

British Library Cataloguing-in-Publication Data
A catalogue record for this book is available from the British Library

Library of Congress Cataloging-in-Publication Data
A catalog record has been requested for this book

ISBN: 978-1-138-02603-2 (hbk)
ISBN: 978-1-138-02605-6 (pbk)
ISBN: 978-0-429-26285-2 (ebk)

Typeset in Avenir
by Newgen Publishing UK

This book is dedicated to those people to whom plants speak more loudly than is common, who take a special delight in the beauty of nature and plants, and who practise designing with plants, whether they be amateurs or professionals. My hope is that it will stimulate and support you in practising your art form.

Contents

Preface	xi
Acknowledgements	xiii
1. The preferred landscape	1
2. The restorative landscape	32
3. Horticultural considerations in planting design	67
4. Functional and aesthetic criteria in planting design	94
5. Space and place	156
6. The elements of design	213
7. Colour	275
Index	319

Preface

This book attempts to synthesise much of the research on how humans interact with their environments and to apply it to the subject of planting design. Its purpose is to support the creation of designed landscapes that will be better loved, more intensively used and more supportive of the needs and preferences of the people who use them. This application of research and scholarship to designed landscapes does not diminish the critical role of creativity and aesthetic judgement in the design process but rather supports it.

For more than a century, experts from many fields have studied the multiple dimensions of human interactions with the landscape. They have produced a large body of research that illustrates the attraction people have to nature, their preferences for certain landscapes, the way in which they mentally process their environments and the wellbeing that they experience from interaction with natural environments.

The results of this research have been applied to understanding the physiology of the brain and the design of computers, artificial intelligence, interior environments and therapeutic landscapes. However, this body of knowledge is not routinely applied by those who might have the greatest opportunity to use it in their work—landscape architects and designers.

It has been argued that landscape architectural practice must become increasingly knowledge-based if it is to achieve its potential in serving society and the environment (Brown and Corry, 2011). There is now a growing trend within the profession to produce multi-functional landscapes and to measure their performance. Current understanding of how humans interact with their environments is one category of knowledge that can be applied to produce more highly functioning landscapes, and the wellbeing that people receive from interacting with the landscape represents one indicator of landscape performance (Mooney, 2014).

Acknowledgements

I have been extremely fortunate in the support I have received while writing this book. Without the input of my former students, a different book would have been written. They encouraged me to write on planting design and contributed images, critique and professional expertise. Yiwen Ruan contributed the original graphics and also organised the images and permissions used throughout the book. I cannot sufficiently express my gratitude for his years of conscientious support. Melody Redekop wrote the section of Chapter 4 on the design of pollinator habitats. Karin England reviewed my drafts and gave detailed comments.

My collaborators—Allyson Mendenhall of Design Workshop Inc.; Andrea Cochran of Andrea Cochran Landscape Architecture in San Francisco; Melody Redekop, Vancouver, BC; Christine Ten Eyck of Ten Eyck Landscape Architects in Austin, Texas; Kongjian Yu of Turenscape in Beijing; Piet Oudolf in Hummelo, the Netherlands; Richard Hartlage of Land Morphology in Seattle; and Shunmyo Masuno, of Japan Landscape Consultants Ltd. in Yokohama, Japan—are some of the most notable landscape architects and designers practising today. Although in most cases we did not know each other before I began the book, they generously agreed to allow me to use their work, supplied images and narratives of their projects and reviewed my drafts. The work of these collaborators and the photographs of their professional photographers brought the book to life. My thanks to the friends and colleagues who introduced me to the collaborators and supplied their own images for the book. Many of the images in the book were taken from Creative Commons copyright-free sources. My sincere appreciation to those excellent photographers who so generously allow their images to be used in this way. Lastly, I must thank my editor and the editorial assistants at Taylor & Francis for their long-suffering support and patience.

Chapter 1

The preferred landscape

This chapter discusses, first from a historical perspective and then on the basis of environmental psychology and neurobiology, the preferences that people have for landscapes. The history of garden development, the ways in which evolution has formed our preferences for landscapes, why we prefer certain landscape types and configurations and the way we mentally process natural landscapes are discussed. This and the next chapter provide the basis of much of the discussion of planting design in the rest of the book.

PART 1: THE PARADISE GARDEN

The Egyptian garden

The oldest existing garden images, found in Egypt (c.3000 BC), depict fruit trees, vines and vegetables flourishing within walled enclosures (Goode and Lancaster, 1986). These early gardens resulted from the application of life-bringing water to an otherwise barren landscape and often contained a pool for irrigation (G. Jellicoe, S. Jellicoe and Waymark, 1975). Over time, Egyptian gardens combined the utilitarian and the pleasure garden. In this form, the gardens retained their original productive purposes but also became places of shady respite from the desert, complete with decorative water features and abundant flowers. This type of multi-purpose garden was not unique to Egypt. In ancient Egypt, Samaria, Persia and throughout the Roman Empire, the farms, vineyards and hunting parks of the wealthy incorporated ornamental gardens that supported social purposes and provided views over the surrounding countryside.

Such gardens arose, in part, from a conception of an afterlife spent in celestial gardens that was common to many ancient cultures. The ancient Egyptians believed that their gods inhabited a world of gardens and groves, and their tomb paintings portray an afterlife in which the deceased share in this divine landscape. The pharaohs, not content to wait for the hereafter, surrounded their palaces with extensive gardens designed in imitation of the home of their father, the sun god Ra, and Egyptian nobility built themselves gardens intended as earthly reflections of the celestial paradise (Wilkinson, 1998).

The Greeks and Romans

The ancient Greeks, like the Egyptians before them, believed in an eternity spent in a celestial garden that they shared with their gods. The Grecian afterlife, or Elysium, is described in the Aeneid as a paradise of fragrant groves and delightful meadows inhabited by the gods and fallen warriors (Carroll, 2003; Ward Thompson, 2011).

Because the ancient Greeks considered the beauties of nature in their native landscape so highly, they felt little need to embellish nature but were careful to consider "landscape beauty within the site and visible from it" when choosing important sites (Crouch, 1993, p. 59, quoted in Ward Thompson, 2011). For example, Greek temples were commonly set on promontories or in sacred groves found in natural woodlands.

Later, groves were planted around important sites (Barnett, 2007) and the academies of philosophers like Plato (c.428–347 BC) and Epicurus (341–270 BC) were located in both natural groves and designed spaces. The Roman historian Plutarch (c.46–120 AD) described the Greek academies as having beautiful gardens where the philosophers and their students walked in the open while discussing nature and the gods or viewed the landscape from covered colonnades (Penfield, 1961; Thielen and Diller, 2012).

The Roman villa

The third century Greek practice of locating academies in beautiful natural and designed settings and of walking in nature while engaging in discussion was later emulated by the Romans in their villa gardens. The letters of Roman statesman Pliny the Younger (c.61 AD–c.112 AD) make it clear that while his estates were productive enterprises, he treasured the respite from the city, mental restoration and thoughts inspired by the beauty of nature that he experienced there. He wrote:

> You desire to know in what manner I dispose of my day in summer time at my Tuscan villa ... About ten or eleven of the clock ... according as the weather recommends, I betake myself either to the terrace, or the covered portico, and there I meditate and dictate ... From thence I get into my chariot ... and find this changing of the scene preserves and enlivens my attention.   (Book nine, Letter 36)
>
> ... the sylvan solitude with which one is surrounded, and the very silence which is observed on these occasions, strongly incline the mind to meditation.   (Book one, Letter 6)

> True and genuine life! Pleasing and honourable repose! More, perhaps, to be desired than the noblest employments! Oh solemn sea and solitary shore, best and most retired scene for contemplation, with how many noble thoughts have you inspired me!   (Book one, Letter 9)
>
> (Gaius Plinius Caecilius Secundus—Pliny II)

The Persian garden

The sacred texts of Judaism, Christianity and Islam depict the Garden of Eden as an earthly paradise created by divine power as the intended home of humanity.

> And out of the ground made the LORD God to grow every tree that is pleasant to the sight and good for food, the tree of life also in the midst of the garden, and the tree of knowledge of good and evil. And a river went out of Eden to water the garden, and from thence it was parted and became four heads.
>
> (King James Bible, Genesis 2:9–10)

In addition to this description of Eden, found in the Torah, Bible and Quran, the Quran refers to paradise as a garden of flowing waters that is the reward of the faithful.

> And give good tidings to those who believe and do righteous deeds that they will have gardens [in Paradise] beneath which rivers flow.
>
> (Quran 2:25)

These sacred texts inspired the Islamic garden and later Christian gardens in Europe.

The Persian garden dates to c.4000 BC and was, like other gardens of the ancient world, a walled garden. Persian hunting parks were known as *pairidaeza*, derived from *pairia*, meaning around, and *daeza* or wall, and are the source of the English word paradise (Carroll, 2003). Very early in its development the Persian garden contained extensive water channels, pools and fountains and many trees (Wilber, 1962).

The classic Persian garden is divided into quadrants by water channels that intersect at the centre of the garden in what is known as the *chahar bagh* or four gardens form. It was this garden tradition that Alexander the Great (356–323 BC) encountered when he conquered the Persian Empire in 331 BC and by the time of his death in 323 BC had transmitted throughout his empire, which stretched from the Nile to the Caspian Sea and from the Balkans to the Himalayas (Carroll, 2003).

The Islamic garden

In 651 AD, the Persian Empire was re-conquered by Muslim Arabs. Under Islamic influence the classic Persian garden became synonymous with paradise. The flowing water channels came to symbolise the four rivers of Eden as described in the Quran, and the *chahar bagh* form became the template for Islamic gardens for the next millennium (Hobhouse, 2004). Muslim Arabs carried this enclosed paradise garden north from Africa to Sicily and Spain and eastward to the Middle East and India, where it was introduced in the form of the Mughal garden in the sixteenth century. In its various incarnations, the Islamic garden incorporated two seemingly contradictory philosophies: Like the earlier Egyptian gardens, it was simultaneously an earthly imitation of an afterlife paradise and a lush oasis intended to delight the senses and facilitate worldly pleasures (Carroll, 2003).

◄ Figure 1.0

The thirteenth-century Court of the Lions at the Alhambra Palace in Grenada, Spain, exhibits the classic *chahar bagh* form of the Islamic garden. The gravel paved areas between the water channels would have been filled with flowers under the care of its Moorish builders.
Source: © Jean-Pierre Dalbéra | Flickr (used under the Creative Commons licence).

Medieval Europe: Gardens of healing

In later times, the walled Persian gardens became the basis for the medieval cloister garden and the Italian villa (Jellicoe et al., 1975). Enclosed gardens similar to the Persian gardens were first built in Europe during in the Middle Ages (c.500–1500 AD). Many of these were monastic cloisters in which the garden enclosure was formed by the walls of the monastery and by covered arcades that provided views into the garden from a protected space (Gerlach-Spriggs, Kaufman and Warner, 1998). Very little is known of the planting of these gardens, and in England many cloisters probably contained little more than grass and trees (Goode and Lancaster, 1986).

Like the Persian garden, the cloister garden symbolised the paradise of holy writ. The garden was divided into quadrants by two paths, symbolising the four rivers of Eden, that intersected at a well or fountain at the centre of the garden (Figure 1.1). Early Christians believed that by virtue of being baptised they could return to Eden, and this garden form symbolised their return to grace (Carroll, 2003).

Many of these cloister gardens were adjacent to the monastery infirmary and were also used as places of healing. Saint Bernard (1090–1153) described the purpose of the courtyard garden of his monastery at Clairvaux, France, and the benefits it gave the convalescent.

> Within this enclosure, many and various trees, prolific with every sort of fruit, make a veritable grove, which lying next to the cells of those who are ill, lightens with no little solace the infirmities of the brethren, while it offers to those who are strolling about a spacious walk, and to those overcome with heat, a sweet place for repose … The lovely green of the herb and tree nourishes his eyes … their immense delights hanging and growing before him … while the air smiles with bright serenity, the earth breathes with fruitfulness and the invalid himself with eyes, ears and nostrils, drinks in the delights of colours, songs and perfumes.
> (Saint Bernard, quoted in Gerlach-Spriggs et al., 1998, p. 9)

The Romantic landscape ideal

In the eighteenth century, the wealthy classes of northern Europe built country estates, similar in purpose to first-century Roman villas. These working farms had extensive designed landscapes and were used by their owners as retreats from city life and for contemplation of the beauties of nature.

In England, Europe and the United States the Romantic philosophic movement played a major role in the development of a new style of landscape design (Rogers, 2007). Major contributors to Romantic thought, like Jean-Jacque Rousseau (1712–1778) and Alexander Pope (1688–1744),

▲ Figure 1.1

The courtyard of Jerónimos Monastery in Lisbon, showing the cruciform paths with a fountain in the centre and cloister walls behind.
Source: Véronique Debord-Lazaro | Flickr (used under the Creative Commons licence).

believed that culture and society corrupted human nature and that contact with nature revealed the essential goodness of human beings by inducing moral thoughts that led to tranquility and wellbeing (Clark, 1943; Neumeyer, 1947). The natural garden that Rousseau described in his novel *Julie* or *La Nouvelle Héloïse* (1761) was widely admired and stimulated a move to a new style of landscape design that imitated nature (Neumeyer, 1947).

The English Romantic garden was the creation of a small group of influential writers, designers and aristocrats. It eschewed formality, instead imitating an idealised nature that was modelled on the Baroque paintings of Claude Lorrain (c.1604–1682), Nicolas Poussin (1594–1665) and Salvatore Rosa (1615–1673). In keeping with the philosophy of Romanticism, these landscapes were intended to evoke the emotions of the visitor. The nature of the desired emotional response and the type of landscape that would produce it was the subject of intense debate. However, taken as a whole, the gardens offered not only the pleasant activities of walking, riding and hunting but also sought to balance complexity and simple beauty so that the overall effect was neither too stimulating nor too dull and uninspiring (Ward Thompson, 2011). In contrast to the formal geometry of the enclosed gardens of the Middle Ages, these large informal estate grounds, or parks as they were called, offered places for contemplation and emotional engagement through imitation of meadow, grove and riverbank that was much like the landscapes of the early Greeks (Gerlach-Spriggs et al., 1998).

City and National Parks

Romantic ideas were also at the root of the City Park and National Park movements. Urban parks, which began in Europe and Britain, spread throughout North America after the completion of Central Park in New York in 1873. The new parks were presented to the public as a means to improve the health, welfare and character of citizens and the tax base of the municipal government (Schuyler, 1986). Frederick Law Olmsted, designer of Central Park and many of the later city parks and park systems in North America, regarded his parks as works of art whose purpose was to serve as an antidote to the detrimental effects of city life. This perspective was influenced by the writings of British Romantic poets and essayists like William Wordsworth, William Gilpin and Sir Uvedale Price and by American transcendentalists like Henry David Thoreau (Scheper, 1989). In his proposal for Fairmount Park in Philadelphia, Olmsted claimed that parks "provide for counteracting the special evils that result from the confinement of life in cities" and help to turn visitors' thoughts "away from the mental contemplation of objects associated with conditions which have produced previous strain or mental fatigue" and that such urban parks supply a "change of scene and suggestion to the mind as shall as much as possible reverse that which is commonly established by the ordinary things of town" (Olmsted, 1871, *Draft Report on Fairmont Park*, in Schuyler, 1986, p. 107).

While the Americans imported the urban park from Europe, the National Park that arose concurrently was an American invention that was later adopted throughout the world. Before such parks could come into being, it was necessary to convince state and federal governments and public sentiment that setting aside large tracts of the national wilderness for conservation and public enjoyment was a worthwhile enterprise. As he had with the development of city parks, Olmsted once again played an important role in convincing lawmakers of the value of wilderness parks. In advocating for the protection of Yosemite Valley and the Mariposa Grove in California he wrote:

> It therefore results that the enjoyment of scenery employs the mind without fatigue and yet exercises it, tranquilizes it and yet enlivens it; and thus, through the influence of the mind over the body, gives the effect of refreshing rest and reinvigoration to the whole system
>
> (Olmsted, 1865)

In this statement, Olmsted is expressing his central belief, inherited from the eighteenth-century Romantics, in the salutary effect of situating the human being in nature—whether that nature is found in the city or in the wilderness. Olmsted understood that city living could result in a kind of mental fatigue that reduced the "capacity to focus" and that urban dwellers could recover this capacity through connection to nature (S. Kaplan, 1995).

This brief and selective review of garden history reveals that disparate cultures have held common conceptions of the human–nature relationship. The notion of an afterlife spent in an ideal landscape has been common to many cultures, and the ideas that natural beauty is to be cherished and that it confers wellbeing have been consistent throughout human history (Ulrich, 1993; Ward Thompson, 2011).

Having created the cultural construct of an afterlife spent in a garden paradise, humans have built for themselves the closest re-creation of that paradise that their means and imaginations allowed. The resulting gardens have facilitated every possible human need and desire. The walled gardens of the ancient Assyrians, Sumerians, Egyptians and Persians offered refuge from the desert, marauding animals and human enemies, but were also pleasure gardens.[1] The Greek philosophers used the natural settings of their academies for discussion, contemplation and learning. First-century Roman villas were refuges from the cares of city life and places of inspiration and restoration in nature. In medieval times, the cloister was a sanctuary and a place of healing. The private parks of eighteenth-century British aristocrats were places of contemplation and emotional and moral uplift, and nineteenth-century city and wilderness parks were intended to benefit the whole person by providing mental restoration.

Through the ages, humans have shown a desire to be in nature and have framed nature as the ideal environment, conducive to mental clarity, tranquility, social interaction and the stimulation of the senses. It seems that the highest conception of the ideal environment that the human mind could conceive has repeatedly been a garden paradise.[2] That this conception has occurred repeatedly throughout human history is indicative of the immense pleasure, engagement and benefits that humans derive from contact with natural settings.

PART 2: THE PERSON IN THE LANDSCAPE

The idea that experiencing beautiful natural settings uplifts the human spirit has been so compelling that it has been transmitted effortlessly between cultures and has arisen spontaneously in diverse times and places. It may now be said that modern scholars and researchers have reaffirmed what earlier civilisations understood through intuition, observation and experience. Numerous studies have demonstrated the high preference that people have for viewing and being in natural environments and the many benefits they derive from contact with nature.

The psycho-evolutionary perspective

To understand why this may be so, consider our evolutionary history. Scientists believe that our earliest ancestor appeared about 45 million years ago and that our line of the hominids separated from other primates about 5 million years ago. Modern humans, living as hunter-gatherers, appeared on the African savannah some 250,000 years ago and initiated rapid technological and cultural advancement (Heerwagen and Orians, 1993; Paivio, 2014). Only about 5,000 years ago, humans in several regions of the world were able produce the food surpluses that allowed some members of society to become specialists and enabled the development of complex urban societies (Childe, 1950; Smith, 2002). Thus, we can say that for 99 per cent of evolutionary history, our forbears have been hunter-gatherers living in intimate connection with the natural environment, and only recently have we become specialised urban dwellers (Wilson, 2007).

Many researchers posit that in the relatively brief span of time since humans ceased being nomads, it is inconceivable that ways of perceiving and thinking developed over millions of years should be extinguished. Although most humans are now urbanites (Heilig, 2012), scholars from different fields consider that today's sophisticated, technologically advanced urban dweller retains the mind of a nomadic hunter-gatherer (R. Kaplan and S. Kaplan, 1982; Wilson, 1984; Appleton, 1996). They speculate that just as our bodies have been shaped by evolutionary selection, so too our brains, behaviours and the nature of our interactions with the natural environment have been heavily influenced by our evolutionary heritage (Berrill, 1962; S. Kaplan, 1972; Öhman and Mineka, 2001). In particular, many researchers believe that our aesthetic response to landscape is a part of our genetic makeup (Wilson, 1984; S. Kaplan, 1979; Appleton, 1996; Heerwagen and Hase, 2001) and that the human mind is comprised of sets of thinking skills that were developed over the course of human evolution as adaptations to our environment (Gerrans, 2002). They study human cognition by attempting to understand how these evolutionary thinking mechanisms function within the human organism today (Buss, 1995).

The biophilia hypothesis

For early humans, quickly assessing and responding to challenges in the environment would have aided survival, while failure to do so might have been fatal. Those individuals who were more likely to survive were also more likely to pass on their genes. Over time, a genetic type that possessed superior adaptations to their environment would have developed and spread within human population (Wilson, 2007).

In 1984, the idea that human emotion and cognition are influenced by evolution was given broader significance by Harvard University biologist Edward O. Wilson. His book *Biophilia* (literally "love of life") was a scientific proposition of a deep human need for connection with the natural environment (Kellert, 1993a) arising from our evolutionary history (Ulrich, 1993). Earlier researchers had cited evolution as effecting human response to nature and our desire and ability to acquire, process, use and remember information about our environment (S. Kaplan and R. Kaplan, 1982). *Biophilia* proclaimed that our evolutionary heritage continues to influence "aesthetic, intellectual, cognitive, and even spiritual meaning and satisfaction" in human beings (Kellert, 1993b, p. 42).

Biophilic writings discuss the human attraction to birds and animals and our biophilic relation to the landscape. Some authors propose that, as hunter-gatherers, the properties of the physical environment would have so strongly influenced human risk and survival that humans would have evolved to seek safe environments and that this tendency continues to influence our preferences for nature (Ulrich, 1993).

Prospect refuge theory

In *The Experience of Landscape* (1974), British geographer Jay Appleton put forward a theory of aesthetics which he called prospect refuge theory. His hypothesis related our visual assessment of landscape and environmental aesthetics to the early humans' need to seek information in the landscape safely (Heerwagen and Orians, 1993). He argued that the positive emotional response that people get from viewing a landscape is a result of their positive assessment of safety in the landscape and that this feeling is at the root of the aesthetic pleasure that people get from viewing and being in the landscape.

Appleton began with the proposition that human beings interpret their environment spontaneously, in an unpremeditated effort to meet survival needs, and that they experience a positive emotional response when they perceive that the landscape will meet their needs and suffer anxiety when support for survival is not found. He imagined that the hunter-gatherer needed to get close to prey without being seen; to be located in the landscape so that if pursued, they could reach safety before being overtaken; and that when engaged in activities which limit watchfulness, such as building fires or eating, needed to be in a location where they would not be seen by an enemy or where they would see the attacker first so that they would have time to escape to safety.

Appleton advanced the hypothesis that when the landscape provides "the ability to see without being seen" (Appleton, 1996, p. 66) it allows people to feel safe in the landscape, allows them to relax and is accompanied by feelings of pleasure. In this, Appleton agrees with environmental psychologists, who also maintain that landscapes that are experienced as providing a sense of security will be seen as aesthetic (Brown, Keane and S. Kaplan, 1986).

Appleton identified three conditions in the landscape that would provide the condition of "seeing without being seen". These he named *prospect*, *refuge* and *hazard*. Prospect is present when the observer has the ability to extend an unobstructed view into the landscape. Refuge occurs when the landscape provides the opportunity to hide. Since prospect and refuge are based on seeking safety, for prospect and refuge to be experienced, threat must also be present in the landscape. Threats that are derived from the configuration of landscape are called hazards. A hazard is any real or imagined threat to one's safety. It might be the presence of a predator in the landscape or "simply a feeling of exposure to an unidentifiable or even imaginary and perhaps non-existent threat" (Appleton, 1996, p. 74). Even when no real threat is present in the landscape, objects in the landscape or their arrangement may symbolise hazard. People enjoy hazard in the landscape and seek it out where it can be experienced without actual danger. For example, standing in the spray of a waterfall adds excitement to our experience of landscape without any actual danger. A tree or overhanging rock may actually protect us from the elements or it may give us the sense of being enclosed and protected against some imaginary threat and thus constitute a refuge. Both natural and man-made objects in the landscape can act as symbols of prospect, refuge and hazard.

Exploring

As well as avoiding predators and enemies, our early ancestors needed to satisfy their basic biological needs for food, water and shelter (Gärling and Golledge, 2000). This required them to evaluate the landscape, or objects in the landscape, for the things that it had to offer them, which are collectively referred to as *affordances* (S. Kaplan, 1988). Finding affordances was important to survival and required exploration.

For early humans, it was not sufficient that the landscape contained affordances. They needed to be able to safely and easily access those affordances. Places with low ability to extend a view (prospect) and a high number of places to hide (refuge) elicit feelings of fear (Fisher and Nasar, 1992) because enemies would be hard to see and have many places to hide. Such places might cause us to leave rather than explore. Conversely, open woodland with scattered trees and shrubs allows one to extend a view, permits ease of movement and offers some places to hide. In such a landscape, hazard is low, prospect is available and refuge is both present and accessible. This type of landscape would entice us to stay and explore. Thus, the decision to explore and to remain in a landscape long enough to carry out certain activities is dependent on the affordances found in the landscape and the safety with which these might be exploited.

Although Appleton's theory is concerned with natural environments, it reveals that the physical organisation of a space is strongly linked to the feeling of safety and aesthetic satisfaction. Recognising this fact, researchers have applied these same principles to the design of urban environments (see, for example, Luymes and Tamminga, 1995; Hagerhall, 2000).

Humans: The knowledge-seeking organism

Environmental psychologists Stephen and Rachel Kaplan are among those researchers who believe that the way we perceive and think and the biases we have regarding information are all part of our evolutionary inheritance

(S. Kaplan, 1972). They understand humans as "knowledge seeking organisms" who have a deep need to understand their environment. This compulsion stems from the fact that humans use environmental information to recognise and evaluate their environment, to predict what is likely to happen and then to act (S. Kaplan and R. Kaplan, 1982). In what has become known as the Information Processing Model, the Kaplans argue that humans are predisposed to understand their environment and be involved in it.

Preference

A habitat is an area of land containing resources, like food and shelter, and conditions, like temperature and rainfall, that allow a species to survive and reproduce (Morrison, Marcot and Mannan, 2006). Poor habitat, having inadequate affordances, will limit the individual's chances of surviving and passing on genes. Therefore, natural selection would have favoured individuals who were able to select and occupy optimum habitats, and this trait would have entered the general population.

In modern society, many affordances have ceased to have survival value, yet people continue to prefer them, seek them out and appreciate them aesthetically (S. Kaplan, 1987; Appleton, 1996). For example, many studies have demonstrated that people prefer natural settings that have water, green vegetation and flowers, as these elements signal the likelihood of finding food and water and support human survival (Ulrich, 1993). From this perspective, human preferences for landscape are understood as the outcome of a complex process that includes perceiving and analysing environments and reacting to them in terms of their potential usefulness.

This is not to say that individuals do not differ in their preferences for landscapes. Researchers of human–environment interaction do not claim that people are "hard-wired" to respond to environments in certain ways. Instead, they contend that our evolutionary history has given us a set of biases toward landscapes that can be greatly influenced by social and environmental learning (Heerwagen and Orians, 1993; Ulrich, 1993).

Researchers are consistent in telling us that the similarities between people, and even across cultures, are more significant than the variations between individuals. While individuals may vary in their aesthetic sensibilities towards landscapes, people have much in common. Reviews of environmental preference research have found that humans consistently prefer views of nature to those of the built environment, that views of the built environment that lack vegetation and water are least preferred (Ulrich et al., 1991) and that scenes that possess high natural content—specifically water, trees and foliage—are strongly preferred (S. Kaplan, 1987). This preference for natural landscapes applies to the continuum of landscape from cities to wilderness (Ulrich, 1993).

In addition to individual differences in aesthetic preference that arise though personal experience or cultural differences, we know that different people pursue different purposes in the landscape and that the same individual will pursue different purposes at different times. However, people's responses to their environments are not so idiosyncratic that is not possible to design environments that meet the needs of the general population. One reason for this is that people have two overarching purposes at all times: To make sense of, or understand, their environment and to explore and be involved in it (S. Kaplan and R. Kaplan, 1982).

The Information Processing Model: Understanding and involvement

Understanding refers to people's need to comprehend their surroundings, to know where they are located and to find their way. It is supported by anything that makes the environment easier to comprehend, map and summarise. Researchers believe that one of the most important affordances that people seek is wayfinding—that is, to discern a path that will permit them to move through the landscape (S. Kaplan, 1979; Appleton, 1996). In finding their way through the environment, people use a mental image of the environment known as a cognitive map (Darken and Peterson, 2002). It is formed in the act of exploring and supports further exploration and involvement.

According to the Information Processing Model, developed by environmental psychologists Rachel and Stephen Kaplan at the University of Michigan, exploration is done to seek affordances and is the expression of our becoming involved. Involvement is the state of mentally processing our environment and includes visually scanning the landscape for preferred positions or routes through the landscape, forming the cognitive map so that we may find our way back to our starting position, inferring what we will experience as we move through the landscape or simply noticing details in the landscape that attract our attention (S. Kaplan, 1988). Involvement requires exploration in order to discover new affordances and to know more. A landscape that challenges us to investigate is one in which we will probably become involved.

The Information Processing Model posits that understanding and involvement are universal human purposes and that environments that support these purposes will be preferred. To support understanding, a landscape should be easy to form images of and to summarise for oneself. This would include such things as having easily recognised sub-areas and clear views to an intended destination. Additionally, for involvement to occur, the environment must contain numerous possibilities that challenge us to select from the available options how we choose to experience that landscape. Such conditions stimulate us and require conscious mental processing. At the same time, if the landscape has so many possibilities that we cannot easily comprehend it, we will choose not to explore and not to become engaged. In order for a landscape to encourage us to make sense and explore, it must be configured so that we can mentally grasp it and summarise it, yet it must contain multiple possibilities like alternative rest stops, paths and views. It must challenge us without being so complex or confusing that we fail to understand, explore and acquire further understanding. The issue here is having what is required in order to be challenged—and this may be implied rather than real—but not being so challenged that we become frustrated or unable to understand (S. Kaplan, 1988).

The preference matrix

The Kaplans were among the first researchers to investigate how the configuration of the components of a view aid understanding and involvement and influence preference. Their premise for doing this was that much of the information about how a person will be able to function in the landscape is drawn from the spatial arrangement of the landscape. Some of this information helps one to understand the landscape, and other information supports the exploration of the landscape (R. Kaplan, S. Kaplan and Brown, 1989).

By asking people to rate their preference for a series of scenes and then analysing the content of those scenes, the Kaplans developed four indicators of landscape preference. Each indicator describes a particular attribute of a landscape's organisation that is predicted to increase preference. Since their research showed that people react to both the flat two-dimensional picture plane of the scene and to the spatial or three-dimensional arrangement of the landscape, they assigned the four components of preference to either the two-dimensional or the three-dimensional aspect of the scene and to supporting either understanding or involvement (Table 1.0).

Those predictors of preference that are found in the flat two-dimensional picture plane of the landscape offer immediate understanding and support for exploration, which leads to involvement. For example, coherence and complexity refer to the configuration of the picture plane or the two-dimensional array. Coherence supports understanding or making sense, while complexity supports exploration and seeking new knowledge or involvement (R. Kaplan, S. Kaplan and Ryan, 1998). In the three-dimensional or spatial categories of the matrix, the quality of legibility supports understanding, as it reveals that we can find our way into the landscape and out

TABLE 1.0 The landscape preference matrix

Preference Matrix			
Level of Interpretation	Spatial Dimension	Understanding	Involvement
Immediate	2-dimensional	Coherence	Complexity
Predictive	3-dimensional	Legibility	Mystery

Source: Adapted from R. Kaplan and S. Kaplan, 1989.

without getting lost, while mystery encourages exploration and leads to involvement.

Coherence

Coherence is a picture plane, or two-dimensional, component of landscape. It includes anything that allows the viewer to mentally organise the view into patterns of light and dark, or a number of coherent zones. A coherent view is one that is arranged into a few clear zones. Since people can easily hold in mind about five sets of information, a picture plane that is organised into five distinct zones or fewer will be more easily comprehended and will be preferred. Conversely, a scene that has a large number of distinct areas does not support coherence and will not be preferred (R. Kaplan et al., 1998). A coherent scene has a visible order that helps people to make sense of it.

Anything that helps to organise the patterns within the scene increases coherence (R. Kaplan and S. Kaplan, 1989). Repeated elements and patterns, clearly defined regions and unifying textures all enhance coherence. A limited amount of contrast also increases coherence, and scenes that have clear boundaries, which would support coherence, are considered more beautiful (Hadavi, R. Kaplan and Hunter, 2015). Coherence has a relationship to beauty because things are considered to be more beautiful if they are simpler to grasp and require less memory storage (Schmidhuber, 2009).

Complexity

Complexity is the exploration component of the picture plane. It refers to the visual intricacy or diversity within the view or scene. The diversity of elements in a scene increases complexity. More complexity should not be understood as simply the result of the number of things in the landscape but rather its overall visual richness. A more complex environment encourages exploration as it gives increased amounts of information and stimulation. Conversely, a scene with very little happening, such as a large flat patch of grass, is likely to be low in preference due to its lack of complexity (R. Kaplan et al., 1998).

Early research on human preference supported the notion that more complex visual arrays would be more preferred but that with increasing complexity a threshold would be reached at which preference would begin to decline. When this was tested in natural environments, a level of complexity at which preference declined was not found (S. Kaplan, 1987). This may be part of the reason why scenes of high natural content are universally preferred.

A highly coherent landscape that lacks complexity may be boring and not invite engagement and exploration. If complexity overwhelms the scene, coherence will be lost and preference may decline. Scenes with high complexity require a clear structure to maintain coherence (S. Kaplan, 1979). From a design perspective, it seems important that coherence and complexity be balanced if the overall scene is to attract our attention but make sense and ultimately be preferred.

It is important that what draws our attention in the landscape supports our purposes. Otherwise our attention will be focused on landscape elements that have nothing to do with affordances and which distract from our purposes. In such instances, the scene will lack coherence even though the picture plane has a strong, clear structure (S. Kaplan, 1988).

Legibility

Legibility refers to aspects of the landscape that make it memorable and distinct. A legible landscape is one in which people will infer that it supports finding their way into the landscape and being able to return (S. Kaplan, 1988). Distinct components that aid memory support legibility. A small number of distinctive sub-areas within a landscape or a few clear landmarks increase legibility and preference (R. Kaplan et al., 1998). In Figure 1.3, the bridge, building and the specimen pine add distinctiveness and act as landmarks, aiding in finding one's way to and from the destination. The landmarks within a scene are the most important aspects of the view in terms of finding our way through the environment (Tversky, 2000). In Figure 1.2, the clear path around the pond helps to orient us in the landscape, suggesting

▼ Figure 1.2

A scene of high coherence and complexity at Ginkaku-ji Temple in Kyoto. This scene has only three zones. These are the foreground and midground of the pond, with its edge of rocks and evergreen azaleas, the background forest and the sky. For the most part, the three zones do not intrude into each other, which increases the coherence of the entire scene. The intricacy of the pond edge and the forms of the pines add complexity to the view. The scene is coherent yet complex. It is high in natural content and contains water. Both its content and its configuration indicate that the scene will be highly preferred.
Source: BruYYZ | Flickr (used under the Creative Commons licence).

▲ Figure 1.3

Ritsurin Koen, Takamatsu, Japan. The visible paths and landmarks add legibility to the scene. Visitors can explore with confidence knowing that they will easily be able to find their way back to their point of entry.
Source: Ray Swi-hymn | Flickr (used under the Creative Commons licence).

a direction of movement and reaffirming that we are moving towards our destination.

Mystery

Mystery is the quality of the landscape that tells the user that more information will be revealed if they venture further into the landscape. It raises our expectation of receiving new but related information about that landscape (R. Kaplan et al., 1989) and encourages exploration and involvement (Figure 1.4).

Early research by the Kaplans showed two kinds of preferred scenes of natural environments: A trail that disappeared around a bend, or a scene of a sunny clearing that was partially obscured by intruding foliage (R. Kaplan and S. Kaplan, 1989). Since both these scenes were high in mystery, a relationship between mystery and preference was indicated in early research.

Landscapes are contiguous elements that change in their elements and character due to changes in natural conditions such as soil depth or moisture. They also change in response to human actions. Humans alter landscapes to produce more of a particular type of affordance. For example, in an agrarian landscape much of the original landscape has been altered so that food production may be maximised. This modification of landscape in support of particular human needs changes the character and configuration of the landscape. However, since the landscape is contiguous, we do not expect to see great changes in the absence of large influences, whether ecological or human-induced. Thus, people use mystery to infer not only

▲ Figure 1.4

Anything that obscures the view but promises a way forward gives the quality of mystery to a view. Anyone encountering this view can predict that something new will be seen if they continue moving forward.
Source: Jean-Marie Hullot | Flickr (used under the Creative Commons licence).

that they will experience something new if they venture deeper into the landscape but also to predict that they will encounter a landscape that is similar to the landscape in which they began.

Mystery deals with exploring and getting new information. As we move through a landscape, the path we take will determine our experience of that landscape—the sequence with which it reveals itself, the amount of new information we can apply to our cognitive maps and the involvement we have within the landscape.

The quality of mystery in the landscape causes us to set up expectations about what we will encounter in that landscape. From a landscape design perspective, this raises the question: Are we more, or less, satisfied if our predictions come true as we venture into the landscape?

Curiosity models: Seeking knowledge and pleasure

In the field of psychology, *curiosity models* are used to explain what motivates people to explore either a cognitive or a real-world domain. The curiosity-driven or knowledge-seeking model has provided the basis of much of the research in environmental psychology. It posits that human beings have such a strong desire to understand that they will accept a poor answer to avoid uncertainty. By seeking out and discovering new knowledge, the uncertainty and anxiety associated with not knowing are removed.

The other widely held curiosity model is what is known as the *optimal arousal* or *pleasure-seeking model*. Proponents of this model argue that humans are stimulus-seeking creatures who are easily bored. They seek to offset boredom by becoming mentally or emotionally stimulated. In this view of human–environment interaction, people explore not to resolve confusion or seek affordances but because seeing, experiencing or learning something new is pleasurable. The model states that if the stimulus provided by the environment is lacking or is too extreme or unusual, it will trigger avoidance behaviour. That is, people seek to find pleasure in their environment, but if finding it is too difficult, they will look elsewhere.

The two models have much in common. In both, innate human curiosity or the desire to see, understand or experience induces exploration that is done to receive a reward (Litman, 2005). In what I have called the knowledge-seeking model, the reward is the removal of uncertainty and with it a change in emotional state from one of anxiety to one of clarity, calmness and the ability to plan a course of action. In the pleasure-seeking model, the reward for exploration is the replacement of boredom with interest and aesthetic stimulus. Underlying both models is the self-satisfaction of achieving a preferred emotional state through acting.

Experimental psychologist Jordan Litman (2005) used current research in neurobiology to provide the rationale for a new curiosity model that combined the knowledge-seeking and pleasure-seeking models. The underlying mechanisms that drive both knowledge-seeking and pleasure-seeking behaviour, he tells us, are *wanting* and *liking*. Wanting and liking are neurobiological systems that interact but which may change independently. These two systems operate in the subconscious and activate exploration, emotions and pleasurable feelings (Berridge, 2009).

If we were to apply the concepts of wanting and liking to food, wanting would equate to appetite or hunger—the need to eat. Liking would equate to the pleasure derived from the taste of the food. Wanting is related to biological need, while liking is not. Understanding the neural systems of wanting and liking enables us to make a distinction between what motivates us and the affective or emotional response that follows. As regards the experience of landscape, we could equate wanting with the felt need to acquire knowledge to support biological needs, while liking would relate to the pleasure or emotional effect experienced in acquiring that knowledge.

Eighteenth-century philosopher Immanuel Kant put forward the idea that aesthetic appreciation is disinterested. By this he meant that we derive aesthetic pleasure from an object because it gives us pleasure and not because it has a useful purpose. The aesthetic experience removes self-interest, and the aesthetic landscape is not sought out for its affordances, except in as much as the aesthetic experience is an affordance (Bell, 2012). For example, viewing a sunset has no utilitarian purpose, yet it produces a strong and consistent aesthetic response in humans. Research has indicated that aesthetic appreciation is the result of receiving something that we like a great deal but which was not greatly wanted (Chatterjee, 2004).

Most environmental psychologists adhere to the knowledge-seeking curiosity model and consider aesthetic pleasure as simply the pleasure that comes from the clarity of knowing. They argue that what we understand, we find aesthetic. However, the pleasure-seeking curiosity model suggests that the aesthetic response of humans to a landscape composition or the pleasure we get from listening to music may be examples of preferences that are not now, and never have been, related to our survival.

It has been suggested that music evolved from the sing-song voices that mothers use to soothe their babies. While this would explain why the creation of music was adaptive to survival, it would not explain why adults continue to appreciate music (Balter, 2004). Most people would agree that we listen to music for the pleasure and emotional stimulation it gives us. Cognitive scientist Steven Pinker (1998) suggests that the invention and use of music was a byproduct of evolution that was never essential to human survival. He considers music to be a non-adaptive behaviour that stimulates other human adaptations such as the brain's ability to organise sound into patterns, or the cadences of speech and the natural rhythms of walking and running (Balter, 2004). Failure to recognise that things like art, music and landscape appreciation are important to quality of life but unnecessary for survival may limit our understanding of the human–environment interaction and ability to design for the human experience.

Prospect refuge theory and the Information Processing Model are rooted in the need to acquire information in order to satisfy biological needs. Human interaction with the landscape is considered to be need-driven and functional. Questions of seeking beauty and aesthetic satisfaction were subsumed into the discussion of preference. Only recently has beauty been considered to be an affordance, since it gives pleasure (Grahn and Stigsdotter, 2010). But seeking beauty in the landscape or emotional arousal through music is not tied to our need for survival. Rather than it being the case that even when affordances have lost their survival value we still seek them out, it seems that the same mechanisms that aided survival have left corollary neural networks that stimulate the pleasure centres of the brain. The implication of this for planting design is that in addition to seeking clarity about their situations, humans seek to become involved with their environments because they find it highly pleasurable. This raises the question: How can we design to maximise that pleasure?

Sequential experience and human expectations

In 1938, the Russian composer Igor Stravinsky gave a series of lectures at Yale University that were subsequently published as *The Poetics of Music*. In *The Poetics*, Stravinsky tells us that when people actively listen to music, they give themselves "up to the working out of the music—participating in and following it step by step" (Stravinsky, 1970, p. 181). The opening bars of a musical composition set up in the listeners an expectation of what will follow, "For the phenomenon of music is nothing other than a phenomenon of speculation" (Stravinsky, 1970, p. 35). For Stravinsky, music was a form of communication in which the listener became a "partner" or co-composer, ultimately identifying with the composer. He wrote: "The listener reacts and becomes a partner in the game, initiated by the creator. Nothing less, nothing more. The partner is free to accept or to refuse participation in the game" (Stravinsky, 1970, p. 177).

Stravinsky tells us that if the listener's expectation is always met, she or he will become bored and refuse to participate. If the listener's expectations are seldom met, this will also lead to the listener "turning off" and failing to participate in the game. What is needed in order to keep the listener involved is a combination of meeting their expectations and giving them pleasing surprises.

Many pieces of music have defined patterns of repetition that help to meet the listener's expectations. Blues songs follow a progression of three chords in a prescribed twelve-bar sequence. The first movement of a classical symphony uses the melodic theme in an introduction, development and recapitulation structure. In Stravinsky's understanding of how we listen to music, the patterns we recognise within a musical composition help us to form our expectations and to stay engaged with the music.

This understanding of how we listen to music has significant implications for how we experience landscape. To experience a piece of art, we must be actively engaged with the art and experience it sequentially (Schmidhuber, 2009). If this is true of the human visually scanning a painting on a wall, how much truer is it for a piece of music or a landscape?

> The plastic arts are presented to us in space; we receive an over-all impression before we discover details little by little and at our leisure. But music is based on temporal succession and alertness of memory. Consequently, music is a chronologic art, as painting is a spatial art. Music presupposes before all else a certain organization in time, a chronology ...
> (Stravinsky, 1970, p. 35)

What Stravinsky wrote about how music is experienced also applies to the experience of landscape. Re-read the above quote substituting the word landscape for music. Is not the experience of landscape also based on temporal succession and the alertness of memory? Unlike paintings, music and landscapes can only reveal themselves to human experience over a period of time. Except in rare instances, a landscape is experienced sequentially, as we physically move through it while actively perceiving and mentally processing it.

Recall that both legibility and mystery in the Kaplans' preference matrix are predictive in that they allow the user to make inferences about what they will encounter in the landscape. Legibility allows the user to predict that they will be able to move through the landscape and return to their starting point. Mystery allows them to predict that more will be revealed as they move into the landscape, but also to make inferences that the landscape that they encounter will probably not be very different in appearance from the one in which they are presently situated. Just like the person listening to the piece of music, the person moving through the landscape sets up expectations that will not always be met. Ideally, in both music and landscape, the person's response to unmet expectations will be something like "I wasn't expecting that, but now that I've heard (seen) it I accept it as an intriguing surprise that causes me to modify my expectations."

The designer of landscape, like the composer of music, must set up and meet the expectations of the listener/user and at the same time must surprise or exceed those expectations in a way that the user/listener can understand, accept and find pleasurable. The landscape designer, like the musical composer, can use patterns and pattern interruption to both meet and surprise the expectations of the user in the landscape. This view is widely held in aesthetic theory, and much of the discussion around explaining the aesthetic experience has dealt with the ideal ratio between the expected and unexpected in the aesthetic object or its balance between order and complexity (Schmidhuber, 2009).

In his 2014 book *Riveted: The Science of Why Jokes Make Us Laugh, Movies Make Us Cry, and Religion Makes Us Feel One with the Universe*, cognitive scientist Jim Davies attempted to give a unified explanation of why people find certain things to be compelling. Among those human characteristics that make things compelling are an attraction to "incongruity, apparent contradictions, novelty and puzzles" (Davies, 2014, p. 10).

▼ Figure 1.5

Pigeons enthusiastically bathing in a London park provide the unexpected delight of a biophilic encounter, rewarding exploration with stimulus and pleasure.
Source: Photo by Patrick Mooney.

Research that tracks people's eye movements as they look at new scenes shows that when a person scans the landscape, their attention is not drawn to what is predictable, but instead to what is incongruous or surprising. As would be predicted by the pleasure-seeking curiosity model, it seems that people seek to be puzzled so that they can solve the problem (Schmidhuber, 2009). The implication for landscape design is that the use of patterns and repetition in the landscape is reassuring and helps to meet people's expectations, and the incongruous will attract their attention and draw them in as they seek to understand the unexpected. If the element that draws our attention has no purpose or function, coherence will be lacking (S. Kaplan, 1988). We will be confounded and are likely to withdraw either mentally or physically, but if the unexpected landscape element ultimately makes sense to us, coherence is maintained and we will remain involved in the landscape experience.

Validating the research

Many research studies have attempted to test and validate these theories of landscape. The preference that people have for natural over built scenes has been well established in multiple research studies (S. Kaplan, 1987; Ulrich et al., 1991). The degree to which the expression of nature dominates a view or environment strongly influences both our preference and the mental restoration we receive from that environment, and many research studies have validated the view that the dominance of nature as opposed to "non-nature" is the critical aspect of human experience in urban open spaces (Grahn and Stigsdotter, 2010). In scenes containing both natural and man-made elements, the natural elements dominate in the most highly preferred scenes (Hadavi et al., 2015).

In tests of the validity of the Information Processing Model, mystery has repeatedly been found to be the strongest predictor of people's preference for natural landscapes (Gimblett, Itami and Fitzgibbon, 1985; R. Kaplan et al., 1989; Gifford, 2007). A review of multiple studies of the Information Processing Model found that for well-designed studies, mystery, coherence and complexity were good predictors of preference. Legibility was found to be a reliable but weaker predictor of preference (Stamps III, 2004). However, it must be said that for all four variables, the results over the years have been inconsistent (Herzog, 1992; Stamps III, 2004). The Kaplans themselves suggest that it is important that having complexity in the landscape not be done at the expense of coherence (S. Kaplan and R. Kaplan, 1982) and have speculated that certain predictors may be effective only in certain types of environments (R. Kaplan et al., 1989).

Researchers have also repeatedly found that certain configurations of landscape that correspond to Appleton's prospect refuge theory were reliable predictors of people's preference for those landscapes. Multiple studies have found that open, park-like settings that allow the users to extend a view or prospect are widely preferred and that people prefer small, enclosed spaces that offer refuge in public spaces. Conversely, a lack of openness in the landscape or the inability to perceive large areas at a glance is related to lack of preference (Hagerhall, 2000; Grahn and Stigsdotter, 2010; Hadavi et al., 2015).

Conclusion

This chapter has presented a number of models, from research, that describe how people experience their environment and what causes them to prefer one landscape to another. In addition to the research discussed here, many researchers have made specific design recommendations derived from their work. These recommendations can seem to be intangible when removed from the context of site and program. Nevertheless, landscape designers and architects need to embrace an evidence-based design if they are to better address the complexity of the person in the landscape, whether it be designing for aesthetic experience or to mitigate the effects of climate change. In an era of multi-functional and performance-based landscape design, the application of factual information derived from scholarly inquiry will assist in achieving better outcomes.

In subsequent chapters, design principles will be drawn from the research models discussed here, and specific planting design recommendations will be made. These will be categorised according to commonly understood aspects of landscape design like spatial structure, colour and texture, and will include recommendations made by the researchers as well as other design recommendations supported by the research but not suggested by the researchers themselves.

Chapter 1 principles

- Throughout history, different cultures have attached importance to the beauty of natural landscapes and believed that contact with nature confers wellbeing. In modern times, researchers have developed environment/behaviour theories confirming the human affinity for nature.
- According to Rachel and Stephen Kaplan's Information Processing Model, people have two overarching purposes at all times: To understand their environment and to be involved with it.
- The Information Processing Model has defined four attributes of preferred landscapes: Coherence, complexity, legibility and mystery. Of these, mystery has repeatedly been found to be the strongest predictor of people's preference for natural landscapes.
- In order for people to make sense of a landscape, to explore it and to become involved with it, it must be easy to understand and yet contain multiple possibilities like alternative rest stops, paths and views.
- Landscapes should not be so challenging or confusing that they frustrate the human need to understand and be involved.

- Anything that helps to organise a view increases coherence. For example, repeated elements and patterns, clearly defined regions and unifying textures all enhance coherence.
- Coherence and complexity need to be balanced if a scene is to be preferred. Scenes with high complexity require a clear structure to maintain coherence.
- It is important that what draws our attention in the landscape supports our needs and wishes. Otherwise we will be focused on landscape elements that confound and confuse us and will withdraw from the landscape.
- People explore their environment to understand it, because a lack of understanding makes them uncomfortable and induces anxiety.
- People also explore landscape for the stimulus of discovering and experiencing something new and pleasurable.
- The landmarks within a scene are the most important aspects of the view in terms of finding our way through the environment.
- Except in rare instances, a landscape is experienced sequentially, as we physically move through it while actively perceiving and mentally processing it. Thus, most landscape design may be considered the act of creating a sequence of experiential spaces.
- A landscape design must set up and meet the expectations of the user and at the same time must exceed those expectations in a way that gives people pleasure, if people are to be involved with that landscape.
- Pattern and repetition in the landscape can help to meet people's expectations.

Notes

1. In the late eighth century BC, the Assyrian King Sargon II coined the term *kirimahu* or pleasure garden (Carroll, 2003).
2. Although the Classical Chinese garden had multiple philosophical origins, the landscape of the gods also played an important role in its development. In Chinese legend, the *Hsien* or Immortals were god-like beings that inhabited an ideal landscape, with its own sun, in vast grottoes beneath the earth or lived on remote mountains and on islands in the eastern sea. These islands were inaccessible to human beings, disappearing if approached. Nevertheless, in the third century BC, the Emperor Ch'in Shih Huang Ti sent an unsuccessful expedition to find the Immortals. Centuries later, the Emperor Han Wu-ti (157–29 BC) hit upon the idea of persuading the Immortals to come to him by re-creating their mountain and island abodes within his extensive gardens. This device has since led to the creation of countless false mountains and Immortals' islands in oriental gardens (Keswick, 1986).

Glossary

Affordance: Any benefit that humans may derive from their environment.

Biophilia: The proposition of a deep human need for connection with the natural environment put forward by Edward O. Wilson in his 1984 book of the same name. He defined it as "the innate tendency to focus on life and lifelike processes" or a tendency to "explore and affiliate with life" (Wilson, 1984, p. 4).

Cognitive map: A mental image of the layout of some portion of one's environment (Darken and Peterson, 2002). It is formed in the act of exploring and supports further exploration and involvement.

Coherence: One of four components of Stephen and Rachel Kaplan's preference matrix. It includes anything that allows the viewer to mentally organise the two-dimensional view into a number of coherent zones. A coherent scene has only a few distinct areas, repeating themes and textures, and limited contrasting textures.

Complexity: One of four components of Stephen and Rachel Kaplan's preference matrix. It refers to the visual intricacy or diversity of visual richness within the view or scene.

Curiosity: The innate human desire to see, understand or experience. It induces exploration that is done to receive a reward (Litman, 2005).

Curiosity-driven model: A curiosity model that hypothesises that humans seek out new knowledge to remove the uncertainty and the anxiety associated with not knowing.

Curiosity models: A model is any representation of the real world. In the field of psychology, curiosity models are used to explain what motivates people to explore either a cognitive or a real-world domain.

Designed landscape: Any landscape that has been modified for human purposes.

Exploration in the landscape: This is done to seek affordances and is the expression of our becoming involved.

Hazard: A component of Appleton's prospect refuge theory; any real or imagined threat to one's safety.

Hunter-gather: A member of a nomadic society that obtains food by hunting or foraging.

Information Processing Model: In this model, developed by environmental psychologists Stephen and Rachel Kaplan, humans are understood as "knowledge seeking organisms" who have a deep need to understand and be involved with their environment. The Kaplans have identified four qualities of landscape configuration—coherence, complexity, legibility and mystery—that aid or support understanding and exploration. The presence of any of these components in the landscape is predicted to increase the preference that people have for that landscape.

Involvement: The state of mentally processing our environment.

Knowledge-seeking model: See *Curiosity-driven model*.

Landscape: This word has many legitimate meanings. Landscape is "an area perceived by people, whose character is the result of the action and interaction of natural and/or human factors" (European Landscape Convention, 2000) and also an area of land having common characteristics. It is used here to mean an area of land having a particular appearance or character. It may vary in size from a region to a small garden and may be designed or largely unmodified by human actions.

Legibility: One of four components of the Kaplans' preference matrix. An increase in legibility refers to aspects of the landscape that make it memorable and distinct, such as defined sub-areas or clear landmarks.

Mystery: The quality of the landscape that tells the user that more information will be revealed if they venture further into the landscape. It is one of four components of Stephen and Rachel Kaplan's preference matrix.

Natural: This term is used here to mean "having high natural content", so a natural scene or environment is not necessarily wilderness but rather a view or place that is high in natural content.

Natural content: This term describes the major components of the landscape—landform, rocks, vegetation and water. Vegetation is in most instances the dominant natural content in the landscape.

Natural environments or **landscapes**: This term should not be understood to mean landscapes that are untouched by human hands, or wilderness. In this book, the term refers to landscapes in which the natural content is dominant. For people in developed nations, research has shown that natural landscapes include wilderness but also include agricultural landscapes, city parks and golf courses (Ulrich, 1993).

Optimal arousal or **pleasure-seeking model**: A curiosity model that understands humans as stimulus-seeking creatures who seek to offset boredom by becoming mentally or emotionally stimulated.

Paradise garden: The concept of an afterlife spent in a garden environment or a garden built to simulate such an afterlife paradise. The Egyptian and Islamic gardens are examples of paradise gardens.

Perception: The process of receiving and interpreting sensory stimulus. Human perception of the landscape involves quickly and unconsciously comprehending the content of a scene or view and assessing the possibilities for action in that landscape (Hadavi et al., 2015).

Pleasure-seeking model: See *Optimal arousal model*.

Prospect: This is present when a person can extend an unobstructed view into the landscape. It is a component of Appleton's prospect refuge theory.

Prospect refuge theory: A theory of aesthetics put forward by British geographer Jay Appleton. In his 1974 book The Experience of Landscape, he hypothesised that a landscape that gives the feeling of seeing without being seen provides a feeling of safety that allows people to relax, and it is accompanied by feelings of pleasure.

Refuge: This occurs when the landscape provides a real or imagined opportunity to hide. It is a component of Appleton's prospect refuge theory.

Romantic philosophy or **Romanticism**: A philosophic and artistic movement that began in Europe in the eighteenth century. It emphasised emotion over reason and intellect and placed a high value on human contact with nature.

Understanding: This refers to the human need to comprehend one's surroundings, to know where one is located in space and to find one's way in the environment. It is supported by anything that makes the environment easier to comprehend, to map and to summarise.

References

Appleton, J. (1996). *The experience of landscape*. New York: Wiley.
Balter, M. (2004). Seeking the key to music. *Science*, 306(5699), 1120–1122.
Barnett, R. (2007). Sacred groves: Sacrifice and the order of nature in ancient Greek landscapes. *Landscape Journal*, 26(2), 252–269.
Bell, S. (2012). *Landscape: Pattern, perception and process*. New York: Routledge.
Berridge, K.C. (2009). "Liking" and "wanting" food rewards: Brain substrates and roles in eating disorders. *Physiology & Behavior*, 97(5), 537–550.
Berrill, N.J. (1962). *Man's emerging mind*. Fawcett Publications.
Brown, R.D., & Corry, R.C. (2011). Evidence-based landscape architecture: The maturing of a profession. *Landscape and Urban Planning*, 100(4), 327–329.
Brown, T., Keane, T., & Kaplan, S. (1986). Aesthetics and management: Bridging the gap. *Landscape and Urban Planning*, 13, 1–10.
Buss, D.M. (1995). Evolutionary psychology: A new paradigm for psychological science. *Psychological Inquiry*, 6(1), 1–30.
Carroll, M. (2003). *Earthly paradises: Ancient gardens in history and archaeology*. Los Angeles, CA: J. Paul Getty Museum.
Chatterjee, A. (2004). Prospects for a cognitive neuroscience of visual aesthetics. *Bulletin of Psychology and the Arts*, 4, 55–60.
Childe, V.G. (1950). The urban revolution. *Town Planning Review*, 21(1), 3.
Clark, H.F. (1943). Eighteenth century Elysiums: The role of "association" in the landscape movement. *Journal of the Warburg and Courtauld Institutes*, 165–189.
Crouch, D.P. (1993). *Water management in ancient Greek cities*. New York: Oxford University Press.

Darken, R.P., & Peterson, B. (2002). Spatial orientation, wayfinding, and representation. In Kay M. Stanney (Ed.), *Handbook of virtual environments* (pp. 493–518). Mahwah, NJ: Lawrence Erlbaum Associates.

Davies, J. (2014). *Riveted: The science of why jokes make us laugh, movies make us cry, and religion makes us feel one with the universe*. New York: Palgrave Macmillan.

European Landscape Convention. (2000). Accessed January 19, 2019 at https://rm.coe.int/1680080621.

Fisher, B.S., & Nasar, J.L. (1992). Fear of crime in relation to three exterior site features: Prospect, refuge, and escape. *Environment and Behavior*, 24(1), 35–65.

Gärling, T., & Golledge, R. (2000). Cognitive mapping and spatial decision making. In R.M. Kitchin & S. Freundschuh (Eds.), *Cognitive mapping: Past, present and future* (pp. 44–65). London: Routledge.

Gerlach-Spriggs, N., Kaufman, R.E., & Warner Jr, S.B. (1998). *Restorative gardens: The healing landscape*. New Haven, CT: Yale University Press.

Gerrans, P. (2002). The theory of mind module in evolutionary psychology. *Biology and Philosophy*, 17(3), 305–321.

Gifford, R. (2007). *Environmental psychology: Principles and practice*. Colville, WA: Optimal Books.

Gimblett, H.R., Itami, R.M., & Fitzgibbon, J.E. (1985). Mystery in an information processing model of landscape preference. *Landscape Journal*, 4(2), 87–95.

Goode, P., & Lancaster, M. (1986). *Oxford companion to gardens*. Oxford: Oxford University Press.

Grahn, P., & Stigsdotter, U.K. (2010). The relation between perceived sensory dimensions of urban green space and stress restoration. *Landscape and Urban Planning*, 94(3), 264–275.

Hadavi, S., Kaplan, R., & Hunter, M.C.R. (2015). Environmental affordances: A practical approach for design of nearby outdoor settings in urban residential areas. *Landscape and Urban Planning*, 134, 19–32.

Hagerhall, C.M. (2000). Clustering predictors of landscape preference in the traditional Swedish cultural landscape: Prospect-refuge, mystery, age and management. *Journal of Environmental Psychology*, 20(1), 83–90.

Heilig, G.K. (2012). *World urbanization prospects: The 2011 revision*. New York: United Nations, Department of Economic and Social Affairs (DESA), Population Division, Population Estimates and Projections Section.

Heerwagen, J., & Hase, B. (2001). Building biophilia: Connecting people to nature in building design. *Environmental Design and Construction*, 3, 30–36.

Heerwagen, J.H., & Orians, G.H. (1993). Humans, habitats, and aesthetics. In S.R. Kellert & E.O. Wilson (Eds.), *The biophilia hypothesis* (pp. 138–172). Washington, DC: Island Press.

Herzog, T.R. (1992). A cognitive analysis of preference for urban spaces. *Journal of Environmental Psychology*, 12(3), 237–248.

Hobhouse, P. (2004). *The gardens of Persia*. San Diego, CA: Kales Press.

Jellicoe, G., Jellicoe, S., & Waymark, J. (1975). *The landscape of man: Shaping the environment from prehistory to the present day*. London: Thames and Hudson.

Kaplan, R., & Kaplan S. (Eds.) (1982). *Humanscape: Environments for people*. Ann Arbor, MI: Ulrichś Books.

Kaplan, R., & Kaplan, S. (1989). *The experience of nature: A psychological perspective*. Cambridge, UK: Cambridge University Press.

Kaplan, R., Kaplan, S., & Brown, T. (1989). Environmental preference: A comparison of four domains of predictors. *Environment and Behavior*, 21(5), 509–530.

Kaplan, R., Kaplan, S., & Ryan, R. (1998). *With people in mind: Design and management of everyday nature*. Washington, DC: Island Press.

Kaplan, S. (1972). The challenge of environmental psychology: A proposal for a new functionalism. *American Psychologist*, 27(2), 140.

Kaplan, S. (1979). Perception and landscape: Conceptions and misconceptions. In *Proceedings of our national landscape* (pp. 241–248). USDA Forest Service General Technical Report PSW-35.

Kaplan, S. (1987). Aesthetics, affect, and cognition: Environmental preference from an evolutionary perspective. *Environment and Behavior*, 19(1), 3–32.

Kaplan, S. (1988). Perception and landscape: Conceptions and misconceptions. *Environmental Aesthetics: Theory, Research, and Application*, 45–55.

Kaplan, S. (1995). The restorative benefits of nature: Toward an integrative framework. *Journal of Environmental Psychology*, 15(3), 169–182.

Kaplan, S., & Kaplan R. (1982). *Cognition and environment*. New York: Praeger.

Kellert, S.R. (1993a). Introduction. In S.R. Kellert & E.O. Wilson (Eds.), *The biophilia hypothesis* (pp. 20–27). Washington, DC: Island Press.

Kellert, S.R. (1993b). The biological basis for human values of nature. In S.R. Kellert & E.O. Wilson (Eds.), *The biophilia hypothesis* (pp. 42–69). Washington, DC: Island Press.

Kellert, S.R., & Wilson, E.O. (Eds.) (1993). *The biophilia hypothesis*. Washington, DC: Island Press.

Keswick, M. (1986). *The Chinese garden: History, art and architecture*. London: Academy Editions.

King James Bible. (2014). *Holy Bible*. Genesis 2:9–0. Accessed November 30, 2014 at www.kingjamesbibleonline.org/book.php?book=Genesis&chapter=2&verse=9.

Litman, J. (2005). Curiosity and the pleasures of learning: Wanting and liking new information. *Cognition & Emotion*, 19(6), 793–814.

Luymes, D.T., & Tamminga, K. (1995). Integrating public safety and use into planning urban greenways. *Landscape and Urban Planning*, 33(1), 391–400.

Mooney, P. (2014). A systematic approach to incorporating multiple ecosystem services in landscape planning and design. *Landscape Journal*, 33(2), 141–171.

Morrison, M.L., Marcot, B., & Mannan, W. (2006). *Wildlife-habitat relationships: Concepts and applications*. Washington, DC: Island Press.

Neumeyer, E.M. (1947). The landscape garden as a symbol in Rousseau, Goethe and Flaubert. *Journal of the History of Ideas*, 187–217.

Öhman, A., & Mineka, S. (2001). Fears, phobias, and preparedness: Toward an evolved module of fear and fear learning. *Psychological Review*, 108(3), 483.

Olmsted, F.L. (1865). Yosemite and the Mariposa Grove: A preliminary report, 1865. In L.M. Dilsaver (2000), *America's national park system: The critical documents*. Lanham, MA: Rowman & Littlefield. Accessed March 7, 2014 at www.cr.nps.gov/history/online_books/anps/anps_1b.htm.

Paivio, A. (2014). *Mind and its evolution: A dual coding theoretical approach*. Hove: Psychology Press.

Penfield, W. (1961). To cultivate the groves of academus. *Canadian Medical Association Journal*, 85(4), 173.

Pinker, S. (1998). *How the mind works*. London: A. Lane.

Pliny II. (n.d.). *The letters of Pliny the younger.* Accessed November 29, 2014 at www.vroma.org/~hwalker/Pliny/PlinyNumbers.html.

Quran 2:25. (n.d.). Accessed November 29, 2014 at http://quran.com/2.

Rogers, E.B. (2007). What is the Romantic landscape? *GHI Bulletin Supplement*, (4), 11–24.

Scheper, G.L. (1989). The reformist vision of Frederick Law Olmsted and the poetics of park design. *New England Quarterly*, 369–402.

Schmidhuber, J. (2009). Driven by compression progress: A simple principle explains essential aspects of subjective beauty, novelty, surprise, interestingness, attention, curiosity, creativity, art, science, music, jokes. In G. Pezzulo, M.V. Butz, O. Sigaud, & G. Baldassarre (Eds.), *Anticipatory behavior in adaptive learning systems: From psychological theories to artificial cognitive systems* (pp. 48–76). Heidelberg: Springer Berlin.

Schuyler, D. (1986). *The new urban landscape: The redefinition of city form in nineteenth-century America.* Baltimore, MD: Johns Hopkins University Press.

Smith, M.E. (2002). The earliest cities. In G. Gmelch & W.P. Zenner (Eds.), *Urban life: Readings in the anthropology of the city* (4th edn.) (pp. 3–19). Long Grove, IL: Waveland Press.

Stamps III, A.E. (2004). Mystery, complexity, legibility and coherence: A meta-analysis. *Journal of Environmental Psychology*, 24(1), 1–16.

Stravinsky, I. (1970). *Poetics of music in the form of six lessons* (Vol. 66). Cambridge, MA: Harvard University Press.

Thielen, A., & Diller, K.R. (2012). Through the lens of attention restoration theory: The pursuit of learning in gardens throughout history. *Undergraduate Research Journal for the Human Sciences*, 11(1).

Tverksy, B. (2000). Levels and structure of spatial knowledge. In R. Kitchin & S. Freundschuh (Eds.), *Cognitive mapping: Past, present, and future* (Vol. 4) (pp. 24–43). London: Routledge.

Ulrich, R.S. (1993). Biophilia, biophobia, and natural landscapes. In S.R. Kellert & E.O. Wilson (Eds.), *The biophilia hypothesis* (pp. 73–137).

Ulrich, R.S., Simons, R.F., Losito, B.D., Fiorito, E., Miles, M.A., & Zelson, M. (1991). Stress recovery during exposure to natural and urban environments. *Journal of Environmental Psychology*, 11(3), 201–230.

Ward Thompson, C. (2011). Linking landscape and health: The recurring theme. *Landscape and Urban Planning*, 99(3), 187–195.

Wilber, D.N. (1962). *Persian gardens and garden pavilions.* Tokyo: Charles E. Tuttle.

Wilkinson, A. (1998). *The garden in ancient Egypt.* London: Rubicon Press.

Wilson, E.O. (1984). *Biophilia.* Cambridge, MA: Harvard University Press.

Wilson, E.O. (2007). Biophilia and the conservation ethic. In D.J. Penn & I. Mysterud (Eds.), *Evolutionary perspectives on environmental problems* (pp. 249–257). New Brunswick, NJ: Transaction.

Additional reading

Kaplan, R., Kaplan, S., & Ryan, R. (1998). *With people in mind: Design and management of everyday nature.* Washington, DC: Island Press.

Kellert, S.R., & Wilson, E.O. (Eds.). (1995). *The biophilia hypothesis.* Washington, DC: Island Press.

Chapter 2

The restorative landscape

Throughout human history, people have understood that contact with landscapes promotes serenity, intellectual inspiration and healing. Today, people living in developed societies still believe that nature supports wellbeing by reducing stress and mental fatigue (van den Berg, Hartig and Staats, 2007). This chapter explores the scientific basis for this belief and examines in greater detail the restorative landscape and wayfinding as a component of that landscape. Restoration is understood as the return to a previous, better condition—as in the restoration of natural habitats and heritage buildings. The restoration that results from contact with nature has been defined as "the process of renewing physical, psychological and social capabilities" (Hartig, 2007, p. 2). People experience an improved emotional state, better cognitive functioning and reduced stress through contact with restorative environments.

Attention Restoration and Stress Recovery Theory

There are two different but complementary models of how the process of engagement with nature achieves these results. In their Attention Restoration Theory (ART), psychologists Stephen and Rachel Kaplan present a model of the human–environment interaction and the attributes of landscape that support restoration (R. Kaplan and S. Kaplan, 1989; S. Kaplan, 1995). They propose that humans have two types of attention: Involuntary attention and voluntary, or directed, attention. Involuntary attention is given spontaneously and without effort of will to such things as unexpected changes in our environment, movement, sounds, bright lights, natural environments and wild animals (S. Kaplan, 1995; Parmentier, 2008). Directed or involuntary attention is the term used to describe the intentional focusing of our thoughts. It requires that we suppress internal and external mental demands so that we may concentrate on a particular purpose like finishing a tax return or finding our way in an unfamiliar city.

Modern urbanites are frequently exposed to prolonged and unrelenting demands that require directed mental attention. Eventually, this can lead to the inability to inhibit internal and external mental demands and focus attention. In this state of directed attention fatigue, people are less able to concentrate, less able to solve problems and more likely to be impulsive, impatient and irritable. Natural environments act as an antidote to this condition because they attract involuntary attention, allowing our inhibitory mechanism to rest and recover, thereby reversing all the negatives associated with directed attention fatigue (R. Kaplan and S. Kaplan, 1989; S. Kaplan, 1995; van den Berg et al., 2007).

Stress Recovery Theory is a second model of environmental restoration that was developed by Roger Ulrich. Stress management is a significant issue because the prolonged experience of stress can lead to a host of physical and emotional disorders. Ulrich's theory presupposes a condition of mental stress, resulting in physiological symptoms such as elevated heartbeat and increased stress hormone levels, together with negative moods and emotions, and predicts that exposure to nature will reduce stress (Ulrich et al., 1991).

Scientific support for the restorative effect of natural environments

Attention Restoration Theory

Research has shown that natural environments are superior to built environments in restoring mental functioning. A study of AIDS caregivers found that the single most powerful factor in avoiding stress-related burnout was "locomotion in nature"—such as walking, running, biking or canoeing—and that the least restorative activity was watching television (Canin, 1991).

Bernadine Cimprich's (1990) study of the psychological health of post-surgery cancer patients revealed that they made considerable improvement after spending twenty minutes three days a week doing restorative activities such as gardening or walking in the woods. Subjects who engaged with nature regularly scored higher on tests of cognitive functioning, were more likely to return to full-time work or start new projects and reported a higher quality of life than those who did not receive the "nature" treatment.

While Cimprich's 1990 study related the frequency and duration of time spent in contact with nature as an influence on restoration, several other studies have found positive effects to be associated with window views of nature, which may be frequent but are generally not prolonged (Moore, 1981; Ulrich, 1984; Talbot and Kaplan, 1991; R. Kaplan, 2001). Researchers found that students whose dormitory windows overlooked natural scenery scored higher on tests of cognitive functioning and self-reported higher functioning in everyday life than those who looked out on views of the built environment (Tennessen and Cimprich, 1995). A study in which apartment dwellers rated views from their apartments and views similar to those from their home found that views of nature were an important influence on the residents' effective functioning, and having trees in the view was associated with feelings of being at peace, while lack of nature in the view from home was associated with feelings of being distracted, which is an indicator of directed attention fatigue (R. Kaplan, 2001). These studies support Attention Restoration Theory by showing that the mental restoration that results from contact with natural environments includes an improved ability to direct attention and feelings of being at peace.

Stress Recovery Theory

In a frequently cited study, Roger Ulrich (1984) found that patients recovering in hospital from gall bladder surgery who looked out of their window at trees used less pain medication, left the hospital sooner and returned less frequently than those who looked out at views of brick walls. A subsequent study exposed subjects to a stressful movie and then measured their recovery from stress using such measures as skin conductance and heart rate. After stress was induced, subjects were shown images of either nature or cities. Those who were shown images of natural environments recovered faster and more completely than those who were exposed to images of the urban environment. In addition, their mood was better. Anger, aggression and fear were significantly lower for the natural group than for the urban group, and positive feelings were significantly higher for subjects who were exposed to images of natural environments. Exposure to views of nature lowered physiological stress levels and brought the subjects to an emotional state that was more positive than their pre-experiment condition (Ulrich et al., 1991).

A Japanese study used the levels of the stress hormone cortisol—found in saliva—blood pressure, pulse and heart rate variability to measure the stress levels of 12 male university students. These measures of stress were taken before and after the students walked for 15 minutes along a prescribed route or sat and watched activity in either a forest or an urban environment. The students who experienced the forest had significantly lower cortisol levels, heart rate and pulse than those subjects who were exposed to urban environments. They also reported feeling calmer and more refreshed by their experience than participants who were subjected to urban conditions. The researchers concluded that exposure to the forest environment was able to reduce people's stress (Park, Tsunetsugu, Kasetani, Kagawa and Miyazaki, 2010).

Synergies between Attention Restoration Theory and Stress Recovery Theory

There is now ample research supporting both Attention Restoration and Stress Recovery Theory. Some researchers consider attentional fatigue to be a result of stress (Ulrich et al., 1991), while others have proposed that directed attention deficit increases vulnerability to stress (S. Kaplan, 1995; Hartig, Evans, Jamner, Davis and Gärling, 2003). As proposed by Stress Recovery Theory, recovery from stress and improved mood can occur very quickly when a person is in a natural environment. Such rapid stress recovery has been measured using both physiological changes and changes in the emotional state of the research subject. Exposure to scenes with natural content and moderate complexity quickly reduces stress, whereas the built environment tends to hinder recovery from stress (Korpela, Ylén, Tyrväinen and Silvennoinen, 2008).

The two theories are based on different explanations of the positive response that people have to nature and measure different restorative outcomes, but both attest to the positive reaction people have to contact with nature (Wolf, Krueger and Rozance, 2014). Attention Restoration Theory is concerned with people's ability to inhibit mental intrusions and direct their attention. Since the fatiguing of the inhibitory mechanism used to direct attention takes place over time, so too its restoration takes place over longer time periods. Researchers have found that contact with nature produces three types of positive effects: Quick but short-lived recovery from stress and mental fatigue; improved recovery from illness or reduced physical illness; and longer-term improvements in wellbeing such as greater happiness, improved cognitive functioning, improved ability to solve problems and reduction in anger and irritability (Velarde, Fry and Tveit, 2007). These findings suggest that restoration from stress and directed attention restoration are complementary in that their positive outcomes occur over shorter and longer time frames, persist for different periods of time and combine to support people's immediate and long-term needs (Hartig et al., 2003).

Engagement, duration, frequency and greenness increase the restorative effect

Engagement

The more involved a person is in the landscape, the greater will be their mental processing of that landscape (Bell, 2012). Researchers tend to agree that our processing of the landscape is an immediate and unconscious act in which we predict how events will unfold in the landscape (Ulrich et al., 1991; S. Kaplan, 1995). When encountering a landscape for the first time, a person will either decide to explore or make the decision to go elsewhere. This first assessment is not based on any conscious rationale and is almost instantaneous. The person must respond favourably to the general impression of the landscape in order to decide to explore. This includes the impression of both safety and aesthetic preference. If the person decides to stay, the next stage in the process is exploration, in order to acquire information or to be stimulated, and this exploration may take a considerable amount of time. In the final stage, the person will decide to remain in the landscape and carry out certain activities on the basis of what they have discovered. This can be a brief visit or it can last a lifetime (Heerwagen and Orians, 1993).

If the first appraisal of the landscape suggests that it has low affordances, the person may choose not to experience that landscape. If they do choose to explore but find making sense and involvement to be difficult, they will probably choose to leave. Conversely, if the first appraisal of the landscape is positive and further exploration proves easy and stimulating, the person will be inclined to spend time in the landscape or to return frequently.

Studies indicate that a higher degree of involvement, or mental engagement, yields greater mental restoration. In a Dutch study, 8 male and 22 female community gardeners were first given a stressful task and then assigned to either 30 minutes of work in the garden or 30 minutes of reading indoors, after which their mood and stress levels were recorded. Those who had gardened returned to their normal stress and mood levels, while those who read retained higher than normal stress levels and exhibited a more negative mood than before being stressed (van den Berg and Custers, 2011).

In a survey of over 4,000 members of the American Horticultural Society, gardeners reported that their greatest satisfaction from gardening was a feeling of peacefulness and tranquility followed by a fascination with nature (R. Kaplan and S. Kaplan, 2005). Gardening is a more active engagement with nature than viewing or walking. The restorative effects found in these two studies may be the result of a higher level of engagement associated with the act of gardening.

◀ Figure 2.0

Pruning spent blossoms in New York City: Even this little gardening activity engages attention and aids restoration. Source: © Grey van der Meer | Flickr (used under the Creative Commons licence, image cropped).

CHAPTER 2 **The restorative landscape**

Duration and frequency

In general, increasing the duration and frequency of contact with natural settings results in higher levels of restoration (R. Kaplan and S. Kaplan, 2005). For example, a Finnish study of the restorative effects of favourite natural places found that the duration and frequency of visits to the natural area were the biggest predictors of the restorative effect. Increasing the frequency of visits from once per week to three times a week and the duration of the visit from thirty minutes to one and a half hours significantly increased the strength of the restorative experience (Korpela et al., 2008).

Greenness

In studies where levels of "greenness" were distinguished, restorative benefits were found more reliably, or were greater, for greener environments. A study of the quality of life of residents of social housing projects in Chicago found that residents of buildings with more trees and grass reported lower levels of fear and less aggression and violent behaviour, including domestic violence. Buildings with higher levels of vegetation had 52 per cent less total crime, 48 per cent less property crime and 56 per cent less violent crime than buildings with low levels of vegetation (Kuo and Sullivan, 2001a). A subsequent study of another Chicago housing project, which used police reports of violent crimes to measure the differences between barren and greener buildings, confirmed the residents' reports in the earlier study (Kuo and Sullivan, 2001b).

A survey of residents in Adelaide, Australia, found that those residents who reported living in greener neighbourhoods were 1.6 times more likely to report good mental health than residents who reported that they lived in neighbourhoods with lower levels of urban nature. The study found that people who reported living in neighbourhoods with greater access to nature also reported a correspondingly higher level of physical and mental health (Sugiyama, Leslie, Giles-Corti and Owen, 2008).

Landscapes that in some way prompt a person to explore, to spend time and to be engaged support restoration. Increasing the level of greenness, the frequency or duration of time spent in the natural environment, or the person's level of involvement will all increase the level of restoration experienced.

The physical health benefits of urban nature

Using reports by Dutch physicians on over 345,000 patients, researchers correlated the levels of mental, cardiovascular, musculoskeletal, respiratory, neurological, digestive and other miscellaneous diseases with access to green space. They used a national land cover database to calculate the percentage of green space, by area, within 1- and 3-kilometre radii of each subject's home and correlated this with physician-recorded incidence of 24 diseases. In areas that were very strongly urban, the presence of green space did not reduce disease. In all other areas, the percentage of green space within 1 kilometre of their home had a strong influence on people's physical and mental health. When comparing people in the least green neighbourhoods (10 per cent green space or less) to people living in the greenest neighbourhoods (90 per cent green space or more), residents of the least green neighbourhoods had a greater incidence of each of the 24 diseases studied, and this effect was more pronounced for lower income people and children. In addition, residents who had only 10 per cent of green space within 1 kilometre of their home were 25 per cent more likely to experience depression and 30 per cent more likely to suffer from anxiety than those living in the greenest neighbourhoods. The researchers concluded that increasing the green space within 1 kilometre of a person's home by 1 per cent was equivalent to lowering their age by 1 year in terms of assessed morbidity or incidence of all diseases (Maas et al., 2009).

Characteristics of restorative environments

Attention Restoration Theory tells us that restoration from directed attention fatigue can be found in places that are high in natural content, are favourite places or that contain a particular set of characteristics (Korpela et al., 2008). There are four attributes of landscapes that increase the restorative nature of natural environments. These are *fascination*, *being away*, *extent* and *compatibility* (S. Kaplan, 1995).

Fascination

Fascination is derived from the natural content of our surroundings and is simply another term for involuntary attention (S. Kaplan, 1995). Aesthetic elements, such as sunlight shining though foliage or clouds drifting across the sky, draw our involuntary attention and we mentally process our environment spontaneously and effortlessly. Because this process requires no effort, it allows our directed attention mechanism to rest and be restored. The Kaplans have labeled this peaceful involvement with the landscape "soft fascination". Soft fascination allows us to explore the landscape, noticing its aesthetic qualities while simultaneously providing the time and place for self-reflection, which enhances the restorative experience. However, Attention Restoration Theory tells us that fascination alone will not lead to the restorative experience. The other landscape attributes that support restoration must also be present (S. Kaplan, 1995).

▶ Figure 2.1

The high natural content in this landscape provides "soft fascination" by engaging our involuntary attention, resting our directed attention and providing a time and place for self-reflection.
Source: © Paul Pitman | Flickr (used under the Creative Commons licence).

Being away

Recovering from mental fatigue requires being in some place other than the source of the fatigue (R. Kaplan et al., 1998). Being away is the quality of a place that causes it to be experienced as outside of one's day-to-day environment. This may be physical, as in geographically separate, or it may be psychological, as in being in a setting that is aesthetically outside of our daily experience and removed from our usual sources of stress. We can experience being away by being physically distant from the demands of daily living or by being aesthetically and psychologically separated from our usual environments.

A green space in the centre of the city or in one's home landscape can constitute a setting for psychologically being away. For example, on

CHAPTER 2 **The restorative landscape**   39

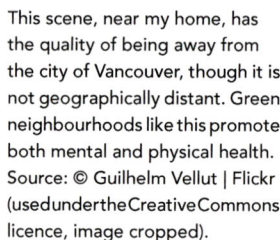

◀ Figure 2.2

This scene, near my home, has the quality of being away from the city of Vancouver, though it is not geographically distant. Green neighbourhoods like this promote both mental and physical health. Source: © Guilhelm Vellut | Flickr (used under the Creative Commons licence, image cropped).

leaving my office each day, I pass through the city centre and cross a bridge to the suburb where I live, in the mountains north of the city. As my journey progresses, I am increasingly surrounded by mature conifers and mountain scenery so that I experience a sense of being away from the city and my work environment upon returning home. Though little geographical distance has occurred, I experience being away due to removing myself from the demands of the workplace and the dramatic change in scenery.

Extent

Landscapes that exhibit the quality of extent support exploration. They have much to see and experience and can occupy our minds for prolonged periods of time (S. Kaplan, 1995). This does not mean that they need to be physically large. As with the quality of being away, extent may be physical or psychological. While larger areas may have more to discover and experience, one can easily imagine a large area of landscape that that does not invite exploration and discovery because it has a single landscape character and is entirely visible from a single vantage point. Such a landscape lacks extent because it has insufficient content and structure to engage our attention for a prolonged period. Conversely, the psychological extent of a landscape can be increased by designing it in such a way that its boundaries are obscured, making it seem larger. Increasing the number of sub-areas within a particular landscape also increases its psychological extent without necessarily increasing its physical size (R. Kaplan et al., 1998). However, for a landscape to have the quality of extent, the sub-areas within that landscape

40   CHAPTER 2 **The restorative landscape**

must be sufficiently connected that they are seen as parts of a larger whole (Laumann, Gärling and Stormark, 2001).

People often explore landscapes mentally as well as physically, and a view or vista is more engrossing if it has extent. As the Kaplans have written, "Even in the depth of winter, in one's mind one can wander around the garden and consider changes to be made come spring" (R. Kaplan et al., 1998, p. 20).

Research has shown that people prefer landscapes that facilitate movement. In a study of people's landscape preferences for work environments, walkable natural areas received the highest rating of all preference factors. Natural areas with mown lawn and widely spaced trees were highly preferred, as were rougher natural areas with clearly walkable paths (R. Kaplan, 2007). Because the walkable landscape facilitates movement and allows the seeking of affordances in safety, this outcome is congruous with prospect refuge theory. Since a legible landscape is one that supports finding one's way into the landscape and being able to return (S. Kaplan, 1988), the preference for visible paths in the landscape contributes to legibility.

Even in situations where people do not physically enter the landscape, it seems that they look for paths through the landscape, for prospects and refuges, for vistas and points of interest (Figure 2.3).

▶ Figure 2.3

When looking across a valley at a distant hillside, we tend to look for patterns of vegetation, possible prospects, refuges and pathways. Views that encourage such mental exploration increase the quality of extent in the landscape.
Source: © Dhilung Kirat | Flickr (used under the Creative Commons licence).

Landscape architect John Simonds posited that humans subconsciously seek a balanced and unified landscape even in the non-designed natural landscape. He applied this concept to finding asymmetrical balance in landscape views and to the associative meanings of the landscape for the particular individual.

> The human eye is constantly darting about, probing and exploring a vague and luminous flux of evolving visual impressions. These are sensed subconsciously. At intervals the mind permits or directs the eye to bring out of optical limbo and into conscious focus certain visual images. This is a creative effort. For the mind demands that the eye "compose" a visual image that is complete and in equilibrium. This is a joint mind-eye effort, for the acceptable equilibrium is not one of form balance, value balance, or color balance alone but one of associative balance as well.
>
> (Simonds, 1983, pp. 190–191)

In places that are not physically large, designers often rely on this process of mental exploration to engage people's attention and give extent. Japanese landscape architect Shunmyo Masuno once confided that he preferred dry waterfalls to those with water because they allowed him to visualise alternative water flows over and down the falls. For him, the dry waterfall had greater extent than did a real waterfall.

In Figure 2.4, the drystone waterfall is the main focal in this landscape view from Tenryu-ji temple in Kyoto. There appears to be a path around the lake leading to a stone bridge over the stream at the base of the waterfall. However, there is no path around the pond to the waterfall. The waterfall, path and stream are illusions. Such a scene has extent because it entices us to mentally explore a landscape that we cannot visit.

Compatibility

A compatible environment is one that supports what the individual wishes to do without undue effort or frustration. It does not confuse or distract and does not place undue demands on directed attention (S. Kaplan, 1995). Natural environments tend to be compatible with our intentions for being in them. For example, when we visit a natural area to enjoy skiing or wildlife viewing, that landscape was chosen in the expectation that it would enable the activity we wish to pursue. The creation of compatible landscapes requires that the designer anticipate the needs and preferences of the users, whether it is giving them a quiet bench from which to watch their children play or a garden that will engage them aesthetically for a number of hours.

▲ Figure 2.4

Psychological extent at Tenryu-ji in Kyoto.
Source: © stockarch.com | (used under the Creative Commons licence).

Case study: The traditional Japanese garden as a restorative landscape

Shunmyo Masuno, Japan Landscape Consultants Ltd.

Shunmyo Masuno is an internationally respected landscape architect and the eighteenth-generation hereditary head priest of Kenkohji Temple in Yokohama, Japan. As a child, visiting the great temple gardens in Kyoto awakened his interest in landscape design. While still in high school, he worked under the supervision of garden designer Katsuo Saitoh, building the garden at Kenkohji Temple, and later served an apprenticeship with him. After graduation in landscape architecture from the Faculty of Agriculture at Tamagawa University in 1975, he completed his Zen training at Sohji-ji Temple in 1979 and in 1982 founded Japan Landscape Consultants Ltd.

Adherents of Zen Buddhism practise the meditative discipline of *zazen* to achieve inner peace and enlightenment. From the twelfth century Kamakura period though the Muromachi period in the sixteenth century, Zen monks also practised calligraphy, brush painting, pottery, poetry and garden design as a means to express their understanding of the essence of Zen. Masuno's practices of *zazen* and the design of gardens is in the tradition of earlier monks, like the famed poet and garden designer Muso Soskeki (1275–1351). Like his predecessors, Masuno considers his designing of gardens to be a religious practice in which he expresses Zen principles. Today, he may be the last Zen priest designing traditional Japanese gardens.

Masuno's work changes in response to its setting and the accompanying architecture. It may be traditional or modern in style, but it always expresses the essence of Zen aesthetics. His landscape designs for the Canadian Embassy and the Cerulean Tower Tokyu Hotel in Tokyo are modern expressions of traditional Japanese stone work and plantings, while his designs for the Japanese garden at the Canadian Museum of Civilization in Hull, Quebec, and Gionji Temple in Miho City, Ibaragi Prefecture, reveal a deep understanding of traditional Japanese gardens.

Shunmyo Masuno's work in bringing the Japanese garden to an international audience has been widely recognised. In 2005, he received an honorary PhD from the University of British Columbia, and in 2012 he was made a Master of Beijing DeTao Masters Academy. In Japan, he received the National Grand Prize from the Japanese Institute of Landscape Architecture in 1997, the Minister's Award from the Ministry of Foreign Affairs in 2003 and the GALA SPA Award in 2005. The Canadian government awarded him a Meritorious Service Medal that same year, and he received the Cross of the Order of Merit from the Federal Republic of Germany in 2006. He has been a professor at Tama Art University since 1998 and has lectured at several Canadian and American universities. He is the author of several books, including *Zen and the Art of Minimalism* and *Zen, the Art of Simple Living*.

▲ Figure 2.5

Plan of Samukawa Shrine. The shrine grounds are a stroll garden with paths around a two-level pond. A series of waterfalls connects the different pond levels. Perimeter tree plantings help to obscure city views and give the visitor a sense of being away. Source: Plan courtesy of Japan Landscape Consultants Ltd.

Samukawa Shrine

Traditional Japanese gardens use native plants to create an idealised depiction of the Japanese landscape. The gardens are heavily influenced by the indigenous religion of Shintoism, in which natural places and elements are considered to have sacred spirits, and by Zen Buddhism, which seeks to understand the essence of the elements of the natural world. They are intended to create a profound experience and are designed as places of repose and reflection. Masuno's design for the Samukawa Shrine, completed in 2009, expresses these aspects of traditional Japanese gardens and also the characteristics of restorative landscapes.

Samukawa Shrine is a Shinto place of worship located in Samukawa city, Kanagawa Prefecture, 60 kilometres south of Tokyo. It was constructed in the eighth century on the site of a sacred spring and is dedicated to two deities that remove misfortune and bring happiness. A grove of ancient trees, some with trunks as large as two metres in diameter, is a major feature of the shrine grounds. When Masuno was asked to redesign the grounds, he faced two significant problems: Over time, the spring had ceased flowing,

CHAPTER 2 The restorative landscape   45

▲ Figure 2.6

Masuno seeks to express the inner spirit of each rock and plant he uses and to combine them to create an atmosphere of tranquility. The garden distills the aesthetic qualities of the native landscape and expresses the mind of its creator. Its deep mountain atmosphere gives visitors a sense of being away, while intricate features like the waterfalls provide psychological extent.
Source: Photo courtesy of Japan Landscape Consultants Ltd.

and a new building, built in 1997, blocked the visitors' view of the sacred grove. As well as creating the appropriate experience for shrine visitors, his design restored the spring and moved the entire ancient grove to a newly constructed 8-metre-high hillside.

Masuno designed a traditional stroll garden for the temple grounds in which paths around the grove and pond connect a tea house, a tea pavilion (used for Ryurei-style tea ceremonies) and a museum. Throughout the garden, grade changes, varying water levels and plantings guide the eye to points of interest and key views. A large stone stage, used for entertainments and festivals, provides panoramic views of the garden (Figure 2.5).

The structure of the plan is created by the relationship of the pond and the grove to the path and the extensive stonework throughout the garden. The water features and plantings of carefully trained pines (*Pinus thunbergii*), broad-leaved evergreens, mosses and ferns create the atmosphere of being in the mountains of Japan. This style of planting uses a restricted native plant palette that is dominated by broad-leaved evergreens like *Camellia japonica*, *Pieris japonica* and *Rhododendron obtusum* (Figure 2.6).

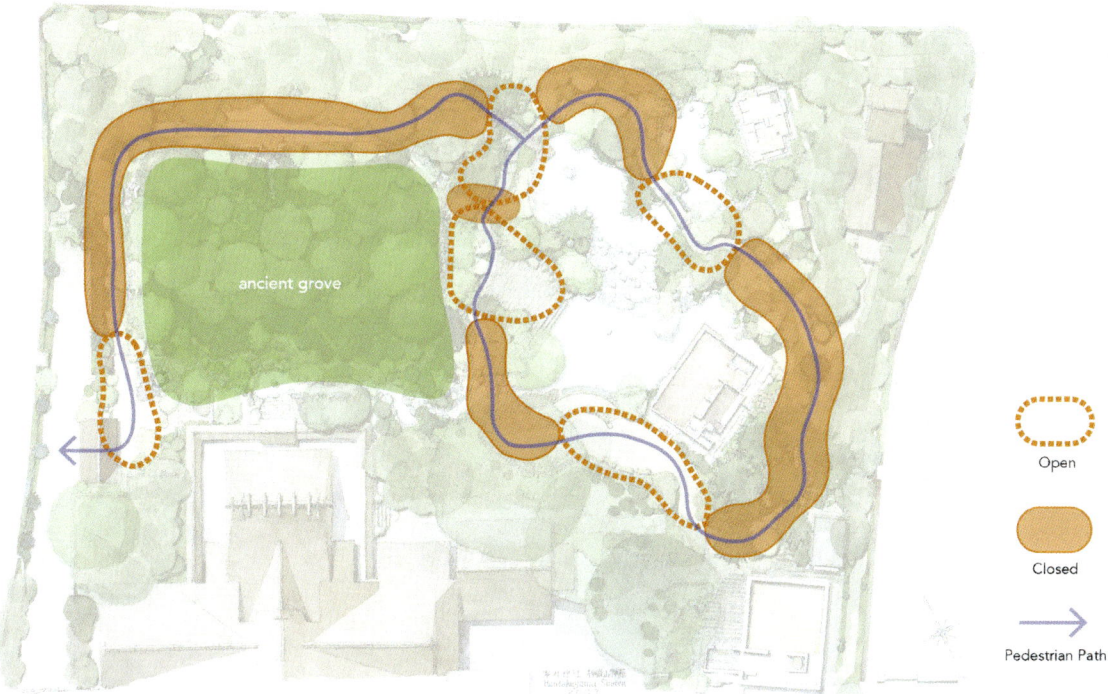

▲ Figure 2.7

This plan shows the sequence of light open spaces and enclosed darker spaces. The pattern of open and enclosed sub-areas is enriched by changing elevations, views and points of interest.
Source: Image courtesy of Yiwen Ruan.

Masuno's intention in designing the garden was to help visitors forget the "urban bustle" and cares of daily living so that they could reconnect with their inner selves (Masuno, 2009). The thick belts of trees on the perimeter of the garden block views of the surrounding city, psychologically locating the visitors in the mountains of Japan.

The garden is conceived as a sequence of light and dark areas. As people move along the path, the space modulates from open to strongly enclosed. Light follows dark. Texture, scents and temperature change and successive points of interest, like waterfalls, streams and bridges, entice the viewer through the garden (Figure 2.7). When in the darker, enclosed spaces, what is not seen allows the person to speculate about what they will encounter as they move deeper into the landscape. This expresses the Zen principle of *yugen* that is entirely congruent with the quality of mystery. Plants play a critical role in shaping the linked sub-areas and in creating their atmosphere, points of interest and successive views. Throughout the garden, visitors discover surprises that keep them engaged with the narrative of the design.

CHAPTER 2 **The restorative landscape**

◀ Figure 2.8

While Figure 2.6 typifies the open section of the garden, where the waterfall is the major view and focal element, this figure shows a different type of view, within an enclosed section of the garden. The enclosed sub-areas possess the quality of mystery that leads visitors to explore and engage. The clear path provides legibility, assuring the visitor that they can easily find their way.
Source: Photo courtesy of Japan Landscape Consultants Ltd.

Samukawa Shrine as a restorative landscape

All the characteristics of restorative landscapes are present in Samukawa Shrine. Fascination is triggered by the luxuriant vegetation and the other natural elements: Topography, water, rocks and the ephemeral qualities of light, sound and movement. These engage our involuntary attention effortlessly, providing the quality of fascination.

The plantings, ponds, streams and waterfalls evoke a natural world that is far away in time and place from Samukawa. Thick plantings that block surrounding views increase this sense of being away. Within the darker areas, the Zen principle of Yugen invites the visitor to contemplate what is to come, and the quality of mystery leads to exploration, discovery and engagement.

The garden has psychological extent because its many points of interest, views and intricate stone work provide a visually rich environment that can engage visitors for extended periods. The light and dark sub-areas of the garden comprise a larger whole and increase the quality of extent.

Visitors come to Samukawa Shrine to enjoy nature, to escape the bustle and stresses of city life and perhaps to enjoy a quiet meditative

▶ Figure 2.9

A view into the garden reveals a serene and unified design and extensive use of broad-leaved evergreens. The Japanese black pines (*Pinus thunbergii*) are associated with mountain scenery, and the rugged stones suggest a distant primal landscape.
Source: Photo courtesy of Japan Landscape Consultants Ltd.

moment in the garden. The garden is a compatible landscape because it enables visitors to effortlessly fulfil their purposes.

Wayfinding and the cognitive map

Human beings require clarity about their situation. If this need to know is thwarted they can become frustrated, anxious and even angry (Spiers and Maguire, 2008). People in the landscape need to understand where they are located and how they may move through that landscape. The ability to discern and remember a path through the environment to a desired destination or to explore successfully has been called wayfinding (Passini, 1981; Kitchin, 1994). Since wayfinding is an ever-present need, it is a fundamental element of compatibility. Recall that a legible scene is one that is easy to survey and form an impression of. A natural environment that is legible aids wayfinding, and this encourages exploration and the mental engagement that leads to restoration.

Humans explore the landscape to find affordances, to have a sense of knowing, to feel safe and to be stimulated. Successful exploration, or wayfinding, is supported by the development and use of an internal mental image of the environment known as the cognitive map (Tversky, 2000;

CHAPTER 2 **The restorative landscape**   49

Darken and Peterson, 2002). A cognitive map contains groupings of environmental information that humans use to simplify and order the complexity of the external world (Kitchin, 1994).

In his classic book *The Image of the City*, urban planner Kevin Lynch developed the idea of cognitive maps, which he referred to as environmental images. In the passage below, he describes the importance of cognitive maps and their relation to wayfinding.

> In the process of way-finding, the strategic link is the environmental image (aka the cognitive map), the generalized mental picture of the exterior environment that is held by the individual. This image is the product both of immediate sensation and of the memory of past experience, and it is used to interpret information and to guide action. The need to recognize and pattern our surroundings is so crucial, and has such long roots in the past, that this image has wide practical and emotional importance to the individual.
>
> (Lynch, 1960, p. 4)

Elements of the landscape that are easily discerned and remembered support wayfinding and the building of a cognitive map. The way in which the cognitive map is formed is determined by the limitations of human rationality and the complexity of the world around us. Because the environment has so much information that is irrelevant to our purposes at any given moment, humans include only the most relevant information in their cognitive maps (Timpf, Volta, Pollock and Egenhofer, 1992). Since most people can only hold about five units or groupings of information in mind at a time (S. Kaplan, 1979), we organise the large amounts of information found in cognitive maps into smaller units called sub-plans (Passini, 1981). When we begin a journey in familiar territory we do not mentally open a visual map of the entire trip and then refer to it at every step of the way. Attempting to do so would engage our entire mental capacity. Rather, we begin with a sub-map that covers the first few decisions of our journey. As we proceed further, the first sub-maps used are put away and new sub-maps turned on at the appropriate places in our journey. All the sub-maps combined constitute the cognitive map used in a particular journey (Timpf et al., 1992). This process allows an efficient use of our limited mental capacity.

Cognitive maps are built up over time in a process in which the individual acquires, simplifies, synthesises and then recalls the locations and relationships between the elements of the spatial environment. The first elements to be selected and retained in building a cognitive map are landmarks (Tversky, 2000). These are distinctive elements that stand out from their surroundings and serve as reference points in the landscape. Next, the routes connecting landmarks are discerned and remembered. The intersections of routes are high-use areas called nodes and, like landmarks, are easily remembered. Both cities and landscapes can be divided into districts or sub-areas that are visually and spatially different from each other and that

▲ Figure 2.10

A legible scene supports wayfinding and encourages exploration and involvement, which contribute to the restorative experience.
Source: © Nicholas A. Tonelli | Flickr (used under the Creative Commons licence, image cropped).

are defined by their edges or the places where one transitions from one district to another. Together, the landmarks, routes, nodes, districts and edges comprise the spatial structure of the city and the landscape. When this structure is learned, a cognitive map has been formed, wayfinding is supported and humans achieve their desired sense of knowing (Lynch, 1960).

The complexity and configuration of the landscape will affect a person's ability to develop and use a cognitive map (Lynch, 1960; S. Kaplan and R. Kaplan, 1982). In new environments, information is added and the cognitive map elaborated as the person moves through the landscape. Developing a cognitive map requires the interaction of human perception and cognition, including the felt or affective response. The cognitive map continues to evolve over long time periods and at any moment is the result of the accrued mapping process (Passini, 1981).

People travelling through an unfamiliar environment form spatial representations of the environment using two different cognitive mapping processes. They can use a route strategy, in which they build their cognitive map by observing and remembering views and landmarks or the sequence of lengths and turns along a path (Lawton and Kallai, 2002), or they can use the survey or orientation strategy of updating their location based on displacements from their point of origin by using local views and landmarks and perhaps such things as the position of the sun (Péruch, Gaunet, Thinus-Blanc and Loomis, 2000; Prestopnik and Roskos-Ewoldsen, 2000). Using the orientation strategy, a person maintains a mental bird's-eye view of their position in the landscape (Dabbs, Chang, Strong and Milun, 1998). In this way, they come to understand the spatial relationship between elements and locations in the landscape and the routes that connect them (Lawton and Kallai, 2002). This is the level of information that allows people to predict and use shortcuts in the landscape (Péruch et al., 2000). It is likely that individuals use a combination of

◀ Figure 2.11
This large distinctive plane tree stands out from its context and provides a memorable landmark in Exbury Gardens, Hampshire, England.
Source: © Lucy Haydon | Flickr (used under the Creative Commons licence, image cropped).

both methods depending on what information is available to them in the landscape (Lawton and Kallai, 2002).

In what has been referred to as the hunter-gatherer model, Silverman and Eals (1992) proposed that since men were the hunters and women the gatherers of food, natural selection would have favoured the development of different spatial abilities in women and men. Tracking and hunting are wide-ranging activities requiring the ability to quickly and accurately form cognitive maps, while foraging would require the ability to recognise and remember the location of objects in the environment. A number of studies have supported this hypothesis. Men preferentially use the orientation strategy and have been shown to more quickly develop accurate cognitive maps of natural environments (Silverman et al., 2000). Women use the route strategy in forming cognitive maps and are consistently better than men in recalling the locations of an array of objects (Eals and Silverman, 1994; Lawton and Kallai, 2002; Prestopnik and Roskos-Ewoldsen, 2000). Women also recall landmarks more accurately, are better at relating landmarks to their location and are more likely to use landmarks when giving directions (Eals and Silverman, 1994). Just as individuals may use both route and orientation mapping strategies, it has been shown that both men and women have foraging-specific navigational skills but that women are more inclined to use these skills (Krasnow et al., 2011).

Transitions

Landmarks and views are easily remembered and are the first elements recognised in the cognitive mapping process. Within views, the most important feature of the view is the landmark (Tversky, 2000). Recall in

▶ Figure 2.12

The recurring drifts of mauve asters and the dried seed heads of the *Echinacea* create a recurrent pattern in the landscape, giving it a visual coherence. Source: Design by James Hitchmough for the Royal Horticultural Society Gardens at Wisley. Image © Gavin McWilliam | Flickr (used under the Creative Commons licence).

Lynch's cognitive mapping process the importance of edges that, he tells us, can act as landmarks.

> An edge may be more than simply a dominant barrier if some visual or motion penetration is allowed through it … It then becomes a seam rather than a barrier, a line of exchange along which two areas are sewn together.
>
> If an important edge is provided with many visual and circulation connections … it becomes a feature to which everything else is easily aligned.
>
> (Lynch, 1960, p. 100)

Such an edge is a transition between two sub-areas of the larger landscape, but it is also an important landmark. Whether large or small, landmarks are noticed and remembered and thus aid in wayfinding. Transitions are those places where a change in orientation occurs. Together, landmarks and transitions are the elements of the landscape that most support wayfinding. In one study, people who watched films of landscape transitions were better at actual wayfinding in the landscape shown than those who watched a film of the views between those transitions (Tversky, 2000). Landscape designers can support wayfinding by increasing legibility and by providing clear landmarks, distinctive sub-areas and transitions.

A pattern-seeking species

Hunter-gatherers needed to be able to quickly assess the landscape for its potential affordances or dangers. Survival of the fittest would have favoured those who could quickly recognise patterns in the landscape that indicated such things as the presence of water, the opportunity for unrestricted movement or places where shelter from the elements could be found. Because pattern recognition was so useful, humans evolved as pattern-seeking organisms that attempt to find order in their surroundings by looking for patterns that fit with the knowledge they have about their world (Bell, 2012); Figure 2.12. Over the course of human evolution, minor changes to a core brain network known as the lateral frontoparietal network enabled humans to excel at pattern recognition (Vendetti and Bunge, 2014). This predilection for finding patterns has become so pronounced in humans that they may identify patterns and causalities that are not really present (Shermer, 2011).

A pattern may be any reoccurring relationship, such as night following day. Detecting patterns in the landscape allows us to classify objects or sub-areas in the landscape, to understand cause and effect, to compress and retain information and to make predictions (Davies, 2014). This ability at pattern recognition is at the heart of deductive reasoning, decision-making, memory and cognitive mapping (Vendetti and Bunge, 2014) and allows us to solve complex and novel problems.

Humans not only recognise simple landscape patterns. They also excel at relational thinking or understanding the relationships between patterns. An example may illustrate how this facility in recognising patterns and the relationships between them allows humans to make complex predictions about their environment that would have aided their survival (Davies, 2014). Consider the predicament of one of our early ancestors who was without water in an arid landscape. She might have used relational thinking to make the prediction "If I move higher, I will probably find one of those dry places without trees. (I have noticed that this pattern is almost always true in this landscape.) The thorny plants that I will probably find there (another pattern I have noticed) can be tapped to give water, but I will need to be careful because the dry place may have scorpions. (This doesn't always happen, but I have noticed it before.)" Note that recognising an individual pattern was of little use in helping our hypothetical ancestor to survive. Only remembering and understanding the relationship between patterns aided her survival.

Psychologists have found that things that require less mental processing and that are easier to understand are more likely to be preferred and even to be believed (Shermer, 2011). A pattern will be remembered as a symbol or an image rather than as all the information associated with the pattern. In this way, pattern recognition allows humans to compress information so that more of it can be stored more easily. This use of patterns to compress information aids us in building cognitive maps, supporting wayfinding and compatibility.

Pattern-seeking and the curiosity model

Whether they are conscious of it or not, humans use patterns to find order in an apparently disordered world (Bell, 2012). This tendency to seek patterns relates to both our knowledge-seeking and pleasure-seeking curiosity models. We are attracted to and will seek to understand anything that is out of place or distinct from its surroundings. We feel pleasure when we make sense of the incongruity, and it is not necessary that a pattern aid survival for us to take pleasure and feel a sense of knowing from discovering that pattern (Figure 2.12). While our innate human curiosity leads us to seek new patterns, too much repetition of the same pattern provides neither new information nor stimulation and will lead to boredom (Davies, 2014).

Case study in pattern in the landscape: Children's Garden, San Francisco, California

Andrea Cochran Landscape Architecture (ACLA), 2002[1]

ACLA's Children's Garden in San Francisco is a three-dimensional pattern in which the clients' four children play in a surreal landscape. From above, the sloping garden appears as a pattern of triangular groundcover beds that define a central zig-zag grass path (Figure 2.13). So different is this from ordinary landscapes that it takes a moment to realise that this animated game board in which children are the moving pieces is a real three-dimensional landscape. When first encountered, this landscape will not meet expectations. It is an example of the unexpected in landscape that gives people pleasure when they have comprehended it. The garden eschews the conventions of backyard gardens in favour of being a world unto itself. It attracts us with its uniquely different forms and materials and gives us pleasure when we understand the relations of its visual pattern to its use.

▶ Figure 2.13

Plan: Children's Playground, San Francisco, 2002, by Andrea Cochran Landscape Architects.
Source: Image courtesy of Yiwen Ruan.

PLANTINGS
A *Abutilon hybrida*
B *Alchemilla mollis*
C Existing *Camellia*
D *Clematis* varieties
   C. armandii
   C. 'Lady Northcliffe'
E Lawn
F Existing *Magnolia*
G Existing *Prunus* tree
H *Salix caprea 'Pendula'* fence with *Rosa 'Sally Holmes'*
I *Sutera 'Gold' n Pearls'*
J *Sutera 'Snowstorm'*

BUILT ELEMENTS
1 Wood deck
2 Willow-twig "bolt" columns, along fence
3 Willow lanterns
4 Decomposed granite
5 Cor-ten steel stair
6 Cor-ten steel edging
7 Wattle fence and railing
8 Sloped lawn strip
9 "Lawn" chair
10 Existing fence around property
11 Living willow fence
12 Moveable willow spheres
13 Willow tunnel "thicket" over existing slide
14 "Lawn Table" and wooden seats

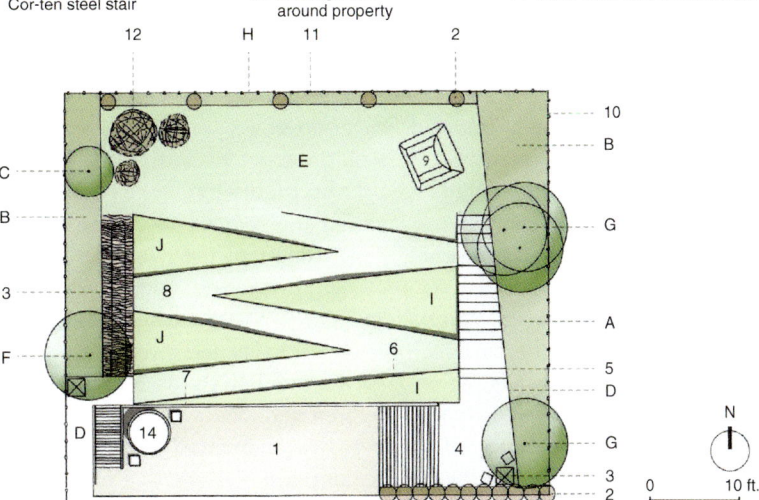

▲ Figure 2.14

Viewed from above, the zig-zag grass path through triangles of colourful groundcover produces a clear pattern of repeated forms, textures and colours.
Source: Photo by Holly Stewart.

▲ Figure 2.15

A different pattern is seen from the bottom of the garden. The slope of the garden is retained with thin retaining walls of Corten steel.
Source: Photo by Holly Stewart.

Preference and restoration

If, as the Kaplans have suggested, preferred environments are also likely to be restorative environments, we would expect to find that the elements of restorative environments would also predict preference (Laumann et al., 2001). Researchers have examined the relation of preferred and restorative landscapes by measuring the effects of the characteristics of restorative environments—fascination, being away, extent and mystery—in supporting restoration and comparing them to the characteristics of preferred landscapes—coherence, complexity, legibility and mystery.

In one study, Norwegian university students were asked to imagine themselves in either a familiar mountain area or downtown Oslo. They were given a questionnaire intended to assess how they rated these two environments for fascination, being away, extent and mystery. The researchers divided restoration and being away into the two categories: Restoration included the categories of relaxation and cognitive restoration, while being away was divided into *escape*, or being physically removed from the demands of work and routine, and *novelty*, which meant being in a novel setting or engaging in an unusual activity. The researchers reported that where the students rated an area as having extent and compatibility, they also confirmed that they found it fascinating. This suggests that adding extent and compatibility increases fascination.

In a follow-up study, the same researchers investigated self-reported preference and restoration. One hundred and fifty-seven Norwegian university students were shown videos of walks through a forest, park, seaside, mountain and an urban area. They then completed a questionnaire in which they answered questions intended to measure their assessment of the four characteristics of restorative environments and their self-reported restoration. The forest and the seaside were found to be more restorative than the urban area. The park rated highest for being away, while the city rated higher than the park for the characteristics of extent, fascination and compatibility. Natural areas scored higher than urban environments on all measures of preference and restoration. Compatibility and fascination were the components of the restorative landscape that most predicted preference, while psychological extent and compatibility most predicted the relaxation effect of a landscape (Laumann et al., 2001).

Dutch researchers hypothesised that people may prefer natural landscapes because they perceive them to be restorative. One hundred participants at Wageningen University were given a psychological test that measured their happiness and stress levels. They were then shown a video intended to induce stress and given the same psychological test once more. They then viewed videos of both natural and urban environments. Participants were asked to imagine walking in the area depicted in the video and to rate the areas in the videos for beauty (a surrogate for preference) and naturalness. After this they were given the psychological test a third time, followed by a mental concentration test.

As might be expected, the subjects rated natural settings as being more natural. Participants showed reduced depression, anger, tension and stress and improved happiness after viewing natural environments. They also performed better on the mental concentration test. Participants who viewed built environments showed a lesser improvement in depression, anger and tension and showed no improvement in happiness and stress levels. The authors concluded that natural environments were most preferred and provided restoration from both elevated stress and mental fatigue.

The researchers found that those individuals who were most stressed after watching the video most preferred natural settings to urban settings and that the more highly an individual preferred an environment the more restorative it was for them (van den Berg, Koole and van der Wulp, 2003). Subsequent research demonstrated that environments that are predominately natural are perceived as being more restorative than those that are predominately built and that the preference that people have for natural environments is due in part to their need for restoration and their belief that natural environments are restorative (van den Berg et al., 2007).

Conclusions

Research evidence confirms the restorative effect of contact with natural environments, including urban nature. Contact with natural environments has been found to reduce stress and to improve mood, social behaviour, cognition and physical health outcomes. The characteristics of restorative and preferred landscapes are intertwined and both have been shown to support broad measures of wellbeing.

Chapter 2 principles applied to planting design

Below are selected principles from this chapter, listed by subject category, with some possible implications for planting designs.

Principles that support restoration

Fascination

Fascination is an essential component of restorative landscapes and is initiated by natural content. Environments that are predominately natural are perceived as being more restorative, and increased greenness is associated with improved social and physical outcomes.

- If, therefore, planting designs are intended to be restorative they should be lushly vegetated. One way to do this is to plant in vertical layers. For example, a planting design could feature low perennials and grasses, taller evergreen and deciduous shrubs and small ornamental trees in a three-layer planting.
- If you wish your planting to activate the restorative response, the area of planting should in most cases exceed that given over to hard landscape elements.

By increasing the level of greenness, the frequency or duration of time spent in the natural environment or the person's level of involvement will all increase the level of restoration experienced.

- Create planting designs that are visually rich, that people will find attractive, will be more engaged with and that they will want to visit more often and stay in longer.

Restorative environments prompt our fascination and possess the qualities of being away, extent and compatibility.

- Restorative planting designs, as well as providing high natural content, should have these other qualities of restorative landscapes.

Being away

The quality of being away, physically or psychologically, removes us from the source of our mental fatigue and aids restoration.

- Use plantings to separate designed landscapes from their surroundings. For example, thick belts of trees can block urban views and reinforce the sense of being away.
- Plantings that are different from those in our usual day-to-day environments also create a sense of being away. Scent is a powerful trigger to memory and emotion (Meyer, 2007). Adding scented plants at entries, path edges and other accessible locations fosters involvement and reinforces the sense of being away.

Extent

Landscapes with the quality of extent give us much to see and experience and can occupy our minds for prolonged periods of time. The quality of extent supports exploration and involvement. Psychological extent is increased by the presence of a few sub-areas, but the sub-areas must be sufficiently connected that they are seen as parts of a larger whole.

- Develop planting designs in which a few distinct sub-areas are linked by transitions where sub-areas meet.

Compatibility

- Wayfinding is an ever-present need and is a fundamental element of compatibility. Landmarks and transitions are the elements of the landscape that most support wayfinding.
- Landscape designers can support wayfinding and engagement by providing clear landmarks, distinctive sub-areas and transitions.

Involvement

Landscapes that prompt a person to explore, to spend time and to be engaged support restoration. If the first appraisal of a landscape suggests that it is not compatible—that is, that it does not meet our needs or is unsafe—we will probably choose to avoid that landscape. When this happens, the restorative experience cannot occur.

- Provide landscapes that are legible, which reassure the user that they can find their way and which support what they wish to do in that landscape.

If people explore a landscape but find it confusing, they will probably choose to leave. Conversely, if their first evaluation is positive and further exploration confirms their expectations, people will be inclined to spend time in that landscape and return frequently.

- Part of our objective in designing landscapes is to make them open and safe and to provide defined paths with clear landmarks and transitions.
- Alternating the degree of enclosure in successive sub-areas of the landscape is a fundamental way to enhance experience and support engagement.
- Use plants to shape different types of spaces that provide a sequence of experiences.

Views

People experience improved wellbeing when the views from their windows overlook natural scenery.

- Planting designers should always consider the view from within the building and strive to make these views high in natural content.

Within views, the most important feature of the view is the landmark.

- Planting designers should create landmarks such as large trees at important places in the landscape, such as the intersections of paths or at major nodes.

Principles that support preference and restoration

Restoration and preference are intertwined. Many people prefer landscapes that they consider to be restorative.

- This suggests that adding the elements of preference (coherence, complexity, legibility and mystery) will contribute to the restorative experience. For example, reinforcing the edge of the path with continuous plantings increases legibility and wayfinding.

Patterns

People feel a sense of knowing and take pleasure in discovering patterns. Therefore, patterns in planting design foster engagement and preference.

- Repetition of the same plants, or even of similar plant placements, creates the kinds of patterns that people love to discover.

Too much repetition of the same pattern will lead to boredom and curtail engagement.

- Use patterns with restraint. For example, use different patterns in different sub-areas, or use patterns in the centre of a view but nowhere else.

Glossary

Attention Restoration Theory (ART): A theory developed by environmental psychologists Rachel and Stephen Kaplan. It proposes that our ability to direct our mental attention is depleted by prolonged mental demands. This results in directed attention fatigue, which leads to reduced cognitive abilities and irritability. Contact with restorative environments triggers fascination, which allows the directed attention mechanism to rest and leads to a recovery of mood and cognitive functions.

Being away: The quality of a place that causes it to be experienced as outside of one's day-to-day environment. It is one of four qualities of a restorative environment that were identified by environmental psychologists Stephen and Rachel Kaplan.

Cognitive map: A mental image of the layout of some portion of one's environment (Darken and Peterson, 2002). It is formed in the act of exploring and supports further exploration and involvement.

Compatibility: A measure of the degree to which an environment supports the intentions of the user.

Compatible environment: See compatible landscape.

Compatible landscape: One that supports what the individual wishes to do without undue effort or frustration.

Directed attention: Synonymous with *voluntary attention*. The term used to describe the intentional focusing of thought. It requires suppressing internal and external mental distractions.

Districts: Areas that have distinct visual properties that differentiate them from their surroundings. They are one of the components of cognitive maps identified by Kevin Lynch (1960).

Duration: The length of time over which something occurs. Increasing the duration of time spent in restorative environments increases the restorative effect.

Edges: Breaks in continuity in the environment that occur where two districts meet. They are a necessary component of cognitive maps (Lynch, 1960).

Extent: A quality of restorative landscapes identified by environmental psychologists Stephen and Rachel Kaplan. Landscapes that exhibit the quality of extent have much for us to see and can occupy our minds for an extended period of time.

Fascination: Synonymous with involuntary attention. The ability to trigger fascination is one of the necessary components of restorative landscapes identified by the Kaplans. Landscapes with a high natural content attract people's attention because of their "soft fascination" and are processed using involuntary attention, which allows recovery from mental fatigue.

Frequency:: A measure of how often something is repeated. Increasing the frequency of contact with natural environments increases the restorative effect.

Greenness: A measure of the amount of vegetation within a particular area. Research has shown that people living in greener neighbourhoods are healthier mentally and physically than those living in less green neighbourhoods.

Involuntary attention: Mental attention which is given spontaneously and without effort to such things as unexpected changes in our environment, movement and natural environments.

Landmarks: Elements in the external environment that are memorable because their physical characteristics differentiate them from their surroundings. They are the first component of the environment that is remembered and are used to develop a cognitive map (Lynch, 1960).

Nodes: Places that are memorable due to either intensity of use or their aesthetic qualities. They occur at the intersection of paths or at landmarks and are one of the five elements of cognitive maps (Lynch, 1960).

Path: See *Route*.

Pattern: Any reoccurring relationship. Visual patterns are produced by the repetition of visual elements. Humans have a predilection for identifying patterns. Finding patterns in the landscape gives people a sense of order that they find pleasurable.

Restoration: The recovery of a state of better physical, psychological and social functioning that accrues from contact with restorative environments.

Restorative environments: Environments that foster recovery from mental fatigue, restore emotional and cognitive functioning and reduce stress. They have the four characteristics of being away, extent, compatibility and fascination.

Route: An established way or track of movement between two points in the landscape. Routes are one of the five elements of cognitive maps. Routes that have clear visual characteristics, have continuity and connect important destinations are more memorable (Lynch, 1960).

Stress Recovery Theory (SRT): A theory developed by Roger Ulrich. Researchers have demonstrated that being in natural environments leads to a decrease in stress, as measured by such things as reduced heart rate, blood pressure and stress hormone levels.

Transitions: These occur at places where the visual character of the landscape changes or where two different sub-areas intersect. Their purpose is to smooth change in the landscape so that the experience of change is not abrupt or inharmonious.

Voluntary attention: See *Directed attention*.

Wayfinding: This refers to the human need to navigate three-dimensional environments. It's a fundamental human need and is a component of compatible landscapes.

Note

1 See Chapter 5 for an introduction to Andrea Cochran Landscape Architects.

References

Bell, S. (2012). *Landscape: Pattern, perception and process.* New York: Routledge.

Canin, L.H. (1991). Psychological restoration among AIDS caregivers: Maintaining self-care (Doctoral dissertation). Ann Arbor, MI: University of Michigan.

Cimprich, B.E. (1990). Attentional fatigue and restoration in individuals with cancer (Doctoral dissertation). Ann Arbor, MI: University of Michigan.

Dabbs Jr, J.M., Chang, E.L., Strong, R.A., & Milun, R. (1998). Spatial ability, navigation strategy, and geographic knowledge among men and women. *Evolution and Human Behavior*, 19(2), 89–98.

Darken, R.P., & Peterson, B. (2002). Spatial orientation, wayfinding, and representation. In K. Stanney & K. Hale (Eds.), *Handbook of virtual environments: Design, implementation, and applications* (pp. 493–518). Boca Raton, FL: CRC Press.

Davies, J. (2014). *Riveted: The science of why jokes make us laugh, movies make us cry, and religion makes us feel one with the universe.* New York: Palgrave Macmillan.

Eals, M., & Silverman, I. (1994). The hunter-gatherer theory of spatial sex differences: Proximate factors mediating the female advantage in recall of object arrays. *Ethology and Sociobiology*, 15(2), 95–105.

Hartig, T., Evans, G.W., Jamner, L.D., Davis, D.S., & Gärling, T. (2003). Tracking restoration in natural and urban field settings. *Journal of Environmental Psychology*, 23(2), 109–123.

Heerwagen, J.H., & Orians, G.H. (1993). Humans, habitats, and aesthetics. In S.R. Kellert & E.O. Wilson (Eds.), *The biophilia hypothesis* (pp. 138–172). Washington, DC: Island Press.

Kaplan, R. (2001). The nature of the view from home: Psychological benefits. *Environment and Behavior*, 33, 507–542.

Kaplan, R. (2007). Employees' reactions to nearby nature at their workplace: The wild and the tame. *Landscape and Urban Planning*, 82(1), 17–24.

Kaplan R., & Kaplan, S. (1989). *The experience of nature: A psychological perspective*. Cambridge, UK: Cambridge University Press.

Kaplan, R., & Kaplan, S. (2005). Preference, restoration, and meaningful action in the context of nearby nature. In P.F. Barlett (Ed.), *Urban place: Reconnecting with the natural world* (pp. 271–298). Cambridge, MA: MIT Press.

Kaplan, R., Kaplan, S., & Ryan, R. (1998). *With people in mind: Design and management of everyday nature*. Washington, DC: Island Press.

Kaplan, S. (1979). Perception and landscape: Conceptions and misconceptions. In *Proceedings of Our National Landscape*. USDA Forest Service General Technical Report PSW-35 (pp. 241–248).

Kaplan, S. (1988). Perception and landscape: Conceptions and misconceptions. In *Environmental Aesthetics: Theory, Research, and Application*, 45–55.

Kaplan, S. (1995). The restorative benefits of nature: Toward an integrative framework. *Journal of Environmental Psychology*, 15(3), 169–182.

Kaplan, S., & Kaplan R. (1982). *Cognition and environment*. New York: Praeger.

Kitchin, R.M. (1994). Cognitive maps: What are they and why study them? *Journal of Environmental Psychology*, 14(1), 1–19.

Korpela, K.M., Ylén, M., Tyrväinen, L., & Silvennoinen, H. (2008). Determinants of restorative experiences in everyday favorite places. *Health & Place*, 14(4), 636–652.

Krasnow, M.M., Truxaw, D., Gaulin, S.J., New, J., Ozono, H., Uono, S., Ueno, T., & Minemoto, K. (2011). Cognitive adaptations for gathering-related navigation in humans. *Evolution and Human Behavior*, 32(1), 1–12.

Kuo, F.E., & Sullivan, W.C. (2001a). Aggression and violence in the inner city: Effects of environment via mental fatigue. *Environment & Behavior, Special Issue*, 33(4), 543–571.

Kuo, F.E., & Sullivan, W.C. (2001b). Environment and crime in the inner city: Does vegetation reduce crime? *Environment & Behavior*, 33(3), 343–367.

Laumann, K., Gärling, T., & Stormark, K.M. (2001). Rating scale measures of restorative components of environments. *Journal of Environmental Psychology*, 21(1), 31–44.

Lawton, C.A., & Kallai, J. (2002). Gender differences in wayfinding strategies and anxiety about wayfinding: A cross-cultural comparison. *Sex Roles*, 47(9–10), 389–401.

Lynch, K. (1960). *The image of the city*. Cambridge, MA: MIT Press.

Maas, J., Verheij, R.A., de Vries, S., Spreeuwenberg, P., Schellevis, F.G., & Groenewegen, P.P. (2009). Morbidity is related to a green living environment. *Journal of Epidemiology and Community Health*, 63(12), 967–973.

Masuno, S. (2009). Samukawa Shrine. Unpublished document, Japan Landscape Consultants Ltd.

Meyer, W.J. (2007). Persistence of memory: Scent gardens for therapeutic life review in communities for the elderly (Master's thesis). Arlington, TX: University of Texas at Arlington. Accessed September 26, 2019 at https://rc.library.uta.edu/uta-ir/bitstream/handle/10106/550/umi-uta-1697.pdf?sequence=1&isAllowed=y.

Moore, E.O. (1981). A prison environment's effect on health care service demands. *Journal of Environmental Systems*, 11, 17–34.

Park, B.J., Tsunetsugu, Y., Kasetani, T., Kagawa, T., & Miyazaki, Y. (2010). The physiological effects of Shinrin-yoku (taking in the forest atmosphere or forest bathing): Evidence from field experiments in 24 forests across Japan. *Environmental Health and Preventive Medicine*, 15(1), 18–26.

Parmentier, F.B. (2008). Towards a cognitive model of distraction by auditory novelty: The role of involuntary attention capture and semantic processing. *Cognition*, 109(3), 345–362.

Passini, R. (1981). Wayfinding: A conceptual framework. *Urban Ecology*, 5(1), 17–31.

Péruch, P., Gaunet, F., Thinus-Blanc, C., & Loomis, J. (2000). Understanding and learning virtual spaces. In R.M. Kitchin & S. Freundschuh (Eds.), *Cognitive mapping: Past, present and future* (pp. 108–124). London: Routledge.

Prestopnik, J.L., & Roskos-Ewoldsen, B. (2000). The relations among wayfinding strategy use, sense of direction, sex, familiarity, and wayfinding ability. *Journal of Environmental Psychology*, 20(2), 177–191.

Shermer, M. (2011). *The believing brain: From ghosts and gods to politics and conspiracies—how we construct beliefs and reinforce them as truths*. New York: Henry Holt.

Silverman, I., & Eals, M. (1992). Sex differences in spatial abilities: Evolutionary theory and data. In J. Barkow, L. Cosmides, & J. Tooby (Eds.), *The adapted mind* (pp. 533–549). New York: Oxford University Press.

Silverman, I., Choi, J., Mackewn, A., Fisher, M., Moro, J., & Olshansky, E. (2000). Evolved mechanisms underlying wayfinding: Further studies on the hunter-gatherer theory of spatial sex differences. *Evolution and Human Behavior*, 21(3), 201–213.

Simonds, J.O. (1983). *Landscape architecture: The shaping of man's natural environment* (No. 712.2) (pp. 190–191). New York: McGraw-Hill.

Spiers, H.J., & Maguire, E.A. 2008. The dynamic nature of cognition during wayfinding. *Journal of Environmental Psychology*, 28(3), 232–249.

Sugiyama, T., Leslie, E., Giles-Corti, B., & Owen, N. (2008). Associations of neighbourhood greenness with physical and mental health: Do walking, social coherence and local social interaction explain the relationships? *Journal of Epidemiology and Community Health*, 62(5), e9-e9.

Talbot, J.F., & Kaplan, R. (1991). The benefits of nearby nature for elderly apartment residents. *The International Journal of Aging and Human Development*, 33(2), 119–130.

Tennessen, C.M., & Cimprich, B. (1995). Views to nature: Effects on attention. *Journal of Environmental Psychology*, 15(1), 77–85.

Timpf, S., Volta, G.S., Pollock, D.W., & Egenhofer, M.J. (1992). A conceptual model of wayfinding using multiple levels of abstraction. In A.U. Frank, I. Campari, & U. Formentini (Eds.), *Theories and methods of spatio-temporal reasoning in geographic space* (Vol. 639) (pp. 348–367). Berlin: Springer Verlag.

Tverksy, B. (2000). Levels and structure of spatial knowledge. In R. Kitchin & S. Freundschuh (Eds.), *Cognitive mapping: Past, present, and future* (Vol. 4) (pp. 24–43). London: Routledge.

Ulrich, R. (1984). View through a window may influence recovery. *Science*, 224(4647), 224–225.

Ulrich, R.S., Simons, R.F., Losito, B.D., Fiorito, E., Miles, M.A., & Zelson, M. (1991). Stress recovery during exposure to natural and urban environments. *Journal of Environmental Psychology*, 11(3), 201–230.

van den Berg, A.E., & Custers, M.H. (2011). Gardening promotes neuroendocrine and affective restoration from stress. *Journal of Health Psychology*, 16(1), 3–11.

van den Berg, A.E., Hartig, T., & Staats, H. (2007). Preference for nature in urbanized societies: Stress, restoration, and the pursuit of sustainability. *Journal of Social Issues*, 63(1), 79–96.

van den Berg, A.E., Koole, S.L., & van der Wulp, N.Y. (2003). Environmental preference and restoration: (How) are they related? *Journal of Environmental Psychology*, 23(2), 135–146.

Velarde, M.D., Fry, G., & Tveit, M. (2007). Health effects of viewing landscapes: Landscape types in environmental psychology. *Urban Forestry & Urban Greening*, 6(4), 199–212.

Vendetti, M.S., & Bunge, S.A. (2014). Evolutionary and developmental changes in the lateral frontoparietal network: A little goes a long way for higher-level cognition. *Neuron*, 84(5), 906–917.

Wolf, K.L., Krueger, S., & Rozance, M.A. (2014). Stress, wellness and physiology: A literature review. In *Green cities: Good health*. Seattle, WA: College of the Environment, University of Washington. Accessed January 4, 2019 at https://depts.washington.edu/hhwb/Print_Stress.html.

Chapter 3

Horticultural considerations in planting design

All landscapes are living systems. Understanding the interactions of plants with soil, water and climate is necessary for the successful implementation of planting designs. This chapter presents an overview of horticultural considerations in the use of plants. Soil formation, structure, textural classes, drainage, water-holding capacity, soil management and plant hardiness are discussed together with macro- and micronutrients.

Soil

Soil consists of natural bodies at Earth's surface, composed of minerals, organic matter and living organisms. It is home to millions of species of bacteria and fungi, most of which are involved in organic matter decomposition and the build-up of soil fertility, and it is the Earth's recycling system where production potential is built up and where so-called wastes and natural toxins are broken down. Soils supply plants with many of their requirements: Water, air, nutrients and support for their roots. Although these functions are vital to the existence of life on Earth, soil is often neglected in the process of designing, creating and managing landscapes.

The importance of matching plants' requirements to a soil's properties cannot be overstated. A great deal of time, energy and expense will be saved though the provision of soils that are supportive of the intended plants. Conversely, planting in inadequate soils is a recipe for frustration, high maintenance, ongoing revision and ultimately failure. Planting designers need to understand the soil that they will be planting in so that they can choose plants that are adapted to the properties of that particular soil and/or manage the soil properties to improve its suitability for the intended plants. An understanding of soil science can assist in these tasks.

Soil formation

There are five factors involved in soil formation: *Climate*, *organisms*, *relief* (or topography), *parent material* and *time*.

Climate: The forces of climate subject rock and stone to weathering, a process in which these materials are broken down into small particles. Such things as the type of rock, the number of freeze–thaw cycles, temperatures, precipitation, rainfall acidity and the movement of the geologic material will influence the rate of weathering.

Organisms: Biota play important roles in soil formation. Plants contribute organic matter to the surface of the soil through leaf litter, twigs, branches and bark, and ultimately their death and collapse. Within the soil, plant roots contribute organic matter from root exudation and annual mortality (Barnes, Zak, Denton and Spurr, 1997). Soil micro-organisms and earthworms control the decomposition of organic matter and make mineral and organic nutrients available. Earthworms mix the soil layers, distributing nutrients and changing the soil texture. Humans till the soil, mixing its layers, move it from place to place and contribute to its enhancement or depletion.

Relief or *topography*: Topography includes local changes in slope, elevation and aspect. Local topographic conditions influence microclimate and erosion, contributing to local soil conditions. For example, on mountain faces it is common to find distinctly different soils and plant species on slopes having different aspects. On north-facing slopes where the snows remain longer and the growing season is shorter, organic matter does not fully decompose. This results in a build-up of a partially decomposed organic layer atop the soil that is acidic and supports acid-loving plants. On south-facing slopes where the organic matter decomposes more fully, a different plant community that is adapted to more heat and less moisture and acidity in the soil will be found.

Parent material: The geologic materials from which soils develop are called parent materials. These can be bedrock or other geologic material at the Earth's surface that has been deposited by glaciation, re-bound in the Earth's crust after glaciation, volcanic activity, wind, water and gravity.

Time: The process of soil formation takes place over many thousands of years. Only after some weathering has occurred can plants and microbes occupy the soil and begin their contribution to its formation. While soils are formed over long time periods, they can be eroded, transported and deposited by wind, water or landslides within time periods as brief as a few seconds.

Soil profile

Most soils have distinct layers called soil horizons. The soil profile is a section through the soil showing all its horizons (Figure 3.0).

The upper layer of a soil has been exposed to the greatest weathering and accumulations of organic matter. This will give it a darker colour and a different texture than the lower horizons. This top layer is the A horizon and is generally referred to as "topsoil". The underlying B horizon will have less organic matter and may be a zone of accumulation where clay particles and

▶ Figure 3.0

The soil profile (after Armson 1977).
Source: Image courtesy of Yiwen Ruan.

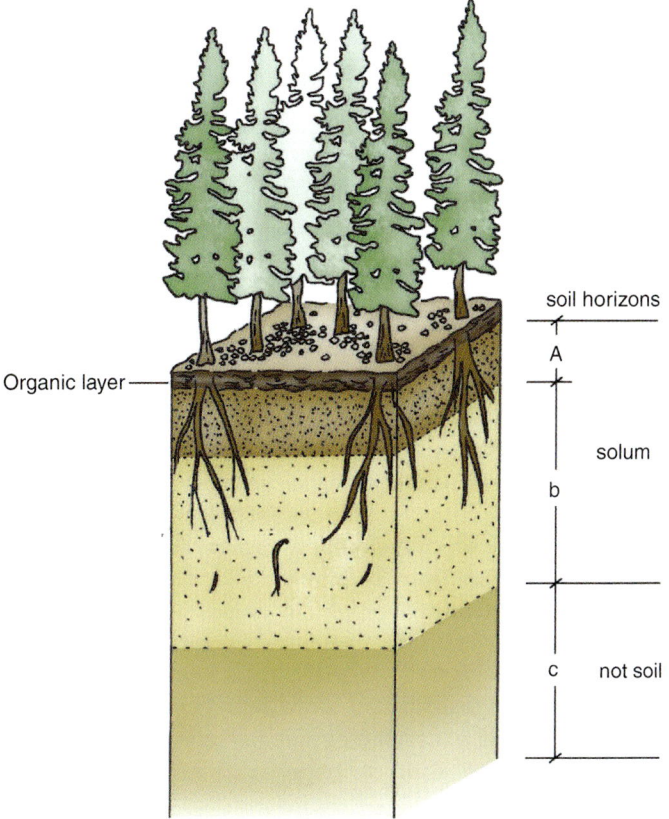

minerals have been washed down, or leached, from the A horizon and accumulated. The A and B horizons make up the solum or soil. The C horizon lies below the B horizon and is usually comprised of the parent material from which the A and B horizons have been formed.

The A horizon, or topsoil, is the best growing medium of the soil profile. Its depth and characteristics will have a great influence on plant growth. Most grasses and herbaceous plants will not extend their roots beyond the A horizon, while trees and shrubs will extend their roots through the A and B horizon to the C horizon. Sometimes the C horizon can be a dense soil layer that is effectively impermeable to water and oxygen. In such cases, the impermeable layer of the C horizon will be the limit of the root zone of the plants.

Soil acts as a reservoir, holding water until the plants need it. Larger soil volumes hold more water and support the growth and longevity of larger trees. Inadequate soil volumes have long been identified as a cause of premature mortality in trees (Lindsey and Bassuk, 1992).

Different models have been developed to estimate the necessary soil volumes for trees (Urban, 1992; Lindsey and Bassuk, 1992). A rule-of-thumb calculation can be done using the guideline that trees require between 20 and 25 square feet of area and a soil depth of 2 feet for every inch of diameter at breast height at maturity. (Diameter at breast height is abbreviated as dbh and is measured at 4.5 feet or 1.37 metres above ground.) For example, a tree that will have a dbh of 24 inches (61 centimetres) at maturity will require 24 × 25 square feet × 2-foot depth = 1,200 cubic feet or 34 cubic metres of soil in its root zone (Virginia Urban Street Tree Selector, n.d.).

Soil fertility and plant nutrients

In order to match plants to a given soil or to manage soil conditions to better support plants, it is advisable to get a soil test. Commercial laboratories will provide a complete analysis of major nutrients in soils and make soil management recommendations. The insurance against costly failures, the direction for plant selection and the advice for soil management that the soil test provides is well worth the modest cost of this service. Make sure to contact the soil test laboratory beforehand and follow their instructions for taking and submitting soil samples in order to get representative and uncontaminated samples. In addition to professional testing, a number of do-it-yourself test kits or electronic meters can be purchased from garden centres, retail nurseries and home improvement stores. The following discussion includes soil attributes that are commonly measured in soil tests and will help the reader to better understand the soil test recommendations.

Soil pH

Before discussing nutrients in the soil, it is necessary to discuss the soil acidity and alkalinity, or pH, since it affects availability of nutrients. The term pH stands for potenz Hydrogen or hydrogen potential. As the number of hydrogen ions (H+) in the soil increases, so too does soil acidity. The acidity or alkalinity of a soil is measured using the pH scale, which ranges from 1 to 14, with a pH of 7 being considered neutral, since it is neither acidic nor alkaline. From pH 7 to 1 the soil is increasingly acidic, and from pH 7 to 14 the soil is increasingly alkaline. Because the pH scale is logarithmic, a soil with a pH of 4 is ten times more acidic than a soil with a pH of 5 and 100 times more acidic than a soil with a pH of 6.

Parent material affects the pH of a soil. Where the parent material is calcareous, such as a limestone or chalk, the soil will be neutral to alkaline. Parent materials like shale, sandstone and granite, which contain acidic minerals such as iron, sulphur and aluminum, will produce more acidic soils. Rainfall also affects soil pH, with areas of high rainfall having pH values ranging from 5 to 7, while a pH range between 6.8 and 9 characterises arid regions.

pH effect on nutrient availability

Soil pH affects the chemical composition of nutrients in the soil and their availability to plants. Worldwide, mineral soils have a pH range from 4 to 10, while a pH range of 5.5 to 6.5 provides optimum availability of plant nutrients. Iron, manganese and zinc are essential nutrients that are less available to plants in the pH range between 5 and 8, and phosphorus is most readily available to plants at around pH 6.5. In acid soils below pH 5, so much aluminum, iron and manganese can be dissolved in soil water that it becomes toxic to plants. In these conditions, other valuable nutrients such as potassium, magnesium and copper are easily dissolved in soil water and leached from the soil. Soil pH also influences soil micro-organisms. Acidic conditions reduce the number of decomposing bacteria, which reduces organic matter decomposition and results in organic matter accumulation and less nitrogen and other nutrients being available to plants.

Although many plants cannot survive below pH 5, some plants are adapted to the low-nutrient conditions that occur in acid soils. These include many conifer trees and plants in the *Ericaceae* family such as the heathers and heaths (*Calluna* and *Erica* species), all rhododendrons and azaleas (*Rhododendron* species), blueberries (*Vaccinium* species) and the strawberry tree (*Arbutus unedo*). Conversely, ericaceous plants cannot tolerate neutral to alkaline soils. In these conditions, micronutrients like iron, which is essential to their growth, become unavailable and the plants will show evidence of chlorosis, or yellowing of the leaves between the veins. This condition will eventually lead to the plants' decline and death (Figure 3.1).

Figure 3.2 shows the effect of pH levels on nutrient availability to most plants.

▶ Figure 3.1

Leaves of a rhododendron plant exhibit chlorosis that may have been caused by planting in a soil with too high a pH.
Source: Photo by Patrick Mooney.

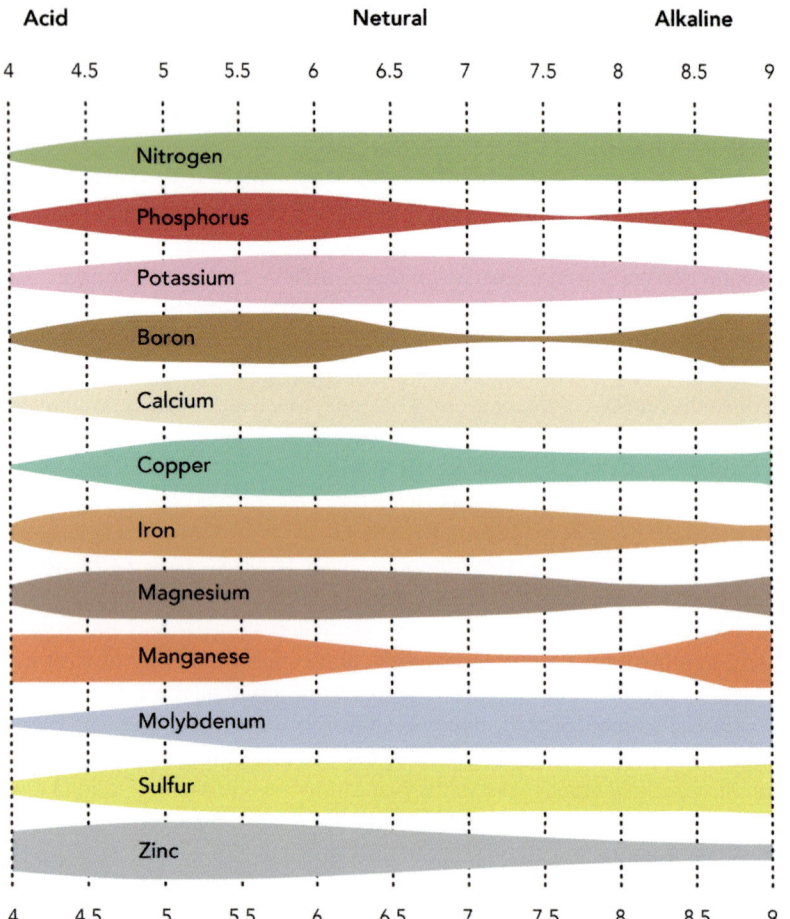

◀ Figure 3.2

The effect of pH on plant nutrient availability.
Source: Drawing by Jiffy Lee and Yiwen Ruan.

Small adjustments to soil pH are possible but require an ongoing management program. In the case of horticultural limes that are intended to raise pH, repeated applications will be needed, because liming materials dissolve in the soil water solution and are leached from the soil. The same principle applies to acidifying soil amendments. Attempting to grow rhododendrons or other ericaceous plants on alkaline soils by lowering the pH through the application of acidifying agents is unlikely to be successful in the long term. It is always preferable to adapt the plantings to the regional and local soil conditions, whether acid or alkaline, clay or sand.

Plant macro- and micronutrients

Plants require macronutrients, which are used in relatively large amounts, and micronutrients, which are also necessary for plant growth but are used in much smaller amounts. Of the nine essential macronutrients, three are not derived from the soil. Plants obtain carbon and oxygen from the air during photosynthesis and hydrogen from water in the soil. With the exception of nitrogen, which is derived almost exclusively from decayed plant matter, the remaining macro- and micronutrient minerals in a soil are derived from its parent material. The minerals present in the soil influence the pH of the soil, and this in turn influences the availability of nutrients.

For adequate plant growth, nutrients must be present in the soil in forms that are available for use by plants and they must be balanced. For example, an excess of calcium in the soil can reduce the availability of iron, zinc and manganese (Brady and Weil, 2010).

The macronutrients

Nitrogen, phosphorus, potassium, calcium, magnesium and sulphur are the macronutrients supplied by soils and are the focus of soil fertility and plant nutrition.

Nitrogen (N)

Nitrogen supports vegetative plant growth and is responsible for leaf and shoot expansion. For this reason, lawn fertilisers are high in nitrogen. In flowering plants, excess nitrogen will reduce flowering and fruiting.

The majority of nitrogen found in terrestrial ecosystems is stored in living and dead plant matter and is unavailable to plants until it undergoes a process known as the nitrogen cycle. This consists of two parts: Mineralisation and nitrification. In mineralisation, bacteria, micro-organisms and fungi in the upper soil layer convert decaying organic matter into ammonium (NH_{4+}). In the process of nitrification, most of the ammonium is converted to nitrate (NO_3) by bacteria belonging to the genus *Nitrosomonas* (Johnson, Albrecht, Ketterings, Beckman and Stockin, 2005). When the microbes die, nitrates which are plant-accessible are released. Nitrates are easily dissolved in soil water, transported by water moving through the soil and may be leached from the soil.

Members of the bean family or *Fabacea* can fix nitrogen through nodules on their roots. These include trees like black locust (*Robinia pseudoacacia*) and shrubs like the red bird of paradise (*Caesalpinia pulcherrima*). A few woody plants that are not in the *Fabacea* family, such as alders, *Alnus* and *Ceanothus*, also fix nitrogen through nodules on their roots. Such nitrogen fixing plants are not only suitable for planting in nitrogen-deficient soils, they are improvers of the soils. Over time, they add available nitrogen to the soil, which can help to support other plants.

The nitrogen found in chemical fertilisers is produced in an energy-intensive process that uses natural gas to capture nitrogen present in the air. The resulting ammonium is used to make nitrogen fertilisers.

Phosphorus (P)

Phosphorus is particularly important in promoting root development, flowering and fruiting, and disease resistance in plants. In acidic soil conditions, phosphorus combines with iron, aluminum and manganese present in the soil, locking the phosphorus in the soil and making it unavailable to the plants. This situation is mitigated if the soil has higher organic matter content. The acids that result from organic decay will also form compounds with iron and aluminum. This means that less iron and aluminum is combined with the phosphorus and the remaining phosphorus remains available for plant growth (Brady and Weil, 2010).

Potassium (K)

Potassium helps to offset the effects of too much nitrogen or phosphorus and is used to balance commercial fertilisers. It aids in water uptake by plants, general plant vigour, disease resistance and root growth. Potassium deficiency may give the same symptoms as drought even where water is available.

Nitrogen (N), phosphorus (P) and potassium (K) are major nutrients found in manures and most commercial fertilisers. The percentage of each of these three macronutrients is shown on the fertiliser container in the order N-P-K, so a commercial fertiliser with the symbol 4-10-10 would be 4 per cent nitrogen, 10 per cent phosphorus and 10 per cent potassium.

Calcium, magnesium and sulphur are classified as secondary plant nutrients because they are required in smaller amounts than the other macronutrients. They are usually present in the soil and need not be supplied by fertilisers. Horticultural lime contains large amounts of both calcium and magnesium. Sulphur is available through decomposing organic matter and in many forms of fertiliser like potassium sulphate, magnesium sulphate and calcium sulphate (gypsum).

Calcium (Ca)

Calcium is essential for the development of plants cells and shoots and root tip growth. A calcium deficiency will result in deformed leaves, stunted roots and failure of fruit to develop. This deficiency can be corrected with the application of gypsum.

Magnesium (Mg)

Magnesium is necessary for photosynthesis, since it is a component of the chlorophyll molecule, and it is essential for the uptake of other nutrients. Its deficiency will result in chlorotic leaves developing near the bottom of the plant and then becoming spotted and dropping.

Sulphur (S)

Sulphur is necessary for the production of chlorophyll, the utilisation of phosphorus and other nutrients and the manufacture of proteins. Its deficiency is indicated by an overall yellowing of the plant and stunted growth (Tucker, 1999).

The micronutrients

The essential plant micronutrients, alternatively known as trace elements, are boron (B), zinc (Zn), manganese (Mn), iron (Fe), copper (Cu), molybdenum (Mo), chlorine (Cl) and cobalt (Co). These nutrients are no less essential to plants than macronutrients but, except for iron and manganese, are found in very small concentrations in soils. Micronutrients are relatively less present in sandy and organic soils and less available under alkaline conditions (Brady and Weil, 2010). Under extended periods of cultivation, the relatively small amounts of trace elements in the soil can become depleted, leading to nutrient deficiencies. As with macronutrients, their availability is influenced by soil pH (Figure 3.2).

The macronutrients are involved in key metabolic processes, such as respiration and photosynthesis, by which plant tissues are created and maintained and energy is produced. They have also been shown to be involved in mitigating the effects of frost and drought. Deficiencies in trace elements lead to abnormal and stunted growth (Kabata-Pendias, 2010).

Cation exchange capacity

An ion is any electrically charged atom or group of atoms. Positively charged ions are called *cations* and negatively charged ions are called *anions*. The cation exchange capacity or CEC of a soil is a measure of the total number of positively charged ions, or cations, that the soil can adsorb, that is, that can be adhered to the surface of the soil particles (Brady and Weil, 2010). It is important because, like pH, it influences the availability of nutrients. Hydrogen (H+) is a cation in the soil, as are many plant nutrients; for example, phosphorus (P+5), potassium (K+1), magnesium (Mg+2), iron (Fe+3), copper (Cu+2) and boron (B+3). During the process of cation exchange, hydrogen ions, present in the soil from root hairs and soil microorganisms, move into solution in the soil, where they replace soil nutrient cations. This results in nutrients being moved into the soil solution, where they are absorbed by plants or may be leached from the soil. The higher the soil CEC, the greater the availability of nutrients to the plants. Cation exchange capacity is considered an indication of soil nutrient availability. It should be noted, however, that CEC is itself influenced by the pH of the soil. As pH increases, CEC increases.

Carbon/nitrogen ratio

The carbon/nitrogen (C/N) ratio is the ratio of the weight of organic carbon in the soil (C) to the weight of the total nitrogen (N) in the soil. The C/N ratio is significant because it influences the available nitrogen in the soil. The C/N ratio in most soils is between 10:1 and 12:1, while the C/N ratio in plants is between 20:1 and 30:1. Because the C/N ratio in plants is so much greater than in soils, adding organic matter which is derived from plants to a soil increases its C/N ratio. This leads to increased activity of decomposing soil micro-organisms and ultimately the formation of humus and the release of nitrates (Brady and Weil, 2010).

Soil types and their characteristics

Different soils vary greatly in their colour, texture, structure and organic and mineral content. These factors influence the soils' ability to support plants.

Soil colour

While the colour of the soil has no direct bearing on productivity, the soil colour is indicative of the minerals, organic matter and available water in the soil. Darker soil colours typically indicate increased organic content in the soil. Soils having a high organic matter content have a negative charge that gives a high CEC and higher nutrient values. Reddish and yellowish soils indicate the presence of iron, and blue-coloured soils are an indication that the soil has a high water table and is saturated throughout much of the year (Soil 4 Teachers, n.d.). Soils that are high in calcite or dolomite will be white in colour and alkaline. For example, chalk is a soft white limestone comprised of calcite ($CaCO_3$) that is usually distributed in shallow, well-drained soils that may have a pH of 7.1 or higher (RHS, n.d.).

Soil texture

Sand, silt and clay are different-sized soil particles. The type of soil particle that predominates in a soil determines the soil's textural classification, so a sandy soil would have predominately sand particles, a silty soil predominately silt particles and so on. Sand particles are between 0.05 and 2.0 millimetres in diameter; silt particles are between 0.05 and 0.002 millimetres and clay particles are less than 0.002 millimetres (or 2 microns). Sandy soils are considered to be coarse-textured, while soils with high clay or slit content are considered to be fine-textured (Brady and Weil, 2010). Loams or loamy soils are soils that have a mix of sand, silt and clay particles. They contain between 7 and 27 per cent clay, 28–50 per cent silt and less than 52 per cent sand (Figure 3.3).

▶ Figure 3.3

Soil particle composition of different soil types.
Source: Drawing by Jiffy Lee and Yiwen Ruan.

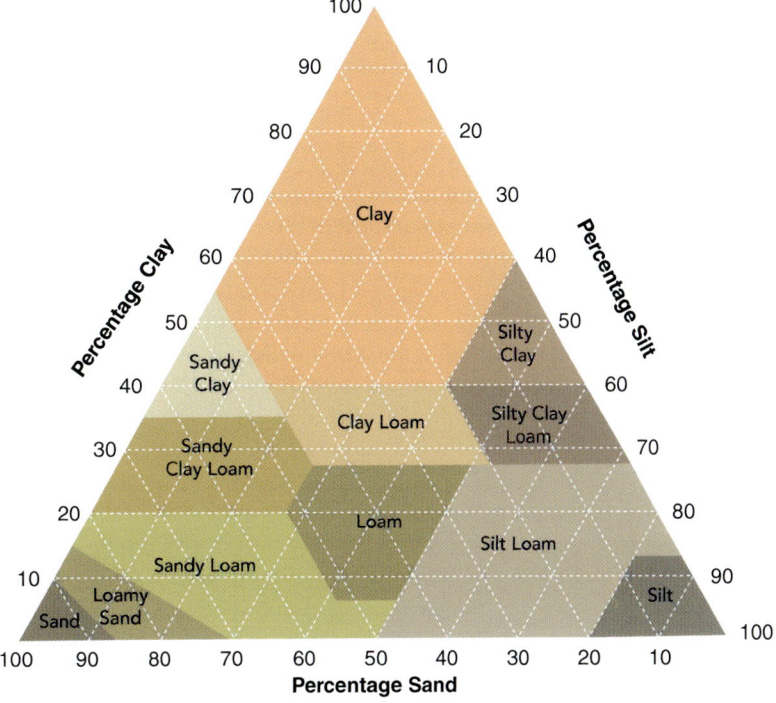

A great deal may be inferred from the texture of a soil. Fine-textured soils that are dominated by clay and silt particles include clay and clay loams, sandy and silty clay loams, and silty clay soils. Soils that are high in clay content have a high water- and nutrient-holding capacity and are likely to be poorly drained. Loams and silts are medium-textured soils that are intermediate in fertility and moisture retention and include very fine sandy loams, loams, silt loams and silts. They combine good fertility and moisture retention with good drainage. Sands, loamy sands and sandy loams are coarse-textured soils that are well drained, less moisture retentive and less fertile than fine- or medium-textured soils. Figure 3.3 shows the per cent range of the different soil particle sizes in soils of all textural classes.

Suppose that our soil test informs us that a particular soil is 40 per cent sand, 30 per cent clay and 30 per cent silt. If we follow the dashed white lines in the diagram from the 40 per cent point on the sand side of the triangle diagonally right to left, the 30 per cent point of the clay side of the triangle horizontally left to right, and the 30 per cent point on the silt side of the triangle diagonally right to left to find the point where the three dashed lines converge, we would discover that our soil is a clay loam. In the same fashion, we could determine that a soil that was 10 per cent sand, 30 per cent clay and 60 per cent silt would be a silty clay loam. From the relative coarseness or fineness of the soil textural class we could infer its drainage and moisture retention. If possible, we would choose the silty clay loam over the clay loam because it is more fertile and better drained than the clay loam.

Soil organic matter content

Organic matter has a significant influence on soil quality compared to the amount present in the soil. It supplies most of the cation exchange capacity of the soil, is the main energy source for soil micro-organisms that fix and release nitrogen, and is a major source of phosphorus and sulphur (Brady and Weil, 2010). Humus is the more-or-less stable portion of soil organic matter that remains in the soil after most of the organic matter has decomposed (Soil Science Society of America, n.d.). The ability of humus to hold water and nutrients is greater than that of a clay soil, so the addition of organic matter and humus to the soil greatly increases both soil moisture and nutrient-holding capacity.

Humus is important to the formation and maintenance of soil structure. Soluble salts, clay, iron and lime will cause soils to aggregate into columnar or blocky structures that reduce plant growth. The addition of organic matter to the soil promotes the formation and stability of soil aggregates—assemblages of soil particles that are bound together within the soil. In the process of soil aggregate formation, decomposition of organic matter by soil microbes produces organic materials that cause soil particles to adhere, forming soil aggregates. Earthworms also release materials that bind soil particles together.

Increased organic matter fosters soil aggregate formation and stability and increases soil biological activity. Like texture, the structure of the soil aggregates fosters root penetration and the movement of water, air and nutrients through the soils. Soil should be managed to preserve the soil structure as this facilitates plant growth.

Available water capacity

Available water capacity is an indicator of a soil's ability to retain water for plant use. It is defined as the water held in soil between its field capacity and permanent wilting point (Soil Science Society of America, n.d.). Field capacity is the water remaining in a soil after it has been thoroughly saturated and allowed to drain freely. The permanent wilting point is the moisture content of a soil at which a sunflower plant will wilt and not recover when removed to a dark, moist atmosphere (Brady and Weil, 2010).

Water capacity may be expressed as a fraction or percentage of total soil volume or as depth in inches or centimetres. In Figure 3.4, it is the area between the field capacity and wilting point lines. This diagram clearly shows the effect of soil texture on the ability of a soil to hold water against the force of gravity. The permanent wilting point will be specific to individual plant species. For example, experienced gardeners will know that

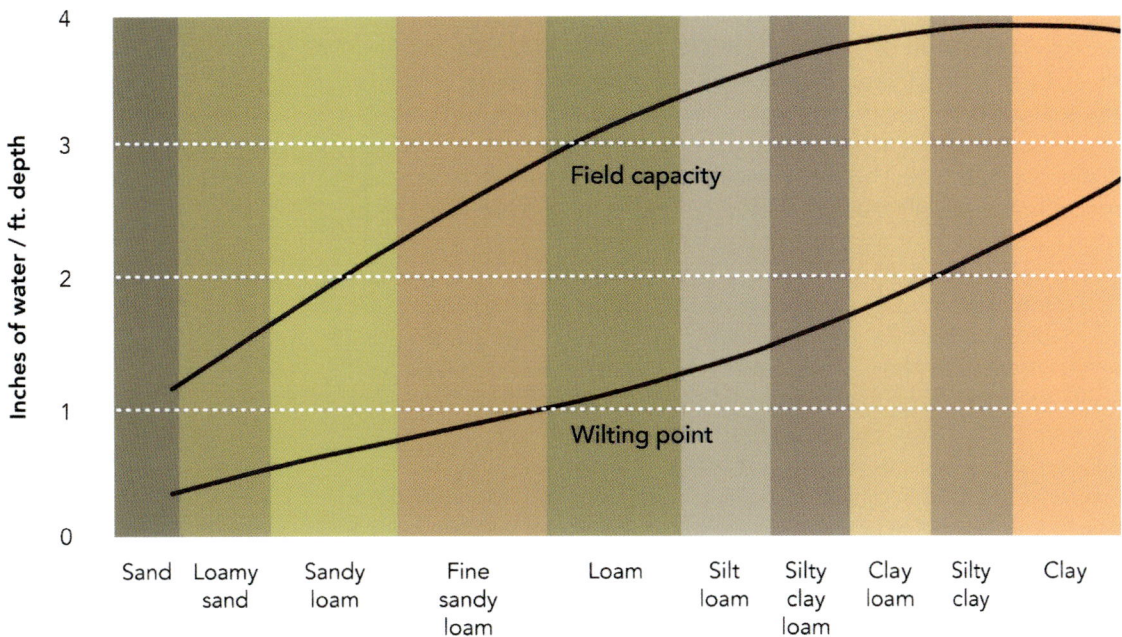

▲ Figure 3.4

Available water capacity, field capacity and the wilting point of soils by soil textural classification (after Zotarelli, Dukes and Morgan, 2010).
Source: Drawing by Jiffy Lee and Yiwen Ruan.

a garden *Phlox* (*Phlox paniculata*) will wilt much sooner than a bearded *Iris* (*Iris germanica*) growing beside it even though they share a common available soil moisture.

Factors affecting available water capacity

There are a number of factors besides the soil textural class that can affect available water capacity. As we have seen, organic matter increases soil's moisture-holding capacity. Compaction and salts in the soil reduce available water capacity. Compaction reduces the volume of water-holding soil pore spaces in the soil, and salts in the soil reduce the ability of plants to take in water through their roots. Shallow soils have lower soil volumes than deeper soils and will have less available water. A high volume of non-porous stones in a soil will also reduce the available water capacity, since they reduce the volume of water-holding soil.

Figure 3.4 demonstrates the lower available water capacity of coarse-textured soils when compared with fine-textured soils and shows that the permanent wilting point is found at higher soil water volumes in finer-textured soils.

Soil management

Soils intended for growing plants should enable the plants' roots to attain a spread and depth sufficient to support the plants, allow water and air to infiltrate through the soil, act as a reservoir of available water and supply the necessary plant nutrients. The ability of a soil to meet these criteria is influenced by its physical, chemical and biological makeup. Physical properties of a soil such as its textural composition and depth will affect root penetration and plant stability and the movement of air and water through the soil. Chemical properties such as pH, available nutrients and nutrient balance will affect the plants' ability to access necessary nutrients, and biological properties such as per cent organic matter and the activity of decomposing bacteria will affect a soil's nitrogen cycling, aggregate formation and stability.

Soils with high clay content are heavy, hard to work and likely to be poorly drained. Because clay particles are less than 2 microns in size, clay soils have very small pore spaces. These small pore sizes attract water molecules and restrict the flow of water and air through the soil. If clay soils are worked when wet, the small platy soil particles will align and the soil will compact. This destroys the soil structure, reducing soil pore spaces so that water and oxygen cannot adequately infiltrate the soil. The original soil structure cannot be regained. For this reason, clay soils should never be worked when wet. However, incorporating organic matter into a compacted clay soil will lead to a build-up of humus that will bind the clay particles into sand-sized soil aggregates that will once again permit air and water to infiltrate the soil.

Course-textured sandy soils are so well drained that they are likely to be moisture deficient and also nutrient deficient, since soluble nutrients are easily leached from sandy soils. The addition and decomposition of organic matter will bind the sand particles into soil aggregates and will aid both moisture and nutrient retention. Because nutrients are easily leached in coarse-textured soils, additional fertilisers or yearly application of organic matter may be required for optimal plant growth.

Most soils will benefit from the addition of organic matter, as it improves soil structure and increases moisture retention and available nutrients.

Organic matter can be added to a soil in three ways:

1. Soil amendments prior to planting
2. Mulching
3. Topdressing

Soil amendments prior to planting

This is the type of treatment that would be appropriate on a site where the soils were heavy compacted clays or low-fertility subsoils and where installing commercial topsoil blends was not possible. A typical treatment would consist of covering the top of the soil with 6–9 inches (15–23 centimetres) of organic matter such as sawdust. This can then be worked into the upper 12 inches (30 centimetres) of the soil using the blade of a bulldozer or a mechanical tiller. The goal should be to establish a soil organic matter level of 4 to 5 per cent. This level of organic matter should yield enough available nutrients that no additional chemical nitrogen fertiliser will be required (Davis and Wilson, 2005).

The larger the wood particles used, the slower the decomposition rate. Nitrogen will be unavailable in the soil until the mineralisation process has been completed. To mitigate this problem, the sawdust or other organic soil amendment can be composted before being added to the soil. If fresh sawdust or woodchips are being added to the soil, it is advisable to add a commercial nitrogen fertiliser to the amended soil to compensate for the lack of available nitrogen while the decomposers do their work. This should be approximately two to three years or longer depending on local climate. In addition, the decomposition process will be accelerated if nitrogen is added to the composting soil amendment.

Fallen leaves, straw, manures, composts, wood ash and bio solids are other organic amendments that are already decomposed or will break down more quickly and can be added in the place of sawdust and woodchips. Bio solids are organic matter that has been recovered from sewage and are usually marketed as a fertiliser. It is often the case that manures and bio solids are high in salts that will effectively dry the soil and may even cause plant mortality. In the United States and Canada, Class A bio solids have been approved for food production but should be tested before use. Under certain conditions the pathogens in the bio solids may rebloom and Class A bio solids may contain allowable levels of ten metals, including the heavy metals cadmium, mercury and lead. The same labs that do soil testing will test organic soil amendments for salts, pH and nutrients. A more specialised laboratory, such as a university laboratory, is usually needed to test for levels of heavy metals.

Wood ash has some phosphate as well as trace elements and small amounts of heavy metals. It is high in calcium carbonate and will raise the pH of the soil to which it is added. It should never be used on acid-loving plants and should be used with caution to ensure it does not adversely affect soil pH.

Peat is partially decomposed plant matter, especially sphagnum moss that develops in wetlands. It is acidic and low in nutrients but is used as a soil amendment in many parts of the world to improve soil structure and moisture retention.

The value of peat lands

Peat lands have many important values other than that of the extracted peat. Objects buried in peat bogs are slow to decay, and peat lands have provided important archeological records. Peat lands support rare species of plants, insects, birds and mammals that are adapted to their acidic, low-nutrient, saturated conditions. They act as sponges that store, filter and then slowly release the water they receive to surrounding areas, helping to reduce flooding and supporting adjacent ecosystems (RSNC, 1990).

Most importantly, peat soils are a significant source of carbon sequestration and so offset the causes of climate change. Although peat lands cover only 2–3 per cent of the global land surface, the carbon stored in peat represents about 20 per cent of all carbon stored in terrestrial ecosystems (Heijmans, Mauquoy, Geel and Berendse, 2008). The amount of carbon stored in northern hemisphere peat lands is equal to about 90 years of global anthropocentric carbon dioxide emissions. When peat is harvested and burned or allowed to compost, the carbon it contains is released into the atmosphere (Hogg, Lieffers and Wein, 1992).

The process of extracting peat entails draining the peat land and removing the upper layers of peat. If the peat land is restored after extraction, peat will regrow at that rate of 6–7 centimetres a century, meaning that if the peat has been extracted to a depth of 2 metres, it would take an estimated 3,000 years before the peat was restored to its original depth (Organic Gardening, n.d.).

Canada, the world's largest peat producer, exports 80 per cent of its 1.2 million tonnes of annual production to the United States, where it is primarily used in agriculture and by home gardeners. The natural peat accumulation in Canada is estimated to be about 70 million tonnes per year, and far exceeds that which is extracted each year (Daigle and Daigle, 2001). In Britain, draining for agriculture and afforestation is a long-standing practice. It is estimated that by 1980, 91.5 per cent of the lowland bog areas of the UK had been destroyed (Barkham, 1993).

Increasingly, the climate change effect of peat extraction is being recognised, and there is growing opposition to the extraction and use of peat. Many horticulturists now recognise that compost and coir (a byproduct of coconut production) and other organic amendments are reliable substitutes for peat.

Mulches

Mulch can be any material that is spread over the surface of the soil between plants. Mulches may be divided into organic mulches such as bark mulch or pine needles, inorganic mulches like decorative pebbles or ceramic mulches, and sheet mulches such as newspaper and cardboard, "landscape fabric" or black plastic sheets.

Mulches help to suppress weeds and retain moisture. They may also be used to protect plantings, especially new plantings, from frost damage by limiting the depth of penetration of frost into the soil. Biodegradable mulches will eventually decompose and their organic matter will be incorporated into the soil by earthworms and leaching. For this reason, organic mulches are another source of organic matter for the soil, improving soil structure, moisture retention and nutrients.

Mulches should be laid to a depth of 2–4 inches (5–10 centimetres). After placing the mulch over clean, weed-free, well-watered soils, care should be taken to pull the mulch back from the stems and trunks of shrubs and trees to avoid softening of the bark and potentially introducing disease to the plants.

Inorganic mulches such as decorative gravels have no soil improvement qualities but do help to retain moisture and give a uniform appearance. Sheet mulches may be organic, like newspaper and cardboard, or inorganic plastic sheet mulches. Organic sheet mulches are used to kill existing vegetation without the use of chemicals and are commonly left in place and incorporated into the new planting. Sheet mulches like landscape fabric are typically black in colour to absorb the sun's rays and warm the soil beneath. They do an excellent job of suppressing weeds and are often used in growing vegetables or other row crops. I don't recommend that they be used in the landscape except as a temporary measure, as they eventually become exposed and unsightly as well as making it impossible to work the soil over which they have been placed without removal. Granular mulches, whether organic or inorganic, can simply be raked away from the areas to be worked and replaced when work is complete.

Topdressing

Topdressing is the practice of adding a layer of soil or compost over a lawn or planting bed. Topdressing lawns increases the rooting depth, reduces water demand and adds nutrients. It improves the appearance of the lawn and can aid establishment or be used to renew a lawn every few years.

Topdressing is often done annually or semi-annually in planting beds. Here its purpose is similar to mulches; it helps to hold moisture, improves the quality of the soil and gives a uniform attractive appearance. Topdressing is usually done with composts or very well-rotted manure such as mushroom compost—the spent manures that have been used to grow mushrooms. Annual topdressing of planting beds will usually be 1–2 inches (2.5–5 centimetres) in depth. Be sure to pull the topdressing away from the base of plants as it can cause stem rot.

Topdressings will have lower weed suppression capabilities than organic mulches but are superior at quickly incorporating organic matter into the soil profile because the topdressing material is already partially decomposed.

Adjusting the pH

Adding lime, or liming, is done to raise the pH of acidic soils. The liming materials are usually finely ground limestone and contribute calcium carbonate to the soil. Dolomite lime is a finely ground limestone that contains both calcium and magnesium, and it is used on soils that are magnesium deficient. The liming material is spread at a recommended rate on the surface of the soil and may be mixed into the soil or allowed to leach over time.

Raising the pH of acidic soil increases the activity of soil microorganisms, speeding organic matter decomposition and the release of nitrogen. Depending on the existing pH of the soil, it may also increase the availability of a wide variety of nutrients, making fertiliser use more efficient (see Figure 3.2). In very low-pH soils the levels of aluminum and manganese may be toxic to plants. Raising the pH by liming changes the chemical form of these minerals and makes them less available to plants, thereby eliminating their toxicity (Atlantic Soils Need Lime, n.d.). Where soils are naturally acidic, lawns may be limed annually to increase nutrient availability and reduce the growth of mosses that thrive in low-nutrient acidic conditions.

Just as adding calcium to the soil will raise soil pH, adding acidic materials like iron, sulphur, ferrous sulphate and aluminum sulphate increases acidity and lowers the pH. Soils with high clay content have a buffering capacity and, whether raising or lowering the pH of the soil, larger amounts of the agent will be needed (RHS, n.d.).

Plant hardiness

Plant hardiness is a measure of a plant's ability to survive in a geographic area having uniform climatic conditions. It is based on a number of climatic factors, but in temperate regions is mostly a measure of the plant's ability to survive minimum winter temperatures. In 1960, the United States Department of Agriculture (USDA) released its the first plant hardiness zone map, based on minimum average ten-year winter temperatures. It is intended as an aid to gardeners and has become widely adopted.

In 1967, Agriculture Canada released a plant hardiness zone map for Canada based on plant survival data. In addition to minimum winter temperatures, it included the length of the frost-free period, summer rainfall, maximum temperatures, snow cover and wind speeds. Plant hardiness maps have now been developed for much of the planet and are mostly based on minimum winter temperature.

In North America, plant hardiness zones are numbered, with lower numbers indicating colder regions and warmer regions having higher numbers. All plants in cultivation have been assigned a plant hardiness zone under the different plant hardiness systems. By matching a plant of known hardiness with a hardiness zone, the risk of loss of the plant due to climatic factors is greatly reduced. For example, bur oak (*Quercus macrocarpa*) has a USDA plant hardiness rating of 3. It may be confidently planted in zones 3–9 but cannot be expected to thrive in either colder or warmer hardiness zones.

The USDA plant hardiness mapping has been applied to Europe and the UK. The maps are periodically revised based on new ten-year average temperatures, and we may expect that climate change will result in significant change in the location of plant hardiness zones in future, with warmer zones generally creeping northward.

In the United Kingdom, the Royal Horticultural Society (RHS) has developed its own hardiness rating system based on minimum temperatures. Table 3.0 compares the RHS and USDA hardiness rating systems.

TABLE 3.0 A comparison of RHS and USDA plant hardiness rating systems (after Gardenia, n.d.).

RHS Hardiness Ratings	USDA Hardiness Zones	Temperatures
H1a	13	>59°F 15°C
H1b	12	50°F to 59°F 10°C to 15°C
H1c	11	41°F to 50°F 5°C to 10°C
H2	10	34°F to 41°F 1°C to 5°C
H3	9	23°F to 34°F -5°C to 1°C
H4	8, 9	14°F to 23°F -10°C to -5°C
H5	7, 8	5°F to 14°F -15°C to -10°C
H6	6, 7	-4°F to 5°F -20°C to -15°C

Source: Table courtesy of Yiwen Ruan.

Plant hardiness ratings and zone maps must be understood as a reliable but general guideline. Microclimatic and soil conditions will also affect plant survival.

Plant communities

A plant community is a group of plants that occur together. The largest community recognised by scientists is the *biome* or formation. A biome is a community of plants and animals that is determined by the precipitation and temperature, and may cover many thousands of square miles/kilometres. For example, the short grass prairie of North America receives little more than 25 inches (64 centimetres) of annual precipitation while the tall grass prairie receives about 30–40 inches (76–102 centimetres) of precipitation annually. Within a biome there will be smaller reoccurring plant communities known as associations. A plant association is a plant community that has a defined species composition and which grows in a uniform habitat condition (Barnes et al., 1997).

Plants within the plant association are adapted to similar climatic and growing conditions but occupy different niches based on their specific needs.

The variation in the growing conditions of the plants is the result of environmental gradients. Environmental gradients are gradual changes in abiotic (that is, physical and not biological) factors through space or over time.

Every plant has a set of requirements and tolerances that influences its establishment, growth and regeneration. For example, a plant may require high levels of light, water and nutrients and have a very low tolerance for salinity. If the plant's requirements are met but its salinity tolerance is exceeded, it will not be able to survive. Salinity tolerance becomes the limiting factor to the plant's establishment in that location, and limiting factors supersede all other factors in plant survival (Brady and Weil, 2010).

Plant communities change with changes in environmental gradients

The Douglas fir (*Pseudotsuga menziesii*) is a large conifer tree that is native to western North America. It is the dominant tree in a number of plant associations throughout its range, and these plant associations change in response to climate, soils and available moisture. Figure 3.5 shows four different plant associations that are positioned along a slope due to changes in growing conditions that result from environmental gradient changes. Each plant association will have a distinct species list, or floristic composition, with some overlap between the different plant associations.

The Douglas fir–Shore pine–*Arbutus* (*Pseudotsuga menziesii* var. *menziesii*–*Pinus contorta* var. *contorta*–*Arbutus menziesii*) plant association is defined by its dominant trees and occurs at the top of the slope. This position has the driest soil moisture regime because soils are shallower and rock outcrops closer to the surface at the top of the slope due to soil erosion. This means that soil volume and available soil moisture are reduced. On water-shedding sites like the top of this slope, dissolved nitrogen is carried downslope by water flowing through the soil as interflow, resulting in a poorer nutrient regime. Further down the slope, water-receiving positions receive eroded soils, giving them deeper, more fertile soils. In Figure 3.5, plants at the bottom of the slope receive more moisture and nutrients and less sun than those that occupy a position further up the slope. Over extended periods of time, the soils at the bottom of the slope become higher in fine soil particles and organic matter and thus more nutrient-rich and moisture-retentive than soils further up the slope. These conditions interact with the requirements of the individual plants to create an ideal position for each of the plant associations shown above. The skunk cabbage (*Lysichiton americanum*), which thrives in the very moist, high-nutrient environment at the bottom of the slope, could not survive in the drier, low-nutrient environment at the top of the slope. Conversely, the white fawn lily (*Erythronium oreganum*) is adapted to the full sun, low-nutrient conditions at the top of the slope and would not survive in the lower slope environment.

Abiotic conditions change over space and time, leading to changes in conditions for plant growth. In this example, soil moisture regime and

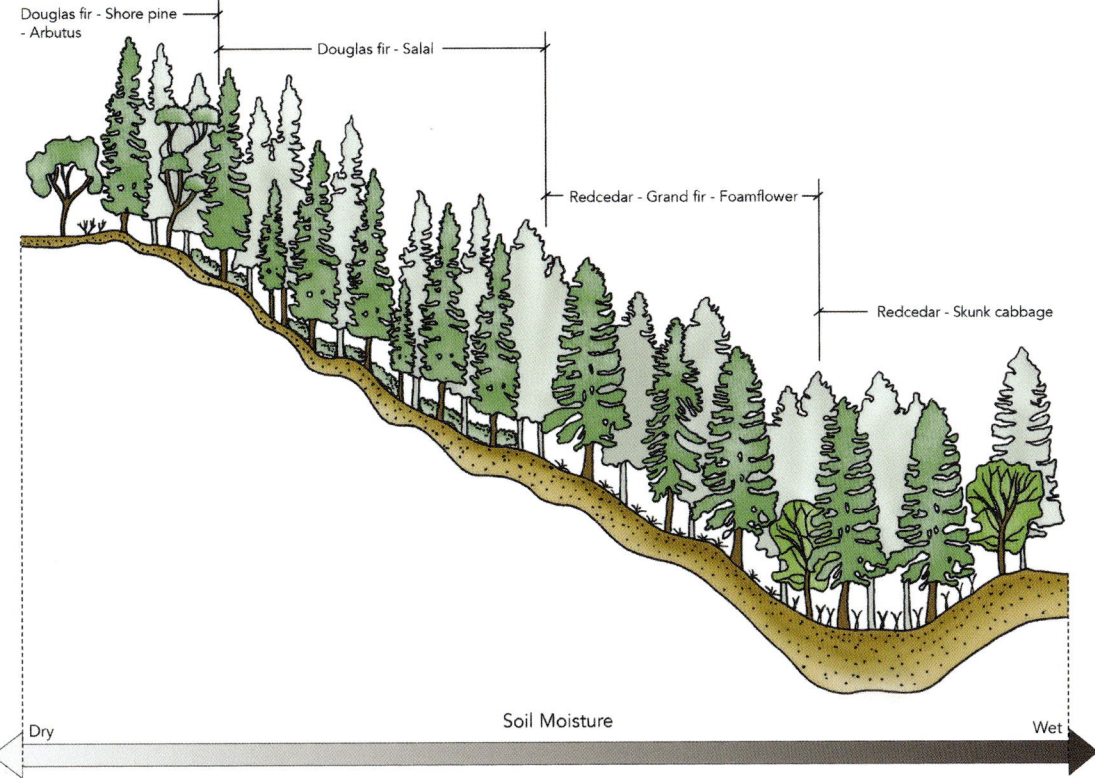

▲ Figure 3.5

Plant associations located along a moisture and fertility gradient (after Nuszdorfer, Klinka and Demarchi, 1991).
Source: Image courtesy of Yiwen Ruan.

depth, fertility, organic matter levels and sun exposure are growing conditions that change over time and along the gradient of position on a slope. Other environment gradients that will affect soil moisture and plant growth include elevation above the water table, depth to the impermeable layer and soil volume.

Whether we are discussing native plants in a natural landscape or non-native plants in a designed landscape, the understanding that each plant has a range of critical abiotic factors that determine where it will thrive is essential to designing with plants and to making appropriate planting decisions. Figure 3.5 illustrates the important concept that all plants have a set of requirements and tolerances that influence their regeneration, growth and location in the landscape and that these growing conditions change in response to environmental gradients. Planting design is the act of creating new plant associations in which:

- The plants have similar growing conditions.
- Individual plants have specific niches and limiting factors.
- The growing conditions change in response to environmental gradients.
- Designed plant associations can form biologically diverse functioning habitats and ecosystems.

Fawn Lily

Skunk Cabbage

Chapter 3 principles

Below are some of the key principles of this chapter.

- Available soil moisture is a function of the volume of soil. It is important to ensure sufficient soil volume for the designed plant community, especially for trees, if they are to survive into maturity (see *Additional reading*).
- Topsoil is the best growing medium of the soil profile. Its depth and characteristics will have a great influence on plant growth.
- Most soils benefit from the addition of organic matter as it improves soil structure and increases moisture retention and available nutrients. This may be done prior to installation or through the use of topdressing or mulching.
- It is always advisable to get an existing soil tested prior to planting so that nutrient deficiencies can be corrected.
- It is also advisable to get manufactured topsoil tested, prior to installation, to ensure that it meets that manufacturer's stated analysis.
- It is not enough for the required nutrients to be present in the soil in forms that are available for use by plants. They must be also be balanced, or in the right proportions to each other. Management guidelines given in a soil analysis are intended to help attain this balanced condition.
- Establishing the pH of your soil and matching plants to that pH is necessary for long-term success of the planting.
- Nitrogen is easily leached from the soil and needs to be replaced. We recommend soil management based on the addition of organic materials by direct incorporation or through topdressing and mulching.

▲ Figure 3.6

Fawn lily and skunk cabbage occupy opposite ends of the soil-moisture–fertility continuum.
Source: © Peter Stevens | Flickr; © John Mason | Flickr. Used under the Creative Commons licence.

- Avoid applying too much nitrogen, as it can cause fertiliser burn and will reduce flowering and fruiting.
- Soils should not be tilled, graded, dug or transported when wet. Especially in fine-textured soils, this will lead to compaction that will permanently destroy the original soil structure.
- With the exception of adding organic matter, it is always preferable to adapt the plantings to the site soil conditions, whether acid or alkaline, clay or sand, than to try to overcome these conditions with continuous soil amendments.
- Natural plant communities are distributed along a set of environmental gradients. In creating designed plant communities, each plant in the community must be adapted to a similar range of environmental conditions.

Glossary

Biome: The largest community of plants and animals recognised by scientists. It is determined by precipitation and temperature and may cover many thousands of square miles/kilometres.

Carbon/nitrogen ratio (C/N ratio): The ratio of the weight of organic carbon in the soil (C) to the weight of total nitrogen (N) in the soil. It is significant because it influences the availability of nitrogen in the soil.

Cation Exchange Capacity (CEC): A measure of the total number of positively charged ions that the soil can absorb. It is an indication of available plant nutrients (Brady and Weil, 2010).

Designed landscape: Any landscape that has been altered spatially or functionally to achieve human benefits (Musacchio, 2009).

Ecological restoration: The process of assisting the recovery of an ecosystem that has been damaged or degraded (SER, 2004).

Ecosystem: A dynamic complex of plant, animal and micro-organism communities and their non-living environment interacting as a functional unit (Convention on Biological Diversity, 2004).

Environmental gradients: Gradual changes in abiotic (that is, physical, not biological) factors in the landscape through space or over time. Factors like altitude, temperature, soil depth, ocean proximity and interflow produce the changes in environmental gradients, like soil moisture regime, microclimate and soil nitrogen levels.

Field capacity: The water remaining in a soil after it has been thoroughly saturated and allowed to drain freely.

Formation: See *Biome*.

Humus: The more-or-less stable portion of soil organic matter that remains in the soil after most of the organic matter has decomposed.

Interflow: Stormwater runoff that flows through the soil profile and that is used by plants or returns to the surface but does not become groundwater.

Landscape: The word *landscape* has many legitimate meanings. Landscape is "an area perceived by people, whose character is the result of the action and interaction of natural and/or human factors" (European Landscape Convention, 2000) and also an area of land having common characteristics. It is used here to mean an area of land having a particular appearance or character. It may vary in size from a region to a small garden and may be designed or largely unmodified by human actions.

Macronutrients: Plant nutrients that are used in large amounts. The principal macronutrients are nitrogen, phosphorus and potassium.

Micronutrients: Plant nutrients that are essential to plant growth but that are found in small concentrations in the soil and used in smaller amounts by plants than the macronutrients.

Mulch: Any material that is spread over the surface of the soil between plants.

Native plants: Plants that are endemic to and which occur naturally in a particular location. That is, they are not introduced.

Parent material: The geologic material from which soils develop.

Peat: Partially decomposed plant matter, especially sphagnum moss, that develops in wetlands. Peat soils are entirely organic and are not derived from mineral parent material.

Permanent wilting point: The moisture content of a soil at which a sunflower plant will wilt and not recover when removed to a dark, moist atmosphere.

pH: Potenz Hydrogen, or hydrogen potential. It is a measure of the acidity or alkalinity of a soil and is measured using the pH scale, which ranges from 1 to 14, with a pH of 7 being neutral.

Plant association: A plant community that has a defined species composition and which grows in a uniform habitat condition. It is a subset of a larger plant community (Barnes et al., 1997).

Plant community: A group of plants that occur together.

Plant hardiness: A measure of a plant's ability to survive under a particular set of climatic conditions.

Plant hardiness zone: An area of uniform climatic conditions. By matching plant hardiness to plant hardiness zones, plant mortality due to climate is greatly reduced.

Soil: This consists of natural bodies at Earth's surface, composed of minerals, organic materials and living organisms, in which most rooted plants grow.

Soil aggregates: Assemblages of soil particles that are bound together within the soil.

Soil horizons: The distinct layers in a soil profile that are created by weathering and other soil formation processes.

Soil profile: A section through the soil showing all its horizons.

Soil texture: A measure of the size of a soil particle. Sands are the largest soil particles, and sandy soils are defined as coarse-textured soils, while soils that are comprised of predominately the finer soil particles of silts and clays are considered fine-textured soils.

Topdressing: The practice of adding a layer of soil or compost over a lawn or planting bed.

References

Armson, K.A. (1977). *Forest soils: Properties and processes.* Toronto: University of Toronto Press.

Atlantic Soils Need Lime. (n.d.). Accessed June 15, 2014 at www.nr.gov.nl.ca/nr/publications/agrifoods/atlantic_soils_lime.pdf.

Barkham, J.P. (1993). For peat's sake: Conservation or exploitation? *Biodiversity and Conservation*, 2(5), 556–566.

Barnes, B.V., Zak, D.R., Denton, S.R., & Spurr, S.H. (1998). *Forest ecology* (4th ed.). New York: John Wiley and Sons.

Brady, N.C., & Weil, R.R. (2010). *Elements of the nature and properties of soils* (p. 383). Upper Saddle River, NJ: Pearson Educational International.

Convention on Biological Diversity. (2004). *Ecosystem approach.* Accessed January 19, 2019 at www.cbd.int/ecosystem/description.shtml.

Daigle, J.Y., & Gautreau-Daigle, H. (2001). *Canadian peat harvesting and the environment* (2nd ed.). Ottawa, ON, Canada: North American Wetlands Conservation Council.

Davis, J.G., & Wilson, C.R. (2005). Choosing a soil amendment (Fact Sheet 7.235). Fort Collins, CO: Colorado State University Cooperative Extension Horticulture.

European Landscape Convention. (2000). Accessed January 19, 2019 at https://rm.coe.int/1680080621.

Gardenia: Creating Gardens. (n.d.). *Hardiness zones of Europe.* Accessed January 20, 2019 at www.gardenia.net/guide/european-hardiness-zones.

Heijmans, M.M., Mauquoy, D., Geel, B., & Berendse, F. (2008) Long-term effects of climate change on vegetation and carbon dynamics in peat bogs. *Journal of Vegetation Science*, 19(3), 307–320.

Hogg, E.H., Lieffers, V.J., and Wein, R.W. (1992). Potential carbon losses from peat profiles: Effects of temperature, drought cycles, and fire. *Ecological Applications*, 298–306.

Johnson, C., Albrecht, G., Ketterings, Q., Beckman, J., & Stockin, K. (2005). *Nitrogen basics: The nitrogen cycle*. Agronomy Fact Sheet Series. Ithaca, NY: Cornell University Cooperative Extension.

Kabata-Pendias, A. (2010). *Trace elements in soils and plants*. Boca Raton, FL: CRC Press.

Lindsey, P., & Bassuk, N. (1992). Redesigning the urban forest from the ground below: A new approach to specifying adequate soil volumes for street trees. *Arboricultural Journal*, 16(1), 25–39.

Musacchio, L.R. (2009). The scientific basis for the design of landscape sustainability: A conceptual framework for translational landscape research and practice of designed landscapes and the six Es of landscape sustainability. *Landscape Ecology*, 24(8), 993–1013.

Nuszdorfer, F.C., Klinka, K., & Demarchi, D.A. (1991). Coastal Douglas-fir zone. In D. Meidinger & J. Pojar (Eds.), *Ecosystems of British Columbia*, Special Report Series (Vol. 6) (pp. 81–93). Victoria, BC, Canada: Research Branch, BC Ministry of Forests.

Organic Gardening. (n.d.). *Questioning peat moss: Consider the environmental costs of using it*. Accessed October 6, 2014 at www.organicgardening.com/learn-and-grow/questioning-peat-moss?page=0,1.

RHS (Royal Horticultural Society). (n.d.). Accessed January 19, 2019 at www.rhs.org.uk/advice/profile?pid=179.

RSNC The Wildlife Trusts Partnership. (1990). *The peat report*. Lincoln: Royal Society for Nature Conservation.

Society for Ecological Restoration (SER) International Science and Working Group. (2004). *The SER international primer on ecological restoration* (version 2). Tucson, AZ: Society for Ecological Restoration International. Accessed August 10, 2019 at www.ctahr.hawaii.edu/littonc/PDFs/682_SERPrimer.pdf.

Soil 4 Teachers. (n.d.). Soils overview, provided by the Soil Science Society of America. Accessed January 20, 2019 at www.soils.org/files/about-soils/soils-overview.pdf.

Soil Science Society of America. (n.d.). Glossary of soil science terms. Accessed May 26, 2015 at www.soils.org/publications/soils-glossary#.

Tucker, M.R. (1999). *Essential plant nutrients: Their presence in North Carolina soils and role in plant nutrition*. Department of Agriculture and Consumer Services, Agronomic Division. Accessed July 27, 2019 at http://cdm16062.contentdm.oclc.org/cdm/fullbrowser/collection/p249901coll22/id/461709/rv/compoundobject/cpd/461718.

Urban, J. (1992). Bringing order to the technical dysfunction within the urban forest. *Journal of Arboriculture*, 18(2), 85–90.

Virginia Urban Street Tree Selector. (n.d.). Accessed March 25, 2014 at http://dendro.cnre.vt.edu/treeselector/faq.shtml.

Zotarelli, L., Dukes, M.D., & Morgan, K.T. (2010). *Interpretation of soil moisture content to determine soil field capacity and avoid over-irrigating sandy soils using soil moisture sensors*. AE460. Gainesville, FL: University of Florida Institute of Food and Agricultural Sciences.

Additional reading

Tree soil volumes

Lindsey, Patricia., & Bassuk, Nina. (1992). Redesigning the urban forest from the ground below: A new approach to specifying adequate soil volumes for street trees. *Arboricultural Journal*, 16(1), 25–39.

Urban, J. (1992). Bringing order to the technical dysfunction within the urban forest. *Journal of Arboriculture*, 18(2), 85–90.

Soil management

The Royal Horticultural Society has an excellent website (www.rhs.org.uk). See information on soil management at this link www.rhs.org.uk/advice/profile?pid=179.

Chapter 4

Functional and aesthetic criteria in planting design

This chapter discusses the myriad of goals and objectives that may be incorporated into landscape design and the role that planting design plays in supporting the entire landscape design program. This includes the functional uses and aesthetic meanings of plants in the landscape.

The design program

In what is known as the design process, designers evaluate the current condition of a site against their intended purposes and then develop a plan to change that site so that it better accommodates human needs (Lyle, 1985). When the intended intervention has been made, the product will be a designed landscape, that is, one that has been changed to meet human purposes (Musacchio, 2009).

Part of the design process is the development of a design program for the site. The program is a description of the intended uses of the site, its component parts and their interrelations and is developed after reviewing all available user and site information (La Gro, 2011). For example, the program for a commercial display garden might include glasshouses, perennial borders, a wildflower meadow and a water garden with associated parking, sales centre and public washrooms.

The program will reflect input from the stakeholders, who will determine the goals for the program. Stakeholders can include the owners/clients, regulatory agencies, the public, special interest groups and the designers. Their collective values influence the goals of the proposed landscape intervention and are played out in the accepted program for the site (Figure 4.0).

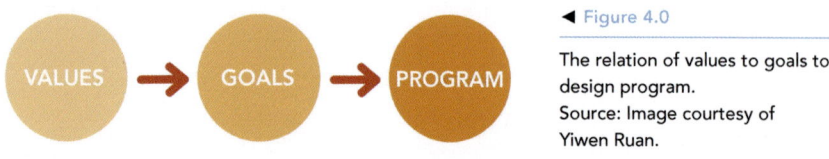

◀ Figure 4.0

The relation of values to goals to design program.
Source: Image courtesy of Yiwen Ruan.

The role of plants in the multi-functional design program

Many books on garden and planting design treat plants as decorative elements, whose sole purpose is to beautify the site and stimulate an aesthetic response in the viewer. These are essential goals of planting design, but plants in designed landscapes also contribute to other valuable functions. These landscape functions are best considered by evaluating the complete range of ecosystem services that may be found in landscapes (Mooney, 2014) and that are supported by plants. Ecosystem services are the services that people receive from nature (Termorshuizen and Opdam, 2009), and landscapes can be designed to deliver a range of essential ecosystem services, such as the water purification and pollination that are necessary for our survival and less tangible benefits like opportunities for recreation, increased wellbeing and aesthetic experience (Mooney, 2014). Landscapes that deliver multiple ecosystem services are considered to be multi-functional and sustainable landscapes (O'Farrell and Anderson, 2010).

Since ecosystem services are increasingly used as the measures of multi-functional landscape performance and sustainability (Selman, 2012), many of today's landscape designers are attempting to produce designs that maximise a range of ecosystem services and their resulting benefits. Chinese landscape architect Kongjian Yu is a world leader in this movement.

Kongjian Yu, China's leading landscape architect

Growing up in rural China, Kongjian Yu endured the social upheaval of the Great Cultural Revolution (1966–1976) and experienced firsthand the environmental degradation of the countryside surrounding his village. After studying forestry and receiving his Masters of Landscape Architecture degree at Beijing Forestry University, he undertook a Doctor of Design degree at Harvard University, where he was influenced by the thinking of noted planner Carl Steinitz. Upon graduation, he worked for the SWA Group for two years before returning to China in 1997, where he founded the firm Turenscape and began teaching urban and regional planning at Peking University (Saunders, 2012).

Today Yu, still an active partner in Turenscape, has won two American Society of Landscape Architects (ASLA) Excellence Awards for general design, an additional nine ASLA Honor Awards and four World's Best Landscape of the Year Awards (World Architectural Festival). He is the founder and dean of the School of Landscape Architecture at Peking University and is a visiting professor at Harvard University. In 2016, Yu was elected as foreign honorary fellow of the American Academy of Arts and Sciences. He lectures widely and has authored many books and articles, including *The Beautiful Big Foot, Landscape as Ecological Infrastructure* and *The Art of Survival*.

Yu believes that conventional urban planning, with its reliance on built infrastructure, has had a negative effect on urban living and the environment.

In response, he seeks to make urban landscapes that are productive rather than ornamental and that heal past environmental damage. His approach, which he calls negative planning, uses a natural ecological infrastructure, instead of conventional built infrastructure, to provide necessary goods and services (Yu, 2006). Ecological infrastructure includes any network of natural lands and working landscapes that is planned and managed to conserve ecosystem functions and provide ecosystem services (Benedict and McMahon, 2006; Eisenman, 2013). Such green infrastructure, as it is sometimes called, preserves and enhances the life support systems of the planet and produces a variety of ecosystem services ranging from water purification to psychological restoration.

Planning and design

In Yu's negative planning, the ecological infrastructure is composed of parks and ecologically critical significant areas and takes precedence over other elements of the plan because its location, size or form determine its functions and benefits. As he has said:

> We can't choose sites for residential areas or office buildings before we figure out the location of rivers, wetlands, wild animal habitats, and cultural heritage sites. Such eco-infrastructure should stay where it is. A green skeleton enables urban design to bring healthy development.
> (Kongjian Yu, quoted in Shuya, n.d., p. 1)

Turenscape's landscapes maintain existing landscape patterns and processes by integrating farmland, wooded areas, shelterbelts and other environmentally significant areas. Greenways are established along existing gorges, waterways, railways and roads, and the natural form of rivers and coastlines is preserved or restored. In addition to their environmental benefits, the award-winning parks designed by Turenscape are intended to be beautiful places that enhance the quality of life for local residents by preserving cultural heritage sites and providing public recreation in an urban natural setting (Yu, 2014).

The aesthetics of negative planning

Designed landscapes that conform to aesthetic norms but have little ecological function are common throughout the modern world. While it is increasingly recognised that alternatives need to be found, the public often demands that traditional landscape appearances be maintained.

Recognising this, Yu has called for the development of a new and productive landscape aesthetic that will be appreciated by ordinary people. This approach might be termed "negative aesthetics" because, just as Yu's

▲ Figure 4.1

Shenyang Architectural University Campus, Shenyang City, China, by Peking University Graduate School of Landscape Architecture and Turenscape. Formerly a rice field. Yu used rice to create a productive landscape. The appearance of the rice crop unifies the campus and establishes the colour, texture and seasonality of the landscape.
Source: Photo courtesy of Turenscape Ltd.

▶ Figure 4.2

The red ribbon bench in Red Ribbon Park in Qinhuangdao City: Its colour and solidity emphasise the ephemeral qualities of the delicate seed heads and waving blades of the adjacent fountain grasses (*Pennisetum alopecuroides*).
Source: Photo courtesy of Turenscape Ltd.

"negative planning" reverses the importance of the urban components by making built infrastructure unimportant and the ecological infrastructure the most important driver of the design, Yu's landscape design reverses the place of aesthetics. His landscapes are designed to produce ecosystem services, and the aesthetics of the plantings follow from the processes of the landscape.

In Kongjian Yu's landscapes, the decisions of what to plant and where to plant are rooted in landscape processes. Massed plantings of grasses and reeds are placed in a particular position to create a specific process and ecosystem service. For example, where the landscape is intended to mitigate polluted water, some of the river's water flows slowly through designed wetlands, dropping its particulate pollutants, while the plants take up heavy metal pollutants, nitrogen and phosphorus. Along the river's edge, native riparian plants stabilise the shoreline, preventing erosion and helping to reduce downstream flooding while providing habitat.

The form of the landscape reveals its functions. For example, where food production is one of the ecosystem services of the landscape, farmland is incorporated into the urban fabric or the entire landscape is given over to food production (Figure 4.1). Where flood mitigation is the goal, residents can observe portions of the designed landscape accepting flood waters during flooding events and then, after the flood, returning to their normal water levels and appearance, undamaged.

One of Yu's aesthetic tools has been that of merging the look of the "rough" and the "refined" by juxtaposing the "soft" planted landscape of native vegetation with colourful "hard" landscape elements like bridges, shelters and seating. Because he uses local species, provided by native plant nurseries, his plantings may seem "natural" and "wild" rather than designed, presenting a rough, even un-designed appearance, while the hard landscape elements are the refined: Sculptural, precise and colourful (Figure 4.2).

The Red Ribbon Park in Qinhuangdao City, China, illustrates this principle. While the ecological infrastructure of the park cleanses stormwater and maintains biodiversity, the Red Ribbon that gives the park its name contains much of the human program of the site. This continuous red bench unifies circulation, seating and lighting (ASLA News, n.d.). It is the focus of human activity and views.

Another key strategy to achieving public acceptance of Turenscape's designs is the provision of seasonal colour. Eye-catching annuals and perennials at key locations draw the eye to distant views and nodes of use in the landscape (Figure 4.3).

Case study: Minghu Wetland Park

Turenscape Landscape Architecture

Perhaps because of these design devices, it seems that the Chinese public is embracing Yu's new landscape aesthetic. The improved condition of the

▲ Figure 4.3

Masses of colour contribute to public acceptance of productive landscapes. In Minghu Wetland Park, people cool their toes in a terraced wetland amidst pink and white cosmos that line the shore.
Source: Photo courtesy of Turenscape Ltd.

landscape may also play a role in public acceptance, for when people know that a landscape is ecologically healthy, it increases their enjoyment of that place (Bell, 2012). Minghu Wetland Park in Liupanshui City is an example of an urban park that has made the landscape more ecologically healthy and is used intensively by local residents.

A little more than 1,000 kilometres northeast of Hong Kong, in the city of Liupanshui, lies the valley of Shuichengh river, surrounded by karst limestone mountains. In the 1960s, the city was developed as an industrial rail-town, exporting coal, steel and cement. Local industries polluted the environment, fertiliser nutrients and sewage from upland settlements and farming terraces drained to the city below, and the river was channelised to reduce flooding. The combined industrial and agricultural activity and the channelisation of the river left a legacy of water and soil pollution and increased downstream flooding.

In 2009, the Liupanshui Municipal Government commissioned Turenscape to address these problems. At the time, the site of what is now Minghu Wetland Park consisted of polluted wetlands, derelict fish ponds, mismanaged corn fields and dumped garbage. Yu's approach was to develop a comprehensive ecological infrastructure intended to purify surface waters and reduce downstream flooding while supporting river flows during the dry season. The concrete straitjacket that had contained the River Shuichengh was removed and the floodplain basin of the river widened to create the wetland park. All surrounding surface waters were directed to a series of wetland terraces in the park. Islands within the wetlands provide

CHAPTER 4 Functional and aesthetic criteria

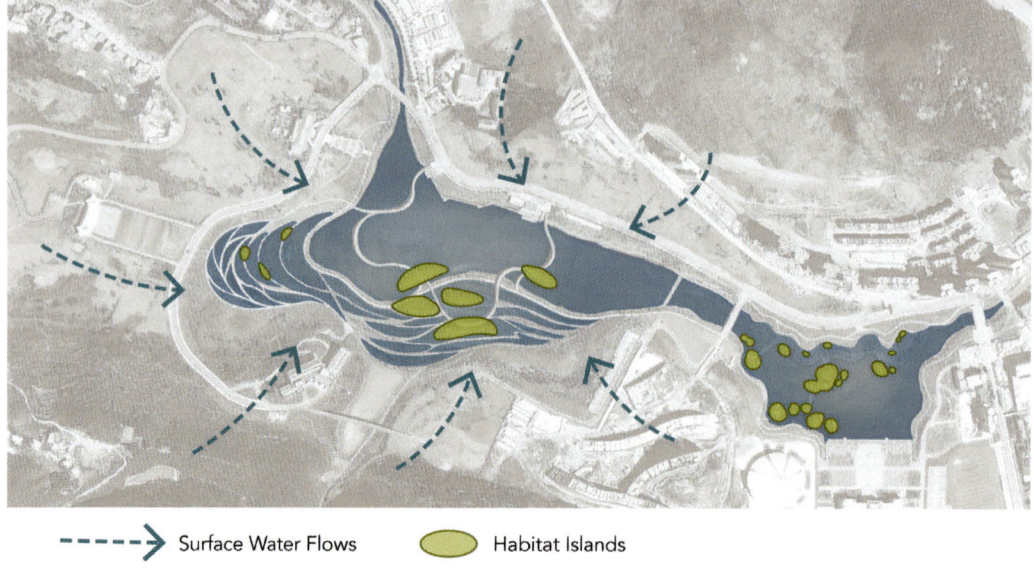

▲ Figure 4.4

All surface water flows are directed to the basin of the Shuichengh River where the curvilinear forms of the terraced wetlands accept and purify water. A number of islands, dispersed throughout the wetland, support biodiversity by providing habitat for a variety of species (after Beals and Zhang, 2015).
Source: Image courtesy of Yiwen Ruan.

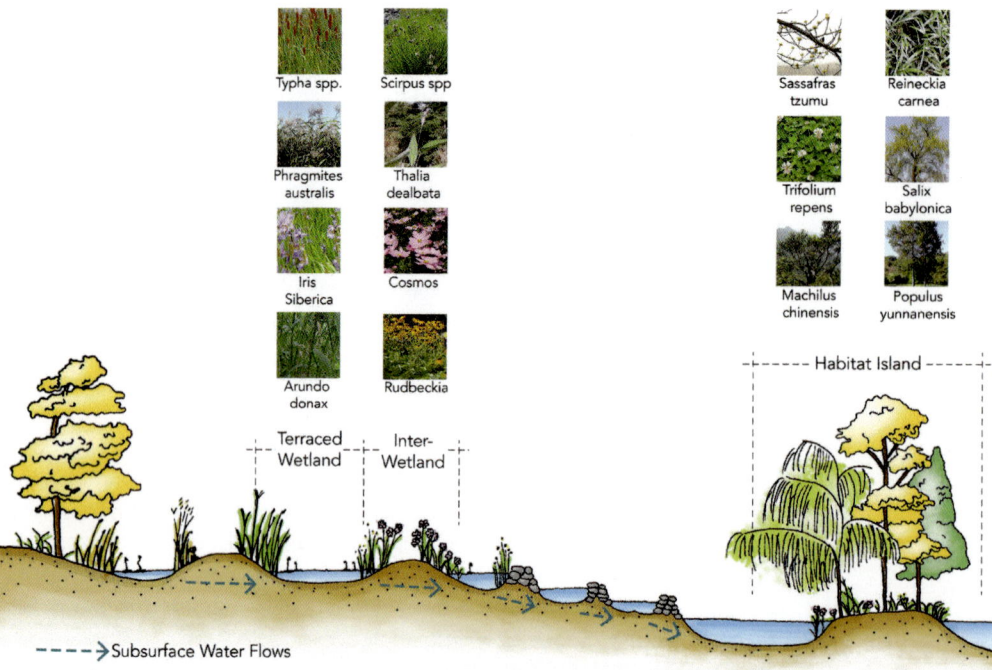

▲ Figure 4.5

The terraced wetlands intercept, slow and purify surface and subsurface flows within the different plant associations. Note that the ecosystem services of water purification and reduced flooding are not provided by the plants alone but through the interactions of water, soils, topography and plants (after Beals and Zhang, 2015).
Source: Image courtesy of Yiwen Ruan.

▲ Figure 4.6

The Rainbow Bridge illustrates Kongjian Yu's practice of juxtaposing colourful and refined constructed landscape elements with rough and productive plantings. The bridge is an iconic focal point that orders the circulation and provides views over the wetland to the surrounding karst landscape.
Source: Photo courtesy of Turenscape Ltd.

habitat for birds, amphibians and small mammals (Figure 4.4). Riparian habitats were restored. Newly created waterfalls along the river's edge oxygenate the water, increasing bio-remediation of polluted water and supporting fish and other aquatic species. The terraced wetlands and retention ponds slow water flows, reducing soil erosion and containing particulate pollution, while the wetland plants take up excess nutrients (Figures 4.4 and 4.5). Within this wetland setting, pedestrian paths, bicycle routes and a pedestrian bridge called "The Steel Rainbow" link pavilions and viewing locations with a wide variety of seating options (Figure 4.6). Opportunities to cycle, walk and sit in a natural setting while viewing the surrounding landscape support the physical and mental wellbeing of the residents.

Minghu National Wetland Park, which was opened in 2012, lessens surface runoff, helping to recharge groundwater flows, reduce flooding and purify the river's waters while supporting active and passive recreation and wildlife viewing (Minghu Wetland Park, n.d.) in a biophilic and restorative setting. The new park provides a vibrant urban waterfront that has become a catalyst for urban redevelopment (Yu, Turenscape and Peking University, 2014).

CHAPTER 4 Functional and aesthetic criteria

Planting and ecosystem services

Many ecosystem services may be supported by the design of the plantings or plant communities within a given site. Ecosystem services that are supported by plants include maintenance of biological diversity, provision of food, carbon sequestration and storage, microclimatic modification, mitigation of air and water pollution, increasing pollination, reduction in flooding, preservation and generation of soils, and support for recreation and physical and mental wellbeing (Mooney, 2014). For example, using vegetation to produce a range of different habitats within a site will increase the biological

TABLE 4.0 Classification of ecosystem services (after de Groot, Alkemade, Braat, Hein and Willemen, 2010) presents a broad classification of types of ecosystem services that may be supported by plants

Ecosystem Service Category	Ecosystem Services
Provisioning services	Food (e.g. fish, game, fruit)
	Water (e.g. for drinking, irrigation, cooling)
	Raw materials (e.g. fibre, timber, fuelwood, fodder, fertiliser)
	Genetic resources (e.g. for crop-improvement and medicinal purposes)
	Medicinal resources (e.g. biochemical products, models and test organisms)
	Ornamental resources (e.g. artisan work, decorative plants, pet animals, fashion)
Regulating services	Air quality regulation (e.g. capturing fine dust, chemicals, etc.)
	Climate regulation (including carbon sequestration, influence of vegetation on rainfall, etc.)
	Moderation of extreme events (e.g. storm protection and flood prevention)
	Regulation of water flows (e.g. natural drainage, irrigation and drought prevention)
	Waste treatment (especially water purification)
	Erosion prevention
	Maintenance of soil fertility (including soil formation) and nutrient cycling
	Pollination
	Biological control (e.g. seed dispersal, pest and disease control)
Habitat services	Maintenance of life cycles (including nursery services)
	Maintenance of genetic diversity (especially through gene pool protection)
Cultural and amenity services	Aesthetic information
	Opportunities for recreation and tourism
	Inspiration for culture, art and design
	Spiritual experience
	Information for cognitive development

Source: Table courtesy of Yiwen Ruan.

TABLE 4.1 Site-level ecosystem services provided or supported by plants

Biodiversity and Ecosystem Service types	Ecosystem Services	Rationale
Biodiversity		
	Biodiversity Maintain or increase	Increasing the number of plant species on a site, by definition, increases its biodiversity. This in turn can increase that number and quality of habitats found on a site and directly influence site biodiversity. Site biodiversity increases as site habitat diversity increases.
	Habitat for wild species	Habitats for wild species are different plant associations that can be created or enhanced through planting design that incorporates native plantings and also by selective use of non-invasive, non-native plants.
	Maintain or increase pollination	Native and non-native plantings can support native and non-native pollinator species.
Provisioning Services		
	Food	Direct food production such as grains, fruits, vegetables and herbs result from the plants being incorporated into the designed landscape. Indirect food production such as wild fish or game may also be enhanced through plantings that create or enhance habitats. For example, riparian plantings provide terrestrial habitat and also support in-stream fish habitat.
	Raw materials (e.g. fibre, timber, fuel wood, fodder, fertiliser)	Even in urban landscapes wood for fuel and construction may be harvested from the urban landscape.
	Ornamental resources (e.g. artisan work, decorative plants)	Wild plants may be sustainably harvested from the landscape for ornamental arts and crafts and decorative elements.
Regulating Services		
Climate and Atmosphere	Carbon sequestration and storage	As woody plants grow they capture carbon dioxide from the air, sequestering and storing carbon (Davies, Edmondson, Heinemeyer, Leake and Gaston, 2011; Paoletti, Bardelli, Giovannini and Pecchioli, 2011).
	Moderation of extreme events	Large vegetated areas may reduce local and regional flooding.

(continued)

TABLE 4.1 (Cont.)

Biodiversity and Ecosystem Service types	Ecosystem Services	Rationale
	Pollution mitigation (air)	Plants reduce particulate and gaseous air pollutants (Paoletti et al., 2011; Tallis, Taylor, Sinnett and Freer-Smith, 2011).
	Local climate and air quality regulation	In addition to reducing air pollution, plants in the landscape can provide shade and reduce urban temperatures.
Hazard Regulation	Reduction in landslide potential	Plants help to increase storm water infiltration, reducing runoff and erosion, while their roots help to stabilise slopes.
	Reduced flooding	Woodlands and forest cover support precipitation infiltration and reduce downstream flooding.
	Noise reduction	Plants help to reduce noise pollution in urban areas by ameliorating noise levels.
	Disease and pest regulation	Plants can provide habitat for predator insects that reduce populations of insect pests.
Water	Waste-water treatment	Plants used in bioswales, rain gardens and riparian corridors capture harmful particulate pollutants from the surrounding urban catchment area that previously went untreated.
Soil	Maintenance of soil fertility	Plants contribute organic matter to the soil that is the source of nitrogen for plant growth.
	Reduced erosion	By covering the soil with their leaves, plants reduce the impacts of precipitation. Their litter increases infiltration into the soil. In these ways plant cover reduces erosion.
Supporting Services		
	Primary productivity	Primary productivity is a measure of the total biomass produced in a given area or ecosystem. In most ecosystems, plants are the major sources of primary productivity.
	Preservation and generation of soils	By reducing erosion and contributing organic matter, plants help to preserve and generate soils.
	Nutrient cycling	Plants cycle mineral and non-mineral nutrients from the soil.
	Maintenance of genetic diversity	Existing and new habitats support native and non-native biodiversity.

TABLE 4.1 (Cont.)

Biodiversity and Ecosystem Service types	Ecosystem Services	Rationale
Cultural Services		
	Social cohesion	Studies have shown that parks moderately support social cohesion (Seeland et al., 2009; Peters, 2010).
	Mental and physical wellbeing	Studies have shown that urban green space contributes to mental and physical wellbeing (Kuo, 2010).
	Recreation	Parks and other vegetated landscapes support a variety of recreational opportunities (Weber and Anderson, 2010).
	Tourism	Urban parks contribute to tourism (Wong and Domroes, 2005; Chaudhry and Tewari, 2010).

Source: Table courtesy of Yiwen Ruan.

diversity of the site (Bolund and Hunhammar, 1999). The use of rain gardens to purify stormwater before it enters the marine environment can increase marine biodiversity. Urban trees and other woody vegetation sequester and store carbon and reduce air pollution (Nowak, Crane and Stevens, 2006). Riparian vegetation will reduce contaminants entering streams and water bodies and will reduce nitrogen contamination of surface waters (Hanson, Groffman and Gold, 1994). Thus, the planting design should be understood not as an overlay of the site design that is intended to make the site more attractive, but as an essential tool for implementing the entire design program that must integrate function and aesthetics, finding synergies between them and developing the design as a unified whole.

Table 4.1 expands on Table 4.0 by showing a range of ecosystem services that may be found in designed and natural landscapes and provides a brief rationale for the contribution of plants in the landscape to the fostering of each ecosystem service listed in the table.

Designing pollinator habitat

Melody Redekop

An introduction to native pollinators

Pollination is a vital ecosystem service that perpetuates habitats and ecosystems in natural and designed landscapes, providing food security for both people and wildlife. Of the many kinds of insect pollinators, bees are considered to be the most effective pollinators of wild vegetation and agricultural crops (Klein et al., 2006; Potts et al., 2010). In recent years, the global decline of managed honey bee (*Apis* spp.) populations has received widespread media attention. Less frequently mentioned is the fact that native bees are facing the same stressors: Pests and pathogens, the use of pesticides, the intensification of land use causing habitat loss, and climate change. Among these concerns, habitat destruction and fragmentation incurred by agricultural land use and urbanisation are the leading cause of native pollinator habitat decline (McKinney, 2002; Winfree et al., 2009).

Urbanisation alters the natural land cover, leaving only scattered remnant habitats in what was once a continuous habitat network. Despite these negative effects, research has shown that cities can support a high abundance and diversity of pollinators (Tonietto, Fant, Ascher, Ellis and Larkin, 2011; Gunnarsson and Federsel, 2014) if the areas surrounding the remaining habitat fragments facilitate pollinator foraging and nesting (Wray and Elle, 2015). This section offers planting designers a number of principles for creating native pollinator habitats in the urban environment. There are three subcategories: Site layout principles (at both the site and the local scale), nesting principles and floral principles.

Site layout principles

Principle 1: Choose a location that receives sufficient sunlight

When creating a new pollinator habitat, choose a site with good sun exposure, since pollinating insects can lose heat quickly to the surrounding air, making an inhospitable flight environment. Furthermore, pollinators "need to be able to see the sky in order to navigate" (Mader, Shepherd, Vaughan, Black and LeBuhn, 2011, p. 100), making open sites with fewer trees an ideal choice.

Principle 2: Allow room for masses or drifts of at least eight different flowering species

To increase visibility to pollinators, place plants of the same kind together. At the site scale, it is best practice to have at least eight different plant species on a single site in order to ensure floral diversity (see Principle 6) and overlapping bloom time (see Principle 7) (Mader et al., 2011). To conserve pollinators' energy for foraging, increase plant visibility to pollinators by grouping plants of the same species in clusters of at least one square metre in diameter (Mader et al., 2011).

Principle 3: At the local scale, ensure that large habitat patches are preserved and create corridors between the large patches

Habitat type and patch size heterogeneity play important roles in species abundance and diversity at the larger scale. Where possible, it is important to have larger habitat patches (over 125 acres or 50 hectares) near or within the urban environment to create a refuge for specialists and other species that are sensitive to habitat fragmentation. The preservation of larger habitat patches and the creation of viable corridors between these patches promote bee species richness in the urban environment (Beninde, Veith and Hochkirch, 2015). These corridors can either be linear connections (roadway easements, railway corridors, etc.) or "stepping stones" comprised of a diverse mosaic of urban gardens, cemeteries, parks and patches of spontaneous vegetation within the urban environment. Although the minimum required area of floral-rich pollinator habitat at the urban scale has not yet been defined, researchers studying bumble bees in ~250-acre (100-hectare) agricultural sites have estimated the required area to be as high as 1–3 per cent of the total area (Dicks et al., 2015).

Nesting principles

Principle 4: Integrate suitable habitat for ground-nesting bees

Around 70 per cent of North America's native bees are ground nesters (Mader et al., 2011). The general decline of ground-nesting bees in urban areas is caused in part by lack of suitable nesting habitat (Matteson, Ascher and Langellotto, 2008). Concrete sidewalks, building footprints, asphalt roadways and parking lots, dense turf and mulch-covered planting beds do not provide nest sites for ground-nesting bees. Above-ground-nesting bees do not face the same degree of habitat loss, because they are able to use existing holes or create their own using wood in houses, fences, or the pithy stems of plants as nesting habitat.

While urbanisation has a greater impact on ground-nesting bees than on above-ground-nesting bees, public attention has been largely focused on providing nesting opportunities ("bee hotels") for above-ground cavity nesters (MacIvor and Packer, 2015). It is worth noting that some of these boxes are more likely to host native wasps than native pollinators (MacIvor and Packer, 2015). There are several ways to promote ground-nesters in the urban environment: (1) retain diverse patches of undisturbed native soil, since different bee species have varying soil preferences ranging from sand to clays, from loose to compact soil and from flat ground to banks (Cane, 2005); (2) create raised planters with bare soil or sand (Fortel, Henry, Guilbaud, Mouret and Vaissière, 2016); and (3) design pockets or mounds of bare soil/sand within the plantings, perhaps surrounded by root barriers or clump-forming vegetation to reduce maintenance.

Principle 5: Provide nesting resources within 330 feet
(100 metres) of floral resources

Well-designed plantings are not enough to create thriving urban pollinator populations. The pollinator plantings must also be close to nesting resources. Bees leave their nests multiple times daily to forage for pollen and nectar for themselves and for their nests (Cane, 2005), and the distance that a particular bee species is able to travel is based on their body size. For example, small-bodied native bees are able to fly only about 500 feet (150 metres) (Mader et al., 2011), while larger-bodied bees like bumble bees (*Bombus* spp.) are capable of flying up to 1.25 miles (2 kilometres) (Cane, 2005). According to the Xerces guide to attracting native pollinators, "a general rule of thumb is to have flowers no more than a few hundred feet (100m) from potential nesting areas" (Mader et al., 2011, p.102) and optimally within the same patch.

Floral principles

Principle 6: Plant diverse floral resources to attract a variety of bees

Bee diversity is directly linked to floral diversity; essentially, diverse floral shapes, colours and sizes attracts diverse species of bees (Potts et al., 2003) The greatest threats to floral diversity in general are monocultures (Kearns, Inouye and Waser, 1998), defined as the practice of growing a single variety of crop or vegetation at one time, commonly seen in agricultural production. For example, researchers found that orchards with a closer proximity to natural areas or uncultivated lands support a greater diversity and abundance of bees than orchards that are adjacent to other orchards (Kearns et al., 1998). Monocultures can also be seen in planting design, where single species are used in large masses for visual effect such as in lawns and traditional plantings which use ornamental trees and shrubs, selected for the conspicuous flowers, fruit or foliage colour.

Principle 7: Overlapping bloom time

To provide continuous food resources for pollinators, planting designers need to use a range of plants that have overlapping flowering times during the season when pollinators are active—early spring until autumn. Plants that flower in early spring are essential for early emerging bee species like bumble bee queens, mining bees (*Andrena* spp.) and mason bees (*Osmia* spp.), and bumble bee queens entering winter hibernation need floral resources in the autumn (Winfree et al., 2011; Potts et al., 2003). By ensuring sufficient forage for different pollinators, bee reproduction will be more successful and populations will increase in the following years. It is best practice to ensure that at least three different plant species are blooming at all times during the growing season and there are no gaps in flowering. For example, in the Pacific Northwest of North America there is often a bloom gap in June. Lupines are an excellent floral resource for long-tongued pollinators like bumble bees and can be used to fill this gap. A coloured plant chart is a very useful tool to ensure that there are always multiple species in bloom and no gaps in flowering (Figure 4.7 and Table 4.2).

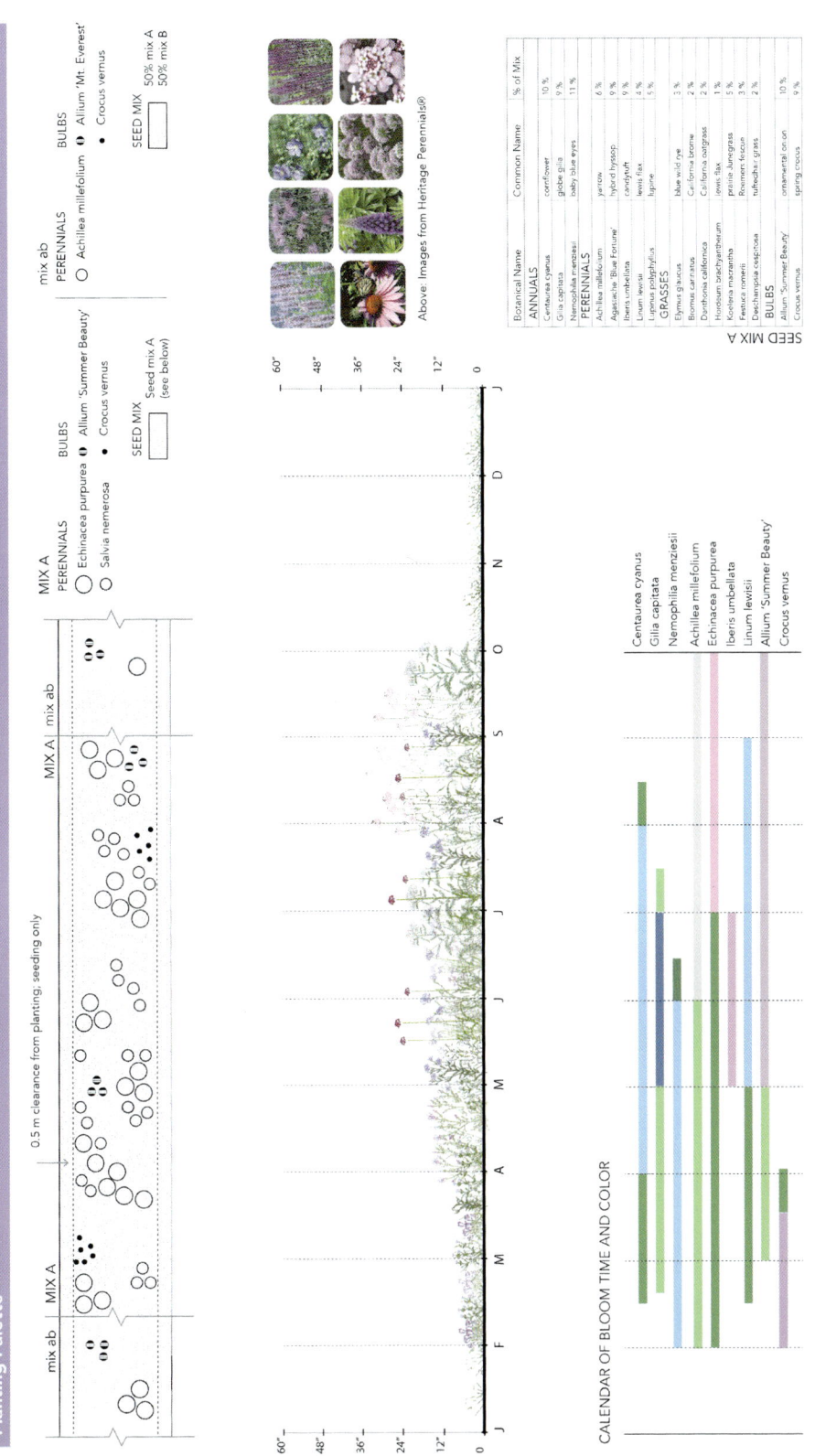

▲ Figure 4.7

In this linear planting, pot-grown perennials are planted into custom seed mixes. Where colour transitions are made between plantings, such as seed mix A and seed mix B (not shown), the two seed mixes are mixed in equal proportions, creating seed mix ab. This bloom chart for a pollinator habitat ensures the long and continuous season of bloom needed by different pollinators. It is a very good idea for novice planting designers in particular to construct bloom charts for their designs to ensure a long bloom period or to create colour harmonies in successively blooming plantings.
Source: Image courtesy of Melody Redekop.

Table 4.2 Typology of different pollinator habitats

	Meadow landscapes		Shrubby landscapes				
	Grassland	**Wildflower meadow**	**Hard surfaces**	**Woodland**	**Woodland edge**	**Old field**	**Hedgerow**
Perception	Perceived as messy and untidy when not in flower (Hitchmough, J., 2004; Nassauer, J., 1995)	Considered aesthetically pleasing; very attractive when flowering, especially when providing a colourful display (Hitchmough, 2004)	Varies depending on the type of hard surface (ex. wall, green roof, or balcony).	Considered attractive, but may be considered unsafe when understory plants and tree canopies are dense (Nassauer, 1995)	May be considered unsafe when understory plants are dense. Considered attractive when flowering	Perceived as seen as messy and untidy in urban landscapes	Perceived as marking the boundary of a property, road, or pathway. Vernacular landscape element
Wildlife	Pollinators (bees, butterflies, moths, flies, etc.); Other beneficial invertebrates; Open grassland birds; Reptiles; Small mammals	Pollinators (bees, butterflies, moths, flies, etc.); Other beneficial invertebrates; Open grassland birds	Pollinators (bees, butterflies, moths, flies, etc.); Open grassland birds; Woodland birds; Reptiles	Hummingbird nesting habitat; Pollinators (bees, butterflies, moths, flies, etc.); Small mammals; Woodland birds	Hummingbird nesting habitat; Pollinators (bees, butterflies, moths, flies, etc.)	Bats; Pollinators (bees, butterflies, moths, flies, etc.); Woodland birds	Bats; Pollinators (bees, butterflies, moths, flies, etc.); Woodland birds; Small mammals
Design Strategies	Maintain a clear, mown strip at pathway edges, indicating that the landscape is cared for and intentional (Nassauer, 1995); Introduce wildflowers in high visibility areas to provide colour and interest	Create long flowering periods with overlapping bloom succession; Create structure using flowers, foliage, and seedheads; Use legible patterns in the planting design	Provide public access to green roofs to promote educational experiences and provide environmental restoration	Maintain unobstructed sightlines; Design defined "gateways" to signify a transition into the woodland area (R. Kaplan, S. Kaplan and Ryan, 1998, p.81).	Place a layer of flowering shrubs and perennials along woodland edges to provide colour and interest	Encourage programmed areas for recreation and public use with defined spaces of shorter, mown grass	Diversify hedgerow by mixing different species, focusing on flowering and fruiting species; Repeat species along the hedgerow to create visual coherence and pattern
Enhancing Biodiversity	Introduce floral resources into areas dominated by competitive grasses (Hitchmough, 2004); Mow areas in rotation to ensure that tall grass habitats are available at all times	Increase floral diversity and abundance; Increase structural height layering and diversity; Mow areas in rotation to ensure that meadow habitats are available at all times	Install green roofs, green walls, and vines where appropriate to help prevent habitat fragmentation caused by urban development (Cane, J. H., 2005); Install diverse types of nest boxes for pollinators	Support canopy height diversity in trees; Maintain the tree canopy to allow sunlight to reach the forest floor, promoting the growth of flowering perennials and groundcovers	Create height diversity between shrubs, grass, and groundcovers; Selectively remove colonizing plant material to promote diversity and prevent natural expansion of woodland	Some maintenance may be needed if the desire is to prevent natural succession towards woodland	Provide a variety of flowering and fruiting hedgerow species to provide diverse resources for wildlife

▲ Table 4.2

Typology of different pollinator habitats
Source: Table courtesy of Melody Redekop (after CABE, 2006).

Principle 8: Native and near-native plants are the most attractive to native pollinators, but adding non-native plants can extend the season of bloom into the late summer

Native pollinators are considered to prefer native and near-native plants. In a recent study, greater numbers of pollinators were recorded on native and near-native plots than exotic plots (Salisbury et al., 2015). While native pollinators may prefer native and near-native plants in spring to early summer, exotic plants provide floral abundance later in the summer (Salisbury et al., 2015; Wray and Elle, 2015). For example, in oak-savannah habitats on Vancouver Island, native vegetation reaches a peak blooming period in May, after which floral abundance decreases dramatically. Researchers studying the urban matrix surrounding the oak-savannah fragments found that nearby urban gardens reached a similar blooming peak in May but did not taper off afterwards (Wray and Elle, 2015). They concluded that pollinators within natural habitats are positively influenced by the availability of floral resources in the urban matrix (Wray and Elle, 2015). In this region, the optimal blend would be to plant predominately native and near-native plants, while including exotic plants with a bias towards summer bloom times (Salisbury et al., 2015). Ideally, the exotic plants would have overlapping bloom times that extend from June into early autumn.

Principle 9: Consider incorporating a floral meadow

Wildflower meadows can provide large areas of optimum pollinator habitat and reduced maintenance costs. They can be integrated into existing lawn areas, roadside verges and other patches of land which require the preservation of open space and sight lines. Seeded wildflower meadows and reduced mowing have both been shown to increase bee species abundance and diversity. A study through the University of Sussex demonstrated that patches of reduced mowing in a suburban public park significantly increased the number of flower-visiting insects. The authors concluded that while reduced mowing was beneficial, the no-mow patches had the highest number of pollinators. They also found that patches of long grass had 50 times more bees, butterflies and moths than the short grass (Garbuzov et al., 2015).

Another study demonstrated that sown wildflower plots attracted 50 times more bumblebees and 13 times more hoverflies than frequently mown control plots (Blackmore and Goulson, 2014). The seeded wildflower plots were a mix of perennials and annuals, which predictably changed in composition by the second year. Since the number of hoverflies declined in the second year (while bumblebees increased), the authors suggest that re-seeding wildflower meadows with annuals on a yearly basis would add floral resources for this important insect group (Blackmore and Goulson, 2014). It is worth nothing that perennial-only seed mixes are also effective and reduce costs by negating the need for re-seeding.

Principle 10: Design pollinator habitat with people in mind

In order for landscapes to be maintained by municipalities and cared for by local residents, they must have meaning for people (Hunter and Hunter, 2008). Landscapes that incite emotional response cause people to feel connected and engaged. The connection that people have to such places causes them care for and maintain the landscape over the long term.

There is promising research indicating that people are supportive of pollinator habitat in the urban environment (Garbuzov, Fensome and Ratnieks, 2015; Glaum, Simao, Vaidya, Fitch and Iuliano, 2017). While concerns may persist that ecological landscape designs are seen as untidy and weedy within the urban environment (Nassauer, 1995), recent studies demonstrate that people are receptive to floral-rich plantings in the urban environment. Given the choice, people even prefer "naturalistic" landscapes over highly manicured vegetation, bedding plants, and even standard mown grass (R. Kaplan, 2007; Glaum et al., 2017). Design strategies such as creating plantings that provide a continual colourful display, ensuring that plantings have structural diversity, maintaining mown edges at the edge of wildflower meadows, creating attractive nesting opportunities, and adding interpretive signage so that people understand the benefits of the landscape can further encourage positive responses to native pollinator habitat.

Private gardens, botanic gardens, cemeteries, green roofs, urban parks, boulevards, roadway easements, riparian areas, industrial areas, brownfield sites and sites of urban agriculture are all suitable locations for the integration of pollinator habitat in the urban environment. These sites provide exciting opportunities for synergistic planting designs that promote pollinator diversity and abundance and provide landscapes with high aesthetic and affective value for people.

Ecosystem services in planting design

If planting design has as its purpose the support of the entire program, then the appropriate use of plants is to support each of the benefits that were intended in the site design program. To do this:

1) The goals of the program need to be understood.
2) The ways in which planting design can contribute to each of the intended goals of the program need to be understood.
3) The ecosystem services that may be added to the official program through the planting design should always be evaluated.
4) Where goals of the program include the provision of ecosystem services, the planting designer must consider how their work can contribute to providing each of the intended ecosystem services in the design program.

Some of the ways in which ecosystem services can be enhanced with the use of plants are discussed below.

Drought-tolerant plants

The provision of fresh water is among the most necessary ecosystem services, and a reduction in the use of potable water for irrigating plants may be considered as an addition to the amount of freshwater available for other uses.

In 1900, only 10 per cent of people lived in cities, while today more than 50 per cent of all people live in cities (UN, 2014). It is projected that by 2030 the number of "megacites" having populations greater than 10 million people will increase from 28 to 41 (UN, 2014) and that by 2050 world population will increase to 9.6 billion persons (UN, 2013), of whom 66 per cent will be urbanites (UN, 2014).

As global population and the size of cities continue to increase, so too does the frequency of severe droughts. Since 1950, the area of the planet experiencing severe drought has increased from approximately 12 per cent to 30 per cent. This trend is thought to be human induced and is predicted to continue with increased drying over Africa, the Middle East, most of the Americas, Australia and southeast Asia (Dai, 2011).

In Britain, it was predicted that river flows in south and east England will decrease by as much as 30 per cent between 2006 and the 2020s (Arnell and Delaney, 2006). In addition, many large aquifers are being extracted at unsustainable levels, putting future water availability at risk in large portions of the planet (Gorelick and Zheng, 2015), and continued climate change will increase water loss from plants and soil while reducing precipitation and snow packs in some areas (Karl, Melillo and Peterson, 2009). We are now in a period of climate change, global population growth, increased urbanisation, increasing demands for food and water (Beddington, 2009) and reduced water availability. Cities will increasingly find that water resources are restricted and water demands increased.

In the United States, residential urban landscapes consume 30 per cent of total household water, and this figure rises to 60 per cent in drier areas of the country. Americans use approximately 58,000 gallons (219,554 litres) of water each year to support their residential landscapes (US EPA, n.d.). Given the increases in drought, urbanisation and population growth, this cannot be considered sustainable. The amount of water available to support urban landscapes will be drastically reduced as other more important demands grow and the amount of available water per urban dweller declines. Already we are seeing widespread efforts to reduce water usage in cities. In Vancouver, British Columbia, and many other cities, residents are restricted to watering lawns only at specified hours and days of the week during the summer months (CBC News, 2014). Under the "Cash for Grass" program in Los Angeles, California, county waterworks districts paid residents one dollar for every square foot of grass that was replaced with water-efficient landscaping (Los Angeles DPW, 2014). In Victoria, Australia, the state government is offering ratepayers $1,500 to install a 1,057-gallon (4,000-litre) rainwater-harvesting tank that is connected to a toilet and laundry (Victoria State Government, n.d.). In Zaragoza, Spain, severe droughts throughout the 1990s led to a spectacularly successful campaign of voluntarily restricted water use. Per capita water use dropped by 34 per cent between 1997 and 2012. Although the city's population grew by 12 per cent between 1997 and 2008, total water consumption fell by 27 per cent (The Guardian, 2014).

In the coming years, it is reasonable to expect that designed landscapes that flourish with little or no irrigation will increasingly be the norm. This does not necessarily mean that all plantings will become drought tolerant, but rather that many more plantings will need to be adapted to the site's soil moisture regime.

There is a range of responses to the demand that landscapes use less water. One very basic response is to provide deep soils that are high in organic matter, as this will greatly reduce water use. Another response has been to create xeric landscapes or xeriscapes (from the Greek word *xeric*, meaning very dry). This can take the form of covering much of the landscape with pavement, gravel and other inorganic mulches. Xeriscapes have the benefit of being very low maintenance, but when replicated over an entire city they can increase the urban heat island effect and add to the negative effects of urban runoff.

However, xeriscapes need not be all rocks and gravel. Many arid areas that have low rainfall and high evapotranspiration support an abundance of native plants that are adapted to the regional climate and that can provide shade, a sense of the regional landscape and habitat for native species. In these regions, the use of drought-tolerant plants may be increasingly required and grass lawn may be replaced with drought-tolerant groundcovers or structured plantings. Such dry land plantings can also provide the sense of urban nature and the biophilic landscape that were discussed in previous chapters.

In wetter areas, the unirrigated landscape is not a xeriscape, since it can be seasonally wet. We have seen that the soil water that is available to the plants at any time is influenced by soil volume and moisture-holding capacity and is the result of the amount of precipitation that the soil has received and the water losses or gains in the soil due to runoff, interflow, evaporation and transpiration. In places where rainfall is abundant throughout most of the year and the landscape is water-restricted only during a seasonal dry period, plants that are adapted to drier conditions but not desert extremes will be suitable. In such areas, lawns may not need to be replaced but simply allowed to turn brown in the dry period and to regain their lush green appearance in the rainy season. Alternatively, purified greywater, reclaimed blackwater or captured rainwater may substitute for potable water use in landscape irrigation systems.

The use of native plants

Native plants have been widely advocated as another response to the need to reduce water use in the landscape because they are adapted to the soils and climate of the region, possess habitat value, are disease resistant and

▲ Figure 4.8

This residential landscape design, by Christy Ten Eyck of Ten Eyck Landscape Architects in Austin, Texas, mixes porous gravel paving and regionally appropriate plants in a xeric landscape that feels alive and welcoming.
Source: Photo courtesy of Ten Eyck Landscape Architects.

are not invasive. However, the use of native plants is not as simple as it might first seem. Within any region there will be a range of soil types, soil moisture conditions and microclimates. It is naive to assume that a plant that is native to a region can be easily grown throughout that region. For example, forest floor plants may require full or dappled shade and moist soils that are difficult to provide in urban conditions. A native plant that is very drought tolerant once established may be drought intolerant until it is established. Some native plants require low fertility and soil moisture in order to thrive. Finally, native plants are not the only plants that have habitat value. Many native species of insects, birds and mammals are adapted to feed on non-native plants, and many non-native plants are not invasive.

Since non-native plants can share all the benefits of native plants, it is more useful to think in terms of regionally appropriate or site-appropriate plants than to restrict the plant palette entirely to native drought-tolerant plants. Regionally appropriate plants include both native and non-native plants and these can be combined to produce the particular aesthetic quality the designer intends without excessive use of water. First and foremost, regionally appropriate plants should be non-invasive and adapted to regional soils and microclimates, and they may provide food or shelter for native insects, birds or animals. The use of these types of plants can be supported with on-site rainwater capture, the use of mulches to conserve moisture and by planting trees that provide shade, thereby reducing water loss of both soils and plants.

CHAPTER 4 Functional and aesthetic criteria   115

Case study: University of Texas at El Paso, Campus Transformation Project

Landscape architects: Ten Eyck Landscape Architects Inc.
Architects: Lake Flato Architects

Christine Ten Eyck

Christine "Christy" Ten Eyck, founder and president of Ten Eyck Landscape Architects Inc. (TELA), is the granddaughter of an architect and daughter of a civil engineer. She and her four siblings spent their formative years in Dallas, Texas; Calgary, Alberta; and Seattle, Washington, where the family enjoyed camping, hiking, skiing and fishing together. Christine's upbringing nurtured a profound love of wild nature and urban design that is expressed in the overriding goal of TELA: To connect urban dwellers with nature and with each other.

Christy received her landscape architecture degree from Texas Tech University in 1981. In 1985, while working in Dallas, she joined friends on what proved to be a transformative experience—rafting the Colorado River through the Grand Canyon. During the trip, she fell in love with the Arizona wilderness and, upon returning to Dallas, quit her job and moved to Phoenix, where she worked for several firms before starting TELA in 1997. Today, TELA is known for multifunctional landscape designs that infuse the city with natural beauty. The firm is now based in Austin, Texas, and its work has been widely published and received many professional awards. Christine Ten Eyck is a sought-after speaker on the subject of sustainable landscapes.

Christine experiences wild landscapes keenly and wishes to share that experience by "bringing the nature back to the city". As part of that process, she studies and seeks to accentuate the path of water through the site, using the appropriate form in each of her designs, whether it be an architectural flume, bioswale, wet meadow and check dam, linear garden or natural drainage feature. During more than two decades of work in Arizona, she came to appreciate and be inspired by ephemeral paths of water through the desert called *arroyos* and the smaller built *acequias*. These were her selected tools for celebrating and managing water at the University of Texas at El Paso. Arroyos are seasonally dry desert creeks that become engorged with water after large rain events, and acequias are built irrigation channels that redirect existing streamflow. In arid landscapes, arroyos and acequias are rare places of flowing water, scented plants and abundant wildlife. To Christine, they are "sacred places in the desert".

University of Texas at El Paso

TELA's design of the University of Texas at El Paso (UTEP) treats water as an experiential resource, celebrates the local ecology and increases ecological function while providing social spaces and a restorative landscape experience.

The problem

The University of Texas at El Paso is located in the foothills of the Franklin Mountain range overlooking the City of El Paso, with sweeping views across the border to Juarez, Mexico. After its founding in 1914, the university gradually replaced the native desert with large buildings, parking lots, open lawns and clipped shrubs. As is true throughout much of the American southwest, development filled and paved over the arroyos because their ecological and stormwater functions were not fully understood or valued. The resulting campus was a hostile environment that mixed pedestrians and cars, lacked exterior social space and provided little protection from the desert sun.

In 2012, Ten Eyck Landscape Architects and Lake Flato Architects submitted a series of concepts that won the competition to create a vision for the 18 acres (7.3 hectares) at the core of the campus. After fundraising, drawings were produced and Ten Eyck Landscape Architects led the multi-disciplinary team through design and construction as the prime consultant of the Landscape Master Plan for the campus core. The 11.5-acre (4.7-hectare) Campus Transformation Project (CTP), commemorating the university's centenary, was intended to create a new campus heart that would be a gathering place for celebrations and recreation and would make the campus centre more pedestrian friendly by ridding it of vehicular traffic. The CTP also needed to mitigate stormwater events and provide a universally accessible and socially engaging campus while re-establishing natural systems and celebrating the university's desert environment.

To fully appreciate the difficulty of fulfilling this mandate, one needs to understand something of the campus and regional landscapes. In El Paso, storms off the Pacific Ocean approach from the southwest, passing over the Gulf of California. As they intersect with the Sierra Madre mountains, they rise and cool, dropping most of their moisture and creating a rain shadow on the eastern side of the mountains. This single fact explains the existence of the Chihuahuan Desert, in which UTEP is situated. Summers are hot and cloudless, with an average daily high temperature of 89°F or 32°C. Although the annual rainfall is less than 10 inches (25.4 centimetres) and typically falls in a few major storms between July and October, the desert hosts a rich shrub and cacti biota (US National Park Service, n.d.). When it does rain, large volumes of water collide with mountainous terrain and exposed soils, leading to low infiltration rates and massive volumes of stormwater runoff. The runoff is heavily polluted due to the build-up of metals and oil from cars on impermeable surfaces, and flooding is common due to the lack of arroyos to distribute and infiltrate the stormwater.

Prior to the Campus Transformation Project, intense rainstorms inundated the Crazy Cat Arroyo, the only remaining arroyo on campus, degrading it and threatening the campus with flooding. A grade change of 60 feet (18 metres) within the campus core and extensive bedrock at or near the surface made achieving the directives of managing stormwater to reduce pollution and eliminate flooding and creating a social and wheelchair-accessible campus very challenging.

The solution: The Campus Transformation Project

Today, at the centre of the UTEP campus, a descending amphitheatre wraps around Centennial Green, an oval of drought-tolerant lawn cut into a hillside and flanked by two new arroyos.[1] Gently sloping paths allow universal access to the campus buildings and landscape. On the southern edge of the Green, Centennial Plaza provides a welcoming introduction to the campus core. The Green and the Plaza are ringed by the Paseo, a broad promenade where students study, enjoy campus entertainment, lounge on seating walls in quiet restorative settings and, in time, will walk beneath a shady arch of native mesquite trees (*Prosopis glandulosa*). Sculptural light standards inspired by the native ocotillo plant (*Fouquieria splendens*) brighten the Green at night, providing an element of safety and prolonging the period of use into the most pleasant part of the day. The Paseo connects to other treed promenades and major pedestrian routes, extending the experience of the campus core to the rest of the campus (Figure 4.9).

Replacing parking lots with a more permeable landscape and building a surface stormwater system reduced the amount of polluted water flowing from the central campus area. Stormwater collected from upper portions of the watershed now moves slowly across the landscape in a series of vegetated arroyos, acequias and detention basins. In addition to the water flowing from impervious surfaces within the project boundary, the surface drainage system manages stormwater from the mountainous area north of the campus and from parking and rooftops located outside the project area. In the new arroyos, boulders of native rock, unearthed during construction, are used with Chihuahuan desert plants to stabilise the soils. The Crazy Cat, the two new arroyos, the acequias and the infiltration basins slow stormwater, reduce flooding risk, recharge the aquifer and act as wildlife corridors. The arroyos enhance the health of the watershed by hydraulically linking the campus to the foothills landscape, reducing pollutants that reach the Rio Grande and supporting a diverse native plant and wildlife community (Figure 4.13).

The Campus Transformation Project sensitively fused open space design with the indigenous desert, weaving the social and the ecological into something new. Aesthetically, the arroyo's native rocks and plants establish a visual presence for the natural system, celebrate the region's heritage and situate the university community within the beauty of the Chihuahuan desert. The network of walkways, waterways and open spaces establishes a comfortable, pedestrian-oriented environment that offers passive and active recreation and is also intended to provide restorative experience.

▲ Figure 4.9

Plan, UTEP Campus Transformation Project.
Source: Image courtesy of Ten Eyck Landscape Architects.

The Campus Transformation Project as a restorative landscape

Researchers report that as the indicators of landscape preference increase, so too do the indicators of restorative landscapes (Han, 2010). For example, the quality of mystery is both the strongest predictor of landscape preference and a consistent predictor of restorative experience (Han, 2010; Gifford, 2007; Gimblett et al., 1985). In the same way, the indicators of restorative landscapes—fascination, extent, being away and compatibility—reliably predict the preference people express for both urban and natural landscapes (Laumann et al., 2001). When people find a landscape that they like, they engage with it mentally and physically; exploring, staying longer and visiting more frequently. These behaviours increase the restorative effect of the landscape.

Fascination

Stephen and Rachel Kaplan's model of restorative landscapes is based on the premise that natural landscapes are inherently fascinating to humans.

CHAPTER 4 **Functional and aesthetic criteria** 119

They draw our attention, are processed effortlessly and restore mental capacity. E.O. Wilson's biophilia hypothesis—that people have an evolutionary inclination to connect with other lifeforms—explains why this is so (Heerwagen and Orians, 1993). The CTP landscape is a lush oasis in the desert. Its high natural content and the passing effects of nature, like grasses swaying in the breeze or songbirds flitting though the trees, activate fascination and satisfy the biophilic response. Focal points like the arroyos, fountains and bridges add complexity, serving to increase fascination.

Extent

For a landscape to express the quality of extent it must exhibit two properties: It must be a big enough space that one may enter and spend time in it, and it must have a quality of connectedness. This means that the different parts of the landscape must be connected and make a recognisable whole, allowing the visitor to experience a unified meaning (S. Kaplan, 1995).

Because a space is perceived or sensed from its boundaries, a unified contiguous edge is critical to a space being perceived as a whole. At UTEP, the central open space of Centennial Green has well-defined edges. A consistent building type[2] is set on a unified landscape edge, comprised of the landforms of the arroyos, the amphitheatre and the belts of mesquite trees that the encircle the Green. The Green itself is unified by its fine-textured ground plane of lawn. From within, no visual clues demarcate where the campus landscape ends and the desert begins. This increases the psychological extent of the space (Figure 4.11).

There is a clear hierarchy of pedestrian walkways and sub-areas in the UTEP campus core. Centennial Green, the Paseo, Centennial Square and the amphitheatre comprise the primary sub-areas, and Geology Green and the Lhakhang Cultural Center are secondary spaces. The Paseo and pedestrian paths to and from Centennial Square are major routes, and the paths that connect the Paseo to Geology Green and the Cultural Center are secondary (Figure 4.9).

Clear boundaries and a unified centre give the campus core the sense of being a unified place. Blending the CTP with its desert context and providing a small number of connected sub-areas gives the user more to explore, physically or mentally, and increases extent.

Being away

The feeling of being away results from experiencing an environment that is distinctly different from one's usual surroundings. The landscape of the CTP, while it might become part of the daily experience of staff and students, is unique. It is a shady retreat filled with water, greenery and wildlife and a contiguous part of the desert landscape. A student seated beneath a tree next to a fountain on the Paseo watches people from a location of prospect refuge while surrounded with markers of the desert. In the arroyos, coveys of quail (*Callipepla gambelii*) scurry between native boulders and desert

▲ Figure 4.10

Before: The UTEP core campus landscape prior to the implementation of the Campus Transformation Project. The landscape did not function ecologically and was not restorative because it was not a landscape where people would choose to spend time.
Source: Image courtesy of Ten Eyck Landscape Architects.

▲ Figure 4.11

In addition to managing water and seeming to belong to the larger landscape, the campus is a restorative landscape. The line where the designed landscape ends and the natural landscape begins is blurred. The space is legible and connected and expresses the quality of extent.
Source: Image courtesy of Ten Eyck Landscape Architects.

▲ Figure 4.12

This setting illustrates many of the attributes of the restorative landscape. The person is immersed in a natural landscape. Although the landscape has identifiable sub-areas, it is seen as a whole, having a distinct boundary. Natural elements—water, rocks, landform, soils and plants—dominate the views and provide fascination. Source: Image courtesy of Ten Eyck Landscape Architects.

plants. Along the Paseo, the cooing of mourning doves (*Zenaida macroura*) drifts from the mesquite trees overhead. It is an experience of the region but distinctly different from any other landscape in the daily experience of the users (Figure 4.12).

Compatibility

A compatible landscape is one that facilitates what the users wish to do. The ability to find one's way is always required, and wayfinding is a necessary component of a compatible landscape. It is supported by elements of the landscape that are clearly differentiated and easily remembered. In the Campus Transformation Project, the clear hierarchy of circulation and spaces provides legibility and supports wayfinding. Buildings, fountains, bridges, light standards and the arroyos are landmarks that help people navigate the campus core.

In terms of both microclimatic modification and social interaction, people require different things at different times. A compatible landscape gives people choice and meets their changing needs. On a cool morning, shelter from wind and exposure to sun are sought. Later that same day, a seat in the shade and a gentle breeze might be needed. At UTEP, visitors can choose between sun and shade locations depending on their preference and current weather conditions. Modifying the microclimate by providing shade, extending use into the cool of the evening and providing restorative and social spaces make the CTP landscape more compatible.

▲ Figure 4.13

Landform, vegetation and rocks recreate the image and function of a desert arroyo.
Source: Image courtesy of Ten Eyck Landscape Architects.

The CTP was designed to give people a choice between social spaces and restorative landscape experience. It contains a high measure of urban nature in a desert environment and is configured to deliver all the attributes of restorative landscapes. Within the CTP, there are more than 640 quiet outdoor seating areas that are intended to provide mental restoration. These areas are located on the edge of Centennial Plaza or in areas that are away from major circulation routes. Each has visual and physical access to native desert and other drought-tolerant plantings. Another 1,880 seats are located in high-use places of social engagement, including garden balconies overlooking the Green, the steps of the amphitheatre and ornamental fire pits that are lit on special occasions (The University of El Paso, Texas, b, n.d.).

Ecosystem services in the CTP

In 2016, the UTEP Campus Transformation Project earned an Honor Award for Excellence in Landscape Architecture from the Society of College and University Planning and became the first project certified under the Sustainable SITESv2 Initiative.[3] The Sustainable SITES award recognises a number of sustainable landscape practices and the ecosystem services delivered by the design of the CTP. The surface drainage system of the arroyos, acequias and detention basins replicate the function of a natural desert drainage system. The system is capable of intercepting 565,370 gallons (2,140 cubic metres) of stormwater runoff daily, which exceeds the 95th percentile storm event. It reduces flooding risk, recharges groundwater and mitigates water pollution (H. Venhaus, personal communication, June 23, 2018). The CTP increased the vegetated area of the campus core by 60 per cent, using a diverse palette of low-water-use and native Chihuahuan desert plants. The extensive desert plantings mitigate the regional climate,

CHAPTER 4 **Functional and aesthetic criteria**

minimise potable water use, provide habitat and contribute to a restorative experience. By providing both social and restorative seating areas within a distinctly regional desert landscape, the CTP delivers the cultural ecosystem benefits of social cohesion, sense of identity, mental and physical wellbeing and recreation (see Table 4.1).

The practice of landscape architecture in the desert southwest of America is still very much in a formative period. In the past, it aped the cultural landscapes of the eastern US, but it is now grappling with the development of a contemporary desert aesthetic. The UTEP Campus Transformation Project is a notable precedent that has demonstrated an ecologically responsive, regional aesthetic for twenty-first-century desert landscape architecture (K. Crawford, personal communication, July 1, 2018). The project delivers a wide range of ecological, social and cultural ecosystem services with minimum water inputs, is a model of public open space in an arid environment and demonstrates that planting design is integral to achieving multi-functional landscapes.

Invasive plant species

Invasive non-native species are by definition species "whose introduction and/or spread threaten biological diversity or have other unforeseen impacts" (Secretariat Great Britain, 2008). Non-native invasive species have been introduced worldwide, sometimes with the intention of the production of food and fibre and other times inadvertently. They have multiple associated costs, including the invasion and alteration of natural ecosystems and communities. Although they have been linked to species extinction, non-native invasive species are only one of multiple threats to native species and ecosystems. Other co-mingled threats include habitat destruction, hunting or collecting and changes in fire regime (Gurevitch and Padilla, 2004). Additional costs include the loss of ecosystem services. For example, invasion of some grass species has changed the frequency of forest fires, which has lessened forest regeneration and increased flooding (Pejchar and Mooney, 2009).

In addition to the ecosystem and ecosystem services losses caused by invasive non-native plants, they have huge economic costs. Introduced plant species have taken grazing lands out of production, reduced agricultural production and increased production costs. Large sums of money are spent annually on eradication and control. Total costs in the United States are estimated at nearly 120 billion US dollars per year (Pimentel, Zuniga and Morrison, 2005) and in Great Britain at £1.7 billion, or more than 2.6 billion US dollars annually. These costs are ongoing and expected to increase in proportion to the area and density of invasion (Williams et al., 2010).

Strategies to combat these invasive species include exclusion of any new introductions of invasive species, early eradication, eradication of existing invasions, and ongoing control rather than eradication of existing infestations (Simberloff, 2003). While the costs of eradication and control are large and will increase, the cost of the continued presence and expansion of invasive species is much greater (Williams et al., 2010).

Invasive plant species may appear to be benign for a number of years before suddenly becoming invasive. Plants that are listed as invasive species in one country or state will not be found to be invasive in other places. It is incumbent on every planting designer to become acquainted with the designated invasive plant species wherever they work and to eliminate these species from their plant palette. A quick search on the internet will connect you to a list of designated or restricted invasive plant species in your area and the best biological or physical control measures for each plant. In addition, any site development should be seen as an opportunity to eradicate invasive species that are present on the site. This is not only a contribution to reducing the problems caused by invasive plant species but also good business, as the continued presence of invasive species will greatly increase ongoing maintenance costs. Finally, it must be recognised that some invasive species have important benefits. For example, stinging nettle (*Urtica dioica*) is considered a weedy invasive species but is an important larval food plant for several native North American butterflies, like Milbert's tortoiseshell (*Aglais milberti*) and the West Coast Lady (*Vaness cardui*), and the butterfly bush (*Buddleja davidii*) is widely classified as invasive but also has value as a nectar source for butterflies (Campbell, Granger and Nyhof, 1995). This is to suggest that in some cases a judgement call is necessary. The habitat value in a particular setting may be weighed against the potential for invasion of an introduced plant species in a particular location.

Plantings to manage stormwater

The soils of natural ecosystems slowly absorb and filter the water that they receive from precipitation and then filter, store and distribute that water. Water may move through the soil profile as what is known as interflow, or it may find its way below the soil profile as groundwater, entering into aquifers where it is stored and released to supply streams, rivers and lakes. Water passing through the soil profile will be cooled and cleansed of particulate pollutants. Plants or micro-organisms in the soil will uptake nutrients and pollutants such as hydrocarbons and heavy metals. This process is necessary to provide the clean, cool water that is the basis of life for many fish and other aquatic organisms.

When humans build cities, they cover the once-absorptive soil with impermeable surfaces like roads, parking lots and roofs and install engineered storm water systems that treat urban runoff water as a waste product to be removed as quickly as possible. As urban development proceeds, the urban watershed becomes progressively "hardened". Several studies have reported that fish and other aquatic species begin to decline when the impervious cover in a watershed reaches between 10 and 20 per cent of the total area, and some authors report some species of fish becoming rare when as little as 2 per cent of the watershed has been made impervious (Wenger et al., 2008).

The negative effects of hardening the urban watershed include increased water volumes and velocities and higher water temperatures and pollutant levels in urban waterways. The large volumes of stormwater delivered to urban streams produce high-velocity stream flows that erode urban streams, reduce in-stream habitat complexity and can flush fish from streams when velocities exceed their natural tolerances. Higher temperatures increase the biological oxygen demand in the stream, thus robbing the water of its natural oxygen levels, and this can be lethal to fish. In addition, untreated urban runoff typically carries oil-soaked soil particles, residue from the brake linings of cars, fertilisers, pesticides and other pollutants that are potentially lethal to fish and other aquatic organisms.

To offset the problems created by urban runoff, it is necessary to retrofit cities so that they mimic the infiltration, filtering and slow distribution of water that occurs in natural systems. The implementation of rain gardens, bioswales and green roofs are some ways to do this.

Plants for rain gardens

Rain gardens are planted closed depressions that collect urban runoff and hold the water until it can infiltrate through the soil. Their purpose is to improve the quality of water of nearby surface waters by reducing high-velocity stream flows, removing pollutants in urban runoff and replenishing interflow and groundwater flows. If enough rain gardens are installed, it can reduce the need to replace urban stormwater systems. The design of a rain garden must incorporate the volumes of runoff it will receive and the soil type in which the rain garden will be placed. To achieve these objectives, a rain garden should:

1) Be a depressed surface that collects and holds precipitation and runoff.
2) Accept water inputs in excess of precipitation that falls directly on the rain garden surface.
3) Contain a water outlet such as a porous bottom or an under drain to prevent soils being saturated for long periods.
4) Contain living plants.
5) Contain living soils.
6) Include an overflow into the storm system to avoid potential flooding.

Criteria 4 and 5 are especially important, as it is the micro-organisms on the plants roots and in the soil that will ameliorate much of the pollutants in the urban runoff intercepted by the rain garden. The plants themselves will remove such things as dissolved fertilisers and heavy metals. The living plants and soils at the bottom of the rain garden are important components because they increase its function.

▶ Figure 4.14
Rain garden plan and section showing the different planting zones (after Hinmann, 2013).
Source: Image courtesy of Yiwen Ruan.

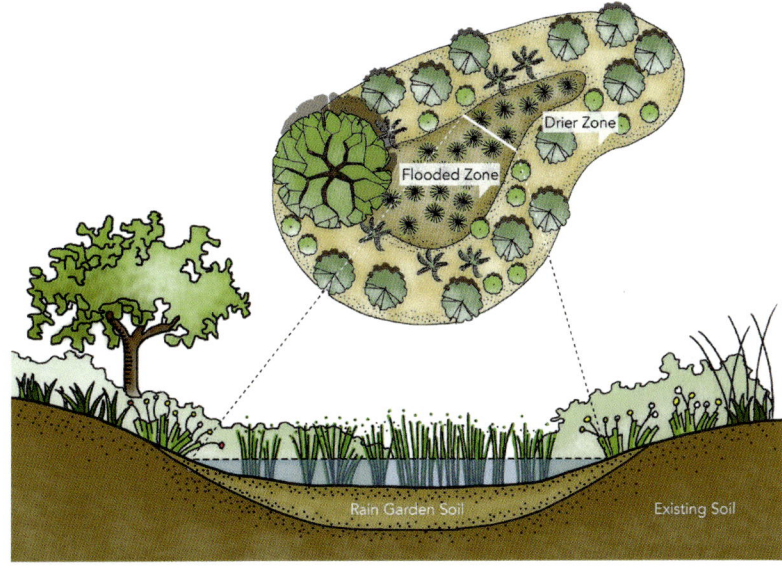

▶ Figure 4.15
In this rain garden in Victoria, British Columbia, *Juncus patens* 'Carmen's Grey', Oregon *Iris* (*Iris tenax*), wild flag *Iris* (*Iris setosa*) and *Cornus sericea* 'Midwinter Fire' occupy the flooded zone, while Chinese silver grass (*Miscanthus sinensis* 'Adagio') and evergreen huckleberry (*Vaccinium ovatum*) are used in the drier zone.
Source: Photo and design, Murdoch Degreeff Landscape Architects.

The plants that are selected for rain gardens should be regionally specific. This is because they must be adapted to extreme moisture conditions. The plants at the lowest levels of the rain garden must be tolerant of being flooded for extended periods of time and then being unirrigated during the annual dry period (Figure 4.14). Native plants that occur in the wettest zones of ephemeral wetlands are good candidates for the parts of the rain garden that will alternatively be flooded and drought stressed. Native sedges (*Juncus* spp.) have proven to be effective plants in the flooded zone of the rain garden, and recent research has identified a number of colourful perennials that can also thrive there (Yuan and Dunnett, 2018). Plants on the sides of the rain garden will seldom if ever be flooded, but need to retain the soils on the side of the rain garden depression and tolerate the regional climate moisture variation.

Plants in bioswales

Bioswales are surface stormwater conveyance channels and may be considered as linear rain gardens. In addition to conveying stormwater, bioswales, like rain gardens, receive, infiltrate, filter and cleanse urban runoff. Bioswales are particularly useful in filtering out particulate pollutants. They are often planted with native grasses and sedges, and the denser the stems of these plants the greater will be the collection of particulates in the bioswale. As in rain gardens, plants at the lowest levels of a bioswale need to be tolerant of alternative flooding and drought and, like rain gardens, additional subgrade drains and overflow drains may be needed.

Plants for green roofs

Green or planted roofs are, like bioswales and rain gardens, part of designed urban water systems that slow the rate of runoff from urban watersheds and reduce water pollution by absorbing atmospheric pollutants. In addition, green roofs can reduce the urban heat island effect, provide wildlife habitat and add building insulation, thereby reducing energy use and interior nose (Fernandez-Cañero, Emilsson, Fernandez-Barba and Machuca, 2013).

Green roofs may be either extensive or intensive. Extensive green roofs have shallow growing media of typically between 2 and 4 inches (50 and 100 millimetres) and thus provide less available soil moisture and nutrients. They are typically planted with low-growing succulents. Intensive green roofs have a growing media that is greater than 4 inches (100 millimetres) in depth and are designed as roof-top gardens that may incorporate paving, structures and a broader range of ornamental and food plants (Torrence, Bass, MacIvor and McGlade, 2013). In either type of green roof, the plant roots stabilise the growing medium against the erosive effects of wind and water while increasing permeability and infiltration, but they may need watering in summer, especially in Mediterranean-type climates (Dunnett and Kingsbury, 2004).

Researchers in Spain found that the public prefers green roofs that have higher plant diversity and a wider range of colours and which mimic traditional gardens. Such plantings are also considered to increase urban biodiversity by providing habitat for vertebrates and invertebrates (Fernandez-Cañero et al., 2013).

Plants for green roofs should:

1) Be tolerant of extremes of sun, drought and wind.
2) Have potential to support native species such as butterflies and ground-nesting bird.
3) Be disease- and pest-resistant.
4) Be selected with reference to the available level of maintenance.
5) Be adapted to the temperature extremes and low nutrients of shallow growing media.
6) Be quick to establish but not so aggressive as to out-compete other green-roof plants (Roehr and Fassman-Beck, 2015).

To date, the most successful plants for extensive green roofs have been succulents. *Sedums* are commonly used, as they have the ability to grow new roots within hours of being planted, to access maximum water and store water within their fleshy stems and leaves. Other recommended succulents for extensive green roofs include hens and chicks (*Sempervivum*), fameflower (*Talinum calycinum*) and iceplant (*Delosperma cooperi*) (Snodgrass and Snodgrass, 2006). Where deeper soils and/or irrigation allow, low perennials and groundcovers like tunic plant (*Petrorhagia saxifrage*) and pinks (*Dianthus deltoides* and *Dianthus carthusianorum*) are recommended (UK Greenroofs Guide, n.d.). To increase the biodiversity of green roofs, experts recommend planting native wildflowers and naturalised meadow plants that are food plants and nectar sources for butterflies and insects (Torrance et al., 2013; Dunnett and Kingsbury, 2004).

Plants for biodiversity and habitats

Many urban regions were built on great rivers, estuaries and migration routes and still support significant biological diversity (Ricketts and Imhoff, 2003; UK Biodiversity Action Plan, n.d.). This is a significant finding, since biological diversity or biodiversity is related to the number and type of ecosystem services that are present in any location (Haines-Young and Potschin, 2010). Generally speaking, where biodiversity is declining, supporting and regulating ecosystem services are also declining (Balvanera et al., 2006). For example, primary productivity, or the amount of biomass produced in an ecosystem, is closely related to biological diversity (Costanza, Fisher, Mulder, Liu and Christopher, 2007). A forest that was growing more vigorously and producing more biomass each year would have higher infiltration of precipitation than a less bioproductive forest and would better perform the ecosystem service of flood control (Haines-Young and Potschin, 2010). In this example, a decline in biodiversity in the forest could indicate a reduction in its bioproductivity and flood control ecosystem services.

Urban regions often retain significant biodiversity, and it is critically important to maintain this biodiversity so that important ecosystem services are not lost. Since we do not know the point of biodiversity decline at which

▲ Figure 4.16

Different species use different habitat types. In western North America, the scarlet tanager finds its habitats in the deciduous forest, while the red-winged blackbird nests in freshwater wetlands.
Source: Photos courtesy of Al Grass.

ecosystem services will be lost, it is prudent to seek to maintain current levels of biodiversity (Kremen, 2005). However, urban regions typically lose biodiversity as they grow, and maintaining regional biodiversity in urban regions is one of the challenges facing environmental designers and planners today. The problem is compounded by the fact that maintaining biodiversity in urban regions is a regionally specific problem that will require direct local knowledge (Cook, 2000; Alberti, 2005).

There are different strategies to maintain regional biodiversity at different scales. It is a general principle of ecology that structural, or physical, diversity increases biodiversity at the scale measured. For example, a tree that was more structurally complex would have more niches that might be occupied by a larger range of birds and insects than a less complexly structured tree (James, 1971; James and Wamer, 1982). At the site level, the diversity of habitats within a site increases site biodiversity. Habitat heterogeneity is a measure of the diversity and variation in vegetative cover that has consistently been positively correlated with avian biological diversity at a site level (Boecklen, 1986; Bühning-Gaese, 1997; Krüger and Lindström, 2001; Tews et al., 2004). Simply put, this means that where the number of different kinds of habitats on a site is increasing, the number of organisms that use those different habitats will also increase.

Consider that the plant associations that we develop in the course of planting design are also habitats. To create a range of site habitats, the designer needs to first consider the types of habitats that could be supported on a given site and their applicability to the intended human use program. This would require them to understand:

1) The environmental gradients present on the site.
2) The range of environmental gradients that each habitat type requires.
3) The plant species found in each habitat type and their individual growing requirements.
4) The key vertebrate and invertebrate species that might occupy each of those habitat types.
5) The suitability of different habitat types to the intended human use.

Achieving these site understandings will usually be a trans-disciplinary effort involving multiple professionals.

Plants for ecological restoration and enhancement

Ecological restoration is the process of assisting the recovery of an ecosystem that has been damaged or degraded (SER, 2004). The type and degree of ecological restoration will vary with the amount and type of degradation that has occurred. Potential restoration objectives include developing a particular habitat type to support biological diversity, preventing erosion, supporting agro-forestry and restoring groundwater recharge. In any ecological restoration for habitat, the designer is seeking to reestablish a plant community that formerly occupied the site in order to provide the necessary habitat. This requires establishing the growing conditions necessary for that plant community.

Site analysis and habitat modelling

It is now considered a fundamental rule of ecosystem restoration that every restoration should be based on modelling the ecosystem type that is being restored (SER, 2004). This involves analysis of both a representative ecosystem site or ecosystem unit and the restoration site. Essentially, the environmental gradients of the two sites must match if the restoration is to be successful.

In addition, enhancing for wildlife involves a two-step modelling process. First, the restorationist needs to research available species/

habitat models for the species in question. Once the site elements and/ or plant community necessary for a species to inhabit a site are known, the restorationist needs to understand the site conditions that will allow those site factors to be developed. This involves the understanding of the environmental gradients that exist or that may be established on the site.

When the basic models have been established, the critical factors within those models can be analysed. This often requires fieldwork and the laboratory testing of soils and water. If the critical environmental gradients cannot be established, the project will need to be modified or even abandoned.

Case study: Iona Island Regional Park freshwater marsh restoration

Background

Iona Island lies within the Fraser River delta in southwestern British Columbia. It is within the Municipality of Richmond in the MetroVancouver Region.

The island is connected to Sea Island, home of Vancouver International Airport, by a causeway and since 1961 has been home to a sewage treatment plant that services much of the surrounding urban area. In 1987, much of Iona Island was set aside for development as a regional park. At West Iona beach, the main parking and use area of the park, two groundwater-fed freshwater marshes had developed from unused sewage lagoons and were popular birding sites. When one of these ponds was filled with material dredged from the Fraser River, important bird habitat and birding opportunities were lost. In addition, the then-proposed expansion of Vancouver International Airport would soon destroy important habitat of the yellow-headed blackbird (*Xanthocephalus xanthocephalus*). This was the only documented breeding habitat for this species in the Fraser River Delta. Although numerous elsewhere in North America, the bird has restricted habitat and was uncommon in coastal British Columbia (Butler and Campbell, 1987).

Design development process

In the spring of 1992, with funding in place, the project got underway with a review of the proposed design. Team members included a coastal engineer, an aquatic ecologist, a civil engineer, a park planner, a landscape architect and a landscape architect/restorationist.

Project goals

The restoration plan sought to restore a freshwater marsh on the recently filled site and to enhance the adjacent freshwater marsh within the newly

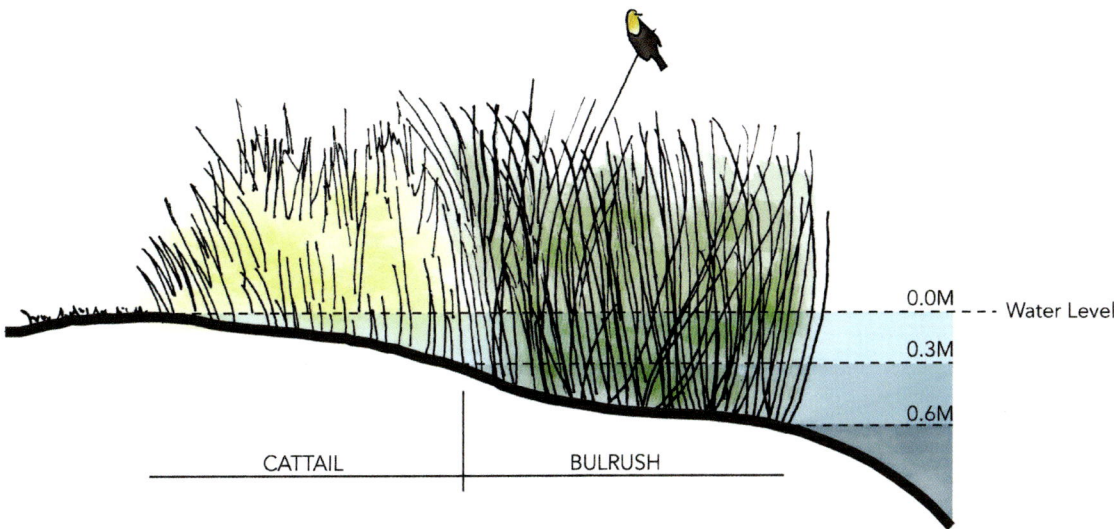

▲ Figure 4.17

The positions of cattail and bulrush plants along a water depth gradient at a pond edge.
Source: Image courtesy of Yiwen Ruan.

created Iona Island Regional Park. The intention was to maximise general avian diversity as well as to provide replacement habitat for the yellow-headed blackbird.

The species/habitat model for the yellow-headed blackbird showed that it nests exclusively in marshes, in hardstem bulrush (*Scipus acutis*) adjacent to open water, and will not nest within a 45-degree angle of influence of a tree or promontory. Males are polygamous and occupy territories in the centre of a marsh, with water depths of 2 to 4 feet (0.6 to 1.2 metres), pushing smaller redwing blackbirds to the peripheries (Orians, 1985). This simple descriptive species/habitat model was used to set the requirements of the nesting sites for the yellow-headed blackbird.

Habitat modelling inevitably led to an examination of what would be required to establish hardstem bulrush. The nearby McDonald Slough was used as the representative ecosystem site. Transects revealed that hardstem bulrush will sprout from a depth of about 2 feet (0.6 metres) and will not grow in much deeper water. Cattails (*Typha latifolia* and *Typha angustifolia*) need to be wet or inundated when making their initial growth but will tolerate drier conditions later in the growing season. In other words, the emergent vegetation positions itself along a moisture regime from wetter to dryer that responds to the seasonal fluctuations in the pond levels (Figure 4.17).

Site analysis revealed that songbirds, raptors, waterfowl and shorebirds would use the wetland. The area around the restored wetland was designed to be an "old field" type of habitat, that is, an open grassy meadow with dispersed shrubs and small trees intended to attract songbirds and raptors. The contouring of the pond bottom and the horizontal placement of each of the emergent plants was done to produce the necessary growing conditions for the emergent marsh vegetation and to limit its growth where open water was required.

Project evaluation

The site was monitored for three years after completion. All the emergent plants throve in their intended locations and did not expand into deeper water. Three years after completion of the restoration, 11 yellow-headed blackbird nests and 54 eggs were recorded in the restored pond. Yellow-headed blackbirds continue to occupy the site. At the same time, general avian diversity increased dramatically in the five years after the restoration was implemented.

The project was, however, contaminated with two exotic invasive species. Scots broom (*Cytisus scoparius*) invaded and colonised the old field area around the pond. In 1998, volunteers cut and removed the broom that was shading out native shrub species. This was followed by several other smaller volunteer broom removals that controlled but did not eliminate the broom.

The second invasive species was purple loosestrife (*Lythrum salicaria*). This introduced invasive plant colonises freshwater marshes, displacing native wetland species. It was brought in with the cattails and bulrushes harvested from Sea Island. It spread quickly and threatened to take over the cattail areas of the marsh. Beginning in 1996, three insect biological controls specific to purple loosestrife and that had been approved by the Canadian government were introduced to the marsh. Although slow to establish, the biological control insects have now eliminated the loosestrife in the restored pond.

The final stage of an ecological restoration is a planting plan of the native plant association, intended to meet the project's goals. Modelling in ecological restoration can result in successfully establishing the intended plant association/habitat. The restoration showed the necessity of eliminating exotic invasive plants from a restoration and the effectiveness of biological controls on purple loosestrife.

Case study: Charlie Mountain Ranch restoration

Design Workshop team members: Mike Albert, Michael Tunte, Ben Roush and Alison Kelly
Architecture: Pearson Design Group Inc.
Structural engineer: KL&A
Landscape contractor: Landscape Workshop Inc.

Design Workshop Inc.: The firm

In 1969, North Carolina State University professors of landscape architecture Joe Porter and Don Ensign started Design Workshop, a consulting practice they named after a collaborative design and planning method they had developed in teaching. Now called DW Legacy Design®, the

▲ Figure 4.18

The Charlie Mountain Ranch lies in a transition zone between subalpine forests and semi-arid oak woodlands that provide habitat for indigenous wildlife.
Source: Image courtesy of Design Workshop Inc.

proprietary process seeks to balance four dominant aspects of landscape architecture: Stewardship of the environment, human community, art and beauty, and economic viability (Design Workshop Inc., n.d.).

Application of the DW Legacy Design process for over 50 years has established an award-winning landscape architecture, land planning and urban design practice with multiple offices in the US, China and the United Arab Emirates. In every project, intensive landscape inventory and analysis is undertaken to foster an understanding of the place, including its existing condition, contextual landscape and historical and proposed uses. In the case of the Charlie Mountain Ranch, application of the process led to the ecological restoration of a historic Colorado ranch.

Charlie Mountain Ranch site inventory and planning

By 2011, the 72-acre (29-hectare) Charlie Mountain Ranch, near Snowmass, Colorado, had been visually and ecologically degraded by decades of poor management. The new owners were committed to restoring its rural character and productivity and engaged Design Workshop to conduct a comprehensive site analysis, leading to a masterplan of the ranch that was done in collaboration with the architect. The site inventory revealed a mosaic of native plant communities, each of which developed in response to changes in topography, soil, solar aspect and proximity to water (Figure 4.19).

The site inventory and analysis revealed a diverse set of plant communities comprised of agricultural meadows, aspen woodlands, mixed conifer forests and an intact cottonwood riparian corridor along the ranch's portion of Snowmass Creek. It also revealed large areas of barren soils and debris

CHAPTER 4 Functional and aesthetic criteria

◀ Figure 4.19

The plant communities of the Charlie Mountain Ranch with their attendant water use. Water conservation efforts were integrated into the master plan to maximise the efficiency of a drip irrigation system. Zone-compatible plantings, by water need, were implemented in the ecological restoration of the ranch.
Source: Image courtesy of Design Workshop Inc.

Before   After

◀ Figure 4.20

Gambel oak stands before and after hand thinning. Thinning reduced wildfire risk and improved habitat values while making the oak stands more resistant to drought, insects and disease. It also made the landscape more legible and restorative.
Source: Image courtesy of Design Workshop Inc.

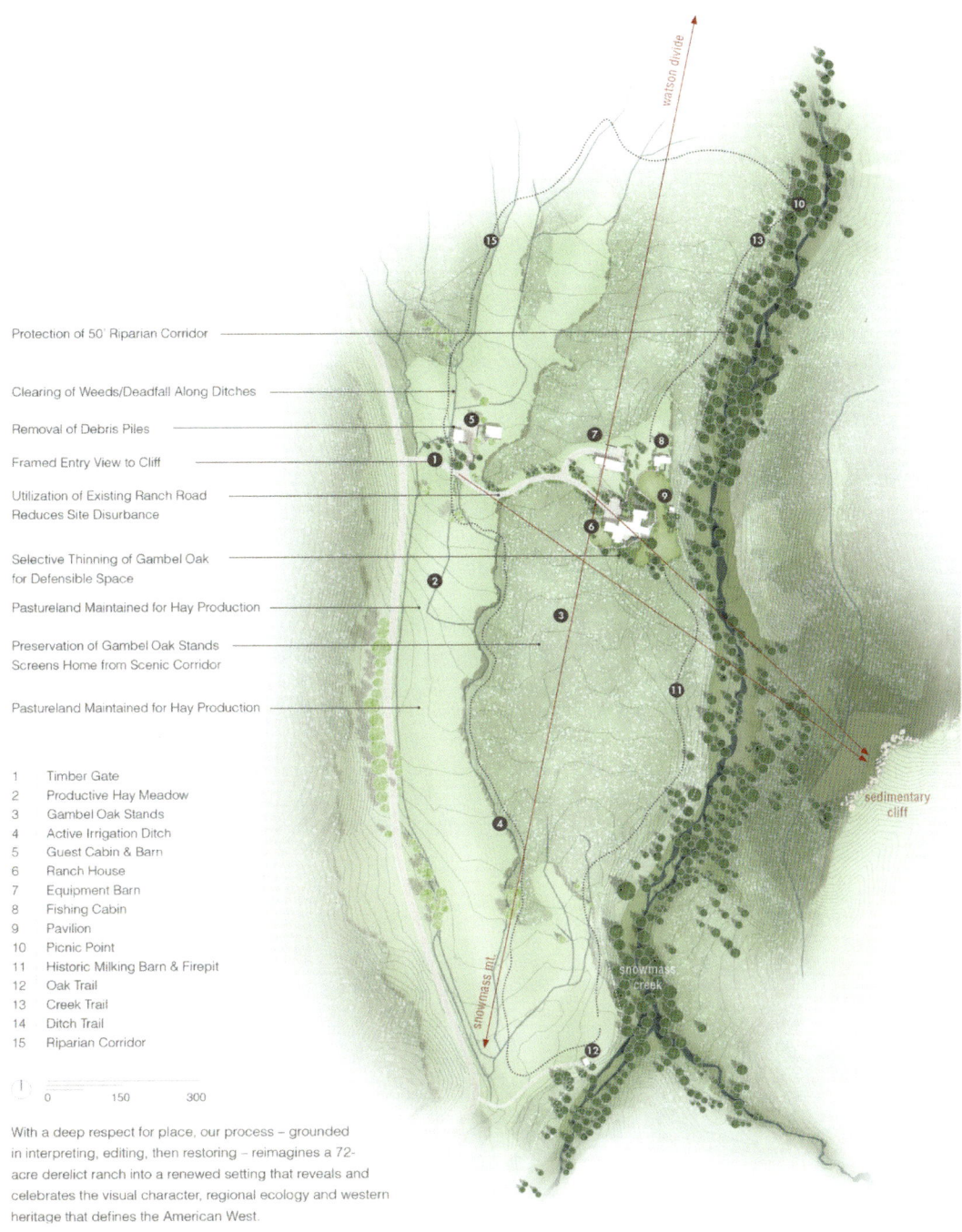

▲ Figure 4.21

Design Workshop's landscape inventory and analysis showed the need for ecological restoration. The interventions of the master plan maintained the historic layout and heritage structures of the ranch, sited new buildings on previously disturbed land, restored drainage ditches, maintained hay pastures and enhanced the ranch's plant communities visually and ecologically. Source: Image courtesy of Design Workshop Inc.

piles, overgrown drainage ditches, meadows contaminated with noxious weeds and impenetrable Gambel oak (*Quercus gambelii*) thickets that presented a fire hazard.

In all landscapes, each plant community is a different habitat serving a different set of species. Each also presents a distinct landscape character with its own colours and textures, seasonal effects, views and qualities of light and space. Recognising that ecology and the visual/aesthetic are inextricably meshed, the landscape architects chose to edit and restore the native landscape of the ranch to enhance both aesthetics and function.

Gambel oak provides habitat for grouse and songbirds and is important winter habitat for deer and elk. However, when left unmanaged, the dense oak stands present a fire hazard and their habitat value is reduced. Thinning reduces fire hazard and improves the growth of herbaceous species beneath the oaks (Kaufmann et al., 2016). At the Charlie Mountain Ranch, the oak thickets were selectively thinned, opening them to sunlight and improving the soil moisture regime. This allowed native bunchgrasses, forbs and wildflowers to flourish, improving habitat values and reducing the risk of wildfire (Figure 4.20). The other plant communities of the ranch—woodlands, meadow and riparian ecosystems—were enhanced with supplemental plantings. These interventions improved the habitat values and visual character of the property.

Rather than having one large building, the master plan called for a cluster of carefully scaled structures to be placed on previously disturbed land. This reduced the potential impacts of further site disturbance and ensured that the resulting structures allowed the majestic landscape to dominate the consciousness of the residents. Design Workshop's landscape architects used inventory and analysis, site planning and design to conserve and enhance the ecological quality of the Charlie Mountain Ranch. Their interventions created a visually imaginative landscape that is more sustainable and livable.

Plant list

Trees	
Populus deltoides	Cottonwood
Populus tremuloides	Quaking aspen
Pinus ponderosa	Ponderosa pine
Picea pungens	Colorado blue spruce
Shrubs	
Cornus servicea	Red osier dogwood
Juniperus communis	Common juniper
Physocarpus opulifolius 'Nanus'	Dwarf Ninebark
Potentilla fruticosa 'McKay's White'	McKay's White *Potentilla*

Rhus aromatica 'Gro-low'	Dwarf fragrant sumac
Chrysothamnus nauseosus	Rabbitbrush
Cercocarpus montanus	Alder-leaf mountain mahogany
Spiraea japonica	Japanese spirea
Rosa woodsii	Woods' rose
Syringa vulgaris cv.	Common purple lilac
Perennials	
Alchemilla mollis	Lady's mantle
Aegopodium podagraria	Bishop's weed
Galium odoratum	Sweet woodruff
Grasses	
Bluegrass sod	
Seed mix: Pitkin County seed mix	
Fescue sod	

The associative meanings of plants in the landscape

In a review of aesthetics as they relate to landscapes, Bourassa (1988) argued that our aesthetic responses are simultaneously biological and cultural, conscious and subconscious, rational and intuitive. Our initial aesthetic response to new environments is immediate, spontaneous and affective (by affective we mean influencing our feelings, moods and emotions). It may activate feelings of like or dislike, engagement or avoidance, that are unmediated by thought (Ulrich, 1983; S. Kaplan, 1987; Appleton, 1996). In these rapid judgments, it is thought that we are responding to the way the landscape is configured—its structure and pattern (Ulrich, 1983). This first affective response I shall call the aesthetic response in order to distinguish it from a separate kind of environmental appraisal that I shall call the aesthetic judgment. Unlike the immediate and innate aesthetic response, the aesthetic judgment is cognitive. In making the aesthetic judgement, the person identifies objects, patterns, characteristics or visual configurations and evaluates the associative meanings, symbols, values and import of the entire landscape or its elements (Ulrich, 1983). It is as if, after an initial affective response to a particular setting, the mind then stops to assess what caused that feeling, to question whether that is the appropriate response and then to reaffirm or modify that response in the face of more detailed information. While the aesthetic response is considered to be innate and cross-cultural, the aesthetic judgment is influenced by such things as cultural norms, age and past experiences (Ulrich, 1983). The aesthetic response and the aesthetic judgment can occur almost simultaneously, and the person perceiving and judging will not necessarily be aware of this

TABLE 4.3 A comparison of aesthetic response and aesthetic judgement

Aesthetic Response	Aesthetic Judgment
Immediate.	May follow the aesthetic response or occur simultaneously.
Is based on formal qualities of the landscape and our innate biological response to landscape.	Based on the values we hold and on the mental associations we have with the landscape and its components.
Is unconscious or subconscious and is not mediated by thinking.	Is a mental judgment, but the individual may be unaware of their thinking.
Considered to be innate and universal.	Is mediated by values, personal history, experiences and culture and is particular to the individual.
Is affective (activates feelings, emotions and moods).	Is affective and will influence how we feel about a landscape setting.

Source: Table courtesy of Yiwen Ruan.

taking place (Bourassa, 1988). Table 4.3 summarises the characteristics of the aesthetic response and the aesthetic judgement.

Our aesthetic response to plants and landscapes

Landscapes, both natural and designed, have aesthetic qualities that have a powerful effect on the user. Aesthetic qualities may be the colours, form, line and patterns within the landscape or the powerful passing effects of sunlight, wind and clouds. It has been consistently demonstrated that people prefer natural over built environments, especially when the landscapes contain water and are open and savannah-like (Ulrich, 1993), and that both cultural and biological factors influence our aesthetic evaluations of landscape (Hartig, 1993). But it is also recognised that these cross-cultural innate preferences for landscape are not "hard-wired". Rather, our evolutionary history has produced in us tendencies and biases that are strongly influenced by culture. For example, Norwegian researchers who studied the relationship between landscape preference and environmental values found that people who were ecocentric, or focused on the environment, preferred wildlands with water and cultural landscapes, while people who were anthropocentric, or human focused, preferred farm environments and tended to be apathetic about the environment. This is one example of how personal values influence aesthetic judgement of landscapes (Kaltenborn and Bjerke, 2002).

The role of knowledge in aesthetic judgements

Our environmental response is the sum of our sensory aesthetic response and our cognitive associative aesthetic judgement, and this is true not only of landscape but also of individual elements in our environment. If we look at a blue vase we may have a positive aesthetic response to its sensory characteristics of form, sheen and colour. If we are asked to choose between two blue vases, one of which is highly ornate and traditional while the other is sleek and modern, our aesthetic judgments will influence our choice. Let's assume that our aesthetic response is to like both vases equally. Our aesthetic judgment about which to choose will be influenced by our personal values and the associations that the style of vase has for us. For example, one individual will choose the ornate vase because they associate it with value and tradition. Another individual might reject the traditional vase as old-fashioned and consider their choice of the modern vase to be an expression of their sophisticated taste. The balance between the relative influence of aesthetic response and aesthetic judgement will vary between individuals, objects and instances. The key idea to take away from this discussion is that, independent of the sensuous qualities of form, line, colour and texture, objects carry associations or meanings that are non-sensory and symbolic and which influence our aesthetic judgements.

The associative meanings of landscapes

For this reason, we will have associations with landscapes that are separate from our aesthetic responses and which are influenced by our knowledge and our familiarity with the landscape. The aesthetic formalist will take pleasure in the artistic composition of the landscape, admiring a pleasantly framed landscape with clearly differentiated foreground, middle ground and background. Another person will seek to understand how processes like glaciation, soil formation, plant colonisation and human disturbances have formed the landscape. These scientific understandings of landscape processes give it personal meaning and allow the individual to comprehend the landscape as a single entity (Rolston III, 1995).

The associations that we have with landscapes may also serve to connect us to former times or distant places. Landscapes present narratives about their origins, cultural modifications and the ongoing human activities on the landscape. Their surfaces have been repeatedly modified for human use without obliterating earlier alterations, so the natural and cultural history of the landscape may be read through its visual appearance. A view or image of a Tuscan landscape can call to mind images of the entire region: Hilltop villas set amongst slim Italian cypresses and surrounded by vineyards in which red poppies grow wild; country roads snaking past fields of golden grain rippling in the herb-scented breeze. This same image may

▲ Figure 4.22

This image of rural Tuscany embodies the sense of the region.
Source: Francesco Carrani | Flickr (used under the Creative Commons licence).

also transport us to an earlier time when agriculture, rather than industry and technology, was the basis of day-to-day existence. This landscape, like every other, carries poignant reminders of the culture that inhabits it. When designed landscapes reference such a place, they conjure up those associations for the users.

The associations of plants

Even individual plants can remind us of a particular region or place. A few rows of lavender can recall to us the scenes and feelings we experienced in a particular Mediterranean landscape. Many pines are drought hardy and spring from inhospitable soils. They are seldom used as street trees and are more suggestive of rural or wilderness settings than of urban centres. For these reasons, a single pine tree can invoke a particular place in our history, such as weekends at the cottage, or hiking in the wilderness.

Plant communities

As well as suggesting or symbolising a particular landscape, plants or groups of plants may bring to mind a particular plant community of which they are a part. In doing so, they suggest an aesthetic character or style for the landscape in which they grow.

Natural selection in plants has led them to develop a form that is optimal for their growing conditions. A *phenotype* is the observed properties of a species, including all aspects of its appearance. A *genotype* is the species' genetic coding, including all its environmental responses. Drought and shade tolerance result from the genotype, but they are visually expressed in the appearance of the plant—the phenotype. Often, this means a balance between water uptake and photosynthesis. In full sun, small leaves are most adapted since they reduce water loss (Parkhurst and Loucks, 1972). Many grey or silver foliage plants are drought tolerant. The fine hairs covering the plant leaves give it silver or grey foliage that reflects sunlight. In addition, the fine hairs on the leaf surface help to still air in the boundary layer. This adaptation reduces water loss and makes the plants more drought tolerant (Plant and Soil Sciences eLibrary, 2014).

Conversely, large-leaved plants such as *Hosta* lily or *Ligularia* will transpire more water and are adapted to moist, shady conditions, where abundant water is available and their large leaves maximise photosynthesis (Givnish and Vermeij, 1976). Even people who are not trained horticulturists will recognise that small succulent plants belong in arid, sunny conditions, that plants with grey foliage are adapted to full sun and that large-leaved plants are often more suited to shady than sunny conditions. Particular plants can suggest a particular region of the world, a certain biome in which they originate or a particular growing condition.

Plants, by their aesthetic associations, may also suggest a particular cultural landscape or style of landscape, and this too is an important part of answering the question: What is appropriate here? Is the style to be formal (and by that I mean geometric and obviously man-made) or is it to be naturalistic—that is, suggestive of a natural environment and minimising the hand of the designer? Boxwood has been used in formal gardens since Roman times and so has a strong association with formality and control of nature. A single boxwood in a pot is suggestive of formal gardens. In recent years, ornamental grasses have been introduced into ornamental horticulture. Their loose look is suggestive of the meadows and prairies in which they originated, so they are often used in more naturalistic and informal plantings. While many plants are strongly suggestive of their style or natural habitat, some plants are neutral and may lend themselves to a range of plant palettes and styles. Broad-leaved evergreen shrubs, like *Abelia grandiflora*, *Viburum tinus* and *Hebes* in particular, may be used in formal or more wild plantings, depending on how they are arranged and what other plants are used. Recognising all the meanings that are associated with plants, the designer should choose plants that carry the same or compatible associations, that suggest the same region, biome or cultural landscape and that belong in the same growing conditions.

Increasingly for pragmatic reasons and also, I think, because we seek authentic experience, designers are responding with landscape designs that are intended to invoke the larger regional landscape, whether in its natural state or the larger culturally modified landscape. Such designs place people experientially in their home place and express the judgement that celebrating the regional landscape is the appropriate response. The resulting designed landscape tells the user where they are located and carries the meaning that it is right and good to be in that place. Designing such a landscape might mean using only native plants, or it might mean mixing native plants with regionally appropriate drought-tolerant perennials to create a sense of the regional but with a longer season of bloom.

When we put together a plant list for a particular project, we are creating a human-made or cultural plant association. This plant association, like plant associations found in nature, should be a community of plants that are adapted to the same growing conditions. If this is done, the plants will not only grow well and visually belong together, they will carry the same associative meanings. In the cultural plant association, just as in nature, there will be microclimatic changes in available soil moisture and sun and wind exposure so that different plants will occupy different niches. The good planting designer will begin by understanding the tolerance of individual plants and, over time through research and observation, become aware of the range of growing conditions that a wide range of plants will tolerate.

The building, the hard landscape and the planting design must all tell the same story. Having been derived from the same values and goals, they present a physical reality that expresses a unified aesthetic and functional vision for the site. This includes the associative meanings of the landscape and the architecture. Each part is harmonious with the other and each supports the other. More than that, as in a chemical reaction, each part is changed in the way it is perceived by the other. In great design, the whole becomes something greater than the sum of its parts. This can only be achieved where there is detailed communication and shared values and vision among all those involved.

In designed landscapes, the goal of the planting designer is to create new or novel plant associations of plants that:

- Combine aesthetically
- Create a sense of unity
- Surprise and delight, adding visual richness to engage our attention and promote exploration
- Help us to connect to place
- Carry the same associative meanings and complement the meanings of the hard landscape
- Are adapted to all of the growing conditions of the site
- Support the goals and ecosystem services of the entire program

Chapter 4 principles

- Planting design is not solely an aesthetic amenity; it is also essential in integrating function and aesthetics and implementing the entire design program.

- Plants, in combination with soil, water and topography, can help to deliver a wide range of ecosystem services and benefits.
- Where goals of the program include the provision of ecosystem services, the planting designer must consider how their work can contribute to providing each of the intended ecosystem services in the program.
- The use of bioswales, rain gardens and native, drought-tolerant and regionally appropriate plants can support reduced water usage and yet be integrated into unified aesthetic landscape designs.
- Invasive plant species are to be avoided and new development should be used as a tool to remove existing invasive species.
- Planting design is a component of ecological restoration, and such plantings should be developed by modelling the ecosystem to be restored.
- Structural diversity increases biodiversity at the scale measured, and at the site level, a diversity of habitat types within a site will increase its biodiversity.
- Aesthetic response to landscape is immediate, spontaneous and affective; it is followed by aesthetic judgement, which is influenced by culture and experience.
- In developing a planting design, the designer needs to consider the aesthetic qualities of all the elements of the landscapes together with their associative meanings so that the entire design will be unified and congruent.

Glossary

Acequia: An irrigation ditch that channels the flow of an existing stream. Acequias were introduced to Spain by the Moors in the eighth century and Spanish colonists brought them to the semi-arid areas of Texas, where agriculture depended on their use (Handbook of Texas Online, 2010).

Aquifer: An underground layer of porous rock, like limestone and sandstone, or permeable materials, like unconsolidated sands and gravels, that store water in their voids. In many places they are the sources of potable water and their continued use will require that the water removed from the aquifer be replaced by new inflows.

Arroyo: A small intermittent stream that is only full following high rainfall events.

Biodiversity: A contraction of the term *biological diversity*. It means the variability among living organisms from all sources including, inter alia, terrestrial, marine and other aquatic ecosystems and the ecological complexes of which they are part; this includes diversity within species, between species and of ecosystems (Convention on Biological Diversity, 2004). The simplest and most intuitive measure of biodiversity is the number of species in a given area. Thus, we may consider biodiversity at different scales, as in global biodiversity or site-level biodiversity.

Biodiversity is not an ecosystem service, but it forms the foundation of the ecosystem services that support human life and wellbeing (Millennium Ecosystem Assessment, 2005).

Biological Oxygen Demand (BOD): A measure of oxygen use by microorganisms to decompose organic waste in water. The presence of large amounts of organic matter, nitrates and phosphates and increased water temperature will increase BOD, reducing the amount of oxygen available for use by fish.

Biomass: The total weight of living organic matter per unit area of landscape (usually measured in $kg/m^2/year$); also the total weight of organic matter in an ecosystem or plant community.

Bioproductivity: A measure of the biomass produced. It is an ecosystem service.

Bioswales: Man-made surface stormwater conveyance channels that treat stormwater runoff.

Design process: The process by which designers evaluate the current condition of a site against their intended purposes and then develop a plan to change that site so that it better accommodates human needs (Lyle, 1985).

Design program: A description of the intended uses of the site, its component parts and their interrelations. It is developed after reviewing all available user and site information (LaGro, 2011).

Ecological infrastructure: Any network of natural lands and working landscapes that are planned and managed to conserve ecosystem functions and provide ecosystem services (Benedict and McMahon, 2006; Eisenman, 2013).

Ecological restoration: The process of assisting the recovery of an ecosystem that has been damaged or degraded (SER, 2004).

Ecosystem services: "The conditions and processes through which natural ecosystems, and the species that make them up, sustain and fulfil human life. They maintain biodiversity and the production of ecosystem goods … (and) are the actual life-support functions such as cleansing, recycling, and renewal, and they confer many intangible aesthetic and cultural benefits as well" (Daily, 1997, p. 3).

Environmental gradients: Gradual changes in abiotic—that is, physical, not biological—factors in the landscape through space or over time. Factors like altitude, temperature, soil depth, ocean proximity and interflow produce the changes in environmental gradients, such as soil moisture regime, microclimate and soil nitrogen levels.

Formation: See *Biome*.

Green infrastructure: See *Ecological infrastructure*.

Green roof or **living roof**: A vegetated roof on top of a man-made roofing structure.

Groundwater: Water that flows beneath the soil profile into underground voids. It is stored in, and moves slowly through, aquifers.

Habitat: The plant association or ecosystem that has the combination of resources (food, cover and water) and environmental conditions (temperature, precipitation, density of competitors and predators) that promote occupancy by individuals of a given species and allows those individuals to survive and reproduce (Morrison et al., 2012).

Invasive plants: Non-native species "whose introduction and/or spread threaten biological diversity or have other unforeseen impacts" (Secretariat Great Britain, 2008).

Regionally appropriate plants: These include both native and non-native plants that are adapted to the growing conditions of a particular region.

Restorationist: A person who conducts ecological restoration.

Runoff: See *Stormwater runoff*.

Species/habitat models: Statements of our understanding of the environmental factors that influence the distribution and abundance of a particular species (Morrison et al., 2012).

Stormwater: Water resulting from precipitation.

Stormwater runoff: Water from precipitation that did not infiltrate into the ground and which instead flows across the landscape. In urban locations it will carry pollutants if left untreated.

Urban heat island: A term used to describe urban areas that are warmer than surrounding rural areas. Changing land surfaces from vegetated, moist and permeable to impermeable, dry and unvegetated increases the heat island effect.

Watershed: An area of land that drains to a single outlet or drainage network.

Notes

1 In working with the UTEP stakeholders, Christine Ten Eyck learned that many students come from low-income families and are the first in their families to attend university. Many had never had access to grass playfields. The client was determined to create a green heart at the campus centre where students could gather, play and celebrate university events. The lawns in the CTP are planted

with 'Tifgreen', a drought-tolerant strain of Bermuda grass (*Cynodon dactylon*). The entire landscape minimises water use and, when complete, will be irrigated with reclaimed blackwater.
2. In 1917, the first UTEP campus building, Old Main, was built in the style of the Himalayan country of Bhutan. Since then, almost all other campus buildings have followed suit. Today the university has cultural ties to Bhutan and an increasing number of its students are from Bhutan (The University of El Paso, Texas, a, n.d.). The consistent Bhutanese style of the architecture provides a clear and unified edge to the central open space of the CTP.
3. The Sustainable SITES Initiative was jointly developed by the American Society of Landscape Architects, the Lady Bird Johnson Wildflower Center and the United States Botanic Garden. It is a voluntary rating system that uses ecosystem-service–based guidelines to assess sustainable landscapes.

References

Alberti, M. (2005). The effects of urban patterns on ecosystem function. *International Regional Science Review*, 28(2), 168–192.

Appleton, J. (1996). *The experience of landscape*. New York: Wiley.

Arnell, Nigel W., & Delaney, E. Kate. (2006). Adapting to climate change: Public water supply in England and Wales. *Climatic Change*, 78(2–4), 227–255.

ASLA News. *Interview with Kongjian Yu, designer of the Red Ribbon, Tang He River Park*. Accessed March 18, 2017 at www.asla.org/contentdetail.aspx?id=20124.

Balvanera, P., Pfisterer, A.B., Buchmann, N., He, J.S., Nakashizuka, T., Raffaelli, D., & Schmid, B. (2006). Quantifying the evidence for biodiversity effects on ecosystem functioning and services. *Ecology Letters*, 9(10), 1146–1156.

Beals, P. and Yuan, Z. (2015). *Liupanshui Minghu Wetland Park, Liupanshui, Guizhou Province, China, by Turenscape, 2012*. Landscape Performance website. Accessed March 18, 2017 at https://landscapeperformance.org/sites/default/files/Vogler-2015-Student-Example-Case-Study.pdf.

Beddington, J. (2009). *Food, energy, water and the climate: A perfect storm of global events?* Lecture to Sustainable Development UK 09 Conference (Vol. 19). Accessed July 25, 2019 at http://citeseerx.ist.psu.edu/viewdoc/download?doi=10.1.1.522.3978&rep=rep1&type=pdf.

Bell, S. (2012). *Landscape: Pattern, perception and process*. New York: Routledge.

Benedict, M.A., & McMahon, E.T. (2006). *Green infrastructure*. Washington, DC: Island Press.

Beninde, J., Veith, M., & Hochkirch, A. (2015). Biodiversity in cities needs space: A meta-analysis of factors determining intra-urban biodiversity variation. *Ecology*, 18(6), 581–592.

Blackmore, L.M., & Goulson, D. (2014). Evaluating the effectiveness of wildflower seed mixes for boosting floral diversity and bumblebee and hoverfly abundance in urban areas. *Insect Conservation and Diversity*, 7(5), 480–484.

Boecklen, W.J. (1986). Effects of habitat heterogeneity on the species-area relationships of forest birds. *Journal of Biogeography*, 59–68.

Bolund, P., & Hunhammar, S. (1999). Ecosystem services in urban areas. *Ecological Economics*, 29(2), 293–301.

Bourassa, S.C. (1988). Toward a theory of landscape aesthetics. *Landscape and Urban Planning*, 15(3), 241–252.

Bühning-Gaese, K. (1997). Determinants of avian species richness at different spatial scales. *Journal of Biogeography*, 24(1), 49–60.

Butler, R.W., & Campbell, R.W. (1987). *The birds of the Fraser River delta: Populations, ecology and international significance*. Delta, BC, Canada: Environment Canada, Canadian Wildlife Service.

CABE Space (2006). *Making contracts work for wildlife: How to encourage biodiversity in urban parks*. London: Commission for Architecture and the Built Environment.

Campbell, S., Granger, L., & Nyhof, M. (1995). *Naturescape British Columbia: Native plant and animal booklet*. Stewardship series. Victoria, BC, Canada: British Columbia Ministry of Environment, Lands and Parks, Naturescape British Columbia.

Cane, J.H. (2005). Bees, pollination, and the challenges of sprawl. In E.A. Johnson & M.W. Klemens (Eds.), *Nature in fragments: The legacy of sprawl* (pp. 109–124). New York: Columbia University Press.

CBC News. (2014). *Metro Vancouver watering restrictions now in effect*. Accessed October 11, 2014 at www.cbc.ca/news/canada/british-columbia/metro-vancouver-watering-restrictions-now-in-effect-1.2660889.

Chaudhry, P., & Tewari, V.P. (2010). Role of public parks/gardens in attracting domestic tourists: An example from City Beautiful from India. *Tourismos*, 5,101–109.

Convention on Biological Diversity. (2004). *Ecosystem approach*. Accessed January 19, 2019 at www.cbd.int/ecosystem/description.shtml.

Cook, E. (2000). *Ecological networks in urban landscapes* (pp. 202–203). Wageningen: Wageningen University.

Costanza, R., Fisher, B., Mulder, K., Liu, S., & Christopher, T. (2007). Biodiversity and ecosystem services: A multi-scale empirical study of the relationship between species richness and net primary production. *Ecological Economics*, 61(2), 478–491.

Dai, A. (2011). Drought under global warming: A review. *Wiley Interdisciplinary Reviews: Climate Change*, 2, (1), 45–65.

Daily, G. (Ed.). (1997). *Nature's services: Societal dependence on natural ecosystems*. Washington, DC: Island Press.

Davies, Z.G., Edmondson, J.L., Heinemeyer, A., Leake, J.R., & Gaston, K.J. (2011). Mapping an urban ecosystem service: Quantifying above-ground carbon storage at a city-wide scale. *Journal of Applied Ecology*, 48(5), 1125–1134.

De Groot, R.S., Alkemade, R., Braat, L., Hein, L., & Willemen, L. (2010). Challenges in integrating the concept of ecosystem services and values in landscape planning, management and decision making. *Ecological Complexity*, 7(3), 260–272.

Design Workshop Inc. (n.d.). Accessed March 17, 2018 at www.designworkshop.com.

Dicks, L.V., Baude, M., Roberts, S.P., Phillips, J., Green, M., & Carvell, C. (2015). How much flower-rich habitat is enough for wild pollinators? Answering a key policy question with incomplete knowledge. *Ecological Entomology*, 40, 22–35.

Dunnett, N., & Kingsbury, N. (2004). *Planting green roofs and living walls*. Portland, OR: Timber Press.

Eisenman, T.S. (2013). Frederick Law Olmsted, green infrastructure, and the evolving city. *Journal of Planning History*, 12(4), 287–311.

Fernandez-Cañero, R., Emilsson, T., Fernandez-Barba, C., & Machuca, M.Á.H. (2013). Green roof systems: A study of public attitudes and preferences in southern Spain. *Journal of Environmental Management*, 128, 106–115.

Fortel, L., Henry, M., Guilbaud, L., Mouret, H., & Vaissière, B.E. (2016). Use of human-made nesting structures by wild bees in an urban environment. *Journal of Insect Conservation*, 20(2), 239–253.

Garbuzov, M., Fensome, K.A., & Ratnieks, F.L. (2015). Public approval plus more wildlife: Twin benefits of reduced mowing of amenity grass in a suburban public park in Saltdean, UK. *Insect Conservation and Diversity*, 8(2), 107–119.

Gifford, R. (2007). *Environmental psychology: Principles and practice*. Colville, WA: Optimal Books.

Gimblett, H.R., Itami, R.M., & Fitzgibbon, J.E. (1985). Mystery in an information processing model of landscape preference. *Landscape Journal*, 4(2), 87–95.

Givnish, T.J., & Vermeij, G.J. (1976). Sizes and shapes of liane leaves. *American Naturalist*, 743–778.

Glaum, P., Simao, M.C., Vaidya, C., Fitch, G., & Iulinao, B. (2017). Big city Bombus: Using natural history and land-use history to find significant environmental drivers in bumble-bee declines in urban development. *Royal Society Open Science*, 4(5), 170156.

Gorelick, S.M., & Zheng, C. (2015). Global change and the groundwater management challenge. *Water Resources Research*, 51(5), 3031–3051.

The Guardian. (2014). *Smarter urban water: How Spain's Zaragoza learned to use less*. Accessed October 11, 2014 at www.theguardian.com/lifeandstyle/2014/jul/30/zaragoza-smarter-urban-water-zaragoza-spain-learned-to-use-less.

Gunnarsson, B., & Federsel, L.M. (2014). Bumblebees in the city: Abundance, species richness and diversity in two urban habitats. *Journal of Insect Conservation*, 18(6), 1185–1191.

Gurevitch, J., & Padilla, D.K. (2004). Are invasive species a major cause of extinctions? *Trends in Ecology & Evolution*, 19(9), 470–474.

Haines-Young, R., & Potschin, M. (2010). The links between biodiversity, ecosystem services and human well-being. *Ecosystem Ecology: A New Synthesis*, 110–139.

Han, K.T. (2010). An exploration of relationships among the responses to natural scenes: Scenic beauty, preference, and restoration. *Environment and Behavior*, 42(2), 243–270.

Handbook of Texas Online. (2010). *Christopher Long, "ACEQUIAS"*. Accessed September 20, 2018 at www.tshaonline.org/handbook/online/articles/ruasg.

Hanson, G.C., Groffman, P.M., & Gold, A.J. (1994). Denitrification in riparian wetlands receiving high and low groundwater nitrate inputs. *Journal of Environmental Quality*, 23(5), 917–922.

Hartig, T. (1993). Nature experience in transactional perspective. *Landscape and Urban Planning*, 25(1), 17–36.

Heerwagen, J.H., & Orians, G.H. (1993). Humans, habitats, and aesthetics. In S.R. Kellert & E.O. Wilson (Eds.), *The biophilia hypothesis* (pp. 138–172). Washington, DC: Island Press.

Hinmann, C. (2013). *Rain garden handbook for western Washington: A guide for design, maintenance, and installation*. Bremerton, WA: Washington State University Extension. Accessed July 29, 2019 at https://fortress.wa.gov/ecy/publications/documents/1310027.pdf.

Hitchmough, J. (2004). Naturalistic herbaceous vegetation for urban landscapes. In N. Dunnet & J. Hitchmough (Eds.), *The dynamic landscape: Design, ecology and management of naturalistic urban planting* (pp. 172–245). London: Spon Press.

Hunter, M.R., & Hunter, M.D. (2008). Designing for conservation of insects in the built environment. *Insect Conservation and Diversity*, 1(4), 189–196.

James, F.C. (1971). Ordinations of habitat relationships among breeding birds. *The Wilson Bulletin*, 215–236.

James, F.C., & Wamer, N.O. (1982). Relationships between temperate forest bird communities and vegetation structure. *Ecology*, 159–171.

Kaltenborn, B.P., & Bjerke, T. (2002). Associations between environmental value orientations and landscape preferences. *Landscape and Urban Planning*, 59(1), 1–11.

Kaplan, R., Kaplan, S., and Ryan, R. (1998). *With people in mind: Design and management of everyday nature*. Washington, DC: Island Press.

Kaplan, S. (1987). Aesthetics, affect, and cognition environmental preference from an evolutionary perspective. *Environment and Behavior*, 19(1), 3–32.

Kaplan, S. (1995). The restorative benefits of nature: Toward an integrative framework. *Journal of Environmental Psychology*, 15(3), 169–182.

Karl, T.R., Melillo, J.M., and Peterson, T.C. (2009) *Global climate change impacts in the United States*. New York: Cambridge University Press.

Kaufmann, M., Huisjen, D., Kitchen, S., Babler, M. Abella, S., Gardiner, T., Darren McAvoy, D., Howie, J., & Page Jr., D. (2016). *Gambel Oak Ecology and Management in the Southern Rockies: The Status of our Knowledge*. Southern Rockies Fire Science Network (SRFSN Publication 2016-1). Fort Collins, CO: Colorado State University. Accessed April 28, 2018 at www.fs.fed.us/rm/pubs_journals/2016/rmrs_2016_kaufmann_m001.pdf.

Kearns, C.A., Inouye, D.W., & Waser, N.M. (1998). Endangered mutualisms: The conservation of plant-pollinator interactions. *Annual Review of Ecology and Systematics*, 29(1), 83–112.

Klein, A.M., Vaissiere, B.E., Cane, J.H., Steffan-Dewenter, I., Cunningham, S.A., Kremen, C., & Tscharntke, T. (2006). Importance of pollinators in changing landscapes for world crops. *Proceedings of the Royal Society B: Biological Sciences*, 274(1608), 303–313.

Kremen, C. (2005). Managing ecosystem services: What do we need to know about their ecology? *Ecology Letters*, 8(5), 468–479.

Krüger, O., & Lindström, J. (2001). Habitat heterogeneity affects population growth in goshawk *Accipiter gentilis*. *Journal of Animal Ecology*, 70(2), 173–181.

Kuo., F.E.M. (2010). *Parks and other green environments: Essential components of a healthy human habitat*. National Recreation and Park Association. Accessed May 25, 2015 at www.nrpa.org/uploadedFiles/nrpa.org/Publications_and_Research/Research/Papers/MingKuo-Research-Paper.pdf.

LaGro, J.A. (2013). *Site analysis: Informing context-sensitive and sustainable site planning and design* (3rd ed.). Hoboken, NJ: Wiley.

Laumann, K., Gärling, T., & Stormark, K.M. (2001). Rating scale measures of restorative components of environments. *Journal of Environmental Psychology*, 21(1), 31–44.

Los Angeles Department of Public Works. (n.d.). *Cash for grass*. Accessed October 11, 2014 at http://dpw.lacounty.gov/wwd/web/Conservation/CashforGrass.aspx.

Lyle, John T. (1985). The alternating current of design process. *Landscape Journal*, 4 (1), 7–13.

MacIvor, J.S., & Packer, L. (2015). "Bee hotels" as tools for native pollinator conservation: A premature verdict? *PloS One*, 10(3), e0122126. doi:https://doi.org/10.1371/journal.pone.0122126.

Mader, E., Shepherd, M., Vaughan, M., Black, S.H., & LeBuhn, G. (2011). *Attracting native pollinators: Protecting North America's bees and butterflies* (p. 371). North Adams, MA: Storey.

Matteson, K.C., Ascher, J.S., & Langellotto, G.A. (2008). Bee richness and abundance in New York City urban gardens. *Annals of the Entomological Society of America*, 101(1), 140–150.

McKinney, M.L. (2002). Urbanization, biodiversity, and conservation. *Bioscience*, 52(10), 883–890.

Millennium Ecosystem Assessment. (2005). Summary for decision makers. In *Ecosystems and human well-being: Synthesis* (pp. 1–24). Washington, DC: Island Press. Accessed April 10, 2014 at https://groups.nceas.ucsb.edu/sustainability-science/2010%20weekly-sessions/session-5-2013-10.11.2010-the-environmental-services-that-flow-from-natural-capital/supplemental-readings-from-the-reader/MEA%20synthesis%202005.pdf/view [April 10, 2014].

Minghu Wetland Park. (n.d.). Accessed April 21, 2017 at www.mhsdgy.com/col/col28739/index.html.

Mooney, P. (2014). A systematic approach to incorporating multiple ecosystem services in landscape planning and design. *Landscape Journal*, 33(2), 141–171.

Morrison, M.L., Marcot, B., & Mannan, W. (2012). *Wildlife-habitat relationships: Concepts and applications*. Washington, DC: Island Press.

Musacchio, L.R. (2009). The scientific basis for the design of landscape sustainability: A conceptual framework for translational landscape research and practice of designed landscapes and the six Es of landscape sustainability. *Landscape Ecology*, 24(8), 993–1013.

Nassauer, J.I. (1995). Messy ecosystems, orderly frames. *Landscape Journal*, 14(2), 161–170.

Nowak, D.J., Crane, D.E., & Stevens, J.C. (2006). Air pollution removal by urban trees and shrubs in the United States. *Urban Forestry & Urban Greening*, 4(3), 115–123.

O'Farrell, P.J., & Anderson, P.M. (2010). Sustainable multifunctional landscapes: A review to implementation. *Current Opinion in Environmental Sustainability*, 2(1), 59–65.

Orians, G.H. (1985). *Blackbirds of the Americas*. Seattle, WA: University of Washington Press.

Paoletti, E., Bardelli, T., Giovannini, G., & Pecchioli, L. (2011). Air quality impact of an urban park over time. *Procedia Environmental Sciences*, 4, 10–16.

Parkhurst, D.F., & Loucks, O.L. (1972). Optimal leaf size in relation to environment. *Journal of Ecology*, 505–537.

Pejchar, L., & Mooney, H.A. (2009). Invasive species, ecosystem services and human well-being. *Trends in Ecology & Evolution*, 24(9), 497–504.

Peters, K. (2010). Being together in urban parks: Connecting public space, leisure, and diversity. *Leisure Sciences*, 32(5), 418–433.

Pimentel, D., Zuniga, R., & Morrison, D. (2005). Update on the environmental and economic costs associated with alien-invasive species in the United States. *Ecological Economics*, 52(3), 273–288.

Plant and Soil Sciences eLibrary. (2014). Accessed July 21, 2014 at http://passel.unl.edu/pages/informationmodule.php?idinformationmodule=1092853841&topicorder=6.

Potts, S.G., Biesmeijer, J.C., Kremen, C., Neumann, P., Schweiger, O., & Kunin, W.E. (2010). Global pollinator declines: Trends, impacts and drivers. *Trends in Ecology & Evolution*, 25(6), 345–353.

Potts, S.G., Vulliamy, B., Dafni, A., Ne'eman, G., & Willmer, P. (2003). Linking bees and flowers: How do floral communities structure pollinator communities? *Ecology*, 84(10), 2628–2642.

Ricketts, T., & Imhoff, M. (2003). Biodiversity, urban areas, and agriculture: Locating priority ecoregions for conservation. *Ecology and Society*, 8(2), 1.

Roehr, D., & Fassman-Beck, E. (2015). *Living roofs in integrated urban water systems.* London: Routledge.

Rolston III, H. (1995). Does aesthetic appreciation of landscapes need to be science-based? *British Journal of Aesthetics*, 35(4), 374–386.

Salisbury, A., Armitage, J., Bostock, H., Perry, J., Tatchell, M., & Thompson, K. (2015). Enhancing gardens as habitats for flower-visiting aerial insects (pollinators): Should we plant native or exotic species? *Journal of Applied Ecology*, 52(5), 1156–1164.

Saunders, William S. (2012) The boy who read books riding a water buffalo. In W.S. Saunders (Ed.), *Designed ecologies: The landscape architecture of Kongjian Yu*, (pp. 60–65). Berlin: Birkhäuser Verlag.

Secretariat, Great Britain Non-Native Species. (2008). *The invasive non-native species framework strategy for Great Britain.* London: Defra.

Seeland, K., Dübendorfer, S., & Hansmann, R. (2009). Making friends in Zurich's urban forests and parks: The role of public green space for social inclusion of youths from different cultures. *Forest Policy and Economics*, 11(1), 10–17.

Selman, P. (2012). *Sustainable landscape planning: The reconnection agenda.* London: Routledge.

Society for Ecological Restoration (SER) International Science and Working Group. (2004). *The SER International Primer on Ecological Restoration* (version 2). Tucson, AZ: Society for Ecological Restoration International. Accessed August 10, 2019 at www.ctahr.hawaii.edu/littonc/PDFs/682_SERPrimer.pdf.

Shuya, Li. (n.d.). *Yu Kongjian: Back to earth.* China Pictorial. Accessed March 18, 2017 at www.chinapictorial.com.cn/en/features/txt/2013-07-02/content_553031_4.htm.

Simberloff, D. (2003). How much information on population biology is needed to manage introduced species? *Conservation Biology*, 17(1), 83–92.

Snodgrass, E.C., & Snodgrass, L.L. (2006). *Green roof plants: A resource and planting guide.* Portland, OR: Timber Press.

Tallis, M., Taylor, G., Sinnett, D., & Freer-Smith, P. (2011). Estimating the removal of atmospheric particulate pollution by the urban tree canopy of London, under current and future environments. *Landscape and Urban Planning*, 103(2), 129–138.

Termorshuizen, J.W., & Opdam, P. (2009). Landscape services as a bridge between landscape ecology and sustainable development. *Landscape Ecology*, 24(8), 1037–1052.

Tews, J., Brose, U., Grimm, V., Tielbörger, K., Wichmann, M.C., Schwager, M., & Jeltsch, F. (2004). Animal species diversity driven by habitat heterogeneity/diversity: The importance of keystone structures. *Journal of Biogeography*, 31(1), 79–92.

Tonietto, R., Fant, J., Ascher, J., Ellis, K., & Larkin, D. (2011). A comparison of bee communities of Chicago green roofs, parks and prairies. *Landscape and Urban Planning*, 103(1), 102–108.

Torrance, S., Bass, B., MacIvor, S., McGlade, T. (2013). City of Toronto guidelines for biodiverse green roofs. Accessed May 21, 2015 at www1.toronto.ca/City%20Of%20Toronto/City%20Planning/Zoning%20&%20Environment/Files/pdf/B/biodiversegreenroofs_2013.pdf.

Ulrich, R.S. (1983). Aesthetic and affective response to natural environment. In I. Altman and J.F. Wohlwill (Eds.), *Behavior and the natural environment* (pp. 85–125). New York: Springer, Plenum Press.

Ulrich, R.S. (1993). Biophilia, biophobia, and natural landscapes. In S.R. Kellert & E.O. Wilson (Eds.), *The biophilia hypothesis* (pp. 73–137). Washington, DC: Island Press.

UK Biodiversity Action Plan (UK BAP). (n.d.). Accessed May 20, 2015 at http://jncc.defra.gov.uk/ukbap.

UK Greenroofs Guide. (n.d.). Accessed May 21, 2015 at www.greenroofguide.co.uk/pdfs/.

United Nations, Department of Economic and Social Affairs, Population Division. (2013). *World Population Prospects: The 2012 Revision, Key Findings and Advance Tables. Working Paper No. ESA/P/WP.227*. Accessed October 20, 2014 at http://esa.un.org/wpp/documentation/pdf/WPP2012_%20KEY%20FINDINGS.pdf.

United Nations, Department of Economic and Social Affairs, Population Division. (2014). *World Urbanization Prospects: The 2014 Revision, Highlights (ST/ESA/SER.A/352)*. Accessed March 29, 2015 at http://esa.un.org/unpd/wup/Highlights/WUP2014-Highlights.pdf.

The University of El Paso, Texas, a. (n.d.). *Bhutan on the border*. Accessed July 8, 2018 at https://admin.utep.edu/Default.aspx?tabid=53233.

The University of El Paso, Texas, b. (n.d.). *UTEP goes green*. Accessed June 5, 2018 at http://gogreen.utep.edu/sustainability.html.

US Environmental Protection Agency. (n.d.). *Water-smart landscapes start with WaterSense*. Accessed October 11, 2014 at www.epa.gov/WaterSense/docs/water-efficient_landscaping_508.pdf.

US National Park Service. (n.d.). *Carlsbad Caverns National Park, New Mexico*. Accessed April 8, 2018 at www.nps.gov/cave/learn/nature/deserts.html.

Victoria State Government. (n.d.). *Living Victoria Water Rebate Program: 1 July 2012 to 30 June 2015*. Accessed October 11, 2014 at www.yvw.com.au/yvw/groups/public/documents/document/yvw1003413.pdf.

Weber, D., & Anderson, D. (2010). Contact with nature: Recreation experience preferences in Australian parks. *Annals of Leisure Research*, 13(1–2), 46–69.

Wenger, S.J., Peterson, J.T., Freeman, M.C., Freeman, B.J., & Homans, D.D. (2008). Stream fish occurrence in response to impervious cover, historic land use, and hydrogeomorphic factors. *Canadian Journal of Fisheries and Aquatic Sciences*, 65(7), 1250–1264.

Williams, F., Eschen, R., Harris, A., Djeddour, D., Pratt, C., Shaw, R.S., Varia, S., Lamontagne-Godwin, J., Thomas, S.E., and Murphy, S.T. (2010). *The economic cost of invasive non-native species on Great Britain*. Wallingford: CABI.

Winfree, R., Aguilar, R., Vázquez, D.P., LeBuhn, G., & Aizen, M.A. (2009). A meta-analysis of bees' responses to anthropogenic disturbance. *Ecology*, 90(8), 2068–2076.

Winfree, R., Bartomeus, I., & Cariveau, D.P. (2011). Native pollinators in anthropogenic habitats. *Annual Review of Ecology, Evolution, and Systematics*, 42, 1–22.

Wong, K.K., & Domroes, M. (2005). The visual quality of urban park scenes of Kowloon Park, Hong Kong: Likeability, affective appraisal, and cross-cultural perspectives. *Environment and Planning B: Planning and Design*, 32(4), 617–632.

Wray, J.C., & Elle, E. (2015). Flowering phenology and nesting resources influence pollinator community composition in a fragmented ecosystem. *Landscape Ecology*, 30(2), 261–272.

Yu, Kongjian. (2006). *The art of survival*. Keynote speech, American Society of Landscape Architects, Annual Meeting and 43rd IFLA World Congress. Accessed March 18, 2017 at www.asla.org/uploadedFiles/CMS/Business_Quarterly/tha%20Art%20of%20Survival.pdf.

Yu, Kongjian, Turenscape, & Peking University College of Architecture and Landscape. (2014). *Slow down: Liupanshui Minghu Wetland Park*. Unpublished document, courtesy of Turenscape Ltd.

Yuan, J., & Dunnett, N. (2018). Plant selection for rain gardens: Response to simulated cyclical flooding of 15 perennial species. *Urban Forestry & Urban Greening*, 35, 57–65.

Additional reading

Tree soil volumes

Lindsey, P., & Bassuk, N. (1992). Redesigning the urban forest from the ground below: A new approach to specifying adequate soil volumes for street trees. *Arboricultural Journal*, 16(1), 25–39.

Urban, J. (1992). Bringing order to the technical dysfunction within the urban forest. *Journal of Arboriculture*, 18(2), 85–90.

Green roofs

Dunnett, N., & Kingsbury, N. (2004). *Planting green roofs and living walls*. Portland, OR: Timber Press.

Getter, K. and Rowe, B. (2008) *Selecting plants for extensive green roofs in the United States* (Extension Bulletin E-3047). East Lansing, MI: Michigan State University.

Roehr, D., & Fassman-Beck, E. (2015). *Living roofs in integrated urban water systems*. London: Routledge.

Snodgrass, E.C., & Snodgrass, L.L. (2006). *Green roof plants: A resource and planting guide* (Vol. 487). Portland, OR: Timber Press.

UK Greenroofs Guide. (n.d.). www.greenroofguide.co.uk/pdfs/.

Chapter 5

Space and place

Organising exterior space is the fundamental activity of landscape architecture, and the use of plants to shape and reinforce space is a critical aspect of planting design. This chapter discusses:

- Shaping space for experience
- Volumetric and cubist space
- A spatial typology
- Using plants to create or reinforce space and place
- Plants as the architectural elements of exterior space
- Circulation, views and movement through space
- A process for conceiving and diagramming the designer's spatial intent
- Implementing this intent in planting design

The primacy of space

The primary activity of the landscape designer is the creation of spaces that respond to human needs and serve necessary functions. Laurie Olin (2013) reminds us that "Landscape architecture is about not bushes and trees but the shaping of space". Planting design, in its role of supporting the entire program, often makes essential contributions to the making of spaces that respond to human needs and fulfil an ecological function.

People experience the world as a sequence of connected spaces that impede or facilitate their purposes and impact their emotions, creating feelings of security, freedom and even joy and delight (Cullen, 1961). As we go about our daily activities, the space around us expands and contracts. This fluctuating sequence of spaces influences our involvement and pleasure in the world around us. The way that a space is enclosed, its size, scale, relation to its context, character and internal and external views are the significant elements of its design that influence our emotional response to that space and our behaviour in it.

Forming or shaping space can be a difficult concept to grasp. However, if the shaping of space is considered to be equivalent to creating outdoor rooms, it becomes apparent that enclosing outdoor areas is necessary to shape space. Enclosing a space gives it a recognisable location and volume and enables us to grasp it mentally.

Space

Positive space

A space makes itself felt from its boundaries, and space is defined by the type and degree of its enclosed edges (Norberg-Schulz, 1988). Strongly enclosed space is referred to as positive space—that is, space that is palpable, experienced and made memorable—while open, less-structured space is referred to as negative space. Positive space is more static and inward-focused than negative space. Positive spaces are places to linger, to meet other people, to socialise (Tuan, 1979).

Very little enclosure is required to create a sense of defined space in the landscape. Even where the physical enclosure seems ridiculously slight, the person in the landscape will feel psychologically enclosed. For example, the act of walking through a gate or under an overarching branch will be felt as a transition between one space and another (Figure 5.0). A campfire set on the open plain defines a small human-scale space around it. Laying a blanket on an open lawn defines the temporarily occupied space of a picnic site (Figure 5.1). In a space that is enclosed on three sides by buildings, something as minimal as a row of shrubs connecting the buildings on the

▶ Figure 5.0

Passing under an archway, lintel or even the branch of an overhanging tree can signal a transition from one space to another.
Source: Photo by Patrick Mooney.

CHAPTER 5 **Space and place**

◀ Figure 5.1

The picnic blanket is sufficient to define the occupied space.
Source: Image courtesy of Yiwen Ruan.

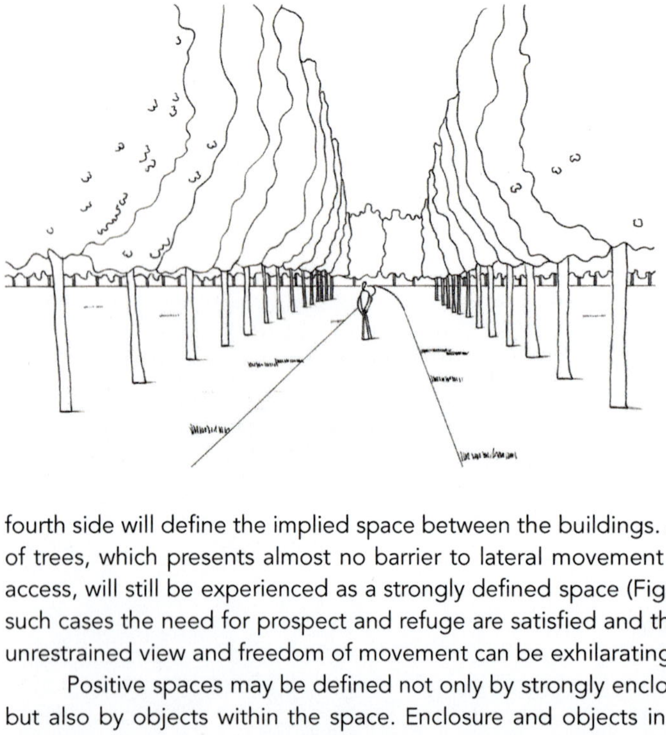

◀ Figure 5.2

The avenue of trees, while it does not impede view or movement, creates a positive space that is separate from its surroundings.
Source: Image courtesy of Yiwen Ruan.

fourth side will define the implied space between the buildings. An avenue of trees, which presents almost no barrier to lateral movement and visual access, will still be experienced as a strongly defined space (Figure 5.2). In such cases the need for prospect and refuge are satisfied and the sense of unrestrained view and freedom of movement can be exhilarating.

Positive spaces may be defined not only by strongly enclosed edges but also by objects within the space. Enclosure and objects in space are used in landscape design to define positive space so that it can be mentally grasped and is easy to visualise and remember. Consider the equestrian statue in the centre of a park or urban plaza. It dominates and makes positive the space around it (Figure 5.3).

For the most part, people seek and enjoy positive space. Perhaps this is so because it is experienced as refuge—a place to pause and rest—or because these designed spaces are programmed for social interaction and

▲ Figure 5.3

Michelangelo's Campidoglio is a strongly defined positive space in which the sense of enclosure will be most strongly felt within a 45-degree angle of influence of the surrounding walls or the central statue.
Source: Image courtesy of Yiwen Ruan.

other human uses. When the physical boundaries grow in height, length and density, views become restricted; the light entering the space will probably be reduced and the sense of enclosure increased. Such a strongly enclosed space can be experienced as a snug refuge or, if the sense of enclosure becomes too great, that small dark space can feel claustrophobic, especially if the ability to move from that space is not easily available.

Positive spaces that are linked and that have memorable views and landmarks facilitate the forming of cognitive maps (Tversky, 2000). They give surety about one's location in the world that is the antithesis of being lost and gives people the confidence to explore, but also to pause, to rest and to relax.

Defensible space

The theory of defensible space posits that defined spaces create territories and bring an area under the control of its residents, even where the boundaries of the space may not actually be barriers to trespass. The physical subdivisions of space, when clearly defined and related to entries, paths and amenities, encourage surveillance and deter crime. Therefore, positive spaces, when combined with the provision of shade, shelter, amenity and convenience, cause people to use and take possession of areas of the landscape (Cullen, 1961) and can also be defensible spaces that inhibit crime and make people feel safer (Hall, 1966).

◀ Figure 5.4

A row of street trees acts as a psychological barrier that separates the pedestrian from traffic and gives an increased sense of security.
Source: Image courtesy of Yiwen Ruan.

Protection from vehicular traffic

Research has demonstrated that pedestrian use and social interaction decline as traffic volumes increase (Appleyard, 1980; Gehl, 2011). For people to feel safe and for children to be allowed to move about freely, pedestrians must be separated from vehicular traffic or traffic speed must be greatly reduced (Gehl, 2011). Plants can play a role in physically and psychologically separating pedestrians from vehicular traffic and increasing the use and benefits of public space (Figure 5.4).

Negative space

The space between positive spaces and objects in the environment is referred to as negative space. Precisely because it is less enclosed and visibly structured, it is also less easily visualised, felt and remembered. This is not to say that that the experience of positive space is positive and the experience of negative space is negative. While negative space does not have a positive feeling of centre that suggests staying in place, its irregular form and multiple exterior views suggest outward movement toward the boundary of the space (Leonard, 1969).

Mixing positive and negative space

Positive spaces may be considered as places to pause and negative space as places to move through. By alternating enclosure and openness, places of repose are followed by places of exploration and movement, producing a sequence of moving and arriving, exploring and pausing. Landscape designers alternate degrees of enclosure to enhance the experience of landscape (Simonds, 1983), and either positive or negative space can be

▶ Figure 5.5
Positive and negative space exist along a continuum. The further apart the two spaces are on the continuum of positive and negative space, the more dramatic the experience of moving between the two spaces will be felt to be.
Source: Image courtesy of Yiwen Ruan.

appropriate, depending on the function of the space and the intended experience of the user.

Space is never static except in a closed room without windows. It always "leaks" from openings in the enclosure, flowing from one space to the next, enticing us to follow the flow, to move from space to space, to explore and become engaged. Rather than focusing on positive or negative space as distinct categories, it is useful when conceiving an intended sequence of experience in the landscape to think about positive and negative spaces as existing along a continuum, from completely enclosed positive space at one end to completely open negative space at the other end of the continuum (Figure 5.5).

Elements of change

> We seek in all cases a unified sequential experience of space modulation … People in motion take great pleasure in the sensation of change—change in texture, light, quality, temperature, scent, visual patterns, expanding or contrasting vistas, and the fluid visual impressions of objects spaces and views.
> (Simonds, 1983, p. 203)

Research has shown that hikers prefer, and will spend more time on, trails that have a greater variety of vegetation (Axelsson-Lindgren and Sorte, 1987; Polat and Akay, 2015). Conversely, a linear space with no rest stops or points of interest will be experienced as a long walk and will not entice users. However, if the street curves away out of view, if there are points of interest and rest stops, if change occurs along the route, it will be experienced as a shorter walk and people will be more inclined to use it (Simonds, 1983; Gehl, 2011). This supports the idea that variety of interest in exterior spaces stimulates people's interest and supports their involvement.

The greater or more surprising the change in the landscape, the more strongly it will be felt and remembered. For example, the effect of entering a larger space will be more acutely felt if the preceding space is small (Simonds, 1983). Conversely, the more alike the two spaces are, the more imperceptible and less remembered the experience of change will be. Yet most change in designed landscapes occurs as a smooth transition. This is so because modulated change is more likely to meet people's expectations.

Recall that mystery is the promise that more information, more stimulus, will be delivered as one moves into the landscape. Mystery is the strongest predictor of landscape preference, and landscapes that have a strong sense of mystery also have a continuity of character. The expectations of the observer are set by the present view. Moving forward, they expect that the landscape they find will be much like the one they are presently in. This expectation gives people the sense that their exposure to the unexpected is under their control (S. Kaplan, 1988). Maintaining continuity of spatial type and aesthetics supports expectations and fosters engagement, while incongruous change can cause people to disengage. Too much continuity can lead to boredom and withdrawal. Therefore, the sense of surprise, the spice of the unexpected, must be introduced within a unified composition in a way that supports the engagement of the user, such as by modulation of space.

When designing a set of linked spaces, the designer must resolve how each space will relate to the spaces to which it is connected, while simultaneously recognising that a person's experience will be affected by much more than spatial enclosure. In addition to space, landscape designers work with scale, view, forms, materials, colour, microclimate and light to balance continuity with surprise and stimulus in the landscape. (See, for example, the case study in Chapter 2—Samukawa Shrine.)

Cubist space

Patrick Condon (1988) has identified two types of space: Volumetric and cubist. Both positive and negative spaces belong to the category of volumetric space. They are spaces that are defined from their boundaries by the enclosing elements and have generally open interiors.

In the early twentieth century, the Cubist art movement used geometric forms and interlocking planes to depict multiple viewpoints simultaneously. In cubist space, Condon tells us, a set of sculptural objects set in space establish the spatial experience. In this type of space, the qualities of a strong sense of enclosure, of arrival and of knowing where one is located that typify volumetric space have been forgone in favour of creating a "quality of experience whereby the moving participant experiences an environmental field that dramatically changes with each step" (Condon, 1988, p. 3).

Cubist space is considered to be an evolution of volumetric space that is found in many modern landscape architectural designs (Booth, 2011). The significance for planting design is that using plants as the sculptural elements seen from multiple viewpoints can create the shifting views that characterise cubist space. Plants can also be used to form a series of

▶ Figure 5.6

Garret Eckbo's 1935 plan for a park in a migrant workers' community was designed for the US Farm Security Administration. Note the lack of continuous boundary walls. Plants are arranged as intersecting vertical or horizontal planes or single objects in space.
Source: Garret Eckbo Collection, Environmental Design Archives, University of California, Berkeley.

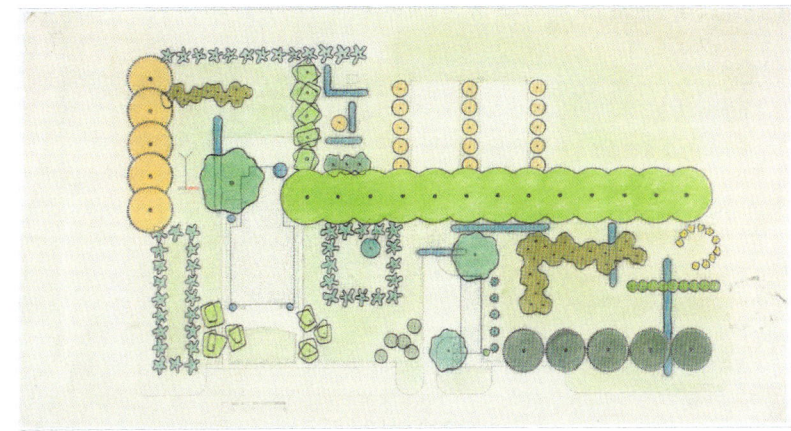

▶ Figure 5.7

In Garret Eckbo's ink perspective of the plan in Figure 5.6, the multiple viewpoints and intersecting planes of Cubist art are transformed into three-dimensional space. By using trees and shrubs of various types to frame overlapping planes, permeable, layered spaces are created within the site.
Source: Garret Eckbo Collection, Environmental Design Archives, University of California, Berkeley.

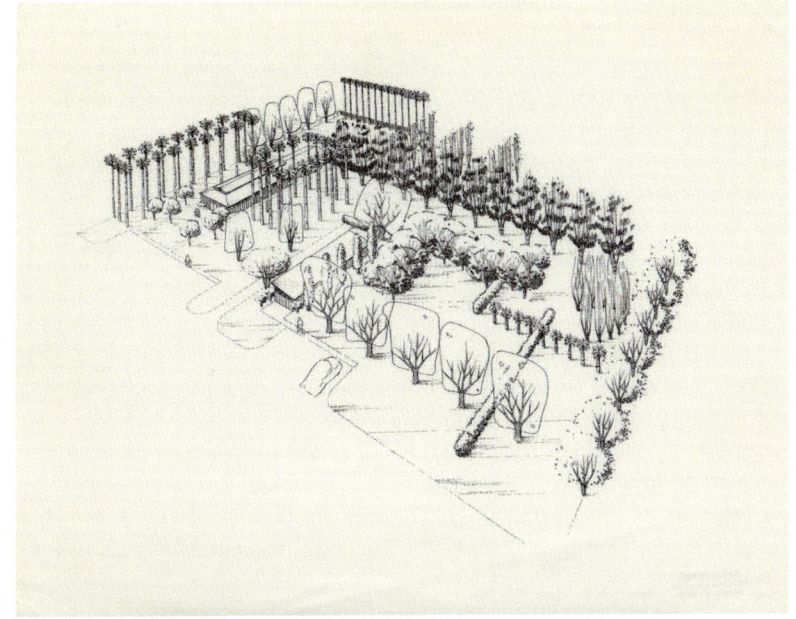

boundaries that make spaces seem more ambiguous and expansive. They may overlap spatial boundaries, making them indistinct, and be layered to create a sense of depth. This type of space encourages exploration and engagement because it cannot be seen from a single vantage point and so has an inherent sense of mystery. Early modernist landscape architect Garret Eckbo has given us perhaps the first recorded example of cubist space created with plants (Figures 5.6 and 5.7).

This type of permeable space is characteristic of the work of landscape architect Andrea Cochran.

CHAPTER 5 **Space and place**   163

Andrea Cochran

Andrea Cochran is the founder and principal of Andrea Cochran Landscape Architecture (ACLA) in San Francisco. Growing up in the northeastern United States, Andrea loved drawing, animals and making tree forts. She enrolled in Rutgers University, with the intention of becoming a veterinarian, only because her parents wouldn't allow her to attend art school (Harvard GSD, n.d.). Her discovery that landscape architecture combined her interests in the fine arts and the sciences led her to complete the Master of Landscape Architecture degree at The Harvard Graduate School of Design in 1979 (LA+D Profile, n.d.; Green, 2011).

After graduation, Andrea worked in public and private practice in the US and Europe before settling in San Francisco in 1981. As a partner in a design–build firm for almost ten years before starting ACLA in 1998, she spent a lot of time on site, mastering the technical skills of site grading and construction and observing how changing qualities of light effect landscape materials (Reid, 2016). This experience continues to shape her design process.

Her designs are carefully considered responses to site, client and context. She begins with a site visit, recording her impressions and applying her artistic sensibilities to discovering how the site might accommodate the client's desires. As the design begins to take shape, she revisits the site, sketching the spaces and recording her perceptions and feelings. Designs are developed using hand sketching, physical models and 3D computer modelling (LA+D Profile, n.d.).

Andrea is primarily concerned with creating a powerful experience of landscape by orchestrating people's movement through a sequence of connected spaces (Harvard GSD, n.d.). Her "sensory and intuitive" design process (Lee, 2015) seeks to realise a unified site in which art, landscape and architecture are seamlessly integrated (ACLA a, n.d.). Artists like Fred Sandback, Donald Judd and Robert Irwin, whose installations blur the line between sculpture and site, and modernist landscape architect Dan Kiley are listed as influences (Green, 2011), and she is a firm believer that the designer's ego must be subservient to serving the client, site and environment (Harvard GSD, n.d.).

ACLA has been widely recognised for the high quality of its work. Each year for the last two decades it has received multiple design awards from professional organisations like the American Society of Landscape Architects (ASLA), the American Institute of Architects, the Society of American Architects, the US Green Building Council, the Cooper Hewitt Smithsonian Design Museum, the Pacific Coast Builders Council, Engineering News-Record and others. In 2016, the firm received the World Landscape Architecture Award for its design for the Windhover Contemplative Center at Stanford University. The following year, ASLA awarded ACLA an Honor Award for the Windhover Center, a second Honor Award for the Telegraph Hill Residence in San Francisco and an Award of

Excellence for the Birmingham Residence in Birmingham, Michigan. The firm's work has been featured in many online and print publications, most notably in the book *Andrea Cochran: Landscapes* by Mary Myers (2009). Andrea Cochran is often asked to speak about her work and has lectured at Harvard and Berkeley Universities and the Isabella Stewart Gardner Museum in Boston.

ACLA employs a simple geometry and refined materials palette to generate a clear, visible order and direct movement through a series of spaces. Each element has a role within the hierarchy of the overall design, and nothing extraneous is included. The firm's landscapes are examples of what the Gestalt psychologists labelled "simple structures", and perceiving them gives us pleasure (see Chapter 6: Gestalt Theory). Because of their uncluttered order, people seem to notice more, see more clearly and become more engaged in these landscapes. Spatial forms, materials, colours and textures draw us through the landscape and lead the eye outward beyond the site. Often, the site is visually connected to its surroundings through the plant selections used in a series of layered spaces (Figure 5.12). Many of these hallmarks of ACLA's designs are evident in the design at Stone Edge Farm.

Case study: Stone Edge Farm, Sonoma, California

Landscape architects: Andrea Cochran Landscape Architecture (ACLA).
ACLA design team members: Andrea Cochran, Principal; Emily Rylander, Senior Associate.
Architects: STUDIOS Architecture.
Landscape contractor/stone mason: Pascual Castillo.
Landscape lighting design: Architecture and Light.

Stone Edge Farm comprises a commercial vineyard, an olive orchard and an organic garden that supplies local gourmet restaurants. In 2001, the owners purchased the adjacent 3.5-acre property to build a retreat from their working farm and residence. The land contained mature California bay trees, oaks and buckeyes and was bordered by a seasonal creek that flooded the property periodically. ACLA's design for the retreat property was installed in 2007 and received an Honor Award from the American Society of Landscape Architects in 2009.

The Retreat program called for a spa building with a media centre, and an observatory to house a 20-inch telescope and a library. The firm's design added a third major structure—a 100-foot-long pyramid constructed of stones unearthed on site. The pyramid balances the other two structures, screens the view of a neighbouring farm and terminates the view along an axis created by a raised lap pool. The three structures are rooted to a ground plane of gravel or meadow by the linear forms of the reflecting pool, lap pool and allées of ancient olive trees that were

PLANTINGS

A Chondropetalum elephantinum
B Cupressus sempervirens
C Euphorbia characias wulfenii
D Mown Grass Lawn
E Olea europaea
F Planting bed
   Acanthus mollis
   Gunnera manicata
   Helleborus argutifolius
G Prunus caroliniana "Compacta"
H Prunus serrulata 'Mount Fuji'
I Rhamnus alaternus
J Schinus molle
K Swale and dry stream bed
   Camassia cusickii
   Camassia leichtlinii 'Semiplena'
   Furcraea foetida
   Ipheion uniflorum 'White Star'
   Iris 'Eleanor Roosevelt'
   Muhlenbergia rigens
   Ornithogalum umbellatum
L Tall grass meadow
   Festuca mairei
   Muhlenbergia capillaris
   Pennisetum spathiolatum
M Mature Quercus and
   Umbellularia californica
N Schizachyrium scoparium

BUILT ELEMENTS

1 Entrance gate
2 Access drive
3 Exposed aggregate concrete stepping-stones
4 Limestone boulder
5 Cor-ten steel shower screen
6 Spa building
7 Ipe wood deck
8 Concrete terrace
9 Raised lap pool
10 Gravel
11 Reflecting pool
12 Observatory
13 Minnesota limestone freestanding wall
14 Boule court with crushed oyster shell
15 Native stone pyramid
16 Playfield
17 Creek

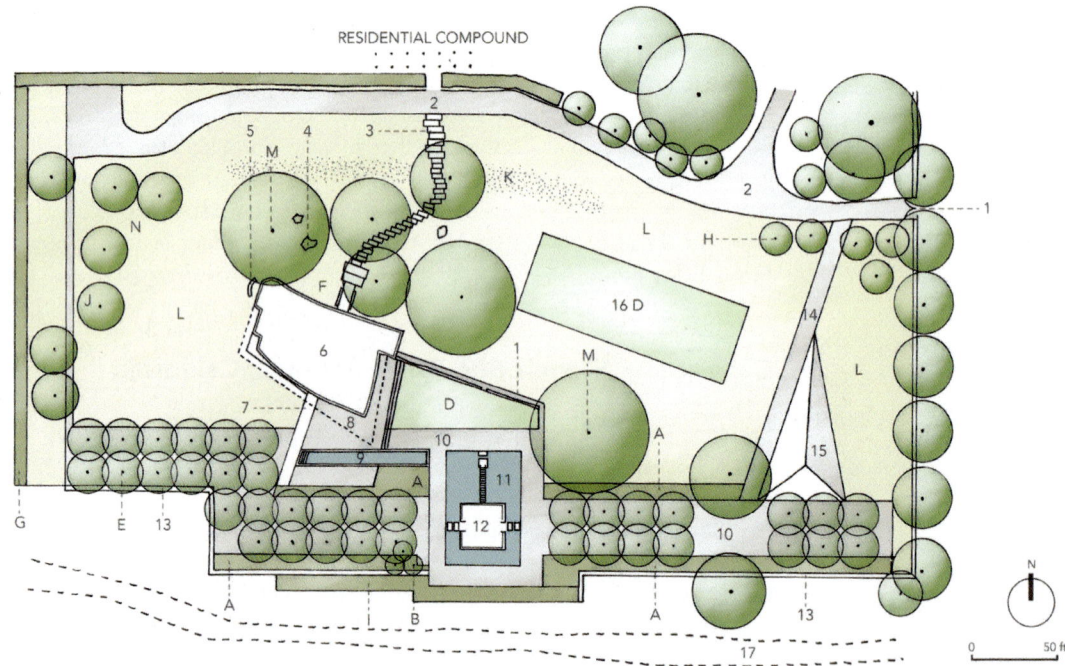

▲ Figure 5.8

The landscape plan of Stone Edge Farm Retreat. Much of the landscape consists of flat planes of gravel (10) and meadow (L). Allées of olive, paired with gravel, define spaces and reinforce circulation and sight lines. Existing mature oaks and California bay trees, set in the meadow, form the image of the quintessential California landscape. Major plantings are drought-tolerant, and more water-intensive plantings (F) and (D) are used sparingly.
Source: Image courtesy of Yiwen Ruan.

transplanted from an orchard in northern California (Myers, 2009). The meadow (Figure 5.9) and the gravel unify the ground plane and divide the site into two zones: The built, higher-use zone of olive allées on a gravel plane (Figure 5.10) and the more contemplative meadow zone of mature trees and ornamental grasses.

The meadow

The meadow dominates the aesthetic impression of Stone Edge Farm and provides the ecosystem service of flood control, as it is graded to absorb intermittent flows from the creek. It was prepared for replanting using the organic gardening practice of sheet mulching instead of applying toxic herbicides. Sheets of recycled cardboard were placed over the meadow

▲ Figure 5.9

The meadow occupies most of the area of the Stone Edge Farm Retreat. Its unified, soft texture and planar form dominate views and give the Retreat its tranquil feeling. The shadow of a mature oak, cast on the stone pyramid, records the movement of the sun throughout the day.
Source: Photo by Marion Brenner.

area until the existing unwanted plants had died. The meadow was then planted with four different grasses: Atlas fescue (*Festuca mairei*), slender veldt grass (*Pennisetum spathiolatum*), little bluestem (*Schizachyrium scoparium*) and pink muhly grass (*Muhlenbergia capillaris*). These drought-tolerant grasses were selected for their thin, narrow leaves and sequence of flowering. The similarity of leaf textures leaves the impression that a single species of grass was planted, unifying the meadow and increasing its contemplative mood. By flowering in sequence, the grasses extend the interest season of the meadow as no single grass could have done. A lawn placed in the meadow as a play area for the clients' son becomes a space within a space (Figure 5.9) (ACLA b, n.d.).

The grove

One approaches the spa building from the adjacent residential compound on a paving-stone path through a grove of mature oaks and California laurel (*Umbellularia californica*). The meandering path provides a time and place to transition mentally from the workaday world of the farm to the tranquillity of the Retreat.

CHAPTER 5 Space and place

▲ Figure 5.10

Ancient olive trees (*Olea europae*) define a space for outdoor dining. The space flows through the permeable edge formed by the trunks of the olives into a grassy meadow that softens and extends the space. These kind of permeable edges and layered spaces are integral to ACLA's designs.
Source: Photo by Marion Brenner.

Because the native oaks are not tolerant of summer water, they were not underplanted with plants that would require irrigation. Instead, a mulch of leaf litter was retained and a dry creek bed was constructed to protect the buildings from flooding by receiving floodwaters from the adjacent creek. The creek bank is planted with evergreen Mauritius hemp (*Furcraea foetida*) and the near-evergreen native deer grass (*Muhlenbergia rigens*). White, blue and purple bulbs provide a sequence of colour along its banks. The spring starflower (*Ipheion uniflorum* 'White Star') blooms throughout the spring. In late spring, two native camas lilies—the creamy-white, semi-double *Camassia leichtlini* 'Semiplena' and the light blue *Camassia cusickii*—flower with the white star of Bethlehem (*Ornithgalum umbellatum*). The purple *Iris* ('Eleanor Roosevelt') flowers in spring and again in fall.

This herbaceous planting is a model of using colour, form and texture to achieve visual unity. The colour palette is a cool, analogous scheme that people find calming and harmonious (see Chapter 7). All the plants have grass-like leaves and all except the *Iris* have star-shaped flowers of similar size. The grassy leaves gradate from the fine-textured spring starflower and star of Bethlehem to the very coarse-textured Mauritius hemp. The *Iris* will naturalise readily, forming drifts between the Mauritius hemp, and will stand out as a dominant plant by virtue of its occupying a larger relative area and having a darker colour and dissimilar flower form. Because the plants share a similar leaf form and texture, they blend, as do the flower forms

CHAPTER 5 Space and place

▶ Figure 5.11

Along the dry streambed, drifts of the purple *Iris* 'Eleanor Roosevelt' and other bulbous plants are naturalised between clumps of evergreen Mauritius hemp.
Source: Photo by Marion Brenner.

▶ Figure 5.12

In this view of the spa building, lines of plants are layered one behind another to the horizon, with the plants forming soft edges to a series of layered spaces. The colour and texture of the olive allée (behind the spa midground) harmonise with the willows that line the edge of the creek beyond, blurring the line where the designed landscape and the agrarian landscape meet. This borrowed landscape dissolves the edge, making the landscape appear larger than it is. The layered plant edges and golden meadows are used to connect the designed landscape to its agrarian context.
Source: Photo by Marion Brenner.

and colours. The formal and textural similarities of the plants have been used to create a visible hierarchy in a unified planting. The coarser architectural foliage of the hemp and the *Iris* dominate the planting, supported by a unified ensemble of secondary plants. Like the mixture of grasses in the meadow, this is an example of increasing unity by combining plants of similar form, texture and colour (See Chapter 6 Principles).

Stone Edge Farm is an exceptional example of minimalist landscape design. This level of simplicity, order and harmony is rare because it is so very difficult to achieve. The work meets the clients' active program needs and provides a feeling of zen-like tranquillity in a beautiful low-water-use landscape that also mitigates flooding.

Form and space

In the environmental design fields, the shape or configuration of built or natural objects in the environment is referred to as *form*. Form has a reciprocal relationship with space, because space is created by the extension of form. Forms interact with space to create enclosure and spatial type, and consistency of form supports unity in design.

In the landscape, a space is defined by a line, whether that line is two-dimensional or in the third dimension (Booth, 2011). For example, the edge of the tree canopy creates an irregular circular line in space. The form that this line circumscribes in the overhead plane defines the three-dimensional space beneath the tree's canopy (Figure 5.36). Different forms are associated with different time periods and historical styles, and a large vocabulary of forms is used to shape and organise space (Olin, 1988). In order for a landscape design to become a unified composition, all elements of the design should, generally speaking, have similar form or orientation (Booth, 2011), that is, they must have a common design language.

In planting design, the forms created by massed plants or the positioning of individual plants should relate to the formal language of the rest of the design, including the architecture and hard landscape forms. For example, if the form of the overall design is based on the grid, then the placement of individual plants and plant masses should, most often, also be placed on the grid or be rectilinear in form. This approach was consistently found in the work of the late Dan Kiley (Figure 5.13).

Scale

In environmental design, the term *scale* refers to the size of the space in relation to the human body. Scale is a function of both the proportions of the vertical enclosure to the horizontal floor and the size of the space. Human-scale space is space in which the size of the space and its proportions make people feel comfortable.

We can all readily remember spaces where the scale of the space did not make us feel comfortable. Kevin Lynch suggests that the walls of an enclosed space should be between one-half and one-third the dimension of the floor of the space and that when a ratio of 1:4 between the dimensions of the walls and floor of a space has been achieved, the sense of enclosure is lost.

Historic evaluation has found that most streets have a ratio of 1:1 to 1:2.5 and urban open spaces a ratio of 1:1 to 1:1.5 (Jacob, 1993). These

▶ Figure 5.13

In Dan Kiley's Fountain Place in Dallas, Texas, the rows of bald cypress (*Taxodium distichum*) are arranged in a grid within the pools of the fountain plaza. On the hard surface areas, the bosque of trees defines the sitting space below.
Source: Photo by Taner Özdil.

▶ Figure 5.14

These plantings create the ideal ratio of walls to floors in exterior space.
Source: Image courtesy of Yiwen Ruan.

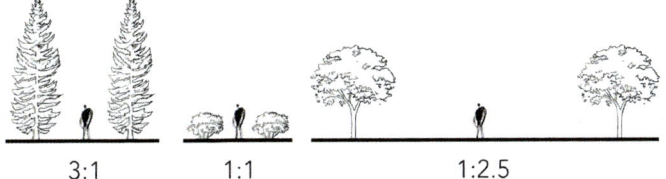

historical guidelines suggest that in order for linear spaces to have a human scale, the ratio of walls to floor should be between 1:1 and 1:2.5, and in open places the ratio should fall between 1:2 and 1:3 in order for people to feel comfortable. However, it is possible for spaces to have these proportions but still not achieve the comfortable fit of human scale because they are either too large or too small.

Smaller spaces, in which a person is more tightly enclosed than in human-scale spaces, are referred to as being "intimate" in scale, suggesting that these are quiet, private or semi-private spaces intended for respite, reflection and meditation. Intimate-scale spaces may be as large as 40 feet (12 metres) in length and width. When its length and width dimensions are less than 10 feet (3 metres), the space created may become uncomfortable. Comfortable human-scale spaces are typically up to 80 feet (24 metres) in width or length, and historically, human-scale urban open spaces have not exceeded 450 feet or 137 metres in the smallest dimension (Lynch, 1960; Jacob, 1993).

When the size of a space exceeds the dimensions of the human scale it becomes supra-human or monumental in scale. Such spaces are not sized to the individual, but to the crowd. Football stadiums and Gothic cathedrals have this scale. Whether in the built environment or in nature, supra-human

CHAPTER 5 Space and place

171

spaces can create a feeling of awe that is grounded in the insignificance of the individual. In nature, larger expansive space gives a feeling of prospect and freedom because the mental traveller within imagines the unrestrained move to the boundary.

In supra-human spaces, people prefer to occupy the boundaries of the space. Only when the edges are fully occupied do people move to the centre. Standing at the edge surveying the open space is an example of prospect refuge theory in action. One's back is protected, people approaching will be visible from a distance and the observer will have time to notice and react (Gehl, 2011).

Spaces of different scales may be created entirely with the use of plants. When the built elements of the spaces fail to provide the size and proportion of the desired scale, plantings can be used to subdivide the space, to reduce the dimensions and to vary the feeling of enclosure. They can also be used as overlapping or interrupting elements of the space to create cubist space within a volumetric space or to create a dynamic tension between the elements in the landscape as seen in Figure 5.7.

A typology of spatial elements

The concepts of space and place have a large literature ranging from phenomenological philosophy to sociology and landscape architecture and architectural discourse. While there is much agreement among scholars, different ideas and terms are used in discussing exterior space. It is not possible, nor desirable, to synthesise this literature here. Rather, a typology of space selectively drawn from the literature for the purpose of application to planting design is discussed. Norberg-Schulz (1980) identified three types of spaces that exist at all scales and one necessary property of space. He called the three types of spaces *centres* or places, *directions* or paths, and *areas* or domains, and prescribed transitions as the necessary property of space (Norberg-Schulz, 1980, in Thwaites and Simkins, 2007). This typology of exterior spatial types has been widely accepted and is used here with the modified terminology of *places*, *matrices*, *paths* and *transitions*. *Views* are added to this typology, because so much of landscape experience is dependent on view that view, like transition, is a necessary property of space.

Places

The formation of "space" also influences the sense of "place". Places are spaces to which some special value or meaning has been attached. This can be a collective social meaning derived from communal use over extended periods of time or it can be an individual value derived from the intensity of use or strength of character and aesthetic distinction of the space (Lynch,

1960; Thwaites and Simkins, 2007). When we talk about a landscape space that is awesome, beautiful or brilliant, it is often because a combination of enclosure, forms, scale, views and character make it so. Such memorable spaces are places that have special meaning to the individual that is created by design and is not the result of prolonged use.

Places that are recorded in the human mind as being differentiated from the general environment, and that are remembered as distinct, support the making of a cognitive map. Most places are positive spaces that the user will be conscious of arriving at, entering and being inside or outside of (Cullen, 1961). Jan Gehl (2011) defines sense of place as occurring when all factors combine to create the sense that the space is entirely pleasant to occupy, while Norberg-Schulz (1980, p. 8) believes that sense of place is a qualitative "total phenomenon, which cannot be reduced to any of its properties".

The matrix

Landscape ecologists divide any landscape into three categories based on land cover. These are *patches*, or areas that are distinct from their surroundings, *corridors* or linear patches, and the general condition of the broader landscape known as the *matrix* (Dramstad, Olson and Forman, 1996). The patches and corridors of landscape ecology are analogous to the places and paths of the experiential landscape. As in landscape ecology, I use the term *matrix* here to describe the general condition of the landscape in which the places and paths are located.

The matrix corresponds to what Norberg-Schulz termed the *area* or *domain*. It is the generally unstructured and mostly negative spaces in which the places and paths are located (Thwaites and Simkins, 2007). Much of landscape architecture is about taking randomly structured space and imposing a perceived order to create a visual/spatial experience. The landscape designer will often be given a space that lacks enclosure or desirable subdivision, or in some way is not yet the space or spaces needed to support the program. The act of landscape architecture lies in shaping that undifferentiated, haphazardly enclosed mixture of positive and negative space into a well-considered series of spatial functions and experiences.

In most instances the newly structured space, whether positive or negative, is built on existing conditions. For example, the existing condition may include a single mature tree that can be saved in a small neighbourhood park. That tree can become a landmark around which the rest of the space is oriented or it may become part of a grove of trees that encloses a perimeter path. What is important is that its inherent spatial opportunities are utilised in some way.

The existing matrix provides the context for any landscape design. Designers need to consider this and to create designs that fit with their matrix or are so completely enclosed that they become a place set aside from the matrix.

Paths

Paths are the routes through adjoining spaces. But paths do more than just connect places; they give the sense of direction in the larger landscape (Thwaites and Simkins, 2007). Although they are primarily directional spaces of movement, paths can have their own hierarchy of space. They may swell to a little opening that is a minor place along the route. Along the way there will be small landmarks, points of interest and places to pause. A path must have a beginning and ending that is in relation to the path itself. It is not enough that each end of the path has a terminus that is in proportion to the path. It must make sense to the user and provide an engaging sequence of experience when traversed in either direction.

For the person in the landscape, the sequence of places generates the sequence of experiences. It is truly said that the path is the locus of the experience of landscape. A person's experience of a place is strongly influenced by the path taken because the path determines their enclosure and what they see and experience. Are they at the exit of a large space, looking through a narrow gateway, or are they hugging the edge of the space, having just entered through the gateway and looking into the space? (Figure 5.15) By keeping the person in the landscape on a predetermined path, the sequence of spaces, views and affordances that make up their experience is delivered in a sequentially prescribed manner.

Because the path determines the user's position in the landscape, designed places need to fuse path and space. If the path is conceived as traversing a sequence of sub-areas of different landscape character, each sub-area along the path can vary in its character, providing modulated change and employing repetition or pattern in the spatial sequence. A sequence of successive characters should be envisioned before the landscape design is realised. After considering the contribution to the character of each segment that could be made by plants, a plant palette for each segment can be created and then applied to the structural sequence envisioned, with appropriate transitions (Figures 5.45–5.49).

Path, view and experience

Scholars of spatial experience emphasise the key role that view plays in the experience of place. In what has been called *sequential view*, the person in the landscape experiences their movement though the landscape as a series of emerging and existing views (Cullen, 1961; Lynch, 1960). The sequential view concept argues that environments should be designed for the experience of the person moving through them by artfully managing enclosure, viewer position and view sequence (Cullen, 1961).

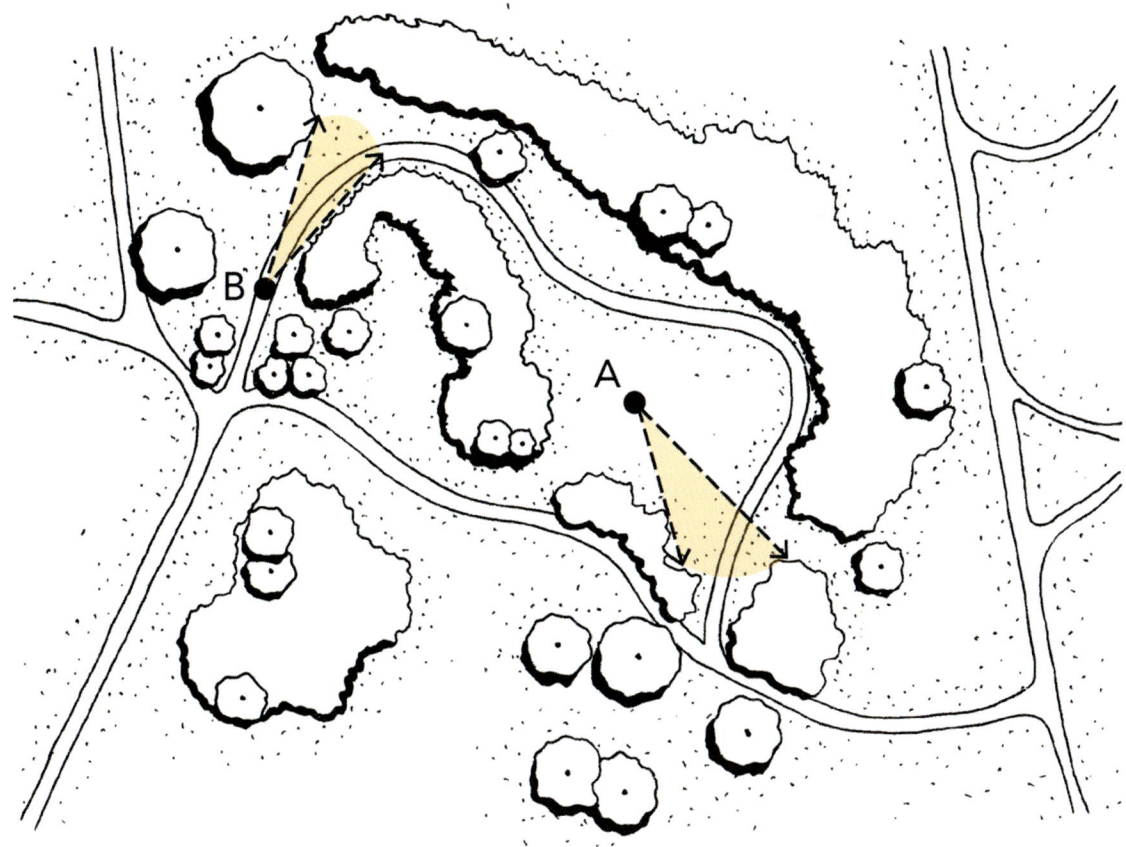

▲ Figure 5.15

The view, sense of enclosure and experience of landscape will be markedly different for person A in the centre of the space than for person B, having just entered the space on the path.
Source: Image courtesy of Yiwen Ruan.

The fact that the view is not seen but is emerging speaks to the presence and importance of mystery in the landscape. In sequential view, it seems that the person moving through the landscape is largely unaware of the evolving landscape until a new view presents itself. The new view is a destination, an indication of leaving one space and entering another (Cullen, 1961; Thwaites and Simkins, 2007) and a landmark marking one's progress through the landscape. Views, spatial enclosure and their sequence largely create the landscape experience. This is not to minimise the importance of materials, qualities of light and composition that give a space its landscape character, but to make the point that the character of the landscape is contained in the view.

Recall that when people look at new scenes, their attention is drawn to what is novel, new or exciting. The conspicuous elements that attract people's attention in the landscape are landmarks, or focal points, and these are the most important features of the views (Tversky, 2000). Landmarks are simply elements that are differentiated from their surroundings by their aesthetics and placement. However, it is important that the landmark that draws our attention also supports our purposes in the landscape (S. Kaplan, 1988). Sight lines that allow people to see and anticipate an open space

CHAPTER 5 **Space and place**

▲ Figure 5.16

Mystery is often nothing more than a blocked or redirected view. The path that curves away and out of view is a classic use of mystery to draw the person into the landscape.
Source: Photo by Patrick Mooney.

that may serve their needs are essential, for unless people can see a space and the access to it they will not use that space (Whyte, 1980). For this reason, a landmark tree, sculpture or fountain should be located where it draws attention to the access of an important use area.

Landscape designers in different cultures and times have understood and used sequential view to entice people through their designs. In Japan, the classical tea ceremony gardens are known as *stroll gardens*; this is sometimes translated as circuit-style gardens. In these gardens, the visitor encounters a series of prescribed views along a circular path that culminates in arrival at a tea house. The different views are often of landmarks such as waterfalls and bridges. As one proceeds through the garden, each view is first a landmark and then a new destination bringing the visitor closer to their final destination.

Such gardens are conceived as a series of linked spaces connected by a path. Mystery is used to draw the person through the landscape, with the person's expectations met and progress marked by the revealing of landmark views (Figure 5.16).

While most views in a Japanese garden are internal to the garden, the designer may also incorporate *shakkei* or "borrowed views" from beyond the garden. The use of borrowed scenery gives the landscape extent. The concept of *shakkei* is not just that the view incorporates scenery from outside the garden, but that the transition from the garden to the surrounding

176　　　　　　　　　　　　　　　CHAPTER 5 Space and place

▲ Figure 5.17

The middle garden of Shugaku-in is traversed by this gravel path through dwarfed Japanese black pines (*Pinus thunbergii*), restricting views over the adjacent rice paddies.
Source: np&djjewell | Flickr. Used under the Creative Commons licence.

▲ Figure 5.18

The stepping stone path from the middle to the upper garden continues the restricted views of the lower garden.
Source: np&djjewell | Flickr. Used under the Creative Commons licence.

area is imperceptible and the garden flows without visible boundary into the larger landscape.

The most extreme example of this is, in the canon of the traditional Japanese gardens, the view from the Cloud Touching Arbour in Shugaku-in Imperial Villa in Kyoto. The garden is conceived as a series of sub-spaces, each having a particular landscape character and type of view. It is divided into the lower garden, the upper garden and the middle garden. The lower garden is where the ladies and men of the court stayed in two small pavilions when visiting the garden. The middle garden consists largely of rice paddies seen though rows of Japanese black pine (*Pinus thunbergii*) that line the path, and the upper garden contains a man-made lake, established though the use of an earthen dam. The designer, ex-Emperor Gomizunoo (1596–1680), created a dramatic and sudden transition by following compressed space and short internal views with expansive openness that reveals a dramatic borrowed view. In this design, the visitor passes from the lower garden though the middle garden and up a steep mountain path to the upper garden. In both the lower and middle gardens the visitor is restricted to relatively short internal views. Arriving at the entry to the upper garden, the visitor passes through a gateway to an open gravel

CHAPTER 5 **Space and place**

◀ Figure 5.19

The visitor arrives at the Cloud Touching Arbour overlooking the upper garden in Shugaku-in.
Source: np&djjewell | Flickr. Used under the Creative Commons licence.

▼ Figure 5.20

Turning 180 degrees from the Cloud Touching Arbour, the visitor is given the first extended view of their visit to Shugaku-in Imperial Villa. In making this abrupt transition in space and view, Gomizunoo capitalised on the opportunity to use *shakkei* on a scale never before seen in Japanese gardens.
Source: Kimon Berlin | Flickr. Used under the Creative Commons licence.

area adjacent to a small rustic structure known as Rin'un-tei, or the Cloud Touching Arbour. From here, visitors are treated to an overview of the upper garden and the surrounding landscape. In so doing, Gomizunoo sublimated all other elements and views in the garden to create a grand climax of borrowed scenery (Kuck, 1989) (see Figures 5.17–5.20). This is the delightful surprise, discussed in Chapter 1, that exceeds the expectations of the visitor and gives pleasure. Even when we have visited the garden multiple times, the impact of this dramatic change in view and spatial enclosure never fails to move us.

This view sequence from Shugaku-in Imperial Villa is intended to demonstrate the integral connection between space, path, view and experience. A succession of spaces and paths is organised to provide only intimate space and closed views, until an unexpected finale of suprahuman space and extended view is revealed, to elicit a particular response from the viewer. This sequence illustrates that the views that designers create in designing for sequential experience are integral to the experience of place.

How to treat a view

There are essentially only four ways to treat a view. It may be blocked, framed, subdivided or filtered. By blocked we mean visually hidden from

▼ Figure 5.21

Top: This panoramic view of Rio de Janeiro illustrates the use of view-blocking and framing to improve a view and focus attention. In the existing view, attention is drawn to the built areas on the left and right foreground and midground rather than Sugarloaf Mountain and Guanabara Bay in the right background. Bottom: The overlapping rectangles show the areas selected for view-blocking. Source: © José Fernandes Jr. | Flickr and Yiwen Ruan. Used under the Creative Commons licence.

 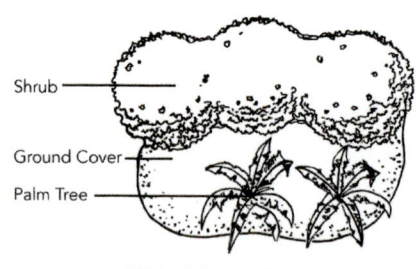

view. Views are most commonly blocked to hide an objectionable view, as when a tall tree canopy is use to screen out an elevated roadway in the distance, but view-blocking may also be done to create anticipation and save a particular view for a later experience, as in the case of Shugaku-in. In framing a view, the designer focuses the users' attention on the view by enclosing it on either side and on the ground and on the overhead plane (Robinette, 1972; Simonds, 1983). This separates that which is within the frame from that which is not, so that the framed view becomes a focal point in the landscape. A subdivided view is most often a panoramic view that is divided into segments by enframement. This may be done to create composed segments or to create a sequence of views by adding variety to what would otherwise be a constant view.

When presented with a wide panoramic view, the designer may want to break it into segments so that it is never fully revealed until the climax of the spatial sequence. If a view is poorly composed, subdividing the view may allow the viewer to experience it as a series of composed views. In this way the designer is able to impose composition on the view. By denying full access to the view, at least temporarily, the designer creates mystery and causes the observer to focus on the view, to mentally process it, whereas if it had been suddenly revealed it might have gone unnoticed.

Partially blocked to slightly obscured views are called filtered views. The architectural equivalent would be a lattice wall with many small openings admitting light and revealing a partially obscured view. This may be done to turn the viewers' attention away from an undesirable view while still admitting light, or simply to allow light, partial views and breezes to enter the space so that it feels open. Partial blocking may be done to

▲ Figure 5.22

View-blocking with vegetation. Top: A mixture of palm trees, broad-leaved evergreen shrubs and groundcovers have been added. These block objectionable portions of the view, make the vista appear more natural and, by partially framing the view, draw the eye to Sugarloaf Mountain. Bottom: The plan of the planting that created the desired composed view.
Source: © José Fernandes Jr. | Flickr and Yiwen Ruan. Used under the Creative Commons licence.

hide undesirable portions of the view and create an overall composition (Figures 5.21 and 5.22).

When places, paths and views are conceived in concert, each place in the spatial sequence may have a degree of enclosure, character and view that is distinct from others in the sequence and yet the sub-areas together create a harmony of experience.

Transitions

Landscape designers should introduce transitions at the places where aesthetics, function and character change. Transitions occur where the properties of two spaces meet. Like landmarks and views, transitions are necessary elements of successful wayfinding (Tversky, 2000). They indicate what is coming and allow people the time and space they need to adjust their expectations (Thwaites and Simkins, 2007). Transitions give a sense of flow and continuity to a series of connected spaces, modulating the change from one area to another and making the experience of change feel effortless, even imperceptible, rather than abrupt or jarring.

Alternatively, as in the example of Shugaku-in above, the purpose of the transition is to create dramatic effect by abruptly revealing an unanticipated event. In such cases, the user is lulled into expecting a continuation of the present landscape mood and character, when suddenly the unexpected is inserted to create a dramatic surprise climax. As in Stravinsky's explanation of the musical listener in Chapter 2, this unpredicted event must delight, so that the person will happily modify their expectations and will want to continue their landscape experience.

Generally speaking, the way to create a transition between two adjacent elements or spaces is to bring shared properties of both spaces into the transition zone. Often this means extending the forms, colours and materials, including plants, of the two spaces into the transition zone. For example, there needs to be a transition between an urban plaza and its connecting streets (Whyte, 1980). In Green Acre Park in New York City there is a trellis that overhangs the street at the entry to the park (Figure 5.23). In this way the spatial enclosure of the plaza overlaps that of the street. Under this trellis, water is introduced as a small fountain that is connected by a runnel to the waterfall that is the climax of the park (Cultural Landscape Foundation, n.d.). The bosque of trees in the park is repeated as a single line of trees on the street so that the canopy of the park is transferred to the street and the space of the plaza begins at the curb. Flowering plants in pots are placed out into the view of the street, effectively transferring some of the verdant living colour of the park to the street views.

Landscapes contain a hierarchy of places, landmarks and views. Within every landscape design there should also be a hierarchy of transitions, with major transitions occurring at important places. Major transitions

▲ Figure 5.23

Green Acre Park, 1971, New York City, by Sasaki, Dawson & DeMay. A combination of hard landscape materials and plants are used to transition between the park space and the street.
Source: Image courtesy of Yiwen Ruan.

should occur whenever the path moves from one sub-area to another. Minor transitions might occur within a sub-area, such as a woodland path, as modulation of the landscape's character. Just as grades must meet at a site boundary, so too must the landscape character and aesthetic qualities. This requires a transition from site to its surrounding matrix. Recognising this, designers seek to make places that fit with their context.

Case study: Design Workshop transitions

Design Workshop is an award-winning landscape architecture, land planning and urban design practice with multiple offices in the United States and abroad. The firm's residential work emphasises regional landscape character and the relationship between landscape and architecture. Design Workshop partner Mike Albert has said:

> Our gardens are identifiable because we interact with the landscape, taking our contextual cues from the climate, physiographic features, textures, patterns and raw materials of the landscape. The end result makes a significant contribution to

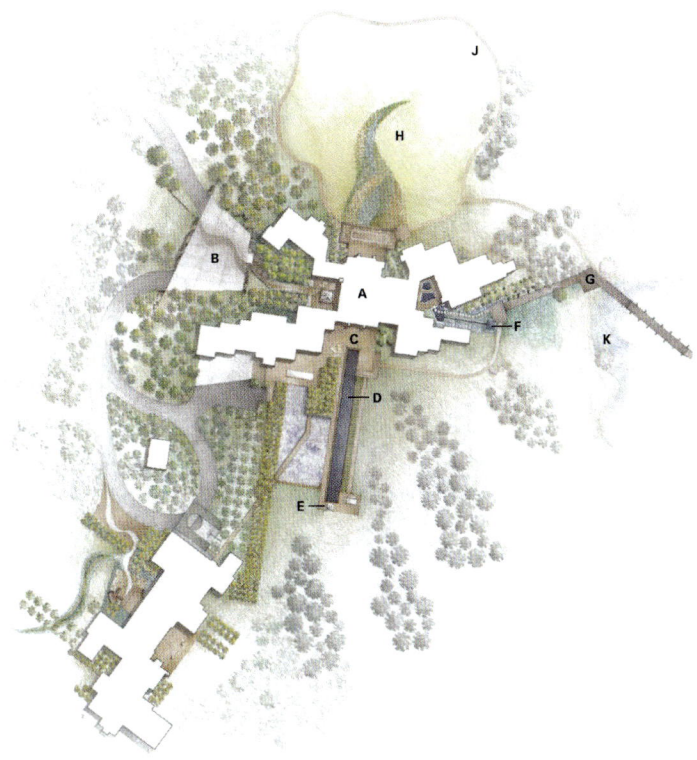

SNAKE RIVER RESIDENCE

A | RESIDENCE
B | AUTO COURT & ENTRY GARDEN
C | TERRACE
D | REFLECTING POOL
E | SCULPTURE
F | WATER RUNNEL
G | BOARDWALK
H | NORTH MEADOW
I | SOUTH MEADOW
J | MEADOW PATH
K | RIPARIAN RESTORATION CORRIDOR

▲ Figure 5.24

Plan of the Snake River Residence. Four separate use areas are located between the wings of the house. The location of the residence and its layout set the stage for different planting designs and characters in each of the four use areas.
Source: Image courtesy of Design Workshop Inc.

establishing a unique design character—otherwise known as regionalism.

Our work is about the interplay between architecture and landscape, how they, together, celebrate the environment … pairing … certain properties of rugged terrain with modern design demonstrates the multitude of steps required to meld what on the surface appears to be elements in opposition.

(Mike Albert, quoted in Zuckerman, 2015)

The celebration of *genius loci* and the fusing of architecture and landscape are demonstrated in different ways in three Design Workshop residential designs that transition from the home, to its garden, to the regional landscape. The homes are set in the expansive landscapes of the American West and enjoy extended views of the surrounding countryside. In each case, the landscape architects recognised the need to create a landscape near the house that was congruous with the architecture and also to transition from the architecture and domestic garden to the surrounding regional landscape. Each transition is conceptually different and subtly and confidently executed. The three residences are: The Snake River Retreat in Wyoming, the Quarry House in Utah and the Charlie Mountain Ranch in Colorado.

CHAPTER 5 **Space and place** 183

The Snake River Retreat

Design Workshop team members: Mark Hershberger, Greg Stewart and Bruce Greig.
Architect: William F. Tull.
Environmental specialist: Biota Research and Consulting.
Contractor: Bill Dziczyc Construction.

The single-storey modernist home is located on Fish Creek, a tributary of the Snake River, near Jackson Hole, Wyoming, and is set amongst mature groves of narrow-leaved cottonwood (*Populus angustifolia*)—the dominant tree species of the region. The four outdoor use areas located between the wings of its cruciform plan are critical in fusing the residence with its landscape (Figure 5.24).

Views

The transition from the modernist house and garden to its natural setting is achieved in multiple ways. One of the key steps in integrating the Snake River Retreat with its rural environment was orienting the home to different views across the river plain to the encircling mountains. The view from each use area received a different planting design, giving it a distinct landscape character. On the north, the living room looks across a meadow of native grasses and wildflowers that has been "edited" by removing cottonwood saplings and adding blue lupins. A meandering stone path hugs the meadow edge where it meets the aspen forest. The view from the interior of the house is evocative of an alpine meadow and differentiates this area from the rest of the site. A sandstone terrace to the south allows extended views to riparian meadows. From another terrace off the great room, an 80-foot (24-metre) reflecting pool brings down the shifting sky, reflecting a totem sculpture and the canopy of distant trees. Between the autocourt and the home's main entry, a stone path passes beneath a bosque of aspens with views to the autocourt and the forest beyond. In each use area, the landscape character is unmistakably of the region, and in each, the foreground views, while different, connect to the natural landscape that forms the background of the view.

Native stone

Design Workshop's regionalist design often employs extensive use of local stone in walls, seating, paving and as sculptural objects in the landscape. At the Snake River Retreat, the native stone is used to bring the sense of the region to the site and extend the architecture into the landscape. The juxtaposition of delicate grasses and quaking aspen leaves with monolithic stone focuses attention on both the hard and soft materials so that their presence in the larger landscape cannot go unnoticed.

Plant selection and placement

The home's landscape is fused with the regional landscape primarily through the plants that were used and the way they were arranged. Meadows of

▶ Figure 5.25

A plan of the home's entry area shows the formal bosque of aspens and the way that this breaks down into groves of aspen and Colorado blue spruce as one moves into the autocourt and the forest.
Source: Image courtesy of Design Workshop Inc.

A Residence
B Entry
C Auto Court
D Aspen Bosque

▶ Figure 5.26

At the main entry, a grid of aspens and grasses captures the modernist sensibility of the house while connecting it visually with the wild landscape beyond.
Source: Image courtesy of Design Workshop Inc.

indigenous grasses like little bluestem (*Schizachyrium scoparium*) and wildflowers (*Lupinus* spp.) replace areas of lawn and combine with native trees and shrubs for a seamless blending of the home landscape and its setting. Nearer the house, quaking aspen, a wild tree that carries no associations with formal gardens, is arranged in a bosque. Between the main entry and the autocourt, the formally arranged aspens are underplanted with a grid of grasses. Although the tree is partially tamed by this arrangement, it brings an air of wildness to the garden. As one moves away from the residence and into the natural landscape, the geometric arrangement of plants dissolves into naturalistic groves, creating an almost imperceptible

CHAPTER 5 **Space and place**

transition from modernist space to native landscape. This designed transition is easily seen in the plan and photos of the autocourt and main entry garden to the residence (Figures 5.25 and 5.26).

Plant list

Trees	
Crataegus douglasii	Black hawthorn
Picea pungens	Colorado blue spruce
Populus tremuloides	Quaking aspen
Populus angustifolia	Narrowleaf cottonwood
Shrubs	
Cornus sericea 'Cardinal'	Cardinal Red osier dogwood
Salix alba 'Vitellinia'	Vitellinia golden willow
Salix discolor	Pussy willow
Salix exigua	Coyote willow
Salix irrorata	Blue stem willow
Salix monticola	Yellow mountain willow
Perennials	
Hosta sieboldiana 'Elegans'	Elegans blue-leaved *Hosta*
Iris siberica	Siberian *Iris*
Linum perenne lewisii	Lewis' prairie flax
Leucanthemum x *superbum* 'Aglaia'	Aglaia double Shasta daisy
Lupinus spp.	Lupins
Parthenocissus quinquefolia	Virginia creeper
Native grasses and riparian plantings	
Agrostis gigantea	Redtop
Carex nebrascensis	Nebraska sedge
Deschampsia cespitosa	Tufted hairgrass
Festuca glauca	Blue fescue
Helictotrichon sempervirens	Blue oatgrass
Juncus torreyi	Torrey's rush
Phleum pratense	Alpine Timothy
Poa compressa	Canada bluegrass
Typha spp.	Cattail
Bulbs	
Muscari ameniacum 'Blue Spike'	Blue Spike grape hyacinth
Narcissus 'Dutch Master'	Dutch Master trumpet daffodil
Tulipa 'Darwin'	Darwin hybrid tulip

The Quarry House

Design Workshop team members: Mike Albert, Darla Callaway and Colten McDermott.
Architect: RKD Architects.
Civil engineer: JVA Consulting Engineers.
Water feature engineer: Cloward H20.
Lighting design: David Craige Lighting Design.

The Quarry House sits on a bluff overlooking the Wasatch Range of the Rocky Mountains in Summit County, Utah. One of the key challenges of the landscape design was fitting the modernist home to its setting. Site analysis indicated that a series of retaining walls would be necessary to limit the disturbed area and provide connection to the natural landscape, but reading the geotechnical engineer's report suggested an alternative strategy to the landscape architect: That of using the bedrock ledges found on the site as natural retaining walls. Over weeks of site investigation, a vein of bedrock outcrops was revealed. While the house provides vistas of the distant mountains, the gathering spaces around the house are enclosed outdoor rooms, sheltered from sun and wind by the home and set against the backdrop of the bedrock escarpment.

Design principles

The landscape architect incorporated a set of design principles to organise the grounds of the house and connect it to the region. To connect architecture and landscape, the forms and materials of the architecture were extended into the landscape. Beginning at the arrival court, stone walls, cascading concrete stairs and paving slabs disperse the materials and forms of the architecture throughout the home landscape. The colours and

▼ Figure 5.27

The Quarry House sits on a bluff overlooking the eastern side of the Wasatch mountain range, known as the Wasatch Back.
Source: Image courtesy of Design Workshop Inc.

textures of the hard materials used in the house and garden reflect those of the surrounding landscape. At the main entry, a glass-walled passage connects two wings of the house, and a suspended concrete slab ties the house and landscape. Quaking aspen trees (*Populus tremuloides*) seen from within the passage connect the views to the arrival area and the distant landscape.

Plantings

A winding drive flows through native sagebrush (*Artemisia tridentata*) and Gambel oak (*Quercus gambelii*) meadows to the autocourt, immersing one in the regional landscape on arrival. Local native plants, like prairie dropseed (*Sporobolus heterolepis*), yarrow (*Achillea millefolium*) and sumac (*Rhus trilobata*) inspired the plant palette of the home's garden, in which massed plantings of Tiger Eyes sumac (*Rhus typhina* 'Tiger Eyes'), Blonde Ambition grass (*Bouteloua gracilis* 'Blonde Ambition'), yarrow (*Achillea* 'Moonshine') and stonecrop (*Sedum acre*) evoke native meadows. The simple massed plantings are appropriate to the modernist house and yet abstract the native landscape.

The rock outcrop

To delineate the boundaries of the domestic garden, the landscape architect utilised the site's indigenous bedrock, revealed during excavation. The

▼ Figure 5.28

Informally placed concrete slabs form a path through a matrix of gold moss–Utah stonecrop (*Sedum acre* evergreen). A multi-trunk specimen of the native Western river birch (*Betula occidentalis*) is a focal point against the bedrock outcrop that connects the garden's aesthetic to the region. These plantings abstract the regional landscape without attempting to mimic it.
Source: Image courtesy of Design Workshop Inc.

geographic feature offers a dramatic backdrop to the domestic garden and serves as a counterpoint to the modern architecture and a transitional boundary between the garden and the natural hillside. In plan, this transition might seem to be abrupt. However, the outcrop is not a wall in the sense of being a barrier separating two different places. Rather, it is a hinge connecting the domestic garden at its base with the natural landscape, seen atop the rocky ledge (Figure 5.28).

Plant list

Trees	
Betula occidentalis	Western river birch
Pinus nigra	Austrian pine
Populus tremula 'Erecta'	Swedish columnar aspen
Populus tremuloides	Quaking aspen (single and multi-stem)
Shrubs	
Artemisia tridentata	Big sagebrush
Chrysothamnus nauseosus	Rabbitbrush
Physocarpus opulifolius 'Summer Wine'	Summer Wine Ninebark
Quercus gambelii	Gambel oak
Rhus typhina 'Tiger Eyes'	Tiger Eyes sumac
Rosa woodsii	Woods' rose
Perennials	
Achillea 'Moonshine'	Moonshine yarrow
Arctostaphylos uva-ursi	Kinnikinnick
Bouteloua gracilis 'Blonde Ambition'	Blonde Ambition grass
Helictotrichon sempervirens	Blue avena grass
Iris pallida 'Variegata'	Variegated sweet *Iris*
Lupinus 'The Governor'	Blue lupine
Penstemon cyaneus	Blue *Penstemon*
Salvia x *sylvestris* 'May Night'	May Night *Salvia*
Sedum acre evergreen	Goldmoss—Utah stonecrop
Sporobolus heterolepis	Prairie dropseed
No-mow fescue native grass seed mix	

Charlie Mountain Ranch

Design Workshop team members: Mike Albert, Michael Tunte, Ben Roush and Alison Kelly.
Architecture: Pearson Design Group Inc.
Structural engineer: KL&A.
Landscape contractor: Landscape Workshop Inc.

The site plan

When new owners purchased the neglected Charlie Mountain Ranch, near Snowmass, Colorado, in 2011, they committed to restoring the ranch and engaged Design Workshop to conduct a comprehensive site analysis and masterplan (see Case Study: Chapter 3). To avoid further ecological degradation, the new structures were situated on previously disturbed land. They are constructed of reclaimed timber and local stone in a vernacular ranch house style and sit on a ground plane of native grasses and wildflowers amid preserved aspen trees.

◀ Figure 5.29

The drive to the main house winds through a grassy meadow infilled with *Rhus aromatica*, *Populus tremuloides* and *Pinus ponderosa*. Trees frame the view, orienting the visitor to the vertical sandstone cliff that dominates the ranch house and garden.
Source: Image courtesy of Design Workshop Inc.

◀ Figure 5.30

The planting was deliberately conceived as monochromatic drifts that would better reveal the textural beauty of the stonework. Massed plantings of Woods' rose (*Rosa woodsii*) interspersed with Bishop's weed (*Aegopodium podagraria*) abut the foundations of the house, giving it a natural setting.
Source: Image courtesy of Design Workshop Inc.

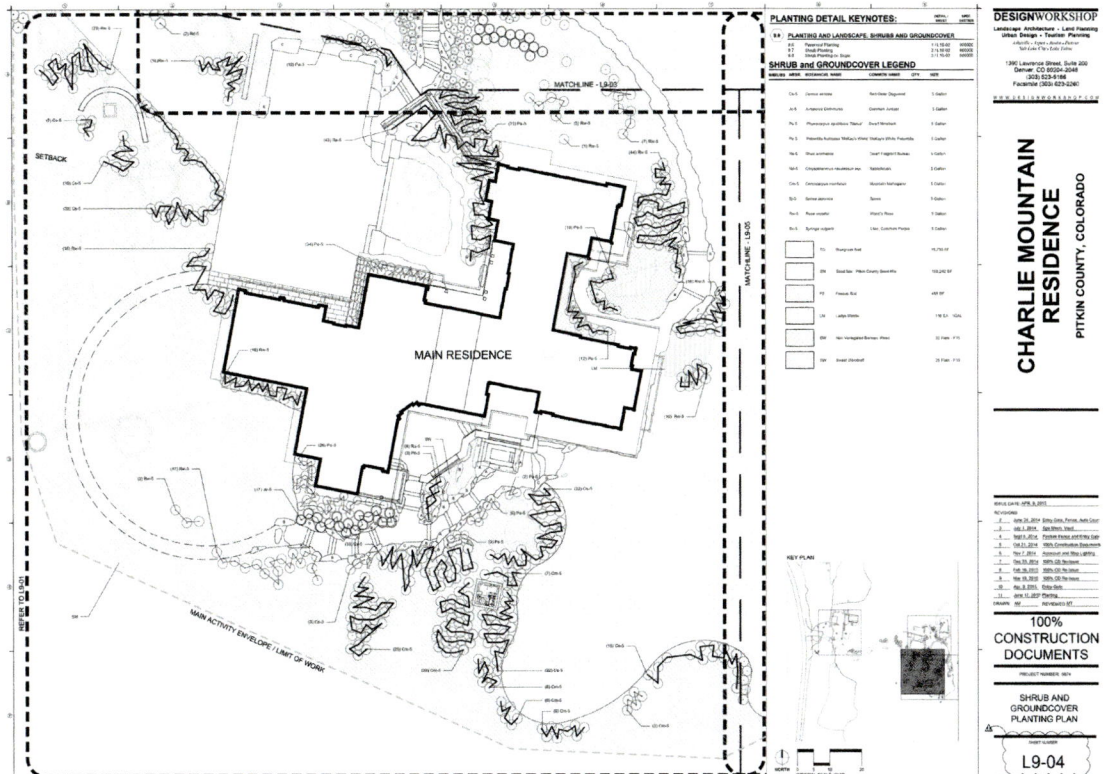

▲ Figure 5.31

The Charlie Mountain Ranch planting plan shows massed shrub plantings bordering the house.
Source: Image courtesy of Design Workshop Inc.

Bringing the wild landscape home

Drifts of native plants bring the wild landscape to the walls of the buildings, so that there is no perceptible demarcation line between the natural landscape and the home grounds. Visitors can easily believe that the buildings, with their lichen-covered stone foundations and ancient timbers, have been here for many years and that native plants have colonised the area around the home right up to the foundation walls. Collectively, the thoughtful attention to detail connects the family and their guests to the beauty and heritage of this mountainous setting.

Plant list

Trees	
Populus deltoides	Cottonwood
Populus tremuloides	Quaking aspen
Pinus ponderosa	Ponderosa pine
Picea pungens	Colorado blue spruce

Shrubs	
Cornus servicea	Red osier dogwood
Juniperus communis	Common juniper
Physocarpus opulifolius 'Nanus'	Dwarf Ninebark
Potentilla fruticosa 'McKay's White'	McKay's White *Potentilla*
Rhus aromatica 'Gro-low'	Dwarf fragrant sumac
Chrysothamnus nauseosus	Rabbitbrush
Cercocarpus montanus	Alder-leaf mountain mahogany
Spiraea japonica	Japanese spirea
Rosa woodsii	Woods' rose
Syringa vulgaris cv.	Common purple lilac
Perennials	
Alchemilla mollis	Lady's mantle
Aegopodium podagraria	Bishop's weed
Galium odoratum	Sweet woodruff
Grasses	
Bluegrass sod	
Seed mix: Pitkin County seed mix	
Fescue sod	

The landscapes of the American West contain diverse plant communities and characters. These three designs refine and emphasise the distinctive character of each site. In different ways, they meld the home and its landscape to the regional landscape. A mix of native and non-native plants are used, not to imitate nature but to create an artistic abstraction of the native landscape.

Shaping space with plants

Much of what I've written about in this chapter can be seen in the work of the Danish–American landscape architect Jens Jensen (1860–1951). Jensen was noted for his expansive spaces that used a sense of mystery to pull people through the landscape (Grese, 1992). Figures 5.32–5.34 illustrate Jensen's plan for Mahoney Park in Kenilworth, Illinois. Figure 5.32 depicts an undulating perimeter pathway around a central space. Along this path, Jensen located three fire pits surrounded by circular stone seating walls that he called "Council Rings". The linear space of the path is tightly enclosed within a belt of trees and shrubs. At a few locations it opens on one side to the small, enclosed spaces of the Council Rings or on the other side of the path to views of and access to the central open meadow space. These

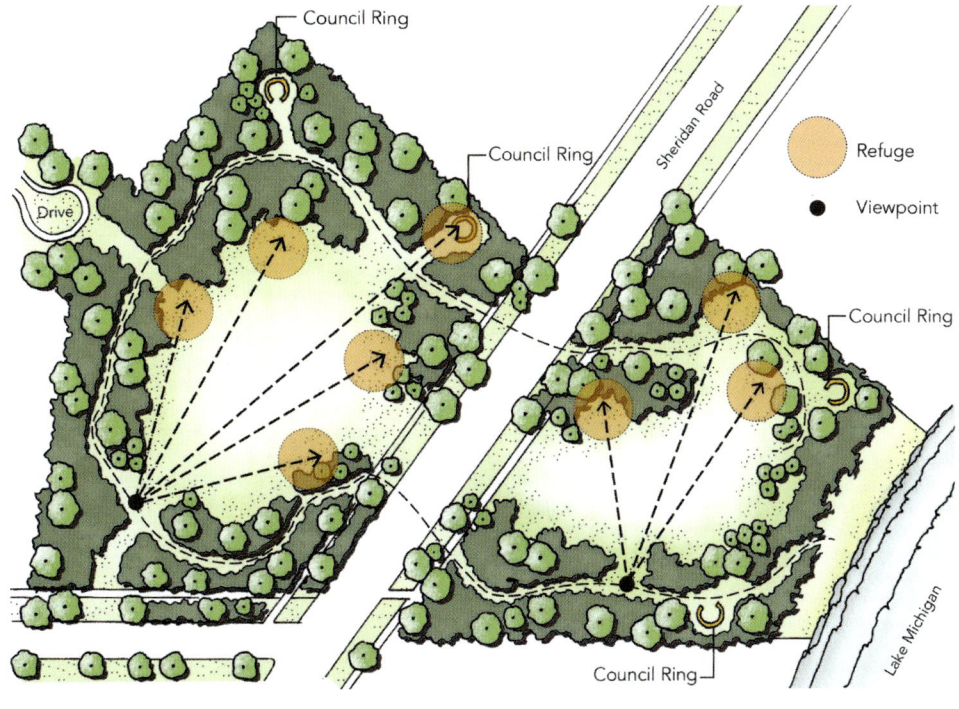

▲ Figure 5.32

Path, view and spatial hierarchy in Jens Jensen's Mahoney Park (after Grese, 1992).
Source: Image courtesy of Yiwen Ruan.

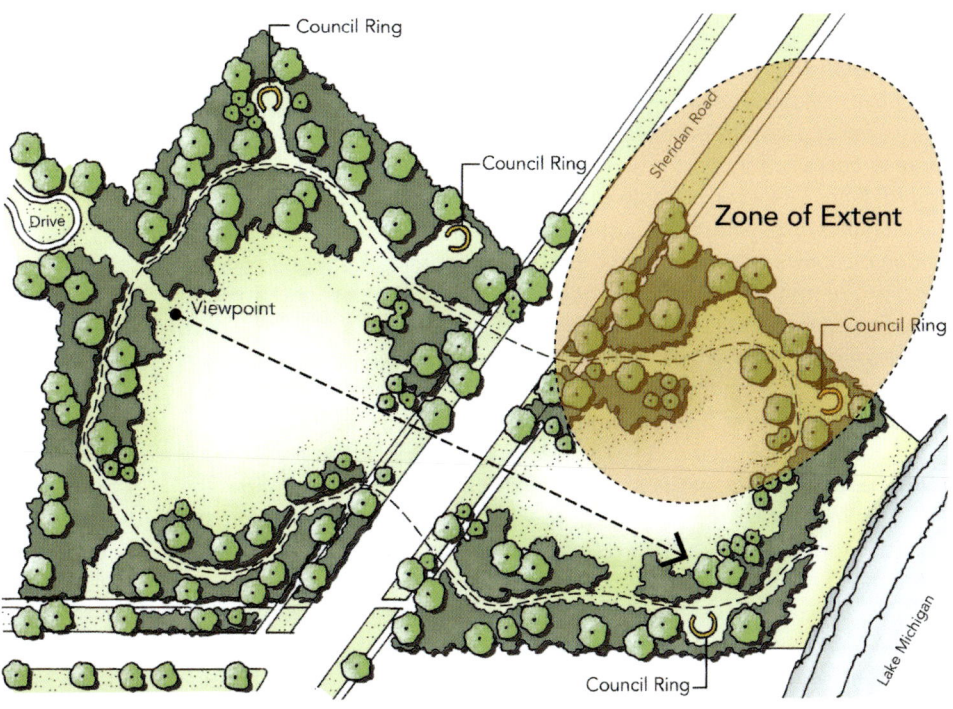

▲ Figure 5.33

The long view of the meadow west–east.
Source: Image courtesy of Yiwen Ruan.

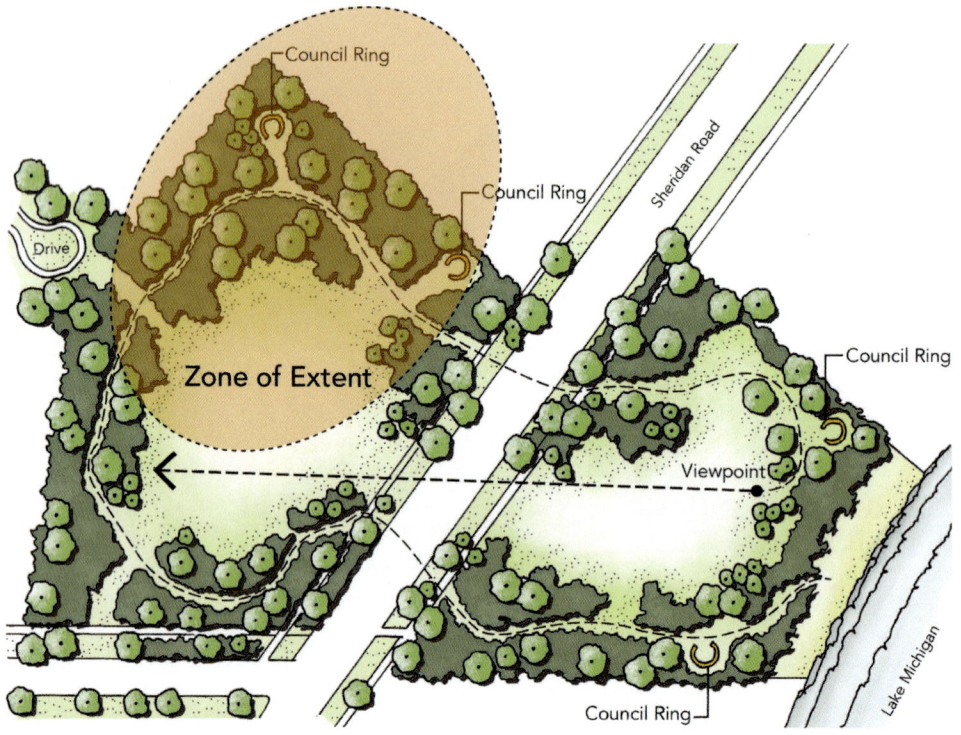

▲ Figure 5.34

The long view of the meadow east–west.
Source: Image courtesy of Yiwen Ruan.

viewpoints along the path reveal a dramatic change in the scale of the spatial enclosure and give the plan a hierarchy of spaces that is created entirely with plants. Views from viewpoints on the path are marked on the plan. The viewer is presented with views to major groves and trees and also to informal coves or bays in the surrounding wall of vegetation that, like the Council Rings, are small intimate-scale places of prospect refuge.

Figures 5.33 and 5.34 illustrate a common technique of Japanese garden designers to give a place extent. At either end of the great central meadow, Jensen placed key viewpoints that maximise the length of the view. The spaces labelled "Zone of Extent" curve away and out of view. This visual deception causes viewers to imagine the space that is not seen as large, or larger than the space that is in view. In this way, Jensen has created imaginary spaces that are larger than the site could contain in reality. The hierarchy of real and imaginary spaces within the park is achieved by using plants to shape spaces and direct views. The spaces range from the tiniest intimate-scale refuges shown in Figure 5.32, to the human-scale spaces of the perimeter path and Council Rings, to the supra-human scale of the meadows and the "Zones of Extent" seen in Figures 5.33 and 5.34. The hierarchy and sequence of spaces, their arrangements and the variation in views along the path give the park psychological extent and much of its ability to engage the visitor.

Plants as spatial elements

> Good space—Enhance it. Bad space—Overpower it with a new geometry.
> (Steve Martino, landscape architect, *Weeds and Walls*)

Plants can be used to create the boundaries of space, to turn undifferentiated space into positive space, to determine views and to orchestrate the sequence of spaces. They can screen or direct a view, enclose a space or be used to filter a view (Austin and Law, 1975). Most architectural elements create a solid wall, but plants can be used to present a subtlety of openness, from the visually and physically impenetrable bamboo thicket to the openness given by the trunks of a row of shade trees. This property of plants to define space while at the same time allowing all degrees of visual penetrability is perhaps the most important and subtle element of using planting design to define spaces and views.

Exterior space differs from architectural space in that it is more irregular, much larger and has a greater ratio of horizontal to vertical dimensions (Lynch, 1960). Landscape designers will often find themselves having to subdivide overly large spaces that would make people feel uncomfortable to provide privacy or human scale, to separate conflicting uses, to assign different parts of the program to designated spaces, to block or compose views, or to create a sequence of experience. They do this by creating new spatial boundaries with plants or hard landscape elements or a combination of the two.

The architectural plant forms

Architectural interior space is defined by ceilings, floors and walls in which openings admit light and views and allow movement between spaces. The boundaries of exterior spaces are analogous to the architectural elements of floors, walls and ceilings and are used to give unstructured space new definition, hierarchy and sequence. Outdoor spaces are defined by vertical elements or walls provided by such things as buildings and street trees, by the floor or horizontal base plane that is composed of such things as paving and lawns, and by the ceiling or overhead plane made up of things like the sky or tree canopy (Ewing and Handy, 2009). The plant forms that define the floors, walls and ceilings of exterior spaces are defined here as *canopy*, *groundcover*, *screen*, *barrier* and *scrim*.

Canopy and ceiling: The overhead plane

The overhead plane encloses the upper surface of a space. In architecture it is the ceiling or roof of the building. In the city it is often a tree.

When trees overarch a space, they are said to canopy that space. The canopy of the tree forms the overhead plane of exterior spaces. As seen in the work of Jens Jensen, the use of trees as groves, avenues and belts can provide a variety and sequence of spaces and define places for various programmatic uses like picnicking, socialising, resting, viewing and active games.

Researchers have found that, in the urban environment, people generally prefer larger to smaller trees (Wolf, 2003) and larger trees in greater numbers around their workspaces (R. Kaplan, 2007) and that areas with tree canopy cover are preferred over areas with more open sky (Buhyoff, Gauthier and Wellman, 1984). In urban environments, sitting beneath trees and watching people passing is the most preferred sitting space (Whyte, 1980).

A canopy is an overhead plane created by plants that people can see and walk beneath. Where the site to be developed is overlooked by adjacent buildings, the use of canopy is often the simplest, and sometimes the only, way to provide privacy. The same tree that defines space and gives a sense of refuge can also provide privacy and shade and can be a focal point or landmark in the landscape.

▼ Figure 5.35

The tree canopy defines the positive space below.
Source: Connie | Flickr. Used under the Creative Commons licence.

▲ Figure 5.36

The canopy defines a space of prospect refuge that is the preferred place to sit and watch people.
Source: Image courtesy of Yiwen Ruan.

When a space is defined by its canopy, the walls and the floor of the space are not demarcated, but the canopy will still define the space (Figures 5.35 and 5.36). This is a good example of how weak enclosure still leaves us with an experiential sense of enclosure and also a reminder that such weak enclosure may be highly desirable from an experiential point of view. Sitting beneath the canopy of the tree, we are shaded, our back is protected and we can look out over the landscape.

Groundcover and floor: The base plane

The base plane is the lowest surface of the space upon which we walk. The floor of an interior room is usually covered in the same material. Outside, a floor of paving defines many spaces. Just as laying a blanket on the grass defines a space, paving a sub-area defines it as a separate zone even if it has no other enclosure. Just as canopy alone can define a space, having only a floor will define a space the size of the floor. Often the base plane material unifies the design and connects the separate sub-spaces (Simonds, 1983).

◀ Figure 5.37

Groundcover: The fine textured groundcover of moss in the temple of Saiho-ji creates a unified ground plane. Source: cdotwright | Flickr. Used under the Creative Commons licence.

Groundcovers are any massed plants that do not limit either view or movement (Austin and Law, 1975). Just like paving, low, massed plants may also define the visual extent of an exterior space. The more unified the plants used on the floor, the more visually unified the space will be. Designers commonly unify the ground plane to unify a space. In Japanese gardens the floor of the space is often a bed of moss. This fine-textured, uniform groundcover creates a calming background to the rest of the scene and balances diverse objects in the space to create a sense of unity (Figure 5.37). Research has shown that people most prefer scenes that have a smooth ground texture with dense stands of trees and the suggestion of a path (R. Kaplan, 2007). This supports the well-known savannah theory, which posits that we most prefer landscapes that are similar to the savannah in which we evolved (Heerwagen and Orians, 1993).

The vertical plane: Screen, barrier and scrim

Vertical elements in the landscape are most noticed, and therefore affect us most, simply because they occupy our field of vision. A single vertical element like an upright plant is like an exclamation mark on the landscape. When it contrasts with its background, it becomes a focal point in the landscape.

In both exterior and interior spaces, the vertical elements influence privacy and filter or block wind, sun and views. Vertical walls are the strongest way to define enclosed space. In exterior spaces, when plants are the chosen vertical elements, they can be backgrounds to objects in the space and provide both enclosure and uniformity (Simonds, 1983). When the walls, ceiling and floor of the space are composed of plants that are uniform or very similar in form, colour and texture this will produce a visually unified space.

Walls and other vertical elements in the landscape, when composed of plants, may be solid or present some degree of openness or visual penetrability. Tall walls that people cannot easily move through or see through are referred to as screens (Figure 5.38), and lower solid plant walls that we can see over but not move through are referred to as barriers (Figure 5.39) (Austin and Law, 1975).

The final, and most interesting, category of vertical elements in the landscape is the scrim (Figure 5.40). A scrim is a tall barrier that we may or may not be able to move through but that we can see through only partially. The term *scrim* is derived from the theatre, where scrims refer to open-weave screens that provide layers of space in a set design. Scrims are opaque, but when they are backlit they reveal the space behind. In architecture, the term scrim is used to describe a visually penetrable screen attached to a building. Such scrims create filtered views and ambiguous spaces that are zones of transition between interior and exterior spaces (Porter, 2004), much like the transition shown in Figure 5.23.

Visual penetrability is a measure of how much sight is available through the vertical elements (Ewing and Handy, 2009) and it seems to be a preferred condition of the landscape. Researchers have found that people prefer forest stands with low tree density and high visual penetrability

▶ Figure 5.38

The screen: The tall, clipped hedges that line the entry to Ginkaku-ji temple in Kyoto are an example of planted screens that block visual and physical access. Source: Jon | Flickr. Used under the Creative Commons licence.

CHAPTER 5 **Space and place**

◀ Figure 5.39

The barrier: The low evergreen azaleas in the foreground surround the pond at Ginkaku-ji, forming a barrier that people can see over but that blocks their movement.
Source: np&djjewell | Flickr. Used under the Creative Commons licence.

◀ Figure 5.40

The scrim: The branches of these Japanese black pine (*Pinus thunbergii*) allow a filtered view that is more open than that permitted by a screen and less open than the view that one would have over a barrier. Such scrims add a sense of mystery to a garden and when layered one behind another create a great sense of depth in the scene.
Source: Fredrik Rubensson | Flickr. Used under the Creative Commons licence.

(Daniel and Boster, 1976). A study of urban park users in Norway found that the most-preferred parks had a moderate tree density, while those with either higher or lower tree density were not as well liked (Bjerke, Østdahl, Thrane and Strumse, 2006). Plant scrims are visually penetrable elements that filter rather than block a view.

Scrims have many uses in the design of experiential space. Even though they do not block views, they can be used to redirect the view away from an objectionable view to a desired view without blocking light entering the space. In small spaces where a screen wall would create a sense of entrapment or claustrophobia, scrims offer an open frame that admits breezes, light and view, making a smaller space feel more open while still creating positive space. When layered one behind another, scrims give a false sense of depth and the distance between the scrims will seem greater. Depending on the plant material used, its maturity and maintenance, the visual penetrability of the scrim can vary greatly.

As discussed above, positive and negative spaces exist along a continuum of spatial enclosure. The different vertical elements of screen, barrier and scrim allow the designer to achieve any degree of opacity in the vertical enclosing elements, thereby allowing an infinite variation in the enclosure of exterior space. The obscured view, however achieved, is used to create physical extent to increase the sense of distance and to add mystery to the landscape.

Figure 5.41 shows the plan of Bryant Park in New York City, by Hanna Olin. A wide bosque of trees frames the central open lawn, providing a thick

▼ Figure 5.41

Bryant Park in New York City, by Hanna Olin.
Source: ©OLIN.

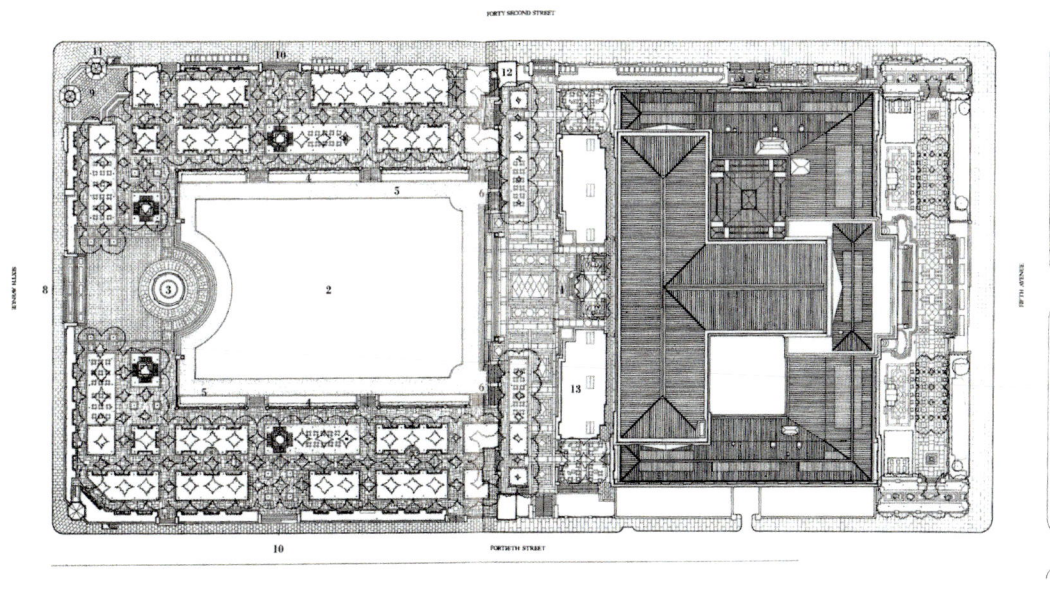

CHAPTER 5 Space and place

▲ Figure 5.42

The bosque at Bryant Park contains an abundance of views, degrees of enclosure and uses within a single program element.
Source: Photo by Patrick Mooney.

edge to the park, creating a strong sense of enclosure and separation from the surrounding streets while permitting views into and from the park.

The area under the canopy of the trees is a scrim is that people can inhabit, a separate, more human-scale space that provides that most ideal urban sitting space—under a tree canopy and overlooking the major circulation. Here is an open yet shaded place of prospect refuge. Beneath the canopy of the London plane trees (*Platanus* x *acerifolia*), park users find a secluded space for resting, reading, eating, socialising and people-watching, that also creates the central open space of the park.

Case study: Mountsier Estate

Landscape designer: Richard Hartlage, Land Morphology, Seattle, Washington.

Plants, landform and built elements can be used alone or in combination to create positive spaces. At the Mountsier Estate in New Jersey, Seattle designer Richard Hartlage combined all these elements to create a memorable positive space.

202   CHAPTER 5 Space and place

▲ Figure 5.43

The edge of an outdoor room at Mountsier Estate is a visually strong and unified composition of landform and ornamental grasses.
Source: Image courtesy of Richard Hartlage, Land Morphology Ltd.

▲ Figure 5.44

The landform of the berm and the concrete walls define the space. The floor is a simple green lawn. This, together with a variety of variegated Harkone grasses (*Hakonechloa macra*) sweeping up the berm, visually unifies the space through the use of texture and colour. The clipped columns of dark green European hornbeam (*Carpinus betulus*) are focal points in the landscape that draw the users' attention and strengthen the imageability or retained metal image of the space.
Source: Image courtesy of Richard Hartlage, Land Morphology Ltd.

Conceiving space in planting design

The preceding discussion makes clear the importance of enclosure to the experience of landscape and the role of views, transitions and landmarks within that framework. Rather than simply beginning to map the subdivision of the space and then create those spaces with plants, the planting designer should develop conceptual spatial solutions, evaluate alternatives and only once a desired concept has been achieved proceed to produce a preliminary and final planting plan. In doing so, it is essential that the planting designer always remember that the purpose of planting design is to support the total program. It must recognise and facilitate the functions and desired experience of all parts of the design.

In the example shown below, the existing hard landscape had clearly defined outdoor rooms. Nevertheless, the opportunity existed to use planting design to change or strengthen the existing spatial structure and views. Figures 5.45–5.49 illustrate a process of conceiving planting design spatially using canopy, groundcover, screen, barrier and scrim to define spaces and then refining that into a planting plan that may be implemented. As a first step in this process, the spatial intent is conceived and diagrammed (Figure 5.45).

Next, the spatial enclosure of all sub-spaces, and by inference the available views, are diagrammed using canopy, screen, barrier and scrim (Figure 5.46).

Next, the plants that will be used to create the spatial concept and landscape character are selected and arranged in a preliminary planting palette. In selecting the plant palette, the colour scheme, level of maintenance required and sequence of bloom must also be considered. Figure 5.47 shows the selected plant palette for each space and transition.

In this process, plants are used to define human-scale spaces, control views and create a predetermined sequential experience along a prescribed path. The process of planting design illustrated above could be achieved using the following steps:

- Establish the program and spatial structure.
- Establish a conceptual structure that supports the functional program and provides a sequence of experience.
- Define the intended character of each sub-area.
- Develop appropriate plant associations for each sub-area and the transitions between them.
- Refine the selected plant associations creating a visible order using form, colour, texture, focal points, transitions and patterns.
- Revise for a balance of unity and diversity with a focus on engaging the user and creating the desired experience.

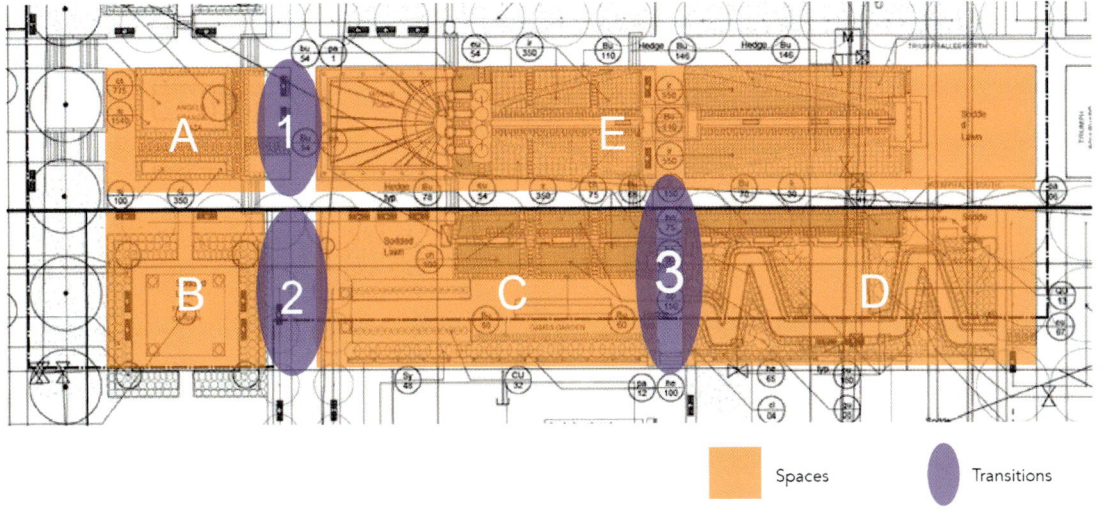

▲ Figure 5.45

Step 1: The intended subdivision of the larger space into sub-areas and the necessary transition spaces are diagrammed.
Source: Image courtesy of Yiwen Ruan.

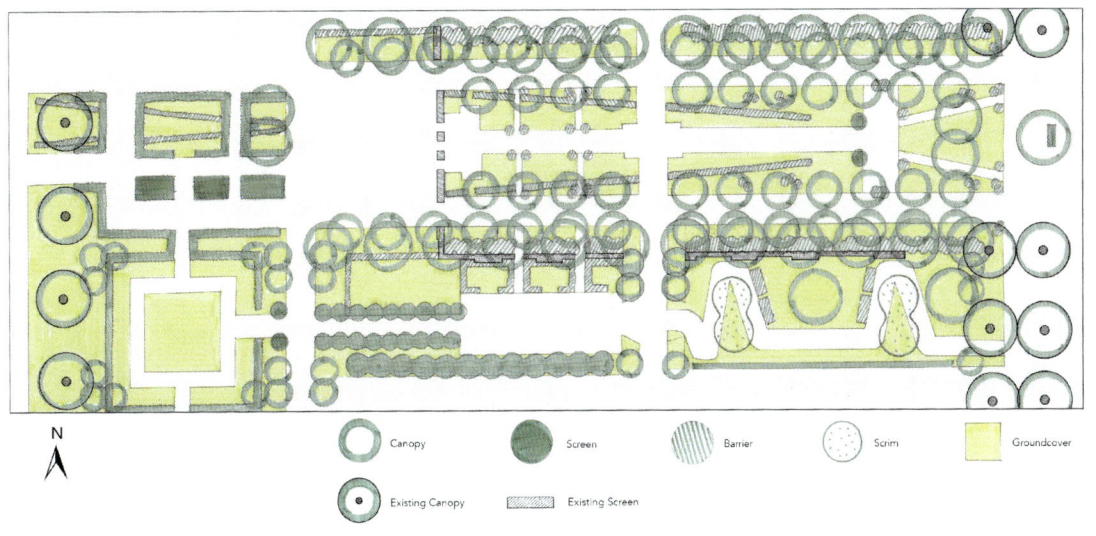

▲ Figure 5.46

Step 2: Canopy, barrier, screen and scrim are used to conceptually define the spaces shown. Where large shrubs or trees are intended to provide canopy or screen, the individual plants are shown in the diagram. Note that rows of tree shown as canopy will also act as scrims that partially block views from the space.
Source: Image courtesy of Yiwen Ruan.

▲ Figure 5.47

Step 3: The plant palette for each sub-area and transition is selected.
Source: Image courtesy of Yiwen Ruan.

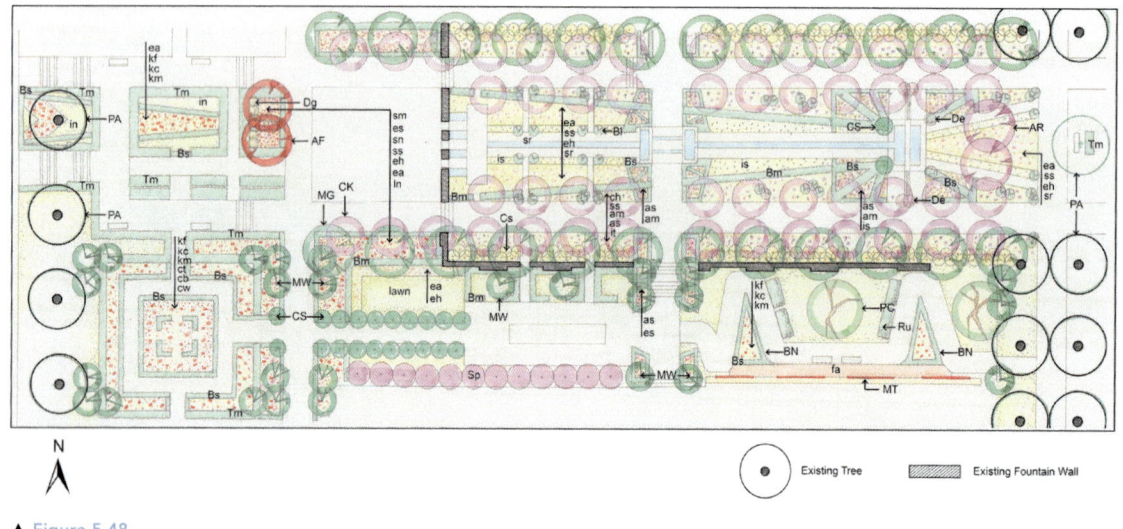

▲ Figure 5.48

Step 4: The planting plan is completed. It shows the cultivar or species of each plant, its location and its size after a set period of time.
Source: Image courtesy of Yiwen Ruan.

Plant List

Quantity	Code	Botanical Name	Common Name	Size	Comments
Trees					
2	AF	Albizia julibrissin 'Fan Silk'	Flame Silk Tree	H: 3m	B&B
2	AR	Albizia julibrissin f. rosea	Pink Silk Tree	H: 3m	B&B
4	BN	Betula nigra	River Birch	H: 6m	B&B
50	CK	Cornus kousa	Kousa Dogwood	4cm cal, H: 7m	B&B
22	CS	Cupressus sempervirens	Italian Cypress	H: 3m	B&B
24	MG	Magnolia grandiflora	Southern Magnolia	H: 15m	B&B
4	MT	Malus transitoria 'Schmidtcutleaf'	Golden Raindrops Crabapple	H: 7m	Espalier Tree
27	MW	Magnolia wilsonii	Wilson's Magnolia	H: 6m	B&B
2	PA	Platanus x acerifolia 'Bloodgood'	Bloodgood London Planetre	10cm cal, H: 20m	B&B
2	PC	Pyrus communis	Pear	H: 7m	B&B
Shrubs					
44	Bl	Blechnum spicant	Deer Fern	10cm pot, H: 1.2m	
200	Bm	Buxus microphylla	Japanese Box	H: 1m	
1200	Bs	Buxus sempervirens 'Suffruticosa'	English Boxwood	H: 30cm	
160	Cs	Cornus sanguinea 'Midwinter fire'	Midwinter Fire Dogwood	H: 1.5m, Spread: 80cm	
6	De	Deutzia elegantissima 'Rosealind'	Rosealind Deutzia	H: 1.5m	
4	Dg	Deutzia gracilis	Slender Deutzia	H: 1.5m	
4	Ru	Ribes uva-crispa 'Invicta'	Invicta Gooseberry	H: 1.5m, Spread: 1.5m	
12	Sp	Syringa pubescens ssp. patula 'Miss Kim'	Miss Kim lilac	H: 2m	B&B
1000	Tm	Taxus x media 'Hicksii'	Hicks Yew	H: 2m	B&B
Groundcovers / Vines / Perennials / Grasses					
250	am	Allium 'Millenium'	Ornamental Onion	H: 40cm	
250	as	Allium schoenoprasum	Chives	H: 30cm	
1500	cb	Crocosmia 'Bright Eyes'	Bright Eyes Montbretia	H: 50cm, Spread: 30cm	
80	ch	Chionodoxa 'Pink Giant'	Glory-of-the-Snow	H: 15cm	
1500	ct	Crocosmia 'Twilight Fairy Crimson'	Twilight Fairy Crimson Montbretia	12cm pot, H: 1m	
1500	cw	Crocosmia 'Walberton Yellow'	Walberton Yellow Montbretia	H: 50cm, Spread: 30cm	
500	ea	Echinacea 'Aloha'	Aloha Coneflower	H: 30cm	
500	eh	Echinacea 'Hope'	Hope Coneflower	H: 50cm	
200	es	Echinacea 'Sundown'	Sundown Coneflower	H: 50cm	
10	fa	Fragaria x ananassa 'Totem'	Strawberry		
150	is	Iris sibirica 'Caesar's Brother'	Siberian Iris	#1 pot, H: 40cm	
150	it	Iris tenax	Toughleaf Iris	#1 pot	
1000	kc	Kniphofia 'Creamsicle'	Creamsicle Red Hot Poker	H: 35cm	
1000	kf	Kniphofia 'Fire Glow'	Fire Glow Red Hot Poker	H: 50cm	
1000	km	Kniphofia 'Mango Popsicle'	Mango Popside Red Hot Poker	H: 75cm	
900	ln	Lysimachia nummularia aure	Creeping Jenny	H: 5cm	
500	sm	Sidalcea malviflora	False Mallow	H: 70cm	
500	sn	Salvia nemorosa 'Pink Friesland'	Pink Friesland Meadow Sage	H: 75cm	
500	ss	Salvia x sylvestris 'Pink Delight'	Pink Delight Sage	H: 60cm	
500	sr	Sidalcea 'Rosaly'	Rosaly Prairie Mallow	H: 100cm	

▲ Figure 5.49

Step 5: The plant list, showing quantities, common and botanical names, sizes and other requirements, is necessary for a nursery or contractor to bid on supplying the plants and installing the landscape. Source: Image courtesy of Yiwen Ruan.

Chapter 5 principles

- The greater or more surprising a change in the landscape, the more strongly it will be felt and remembered.
- Maintaining continuity of spatial type and aesthetics in the landscape supports expectations and fosters engagement.
- Incongruous or too-frequent change in a landscape can cause people to disengage from that landscape.
- When designing a set of linked spaces, the designer must resolve how each space will relate to the spaces to which it is connected.

- Linear spaces that have a ratio of walls to floor of between 1:1 and 1:2.5 are human-scale spaces that make people comfortable.
- In open spaces, the ratio of walls to floor should fall between 1:2 and 1:3 in order for people to feel comfortable.
- When the built elements of the spaces fail to provide the size and proportion of the desired scale, plantings can be used to reduce the dimensions and provide the desired scale and feeling of enclosure.
- Landscape architecture is the act of shaping undifferentiated, haphazardly enclosed mixtures of positive and negative space into well-considered series of spaces, functions and experiences.
- By artfully managing enclosure, viewer position and view sequence, environments can be designed to create an intended experience for the people moving through them.
- The character of the landscape is contained in the view.
- When places, paths and views are conceived in concert, each place in the spatial sequence may have a degree of enclosure, character and view that is distinct from others in the sequence and yet the sub-areas together create a harmony of experience.
- In defining spaces and views for the experience of the user, the ability of plants to define space while at the same time allowing all degrees of visual penetrability is perhaps the most important and subtle element available to the planting designer.
- The farther apart two spaces are on the continuum of positive and negative space, the more dramatic will be the experience of moving between them.

Glossary

Barriers: In planting design, solid plant walls that we can see over but not move through are referred to as barriers.

Borrowed view: The practice in traditional Japanese garden design of incorporating views from outside the garden so that the garden flows without visible boundary into the larger landscape.

Bosque: A grove of trees planted in intersecting rows at right angles with even spacing. Used in this way, the trees of the bosque define the horizontal plane and the vertical extent of the space (Arnold, 1980).

Canopy: The overhead plane, created by plants, that people can see and walk beneath.

Corridor: A linear patch such as a long perennial border or a high-voltage transmission corridor.

Cubist space: Space that is not strongly enclosed and in which the objects in the space, including plants, establish the spatial experience.

Defensible spaces: Areas in which the site planning and design promote use and surveillance by local people, which in turn inhibits inhibit criminal activity.

Filtered view: A view that is partially blocked.

Form: The shape or configuration of built or natural objects in the environment. Forms interact with space to create enclosure and spatial type, and consistency of form supports unity in design.

Framed view: A view which is enclosed by a vertical element on both sides as well as on the ground plane and overhead plane. Its purpose is to focus the viewers' attention on a specific view.

Genius loci: In contemporary environmental design, *genius loci* refers to the "spirit of place", meaning the distinctive atmosphere and sense of place of a particular site or location.

Groundcovers: Any massed plants that do not limit either view or movement.

Hierarchy: A structured way of organizing the elements of a design so that it is easily perceived. In the landscape, hierarchy creates levels of importance, such as major and minor paths, focal points and spaces, or allows selected colors and forms to dominate the view. Its use allows people to understand so that they will explore and experience the landscape.

Human-scale space: Space in which the size of the space and its proportions make people feel comfortable.

Intimate-scale space: Smaller than a human-scale space. Can support calming, meditative activities and prospect refuge or act as a spatial contrast with a larger human-scale space.

Landmark: An element in the landscape that attracts attention because it contrasts aesthetically with its surroundings. Landmarks serve as reference points in the landscape and help people to form cognitive maps.

Landscape character: The recognisable pattern of elements such as vegetation type(s), enclosure, materials and built form that distinguish one landscape from another (Tudor and England, 2014).

Matrix: The matrix corresponds to what Norberg-Schulz termed the *area* or *domain*. It is the generally unstructured and mostly negative spaces in which the places and paths are located (Thwaites and Simkins, 2007).

Monumental scale: When the size of a space exceeds the dimensions of the human scale it becomes supra-human or monumental in scale. Such spaces are used by large groups and, whether built or natural, can inspire a sense of awe in the landscape.

Negative space: This is less enclosed and has a less structured or weaker sense of enclosure than positive space.

Patch: A relatively homogeneous area of land that is differentiated from its surroundings, usually by its vegetative cover.

Paths: The routes through adjoining spaces. Because they control the position of the person in the landscape, they have a major influence on the landscape experience.

Places: Spaces to which some special value or meaning has been attached. This can be a collective social meaning derived from community use over extended periods of time, or it can be an individual value derived from the intensity of use or strength of character and aesthetic distinction of the space.

Positive space: Strongly enclosed space. This enclosure makes it more easily visualised and remembered.

Scale: The size of the space in relation to the human body.

Screen: In planting design, a screen is a tall wall that people cannot easily move through or see through.

Scrim: In planting design, a scrim is a tall barrier that we may or may not be able to move through but that we can see through only partially.

Sequential view: The sequential view concept argues that landscapes are experienced as a sequence of existing and emerging views and that environments should be designed for the experience of the person moving through them by artfully managing enclosure, viewer position and view sequence (Cullen, 1961).

Shakkei: See *Borrowed view*.

Subdivided view: Most often a panoramic view that is divided into segments by enframement.

Supra-human scale: See *Monumental scale*.

Transitions: Places where aesthetics, function and/or character change. They are an inherent property of sequential spaces.

Visual penetrability: A measure of how much sight is available through the vertical elements.

References

ACLA a, Andrea Cochran Landscape Architecture. (n.d.). Accessed August 9, 2018 at http://acochran.com.
ACLA b, Stone Edge Farms. (2009). *American Society of Landscape Architects Award Submission*. Unpublished document, Andrea Cochran Landscape Architecture.
Appleyard, D. (1980). Livable streets: Protected neighborhoods? *The ANNALS of the American Academy of Political and Social Science*, 451(1), 106–117.
Arnold, H.F. (1980). *Trees in urban design*. New York: Van Nostrand Reinhold.
Austin, R., & Law, D. (1975). *The elements of planting design*. Interiors Exteriors.

Axelsson-Lindgren, C., & Sorte, G. (1987). Public response to differences between visually distinguishable forest stands in a recreation area. *Landscape and Urban Planning*, 14, 211–217.

Bjerke, T., Østdahl, T., Thrane, C., & Strumse, E. (2006). Vegetation density of urban parks and perceived appropriateness for recreation. *Urban Forestry & Urban Greening*, 5(1), 35–44.

Booth, N. (2011). *Foundations of landscape architecture: Integrating form and space using the language of site design*. Hoboken, NJ: John Wiley & Sons.

Buhyoff, G.J., Gauthier, L.J., & Wellman, J.D. (1984). Predicting scenic quality for urban forests using vegetation measurements. *Forest Science*, 30(1), 71–82.

Condon, P.M. (1988). Cubist space, volumetric space, and landscape architecture. *Landscape Journal*, 7(1), 1–14.

Cullen, G. (1961). *The concise townscape*. London: Architectural Press.

The Cultural Landscape Foundation. (n.d.). *Green Acre Park, New York, NY*. Accessed July 17, 2015 at https://tclf.org/landscapes/greenacre-park.

Daniel, T.C., & Boster, R.S. (1976). Measuring landscape esthetics: The scenic beauty estimation method. *USDA Forest Service Research Paper* (Vol. RM 167).

Design Workshop Inc. (n.d.). Accessed March 17, 2018 at www.designworkshop.com.

Dramstad, W., Olson, J.D., & Forman, R.T. (1996). *Landscape ecology principles in landscape architecture and land-use planning*. Cambridge, MA: Harvard University Graduate School of Design.

Ewing, R., & Handy, S. (2009). Measuring the unmeasurable: Urban design qualities related to walkability. *Journal of Urban Design*, 14(1), 65–84.

Gehl, J. (2011). *Life between buildings: Using public space*. Washington, DC: Island Press.

Green, J. (2011). *Andrea Cochran: "It's hard to sell nothing"*. The dirt: Uniting the built & natural environments. American Society of Landscape Architects. Accessed August 9, 2018 at https://dirt.asla.org/2011/04/27/andrea-cochran-its-hard-to-sell-nothing/.

Grese, R.E. (1992). *Jens Jensen: Maker of natural parks and gardens*. Baltimore, MD: Johns Hopkins University Press.

Hall, E.T. (1966). *The hidden dimensions*. New York: Doubleday.

Harvard GSD. (n.d.). *Alumni Q+A: Andrea (Andie) Cochran MLA '79*. Harvard Graduate School of Design. Accessed August 9, 2018 at www.groundedvisionaries.org/gsd_news/alumni-qa-andrea-andie-cochran-mla79/.

Heerwagen, J.H., & Orians, G.H. (1993). Humans, habitats, and aesthetics. In S.R. Kellert & E.O. Wilson (Eds.), *The biophilia hypothesis* (pp. 138–172). Washington, DC: Island Press.

Jacob, A. (1993). *Great streets*. Cambridge, MA: Massachusetts Institute of Technology.

Kaplan, R., Kaplan, S., and Ryan, R. (1998). *With people in mind: Design and management of everyday nature*. Washington, DC: Island Press.

Kaplan, S. (1988). Perception and landscape: Conceptions and misconceptions. *Environmental Aesthetics: Theory, Research, and Application*, 45–55.

Kuck, L.E. (1989). *The world of the Japanese garden: From Chinese origins to modern landscape art*. New York: Weatherhill.

LA+D Profile. (n.d.). *Andrea Cochran. Landscape Architects and Designers Profiles*. SUNY College of Environmental Design and Forestry. Accessed August 9, 2018 at http://ladprofile.weebly.com/andrea-cochran.html.

Lee, L. (2015). Andrea Cochran's bold landscape designs are natural wonders. Dwell. Accessed August 9, 2018 at www.dwell.com/article/andrea-cochrans-bold-landscape-designs-are-natural-wonders-14f94579.

Leonard, M. (1969). Humanizing space. *Progressive Architecture* (50), 128–133.

Lynch, K. (1960). *The image of the city*. Cambridge, MA: MIT Press.

Martino, S. *Weeds and Walls*. Accessed July 1, 2015 at http://stevemartino.blogspot.ca.

Myers, M. (2009). *Andrea Cochran: Landscapes*. New York: Princeton Architectural Press.

Norberg-Schulz, C. (1980). *Genius loci: Towards a phenomenology of architecture*. New York: Rizzoli.

Norberg-Schulz, C. (1988). *Architecture, meaning and place: Selected essays*. New York: Electra/Rizzoli.

Olin, L. (1988). Form, meaning, and expression in landscape architecture. *Landscape Journal*, 7(2), 149–168.

Olin L. (2013). Quoted by Adele Chatfield-Taylor in *The cultural landscape foundation pioneers of American landscape design: Laurie Olin reflections*. Accessed June 15, 2016 at http://tclf.org/sites/default/files/atoms/files/Olin_Reflections.pdf.

Polat, A.T., & Akay, A. (2015). Relationships between the visual preferences of urban recreation area users and various landscape design elements. *Urban Forestry & Urban Greening*, 14(3), 573–582.

Porter, T. (2004). *Archispeak: An illustrated guide to architectural terms*. London: Routledge.

Reid, G. (2016). *Designer profile: Andrea Cochran*. The Plant Hunter. Accessed August 9, 2018 at https://theplanthunter.com.au/artdesign/designer-profile-andrea-cochran/.

Robinette, G. (1972). *Plants, people, and environmental quality: A study of plants and their environmental functions*. Washington, DC: US Department of the Interior, National Park Service.

Simonds, J.O. (1983). *Landscape architecture: A manual of site planning and design* (2nd ed.). New York: McGraw-Hill.

Thwaites, K., & Simkins, I.M. (2007). *Experiential landscape: An approach to people, place and space*. London: Routledge.

Tuan, Y.F. (1979). *Space and place: Humanistic perspective* (pp. 387–427). Dordrecht, The Netherlands: Springer.

Tudor, C., & England, N. (2014). An approach to landscape character assessment. Natural England. Accessed June 16, 2016 at www.gov.uk/government/uploads/system/uploads/attachment_data/file/396192/landscape-character-assessment.pdf.

Tverksy, B. (2000). Levels and structure of spatial knowledge. In R. Kitchin & S. Freundschuh (Eds.), *Cognitive mapping: Past, present, and future* (Vol. 4) (pp. 24–43). London: Routledge.

Whyte, W.H. (1980). *The social life of small urban spaces*. Washington, DC: Conservation Foundation.

Wolf, K. (2003). Freeway roadside management: The urban forest beyond the white line. *Journal of Arboriculture*, (29), 127–136.

Zuckerman, L. (2015). Enchanting exteriors. Big Sky Journal. Accessed March 17, 2017 at http://bigskyjournal.com/enchanting-exteriors/.

Chapter 6

The elements of design

Human nature

Previous chapters described *homo sapiens* as a knowledge-seeking species that is adept at using environmental information to navigate three-dimensional space (Bell, 2012). But humans are also stimulus seekers who find pleasure in exploring the landscape. Although space and spatial sequence are the primary determinants of landscape experience (S. Kaplan, 1988), the aesthetic qualities of the landscape are immensely important in enabling people to organise the information they see and in providing the stimulus and restoration that they seek.

The elements of design

In this chapter, I employ the long-standing tradition of applying art and perceptual theory to planting design (Jekyll, 1908; Hobhouse, 1985; Robinson, 1940; Bell, 2004). Line, form, mass, texture and colour comprise the elements of design,[1] and designers need to understand how these visual building blocks interact in the viewer's perception. Additionally, planting designers need to be able to envision the design elements of plants (Robinson, 2004) at all stages of growth and with all seasonal effects[2]. To begin, it is necessary to establish a common vocabulary.

Line

A line is the continuous element linking points in space. The edge of a tree or shrub, when it contrasts with its background, becomes the line that describes the shape of the plant. Different kinds of lines suggest different moods and movements (Robinson, 1940; Arnheim, 1974; Robinson, 2004).

Form

The form of any object, including a plant, is its three-dimensional shape. Circles and squares are flat two-dimensional shapes that, when given

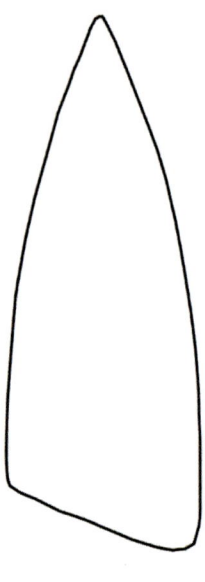 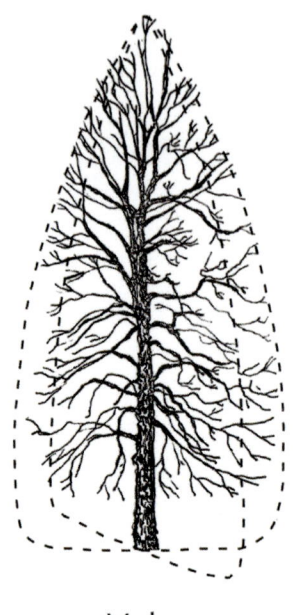 

Form Volume Mass

▲ Figure 6.0

The line of the silhouette produces the shape of the plant. When that shape is filled by the branches of the plant, its form and volume are seen, but it is the way that the volume is filled; the colour and density of the branches and foliage that gives the tree its visual mass or weight.
Source: Image courtesy of Yiwen Ruan.

three-dimensional form, become spheres and cubes. When we speak of the form of a plant, we are talking about the characteristic three-dimensional shape of a mature open-grown example of that plant (Hightshoe, 1987). Different authors describe the forms of plants differently, and the form of many plants changes considerably as they mature. It is essential that the planting designer be familiar with the forms of the plants they wish to use and able to visualise how these forms might be harmoniously combined.

Mass

Mass should be understood as filled form. When the shape of a plant is expressed in three dimensions by its branches, the tree form has a volume. But it is the density of the way in which the volume of the tree is filled with foliage that gives the tree its visual mass. The greater the visual mass of an object, the greater its visual weight in a composition (Figure 6.0).

Texture

Plant texture is the visual impression of smoothness or roughness of the surface of the plant. It is created by shadows cast by the foliage of the plant. Texture is primarily a function of leaf size, with larger leaves producing a coarse texture and smaller leaves a more fine-textured surface, but visual texture is also a function of the arrangement and density of the leaves on the plant.

▶ Figure 6.1

This illustrates that shadows caused by the density and arrangement of the branches and leaves create the visual texture of the plant. The unclipped cedar (*Thuja occidentalis*) on the left has a coarser texture than the same plant on the right, after trimming. Shearing results in a surface that has smaller shadows, producing a finer visual texture, although the size and shape of the leaves is unchanged.
Source: Photos by Patrick Mooney.

Leaves that are further apart cast bigger shadows, resulting in a coarser texture than if the same leaves were more closely spaced on the plant. Clipping smooths the surface of the plant by removing shadows between the branches of the plant, making the plant appear more fine-textured (Figure 6.1).

Unity, complexity and preference

The best landscape designers begin with the intention of creating a particular atmosphere or experience. Because unity and variety are the basis for all design principles (Robinson, 2004), that feeling or impression requires that a person's visual interest be aroused within a unified composition (Robinson, 1940). This can be done in countless ways. For example, repetition increases the perception of unity, as does creating a hierarchical order by subordinating some elements of the design so that others may be more prominent (Hawthorne, 2009). Regardless of how the sense of variety within unity is created, its presence makes people more likely to engage with the landscape.

Gestalt theory

In the early 1920s, a group of German psychologists developed a set of principles that we now call Gestalt theory. *Gestalt* means "unified whole", and Gestalt theory deals with the ways in which humans organise their perceptions in a visually haphazard world. The theory is based on the premise that since all perception manifests the human need to understand, people prefer orderly and simple structures and seek order in their surroundings by perceiving a structured whole from individual parts. Subsequent research led to the development of a number of principles that describe how people perceive the world. These principles can be applied to make visual compositions that are easily perceived and that will be preferred.

While Gestalt theory has been absorbed into various schools of psychology, it has had enormous influence on the study of perception. Many commonly accepted principles of artistic composition are derived from, or are supported by, the research and writings of the Gestalt psychologists.

Simplicity and unity in planting design

Perception is the act of organising what is seen so that it may be understood. Gestalt theory posits that in the act of perception, people consolidate what they see into the simplest structure that will contain the necessary information. Finding this simple structure gives them a sense of knowing that brings pleasure. When confronted with a view containing multiple forms, textures, colours, patterns and focal points, people will attempt to compose it into a simple understandable structure. If this proves too difficult, they will quickly forget what they were unable to perceive (Mallet, 2011).

The purpose of a designed planting is not only aesthetic. It must also fulfill necessary programmatic functions like shaping space, hiding objectionable views and preventing soil erosion. Simple structures are unified hierarchical compositions in which every function and detail is assigned a place and a role and nothing extraneous is included. The plan for Bryant Park (see Figure 5.41 in Chapter 5) provides an excellent example of a complex program and detailed design set within a seemingly simple composition.

Texture and form

Consideration of textural unity is a primary way to achieve visually unified plantings, and repetition of a single plant is often used to create this unity. For example, the use of a single groundcover produces a visually unified ground plane and is common in the traditional Japanese garden (see Figures 5.17 and 5.37). Fine textures, like moss and raked gravel, have been shown to increase preference as they enhance legibility and coherence (S. Kaplan and R. Kaplan, 1982), and fine-textured green spaces tend to be calming and restorative (Figure 6.4).

Conversely, it is widely recognised that combining plants that have different aesthetic qualities can lead to visual disorder. The traditional prescription for this ailment has been a design directive not to use too many plants. Many modern designers follow this advice, using plants in a graphic manner, often deploying massed blocks of a single plant to unify colour, form and texture. However, unity does not necessarily require a restricted plant palette. The knowledgeable use of a range of different plants with similar textures and forms will produce a unified composition.

Failure to adequately consider plant form and texture as unifying elements is perhaps the most common error in planting design and results in landscapes that are visually chaotic. Such landscapes are not likely to be places where people spend time and so will not function as restorative landscapes. Conversely, artistic consideration of plant form and texture can be used to unify planting design, add variety and interest and connect the site to its context. Andrea Cochran's design of Alexander's Crown is a good demonstration of these concepts.

Alexander's Crown, Sonoma County, California: Andrea Cochran Landscape Architecture (ACLA)

ACLA design team: Andrea Cochran, Principal; Sarah Keizer, Senior Designer.
Architect: Howard Backen.

Alexander's Crown, a home and garden in the California vineyard of the same name, is the rural retreat of a family of vineyard and winery owners. In keeping with the owner's environmentally sustainable farming practices, the garden uses drought-tolerant plantings that support local biodiversity. Many of the garden rooms that comprise Alexander's Crown are places of prospect refuge from which vistas over the Alexander Valley connect the garden to its setting (Figure 6.2). (See Chapter 1 for a discussion of prospect refuge theory).

In response to the owner's desire for a Provençal-inspired garden, the landscape architects selected a variety of plants of Mediterranean origin that were suitable for the California climate. Near the house, fine-textured, grey-foliaged plants like lavender (*Lavendula* 'Grosso' and *L.* 'Hidcote Giant'), lavender cotton (*Santolina chamaecyparissus*), germander (*Teucrium*

▶ Figure 6.2

Little Ollie dwarf olive (*Olea europaea* 'Montra') (foreground to midground left) and Mediterranean spurge (*Euphorbia characias* subsp. *wulfenii*) (foreground left and midground centre) accentuate the contrast of the germander (*Teucrium fruticans* 'Compactum') (foreground centre and around the base of the olive tree (*Olea europaea*) in the centre midground). Form and texture are held constant by clipping the shrubs into rounded topiary, while the contrasting foliage colours of the *Euphorbia* and the form of the olive tree supply elements of contrast. Left unclipped, the *Euphorbia*'s soft mass moves in the wind and provides contrast to the dense, mounded shrubs. The rounded forms and subdued grey-greens of the shrubs echo the forms and colours of the trees on the distant valley walls, tying the garden to the native landscape.
Source: Photo courtesy of Marion Brenner.

▲ Figure 6.3

The multi-stemmed trunks of four Swan Hill fruitless olives (*Olea europaea* 'Swan Hill') express the principle of continuity, drawing the eye upward. They are focal points in the landscape by virtue of their form and they balance the mass of the dwarf olive hedge. This produces a visual balance that does not require the mind to edit what the eye sees. Source: Photo courtesy of Marion Brenner.

fruticans 'Compactum') and false dittany (*Ballota pseudodictamnus*) contrast with coarser-textured broadleaved evergreens like dwarf olive (*Olea europaea* 'Montra'), white oleander (*Nerium oleander*), laurel (*Laurus nobilis* 'Saratoga') and white rock rose (*Cistus* x *hybridus*). A number of native Californian plants, including the California lilac (*Ceanothus griseus* var. *horizontalis* 'Yankee Point'), Matilija poppy (*Romneya coulteri*), cow parsnip (*Heracleum lanatum*) and deer grass (*Muhlenbergia rigens*) add interest and connection to the regional landscape.

The flower colours are mostly the muted blue-purples of the Mediterranean subshrubs combined with the whites of climbing Iceberg rose, rock roses, Matilija poppy, cow parsnip and oleander. This allows much of the garden's aesthetic, like its French inspiration, to be determined by the form and foliage of the plants. The landscape architects at ACLA are acutely attuned to the differences between shades of green and use this awareness to bring both harmony and interest to this composition. In the Alexander's Crown garden, dark, glossy green and grey foliage are mixed with the blue-green leaves and chartreuse flowers of the Mediterranean spurge, which provide an eye-catching colour contrast. The grey-green germander and olive trees stand out from darker and brighter foliage and help the garden foreground to blend with the surroundings (Figure 6.3).

The Alexander's Crown garden is a series of restful garden rooms with vistas over the Alexander Valley. The unity of form and texture achieved by using fine-textured, rounded shrubs makes the exposed trunks of the trees sculptural focal points that lighten and balance the plant composition.

Grouping

Anything that helps the viewer to see the visual array as consisting of a few major elements aids in perception (S. Kaplan, 1975). For example, organising plants into distinct areas that have reoccurring colours and textures while limiting contrasting textures increases coherence and the sense of unity (Kuper, 2017) (Figure 6.7). Similarly, when objects are arranged in groups, the number of elements in the view is reduced and unity is supported. Plants may be grouped in three ways: By placing in them in close proximity to each other, in a similar fashion or by selecting plants that are visually similar.

Grouping by proximity

Determining the distance between repeated elements like columns, windows and street trees establishes recognisable groups of these elements and sets up visual rhythms and patterns that establish visual unity. Forming groupings based on proximity requires the designer to judge the distance at which elements cease to belong to the group and become isolated or part of another group. In creating multiple plant groupings, the objective should be to maintain a visual hierarchy between the groups, with some groupings being more prominent than others. This can be accomplished by placing some groups of plants in positions where they are seen more often, are in the centre of the view, or by simply making the plant group larger.

Plants that are not visually similar will form a perceptual group when placed in proximity to each other. If the plant combination is repeated throughout the design, the repetition of the various colours, forms and textures creates a recognisable pattern. Even dissimilar objects will form a group when placed together. The rock and tree grouping at the Dr Sun-Yat Sen classical Chinese garden in Vancouver (Figure 6.29) is an illustration of the fact that objects of very different size, materiality and shape are seen as a group when placed in proximity.

Visually similar groups

Things that have similar visual characteristics are also seen as belonging together, or forming a group, even when they are dispersed within the

◀ Figure 6.4

This small square in the Tuileries in Paris is defined by its plant groupings. The central linden trees (*Tilia cordata*) and the *Taxus* hedge form groups because of their visual similarity and similarity of placement. The lawn unifies the ground plane. The visual array is a simple structure consisting of a few major elements.
Source: Photo by Patrick Mooney.

overall structure (Arnheim, 1974). For example, in Figure 6.24, the triangular arrangement of the large shrubs forms a group within the overall plant grouping because of their visual similarity. Forming the edges of a space with similar plants will unify that edge and increase the unity of the overall composition, allowing more diversity elsewhere (Figures 6.25 and 6.26). Merely making all the trees in a composition the same species can supply enough unity that the rest of the planting can be more varied (Mallet, 2011).

When a planting incorporates a variety of trees, it is important that the trees form visually similar groups. The selected trees should have similar forms and textures and harmonious summer and autumn foliage colours. Interest can be added to this unified composition by inserting a few trees of contrasting character in key positions.

Grouping by placement

In a symmetrical planting, the plants that balance each other are examples of objects that form perceptual groups because of similarity of placement. For example, the two potted shrubs on either side of the front door in Figure 6.8 form a perceptual group because of their visual similarity but also because of their similarity of placement. An allée of trees or the shrubs of a hedge make a group because of their similarity of placement and because they are visually similar. Creating plant groupings by using more than one grouping technique reinforces the unity of the group (Figure 6.4).

Figure–ground

When an object is easily distinguished from its background, confusion is removed and preference increases (Arnheim, 1974). In most landscape views, some objects stand out from the backgrounds and some become

▲ Figure 6.5

Texture, grey foliage and white flowers are the unifying elements in this scene. The foliage colour gradates from the grey foliage of the snow-in-summer in the foreground to the grey-green lamb's ears behind and then to the green-foliaged rose in the centre background. Like colour, texture gradates from the fine-textured snow-in-summer, to the medium-textured rose, to the more coarsely-textured lamb's ears. The stone wall is harmonious with the grey-foliaged plants and provides a ground for the figure of the rose, making the rose the focal point of this unified landscape vignette. Gradation of foliage colour and texture maintain unity, and a few plants arranged in a figure–ground relationship produce a simple unified structure.
Source: Photo courtesy of Deborah Carl Landscape Design.

the background. This is referred to as the figure–ground relationship. The object is the figure, and the background against which the figure is seen is the ground. A strong figure–ground relationship creates focal points that can also serve as landmarks. Repetition of the figure–ground creates patterns that support both unity and preference. Our propensity to find figure–ground relationships explains why focal points and patterns capture our attention (Figures 6.5 and 6.6).

Harmony

Harmony is the viewer's perception that the various elements of a design combine to create a pleasing impression. It is achieved by combining and repeating both similar and contrasting elements.

To achieve a quality of unity, many planting designers follow the general rule that as long as one aesthetic element is maintained—for example, a consistent colour scheme—all other aspects of a design may be varied (Robinson, 1940). In reality, more than one design element in any design needs to be sustained if any real sense of unity is to prevail. In plantings where greater visual unity is desired, only a few plants or groups of plants should

◀ Figure 6.6

Silhouetted against the Paris sky, the form of this pine is isolated by contrast with its background. This figure–ground relationship creates a focal point in which the amplification of the visual characteristics of the pine activates the brain's pleasure centre.
Source: Photo by Patrick Mooney.

vary in form or texture, while the other aesthetic qualities of all other plants should be kept constant. As a general rule, the more elements of design that are fixed by the designer, the greater will be the sense of order and harmony.

The use of gradation in design

Recall from the previous chapter that transitions are used to modulate change in the landscape. Gradation is a way of transitioning from one condition to another by incremental steps. Such transitions help to make changes in the landscape less noticeable at a conscious level, and all design elements can be used to make gradated transitions in the landscape.

Where a calming, restorative experience is the objective of the design, the use of gradation contributes to these feelings of harmony and unity that support restoration.

Textural gradation is a simple and subtle way of making transition in the landscape and can also be used to add extent to a view. Because a plant in the distance will appear to be more fine-textured than the same plant seen nearby, landscape designers often employ coarse-textured plants in the foreground and more finely textured plants in the background to achieve a false sense of depth. This effect is felt even in a relatively narrow planting bed. Where the space in view is larger, allowing for a gradual change from bold textures to medium to finer textures, the perception of extent will be even greater.

Plant forms

A form that is described by a simple line will be more easily be read as a figure, and the simple symmetrical or asymmetrical shapes of trees are likely to be perceived as figures (Arnheim, 1974). Beginning with prehistoric cave drawings, artists have learned that amplifying the visual characteristics of an isolated element, even using deliberate exaggeration, while excluding extraneous detail activates the brain's limbic system or pleasure centre (Ramachandran, 2003) (Figure 6.6).

A plant can be a figure against a ground of sky, as in Figure 6.6, or it can become a figure when seen against contrasting plants or built structures. In most views, the background will occupy more of the picture plane than the figure. The background, whether complex or simple, must be uniform enough that it does not create its own figure–ground relationships, as this will destroy the viewers' ability to isolate the figure. This would suggest either the use of comparatively few plants in the ground or careful attention to form, texture, colour and repetition in order to establish a unity in the background.

Students, office workers, apartment dwellers and the elderly are just some of the people for whom the view from above provides their common interaction with nature (R. Kaplan, 1984). Such views can have powerful restorative effects, and planting designers need to consider both the ground plane view and the aerial view in their designs. In the view from above, the paving often becomes the figure while the various hues, textures and forms of the plants provide the ground. These views are figure–grounds that are easily perceived and that will be preferred.

Juxtaposition

The figure–ground relationship is always one of contrast, but it may also be a juxtaposition, that is, of pairing dissimilar elements so that their essential qualities are revealed more strongly. In Figure 6.29, the plant and rock grouping in the classical Chinese garden, the rock is masculine—solid, unchanging and settles into the earth—while the tree is feminine—translucent, dynamic and upward-reaching. By juxtaposing the two, the viewers' recognition of the qualities of each element is heightened. The rock and the tree provide context for each other.

Juxtaposition is one of the strongest triggers of attention available to the designer, as it causes the viewer to make a mental note of the relationship between the elements. The juxtaposition of plants that show transitory effects, such as movement or seasonal colour, with unchanging rocks is a particularly effective juxtaposition because the characteristics of the two elements differ so greatly and yet their combination is so natural. When the juxtaposed group is a figure–ground relationship, as in Figure 6.29, the composition absolutely demands our attention.

◀ Figure 6.7

In this thyme lawn, designed by landscape architect Karin England, the mother-of-thyme (*Thymus serpyllum*) becomes the figure against the ground of the other thymes when it is in bloom. When all the thymes have finished blooming, the central river of grey-green woolly thyme (*Thymus pseudolanuginosus*) becomes the figure against the uniform green ground of the other thymes. People are attracted to such patterns of repeated colours, forms and textures.
Source: Photo by Karin England.

Repetition and gradation

Because repeated forms, lines or textures in the landscape increase coherence (R. Kaplan et al., 1998), repetition of plants or plant groupings that have the same or similar aesthetic qualities helps landscapes to appear unified. A group of the same type of plants scattered across the view is a visual rhyme, a pattern of repeated colours, forms and textures that attracts attention and simplifies perception (Figures 6.7 and 6.40).

Consistent spacing of similar plants, especially plants having a vertical form, such as an allée of trees, introduces an even, measured rhythm and a predictable order that unifies the landscape. Gradual changes in placing of similar plants varies the rhythm and can provide change and even a false perspective in the landscape. If the repetition of plant groupings is interrupted or unpredictable, the effect is more spontaneous—like jazz rather than a march—and the experiential effect will seem more impromptu and stimulating. However, care must be taken that the unpredictable rhythms do not cause the overall structure to break down.

Symmetry and balance

Balancing visual mass

Balance is a goal of most artistic works (Robinson, 1940) and is produced when the visual weight of objects in the scene are in equilibrium (Arnheim,

▶ Figure 6.8

Symmetrical compositions are instantly recognisable as being balanced and are preferred. In this scene, both the architecture and landscape are symmetrically balanced. If we were to draw a vertical line through the centre of the image, each side of the composition would approximately repeat the other and the visual weight of objects on either side of that vertical line would be in equilibrium with each other. Symmetry is not only about order, repetition and balance. A symmetrical form or composition is perceived as being formed around a centre and conveys a particular sense of simplicity (Davies, 2014).
Source: Image courtesy of Yiwen Ruan.

1974). In traditional architecture and landscape architecture, symmetry is often used to organise and balance design. In a symmetrical landscape, each side of a plan or perspective view is a mirror image of the other. Symmetrical compositions are highly attractive to humans (Cárdenas and Harris, 2006) and are perceived as being balanced, stable and complete (Figure 6.8). Conversely, unbalanced compositions appear arbitrary, unfinished and unstable (Arnheim, 1974).

Asymmetrical balance

Visual compositions can also by balanced asymmetrically (Figure 6.9). Asymmetrical balance is not as immediately apparent as symmetrical balance, and asymmetrical compositions often have unresolved tensions and suggested movement that are more intriguing than the static balance found in symmetrical compositions.

Humans will seek to understand anything seems to be unusual or out of place and will find pleasure in making sense of an apparent incongruity (Davies, 2014). When presented with an asymmetrical composition, the onlooker will try to make sense of it. When the balance in the view is understood, it becomes a source of pleasure. Many people, especially artists and those with artistic tendencies, report a preference for asymmetrical compositions (Barron and Welsh, 1952; Eisenman and Coffee, 1964).

Neither symmetry nor asymmetry is to be preferred. Symmetrical compositions are simple, balanced and strong. They are associated with tradition and order. Asymmetrical compositions can be more complex, dynamic and interesting. While too much symmetrical balance can become boring, asymmetrical balance can dissolve into disorder (Mallet, 2011).

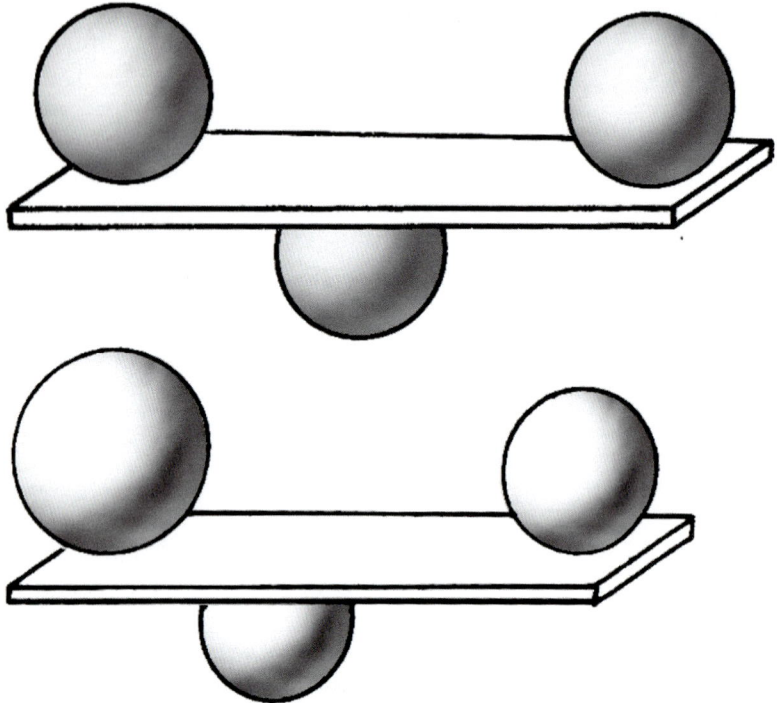

◀ Figure 6.9

Symmetrical and asymmetrical balance. On the left, symmetrical balance is achieved when objects of equal visual weight are placed equidistant from a central balancing point. On the right, asymmetrical balance is found by placing the larger visual weight closer to a balancing point that is not central.
Source: Image courtesy of Yiwen Ruan.

Balancing opposing forces in a visual composition

The size, form and density of an object give it its visual mass and weight. Its weight and placement in relation to other objects can give it a suggested movement. The greater the weight of an object, the greater will be the force of movement or of stability that it embodies. Just as visual weights need to be balanced, so too do visual tensions and suggested movements (Arnheim, 1974). Once we understand these forces, they may be resolved by balancing them or left unresolved to intentionally provide visual tension and suggested movement.

A few diagrams will suffice to illustrate the forces of suggested movement and their resolution. The circle and the square are balanced geometric shapes that do not suggest movement. The circle centred in the square is a perfectly balanced geometric composition (Figure 6.11). But if the circle is moved even slightly off centre it will suggest movement (Figures 6.10 and 6.12, after Arnheim, 1974).

In Figure 6.13, the two circles are individually out of balance, but because they are of equal weight and are equidistant from the centre of the square, they are seen as balanced around the centre of the square. If they are offset, as in Figure 6.14, the circles will be perceived as moving toward the left frame of the square.

The forces of suggested movement illustrated in Figures 6.10–6.14 appear in both two- and three-dimensional art and environments. These felt

▲ Figures 6.10, 6.11 and 6.12

In Figure 6.10, the circle will be seen as if drawn by an unseen force toward the centre of the square. Figure 6.11 will be seen as balanced and lacking movement because the circle centred in the square is a balanced, stable form. In Figure 6.12, the circle will be seen as having broken free of the pull to the centre and being drawn to the upper right boundary of the square.
Source: Images courtesy of Yiwen Ruan.

▶ Figures 6.13 and 6.14

In Figure 6.13, the two circles centred on the square are in balance, but in Figure 6.14 they suggest movement away from the centre.
Source: Images courtesy of Yiwen Ruan.

 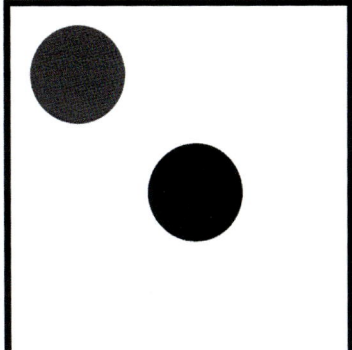

directional movements are not logical but they are nevertheless real aspects of human perception.

Figure 6.15 is a plan of a former agricultural field bounded by woodlots on two sides. Through biotic succession, the pioneer woody vegetation of the woodlots has begun to invade the abandoned field. That is the scientific explanation for how the landscape configuration came to be. Perceptually, the trees have straggled out of the forest and are moving towards the centre of the field. The trees closest to the mass of woodlot trees have a strong pull back to the woodlot. The further they become from the mass of the woodlot trees, the less they are pulled back to the mass until finally they break free. Until this happens, there is a felt tension between the object and the mass, boundary or centre that is

CHAPTER 6 **The elements of design**

◀ Figure 6.15

Woody plants colonize an abandoned field.
Source: Image courtesy of Yiwen Ruan.

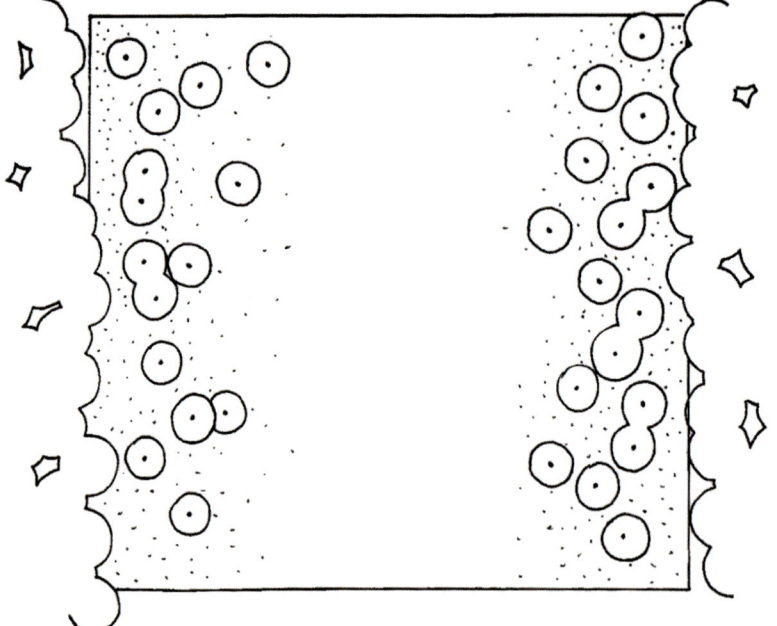

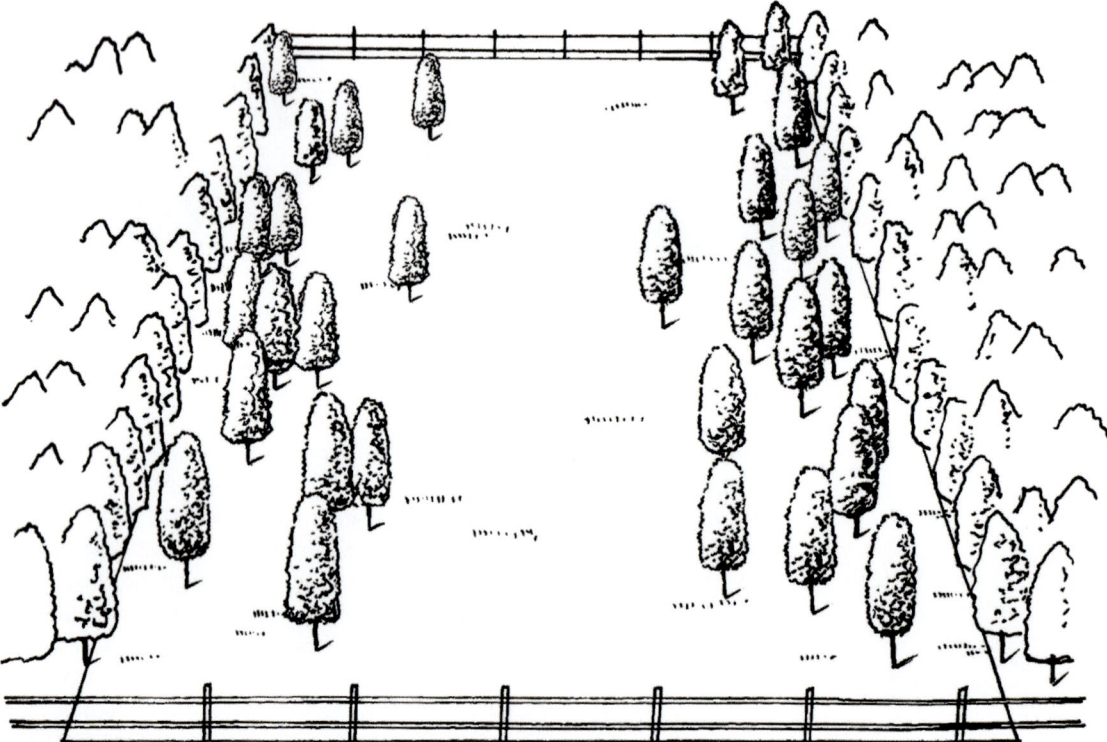

▲ Figure 6.16

Perceptually, the trees are pulling away from the woodlots on either side and moving towards the centre of the field.
Source: Image courtesy of Yiwen Ruan.

attracting it. Experiencing this unresolved tension is one of the most intriguing effects in landscape, and this two-dimensional expression of perceptual forces, seen in plan, is even more strongly felt in the third dimension (Figure 6.16). This suggested movement creates a tension and a transition within the field, and even a single tree judiciously placed on a lawn next to a row of trees can express this directional force and suggested movement in the landscape. Understanding such forces allows the planting designer to resolve or diminish tensions to the point that the perceptual forces in the landscape are in equilibrium and the composition is balanced, or to leave the plant composition slightly unbalanced in order that the viewer may experience the felt tension of these unresolved forces.

This understanding of the forces and suggested movement that occurs between objects in space is the basis for the stone assemblages of traditional Japanese gardens, in which the forces inherent in each rock are resolved through finding equilibrium with other stones in the group. Understanding how these compositions are balanced is instructive in achieving balance in planting design.

When traditional Japanese garden designers conceive a composition of stones, they begin with the understanding that each stone has a force running through the axis that is established by its form (Figure 6.17). The larger the mass of the stone and the more of the mass that is concentrated around the centre, the greater will be its stability and visual weight (Arnheim, 1974). Stones of greater visual weight have greater force of movement and therefore need greater opposing forces to be in balance.

▶ Figure 6.17

The shape and mass of an object generates directional movement along the axes.
Source: Image courtesy of Yiwen Ruan.

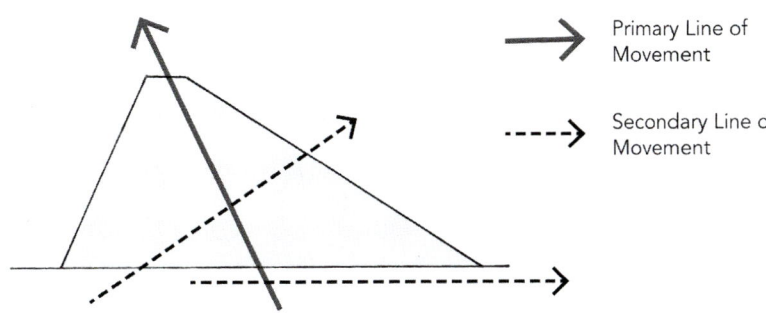

▶ Figure 6.18

This tall vertical stone implies both upward and downward movement along its vertical axis but is balanced in itself. Such stones are often used as the central stone in a rock grouping (Masuno, 1994).
Source: Image courtesy of Yiwen Ruan.

◀ Figure 6.19

This stone suggests movement to the left and is not balanced.
Source: Image courtesy of Yiwen Ruan.

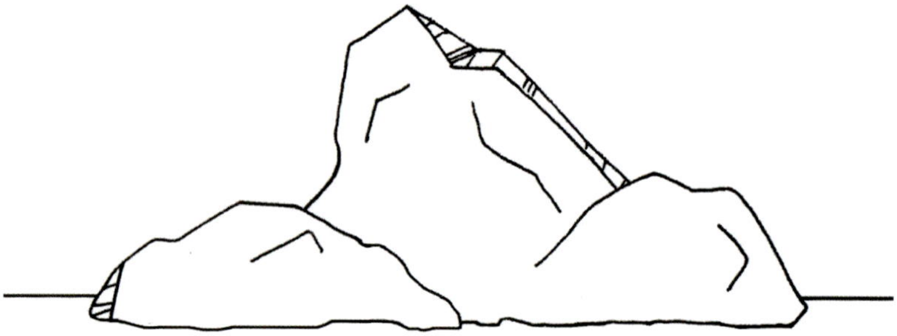

◀ Figure 6.20

When the stone in Figure 6.19 is combined with a second stone, the two stones push and pull each other in opposite directions, becoming a balanced grouping. Although the composition is balanced, its balance is imperfect and slow movement to the left is still present (Masuno, 1994). It is this imperfect balance and suggested movement in asymmetrical compositions that piques the interest of the viewer to make sense.
Source: Image courtesy of Yiwen Ruan.

▲ Figure 6.21

This typical arrangement of five stones resolves the tensions between the stones and is asymmetrically balanced. Each stone anchors the central vertical stone to achieve a balanced composition. The objective of the whole arrangement is to balance the directional movement of all five stones. When this is achieved, an overall equilibrium is present.
Source: Image courtesy of Yiwen Ruan.

▲ Figure 6.22

In this view of the dry-stone garden at Ryoan-ji temple in Kyoto, there are two large stone groupings on the left and three smaller groupings on the right. The asymmetrical balance of the whole composition is stable because the mass of stones in the two larger groupings has the visual weight to balance the three smaller groupings on the right (Kuck, 1984). At the same time, the individual rock groupings pull toward the boundaries, much like the circle in Figure 6.12, so that this group of rocks has a great deal of suggested movement.
Source: Photo courtesy of Melody Redekop.

Balance in planting design

As in the stone groupings described above, plant compositions also need to be balanced and just as the individual stones have movement suggested by their forms, placement and visual weights, so too do plants. There is, however, a fundamental difference between a balanced composition of stones and one of plants. When attempting to balance a stone grouping, the visual weight of each stone will primarily be influenced by its volume and form, because similar stones have similar visual density. The visual density of a plant will change with its form, colour and leaf density. A compact form, denser foliage and darker-coloured foliage give a plant more visual weight than another plant of the same size with lighter-coloured, more open foliage and form (Figure 6.23).

Asymmetrical balance in plan and elevation

Many designers arrange plant groupings using the framework of the scalene triangle, that is, a triangle with unequal sides. This is done to achieve a natural look and asymmetrical balance (Figure 6.24), but care must be exercised that rather than producing a natural effect, the opposite is not achieved (Robinson, 1940).

Landscape designers need to take care to design balanced views rather than balanced plan graphics. Since it is not possible to compose and balance every view, the goal should be to compose and balance the views

CHAPTER 6 **The elements of design**

◀ Figure 6.23

The compact form, darker green and leaf density of the evergreen shrubs lining the path give them increased visual weight and stability that grounds and balances the open form of the larger, but visually lighter, trees and shrubs. This balance is imperfect and will change as the plants grow.
Source: Image courtesy of Yiwen Ruan.

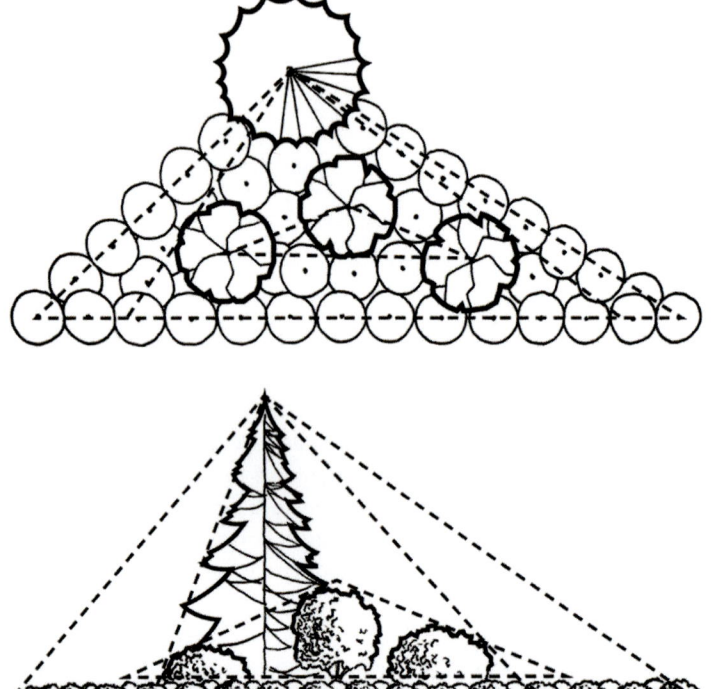

◀ Figure 6.24

Plan and elevation of an asymmetrically balanced plant grouping based on the scalene triangle. As in the rock groupings of Ryoan-ji temple (Figure 6.22), the objective is not just that the individual plant groupings are balanced asymmetrically, but that a balanced composition is achieved between all the plant groupings. When seen in elevation, the forms of the plants overlap and the plants form a group based on their proximity. This grouping effect will, of course, be reinforced if the plants share aesthetic similarities.
Source: Image courtesy of Yiwen Ruan.

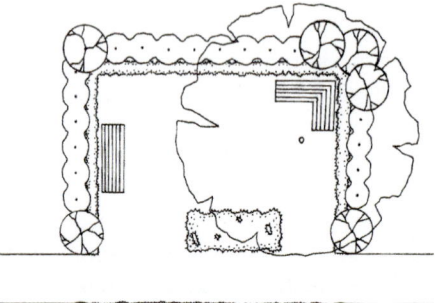

◀ Figure 6.25

Plan view of balance amongst plant groupings.
Source: Image courtesy of Yiwen Ruan.

▶ Figure 6.26

Perspective of the balanced landscape seen in plan view above. Low evergreen shrubs and groundcovers create a uniform edge to this space. The large, visually heavy shrubs at the corners balance each other and anchor the composition. The entire shrub massing balances the upward thrust of the tree that canopies the space. The grassy foliaged plant in the foreground defines the space, increases balance and separates an area for circulation.
Source: Image courtesy of Yiwen Ruan.

that are seen most often or that have greater importance in the sequence of experience. For example, in the traditional Japanese stroll garden, the purpose of the plan is to create a series of major views that are composed and balanced. The spaces between these composed views often have little sense of order. The effect of this is to make the discovery of the composed view that much more striking, as it creates the experience of order arising suddenly from disorder.

Continuity

The Gestalt principle of continuity states that people perceive a line as having movement in a particular direction, and will continue that line of movement by following it with their eyes or body. The eye will come to rest where lines in the landscape converge, and this is where important elements should be placed. Different lines suggest different speeds and directions of movement. The straight line is characteristic of man-made shapes, rarely occurs in nature and is most strongly suggestive of extension of direction and movement (Arnheim, 1974). Curved lines are preferred over straight lines and are associated with pleasantness and warmth (Rodenas, Sancho-Royo and González-Bernáldez, 1975; Aronoff, Woike and Hyman, 1992; Bar and Neta 2006).

> Some of the tree trunks and branches may show definite directions … but there is much in the landscape that the eyes are simply unable to grasp. And it is only … as a configuration of clear-cut directions, sizes, geometric shapes, colors, or textures that it can be said to be truly perceived.
>
> (Arnheim, 1974, p. 46)

The forms of plants express lines of movement. For example, conifers that have straight vertical axes and conical forms are strongly suggestive of upward movement. When the lines of the tree branches are ascending but the tree form is ovoid, the suggestion of upward movement is weaker. Trees that have horizontal branching, like giant dogwood (*Cornus controversa*) and Cedar of Lebanon (*Cedrus libani*), suggest a leisurely extension, especially in winter when their branches are most clearly revealed, and may be used to mirror the horizontality of the hard landscape or architecture.

One application of the principle of continuity is the use of trees and shrubs that have uncluttered lines or that can be pruned to bring them to this condition. Such plants have clear directional movement. They draw the eye upward and have a light, airy mass (Mallet, 2011). When used with deciduous shrubs like *Forsythia*, *Deutzia* and *Weigelia*, or with dense, massed evergreen shrubs that are visually heavy, the directional plants provide balance and lightness.

Objects in space, particularly vertical objects, draw us towards them. Where there is a sequence of trees along a path, the user is pulled through the space, moving from tree to tree in either direction (Figure 6.30).

The principle of continuity can be used to influence how people move through the landscape. Plantings that make the path a figure against the ground of the rest of the landscape will highlight the line of movement (R.

◀ Figure 6.27

In summer, the foliage of the tree partially obscures the line of movement.
Source: Image courtesy of Yiwen Ruan.

◀ Figure 6.28

In winter, the exposed form of the tree more strongly suggests ascending movement.
Source: Image courtesy of Yiwen Ruan.

▶ Figure 6.29

This rock and plant composition in the Dr Sun Yat-Sen Classical Chinese Garden in Vancouver is an example of juxtaposition, asymmetrical balance and unresolved tension. The magnolia tree and rock form a group because of their proximity. The forms of both the rock and the tree have an upward movement, but the mass of the rock also pulls downward, anchoring the composition. At this time, the magnolia is too small to escape the downward pull of the rock. Left unpruned, there would come a time when the rock would be too small to balance the upward directional movement of the tree. The unresolved tension between the ascending movement of the tree and the downward pull of the rock is part of the attraction of this pairing.
Source: Photo by Patrick Mooney.

▶ Figure 6.30

The strong vertical mass of the Western red cedar (*Thuja plicata*) trunks pull the person through the landscape.
Source: Photo by Patrick Mooney.

Kaplan et al., 1998) and linear repetition of plants along the edge of a path visually reinforces the desired line of movement along the path (Figure 6.23).

Drifts, blocks and matrices

Planting in drifts, blocks and matrices are common techniques used in planting design that create simple perceptual forms.

Drift planting

Gertrude Jekyll planted multiple plants of the same kind in long, narrow, overlapping masses she called drifts (see Figure 7.6 in Chapter 7). When viewed obliquely, drifts have the effect of layering plants one behind another, giving the sense that the plants are intermingled. Drift plantings create an impression of naturalness while expressing a visible order.

Block planting

Early modernist landscape architects like Tommy Church (1902–1978), Roberto Burle Marx (1909–1994) and Garret Eckbo (1910–2000) pioneered the use of massed plantings to define space and for simple visual appeal. A block planting is a planted area composed of a single species or cultivar (Kingsbury and Oudolf, 2016). They may be straight-lined geometric or curvilinear in shape. The modern practice of planting large monocultural blocks of plants can be understood as an evolution of the drift. Block plantings are simple compositions that provide visual unity and are easily perceived. Because they do not overlap and are not narrow and linear like drifts, the sense of intermingling is generally not felt in block plantings.

Block plantings of woody plants and groundcovers or grasses and perennials are desired solutions where simplicity, clarity and low maintenance are the order of the day, and they have become a common practice within the landscape architecture profession. For example, blocks of grasses are often used to complement modernist architecture. Their lightness and movement contrast with and heighten the materiality of buildings and plazas, and the use of simple textural masses mirrors the minimalism of the building or hard landscape. However, when using block plantings, designers need to be mindful that too much unity and too little complexity can result in a design that fails to engage.

Unlike more complex plantings, block plantings can be maintained by less skilled horticulturists (Hartlage and Fischer, 2015). However, in a mass comprised of a single plant, any other plant is particularly noticeable. So while block plantings may be easier to maintain, they demand a more perfect, weed-free appearance to achieve a unified effect.

Case study: Wayne Ferguson Plaza, Design Workshop Inc.

Design Workshop team: Steven Spears, Principal-in-Charge; Alex Ramirez, Project Manager; and Philip Koske.

Wayne Ferguson Plaza in Lewisville, Texas, is an intriguing example of the use of block and drift plantings in a modernist design.

Historic Lewisville is a rapidly growing community a half-hour drive north of Dallas, Texas. In 2011, the introduction of a commuter rail service to Dallas became a catalyst for transforming the historic downtown or "Old Town" of Lewisville into a cultural and community gathering space and commercial destination. The main components of this plan were the City Hall, a new Center for the Creative Arts and the refurbishing of the Main Street streetscape. In 2015, Wayne Ferguson Plaza linked these elements with a distinctive green precinct. The new 1.5-acre (0.6-hectare) multi-functional park and plaza provides a performing arts stage and facilities for multi-generational community events (Figure 6.34).

Ecosystem services related to planting

In a former parking lot, 113 new trees sequester more than 7,300 lbs (3,311 kg) of atmospheric carbon and intercept 31,700 gallons (120,000 litres) of stormwater annually. Collected stormwater runoff is treated in rain gardens (Figure 6.31). Tree canopies cover 40 per cent of the site surface area, providing essential shade and reducing the urban heat island effect. A post-construction survey of people in the Old Town core reported that the new plaza promotes the heritage of the Old Town, fosters multi-generational socialisation, reduces stress and improves quality of life. The planting design is seen as integral to the sense of identity and safety that is generated by the Wayne Ferguson Plaza (Özdil, Pradhan, Munshi and Khoshkar, 2017).

Wayne Ferguson Plaza was intended to strengthen the historic identity of Lewisville while providing flexibility for a wide range of events in a more contemporary setting. The theme of the design was "Sky, Rain and Prairie". This concept is expressed in the most prominent water feature on site, which parallels the major pathway and reflects the sky above (Figure 6.32). This feature and its adjacent plantings were inspired by the ephemeral streams of the Texas prairie (Figures 6.32 and 6.33).

The planting of Wayne Ferguson Plaza mixes formal and informal arrangements of the mostly native plant palette. The site is rectilinear, as dictated by the grid of the city streets. Formal avenues of Mexican sycamores (*Platanus Mexicana*) and Texas red oaks (*Quercus texana*) line the Historic Promenade and Pedestrian Alleyway (Figure 6.34). A regularly spaced arc of Forest Pansy redbud trees (*Cercis candensis* 'Forest Pansy') reinforces the boardwalk (Figure 6.32). Within the Prairie Grass Garden, native live oaks (*Quercus virginiana*) and thornless honey locust (*Gleditsia triacanthos* var. *inermis*) are arranged in an informal grove pattern that is underplanted with

◀ Figure 6.31
Collected stormwater runoff is treated in rain gardens planted with common rush (*Juncus effuses*). Between the rainfall interception provided by the trees and the directing of runoff to these rain gardens, peak stormwater flows from a 2-inch rainfall event are reduced by 32 per cent (Özdil et al., 2017).
Source: Image courtesy of Design Workshop Inc.

▼ Figure 6.32
Pedestrian movement along the boardwalk is reinforced by an arc of reflective water on one side and of redbud (*Cercis canadensis* 'Forest Pansy') on the other. The trees form the physical and psychological edge to the space, buffering views of the street and helping to set the user in an immersive landscape.
Source: Image courtesy of Design Workshop Inc.

▶ Figure 6.33

Delicate grasses and blocks of native stone convey the character of the Texas prairie.
Source: Image courtesy of Design Workshop Inc.

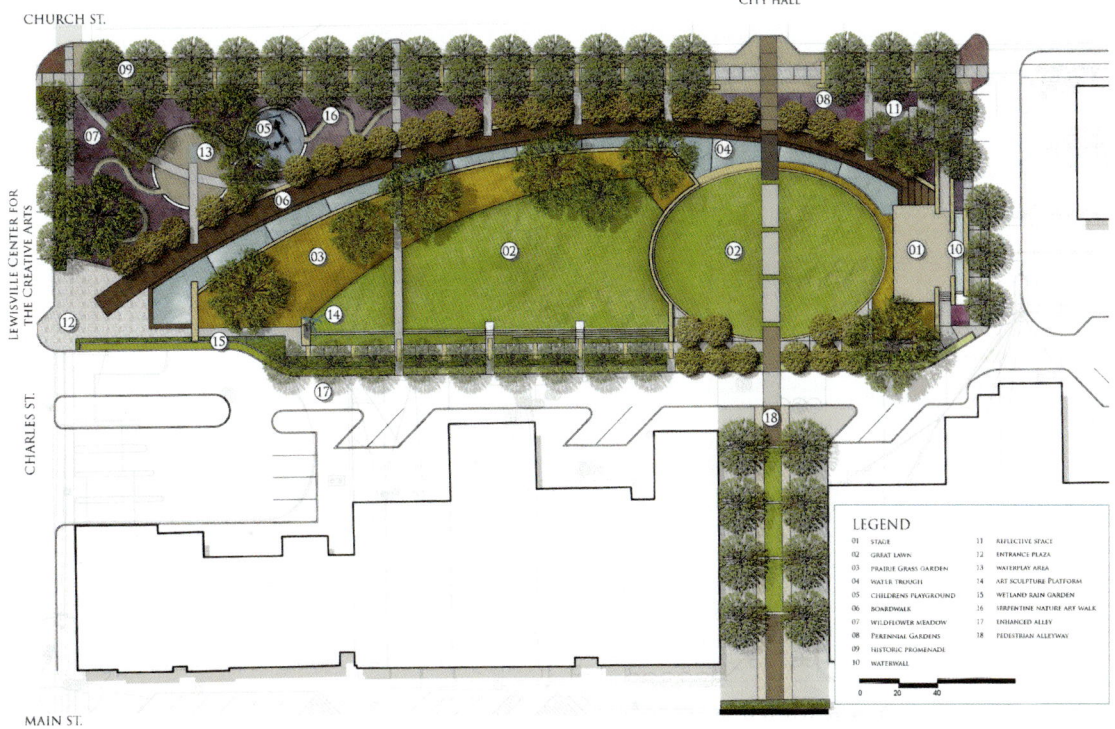

▲ Figure 6.34

Wayne Ferguson Plaza linked Main Street businesses, City Hall and the Lewisville Center for the Creative Arts with a cohesive multi-functional green precinct.
Source: Image courtesy of Design Workshop Inc.

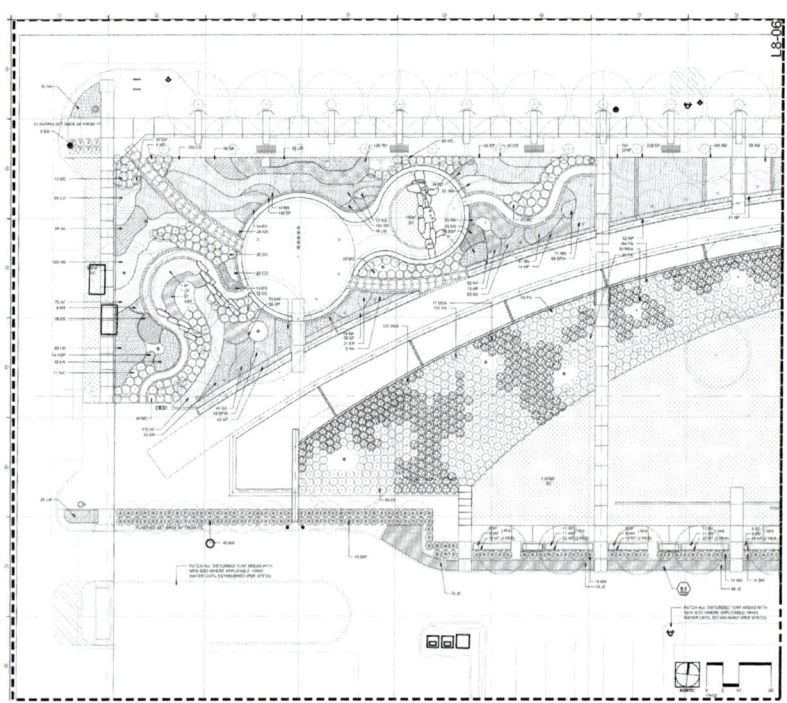

◀ Figure 6.35

This construction drawing of the western portion of Wayne Ferguson Plaza shows perennial, grass and shrub plantings. Plantings of grasses and perennials are a mixture of block plantings south of the boardwalk and drift plantings to its north.
Source: Image courtesy of Design Workshop Inc. Image cropped.

irregular masses of native grasses (*Muhlenbergia capillaris* and *M. emersleyi* 'El Toro') and non-native grasses (*Pennisetum alopecuroides*) (Figure 6.35). A path through the wildflower meadow connects the corner of Church and Charles Streets with the boardwalk (Figure 5.34). In the meadow, overlapping drifts of coreopsis, purple bee balm, white yarrow and butterfly iris evoke the native prairie (Figure 6.35). The repetition of the urban grid in the hard and soft landscape creates a simple modernist form for Wayne Ferguson Plaza. Within the Plaza, a mixture of block and drift plantings break loose from the grid in a more informal, naturalistic arrangement that softens the urban forms and calls to mind the regional landscape.

Plant list

Trees	
Cercis candensis 'Forest Pansy'	Forest pansy redbud
Gleditsia triancanthos var. *inermis*	Thornless honey locust
Lagerstroemia indica x *fauriei* 'Natchez'	Natchez crape myrtle
Prunus mexicana	Mexican plum
Platanus mexicana	Mexican sycamore

Quercus texana	Texas red oak
Quercus virginiana	Live oak
Quercus virginiana 'High Rise'	High Rise live oak
Shrubs	
Buxus microphylla	Boxwood
Camellia sasanqua 'ShiShi Gashira'	ShiShi Gashira *Camellia*
Spiraea x *bumalda* 'Anthony Waterer'	Anthony Waterer spirea
Grasses	
Muhlenbergia capillaris	Gulf muhly
Muhlenbergia emersleyi 'El Toro'	Bull muhly grass
Pennisetum alopecuroides	Fountain grass
Perennials and groundcovers	
Achillea filipendulina 'Cloth of Gold'	Cloth of Gold yarrow
Achillea millefolium	Common white yarrow
Aquilegia cv.	Columbine (yellow)
Aquilegia cv.	Columbine (red)
Coreopsis lanceolata	Lance-leaved coreopsis
Dietes grandiflora	Butterfly iris
Evolvulus glomeratus 'Blue Daze'	Blue Daze *Evolvulus*
Echinacea purpurea	Purple coneflower
Echinacea purpurea 'White Swan'	White Swan coneflower
Hemerocallis 'Autumn Red'	Autumn Red daylily
Heuchera 'Purple Mountain Majesty'	Purple Mountain Majesty coral bells
Lantana montevidensis 'Alba'	White trailing *Lantana*
Monarda sp.	Bee balm (purple)
Penstemon digitalis 'Husker Red'	Husker Red *Penstemon*
Rudbeckia hirta	Black-eyed Susan
Sedum 'Autumn Joy'	Autumn Joy *Sedum*
Salvia nemorosa 'East Friesland'	East Friesland garden sage
Liriope sp.	Evergreen *Liriope*
Water plants	
Equisetum hyemale	Horsetail
Juncus effusus	Common rush
Bulbs	
Narcissus papyraceus	Paper-white daffodil
Narcissus 'Grand Primo'	Grand Primo daffodil
Turf	
Tifway 419 sod	Tifway 419 Bermuda grass

Matrix planting

A matrix is the set of conditions that provides a system in which something grows or develops (Cambridge English Dictionary, n.d.). Matrix planting is a variation on block planting in which a uniform mass of a single plant or a few plants forms a matrix into which a limited number of more visually interesting so-called primary plants are inserted, individually or in small groupings (Kingsbury and Oudolf, 2016). Matrix plantings create a figure–ground relationship that causes viewers to mentally engage the landscape (Figure 6.40). Because the figure–ground establishes a focal point, matrix plantings are easily read perceptual structures. Dutch landscape designer Piet Oudolf uses matrix plantings extensively in his work.

Piet Oudolf

Dutch landscape designer Piet Oudolf has been highly influential in introducing innovative plantings to public spaces and increasing the popularity of a more natural aesthetic in modern planting design. His design of The Battery in New York City (2003) and collaborations with notable American landscape architects Kathryn Gustafson, Jennifer Guthrie and Shannon Nichol of the firm Gustafson Guthrie Nichol Ltd. (GGN) on the Lurie Garden in Millennium Park, Chicago (2004), and with James Corner of Field Operations on the High Line Park in New York City (2009) have drawn worldwide acclaim and demonstrated that perennial plantings may be significant components of successful public spaces. He is widely regarded as the most influential planting designer of the last three decades. Piet's work includes gardens and parks in Continental Europe, the United Kingdom, the United States and Canada. In addition to designing and introducing new plants to cultivation, Piet has co-authored a number of books with Henk Gerritsen, Michael King, Noel Kingsbury and Rick Darke that explain the philosophy, concepts, practices and plants used in his work. Many of the design principles presented in this chapter can be seen in his work. He lectures widely and has taught in the landscape architecture program at Harvard University's Graduate School of Design. Since 2012, he has been a visiting professor at Sheffield University.

Among the many honours Piet has received is the Gold Veitch Memorial Medal, awarded in 2002 by the Royal Horticultural Society for his contribution to advancing the science and practice of horticulture. In September 2012, he was awarded an honorary fellowship by the Royal Institute of British Architects for his contributions to architecture in the broadest sense. The following year, Her Majesty Queen Máxima of the Netherlands awarded him the Prince Bernhard Culture Fund. This is the highest Dutch culture award and recognises exceptional contributions to the arts and cultural and natural conservation. In receiving this award, Piet was recognised for his achievements in gardening and landscape design and the influence of his designs in his home country and abroad.

Influences and origins

Petrus "Piet" Oudolf was born in 1944 in Haarlem and grew up in Bloemendaal, near Amsterdam, where his family ran a restaurant and bar. As a child, he visited Thijsse's Hof, a small local *heempark*[3]. Perhaps it was here that he first experienced his personal emotional response to natural-looking landscapes designed with native plants.

In his mid twenties, Piet decided not to join the family business, opting instead to take qualifications in landscape construction and start a landscape design-build business. As his business developed, Piet became increasingly focused on the untapped potential of perennials and grasses but found that he could not obtain the plants he wanted in sufficient numbers. In 1982, Piet, his wife Anja and their sons, seven-year-old Hugo and Pieter, aged nine, moved to a traditional farmhouse on 3.2 acres (1.3 hectares) of land outside the village of Hummelo in the eastern Netherlands. Anja cultivated a variety of previously unknown cut flowers for sale to local florists, while Piet renovated the family home and established the nursery. Known simply as Hummelo, it became a place of connection for leading garden designers and provided the testing ground for new plants and Piet's evolving planting style.

That first year, Dutch plantsman Henk Gerritsen discovered Hummelo and the wilder-looking plants that only Piet was growing. At his own nursery and garden, Henk was using plants in a way that emphasised their character, structure and all-season appearance. The two men bonded over their common interest in natural-looking perennials and naturalistic planting, and together they developed new ways of conceiving planting design. *Droomplanten* (Dream Plants), published in Dutch in 1994 and republished in English in 1999 as *Dream Plants for the Natural Garden*, documented their philosophy, design principles and plant palette (Oudolf and Kingsbury, 2015).

In the late 1990s, a desire to achieve a more natural aesthetic coupled with an interest in plantings that increased pollinator and bird habitat arose in Europe and North America. Since then, the cumulative work of leading designers on both sides of the Atlantic has given rise to the New Perennial Movement,[4] and today, much more than at the start of the century, grasses and perennials are used in all manner of situations and the interest in naturalistic plantings among the public, gardeners and landscape professionals has never been greater. While the simple, modernist block planting endures, designers like Piet Oudolf continue to experiment with ways of adding complexity and a sense of naturalness to planting design.

The naturalistic, perennial-focused New Perennial Movement, of which Piet has been a formative influence, had its origins in the work of the German plant breeder Karl Foerster (1874–1940). Beginning in the early 1900s, Foerster created a style of gardening that used large drifts of ornamental grasses and perennials in a naturalistic fashion and began introducing new perennials, like the now-well-known Karl Foerster feather reed grass (*Calamagrostis* x *acutiflora* 'Karl Foerster') and a selection of the native

American orange coneflower (*Rudbeckia fulgida* var. *sullivantii* 'Goldsturm') from his nursery in Potsdam-Bornim. Foerster's planting style was taken up by Dutch landscape architect Mien Ruys (1904–1999), who combined loose perennial borders with massed plants and clipped evergreens. She, in turn, influenced the American landscape architects Wolfgang Oehme (1930–2011) and James van Sweden (1935–2013) in the 1990s. Piet too was influenced by the work of Foerster and Ruys but found his own unique expression.

Intentions

The constant in Piet's designs is that they are inspired by nature. Because he felt that traditional landscapes did not provide the emotive response he wanted, Piet set out to create alternatives in which people would experience something more akin to a natural landscape. His designs emphasise the ephemeral, changing with the breeze, the movement of a cloud and the seasons. Each is a unique composition that engages our interest and, especially in winter, challenges our conception of beauty in the landscape.

If the experience of traditional gardens did not suit Piet, neither did the standard garden perennials. Over centuries of cross-breeding and selection, they had lost any semblance of their wild forebears, becoming garish and requiring a high level of maintenance. A landscape composed of these plants would not produce the sense of naturalness that he sought. At the same time, many native or wild plants that Piet would have wished to use were also not suitable. In good soils, they would grow leggy and flop over. Many had small blossoms, short bloom times and limited colours. Piet needed plants that could be easily grown in typical garden soils and were interesting year round, but that still carried the association of the natural landscape.

In the 1990s, he began developing a new generation of perennials and grasses that combined vigour, drought tolerance and four-season interest with a more natural appearance. The Oudolfs ordered and tested seeds from around the world. Piet visited nurseries in Europe, especially Germany but also England and the US, eventually introducing more than 70 plants, including *Salvia verticillata* 'Purple Rain', *Echinacea* 'Fatal Attraction', *Geum* 'Flames of Passion', *Astrantia* 'Claret', *Stachys officinalis* 'Hummelo' and *Salvia* x *sylvestris* 'Dear Anja' (McGrane, 2008).

When selecting plants for introduction to cultivation or use in his designs, Piet considers the whole plant: Its form, texture, silhouette, seed heads, longevity, appearance through its entire growth cycle and maintenance requirements. Many of the plants he uses have more than one season of interest. For example, *Veronicastrum* 'Fascination' flowers from early to mid summer but maintains structural interest throughout the winter. Himalayan mayapple (*Podophyllum hexandrum*) and chestnut-leaved *Rodgersia* (*Rodgersia aesculifolia*) have leaves that are most interesting as they are opening. Umbrella plant (*Darmera peltate*), red-leafed *Mukdenia* (*Mukdenia*

▶ Figure 6.36

Culver's root (*Veronicastrum virginicum*) in flower.
Source: Photo by Benjamin Vogt.

rossii) and Arkansas blue star (*Amsonia hubrechtii*) have foliage that colours in the autumn, and sticky Jerusalem sage (*Phlomis russeliana*) maintains a striking form and interesting seed heads through the winter (Figure 6.37).

Above all, the plants Piet uses need to have a natural appearance. Many possess a proportion of foliage to flower that is similar to plants found growing wild. Unlike the large double blossoms of many cultivated plants, their flowers are often clusters of smaller florets, as seen in queen of the prairie (*Filipendula rubra*) or Wallich milk parsley (*Selinum wallichianum*). Such plants possess a simple elegance that speaks of the wild landscape.

Eventually, as his introductions and other similar plants became widely available, Piet found that he no longer needed to grow the plants used in his designs. This contributed to the decision in 2010 to close the nursery so that Piet could concentrate on his design work. Anja continued to organise the many groups of garden enthusiasts that visited Hummelo each year (Oudolf and Kingsbury, 2015) until October of 2018, when the Hummelo garden was closed to the public (Spencer, 2018).

Cultivating wildness

Piet wishes to re-create the experience of a natural landscape, but he does not attempt to copy nature. Instead, he combines plants from different

▲ Figure 6.37

Winter seed heads of Culver's root (*Veronicastrum virginicum*), left, with *Phlomis russeliana* in the foreground, right, at Hummelo. Culver's root is a native American prairie plant that is attractive to pollinators. The persistent seeds are eaten by birds in the winter and early spring. *Phlomis* is also a good pollinator plant and in winter its seed heads are used by hibernating spiders.
Source: Photo courtesy of Piet Oudolf.

parts of the world that grow in similar conditions, because he believes that such plants "look well together" (Oudolf, 2015). One reason for this is that a plant's appearance indicates its environmental requirements (see Chapter 3, Plant Associations). At one extreme, full-sun, drought-tolerant plants tend to be glaucous, finely textured and compact, like the lavenders (*Lavendula* sp.) or lavender cotton (*Santolina chamaecyparissus*), while plants of the moist woodland are inclined to have a more open form and green foliage, like goat's beard (*Aruncus dioicus*). Shade-tolerant plants are often large-leaved, like yellow waxbells (*Kirengeshoma palmata*), and perennial plants like *Knautia*, *Thalictrum* and *Sanguisorba* seem harmonious when planted with grasses, because meadows are their natural habitat. Piet's ecological plant associations convey the impression of the landscape type from which the plants originate, because the plants are linked aesthetically and ecologically.

Grasses play a significant role in many of Piet's landscapes. Experientially, they call to mind the larger landscape of roadside verges, abandoned fields, meadows and clearings. A landscape dominated by grasses is unified and calming (King and Oudolf, 1998) and may be embellished with contrasting perennials and woody plants to add interest and complexity. Grasses are hardworking, utilitarian plants. They tolerate stress better, live longer and require less care than perennials. On a site where markedly different site conditions exist, designers can create a unity of form and texture by combining grasses with their relatives, the sedges and rushes, and other grass-like plants that are adapted to different site conditions.

Piet's landscapes are planned to the smallest detail yet feel uncontrived. The essence of the "wildness" expressed in his landscapes is that the hand of the designer is, at least subliminally, hidden from the user's awareness. This is, in part, because the plants look natural. They do not shout that they have been cultivated for showiness. Piet strengthens the feeling of naturalness that is inherent in the plants he uses by arranging them informally in drifts, in blocks of different sizes, or as intermingled layers.

Although I am not aware of research to support the idea, I suspect that plantings of natural-looking plants in ecological plant associations allow people to be transported to a favourite natural landscape, to engage in the fantasy that the landscape is natural and to experience it more fully. If so, this greater level of engagement would lead to a more restorative experience.

Complexity and unity

In the act of perception, the brain organises what the eye sees. It looks for distinction so that it may remember. Too much sameness is dismissed because nothing can be singled out. Too much complexity defeats the brain's attempt to distinguish order. Good design aids perception by placing complexity in a unified setting. Piet's designs are unusually complex, yet he has found ways to organise his plantings so that their complexity entices rather than overwhelms.

Pensthorpe

Pensthorpe Waterfowl Park in Norfolk is a conservation trust dedicated to protecting farmland and conserving wildlife. It exposes visitors to meadow, marsh and woodland habitats with the goal of inspiring conservation of the English countryside. The 1-acre (0.4-hectare) Millennium Garden at Pensthorpe opened in 2000 and was Piet's first public commission in England. Piet recognised that his design needed to fit the rural character and scale of its setting. To accomplish this, he used a greater proportion of grasses than had been seen in Britain up to that point in time and bold blocky drifts of perennials of about 10 feet (3 metres) by 13 feet (4 metres) (Stuart-Smith, 2013). The grasses lend the garden a rural character, and the scale of the drifts helps the garden to blend into the surrounding countryside.

In the Millennium Garden, the perennial plants and grasses are variations on a theme composed of a few colours, textures and forms. In late summer, the pinks, magentas and purples of plants like *Echinacea* 'Rubinglow', *Astrantia major* 'Roma', *Monarda* 'Oudolf's Charm' and *Lythrum salicaria* 'Blush' stand out against the parchment-coloured *Deschampsia caespitosa* and *Molinia* 'Transparent'. The spiky flower forms of the *Astilbe*, *Sanguisorba* and *Persicaria* flowers and the low, mounded forms of the *Deschampsia*, *Nepeta* and *Persicaria* plants provide a unity of form and texture. Repetition of sets of plants from foreground to background creates

▲ Figure 6.38

This view of Millennium Garden at Pensthorpe is framed with *Wisteria* vine. In the foreground centre is the purple tall *Verbena* (*Verbena bonariensis*). On the left foreground, red thunder burnet (*Sanguisorba officinalis* 'Red Thunder') is backed with blocks of tufted hair grass (*Deschampsia cespitosa*) and Purpurlanze *Astilbe* (*Astilbe chinensis* var. *taquetii* 'Purpurlanze'), repeated to the distant background. In the right foreground is the pink *Echinacea* (*Echinacea purpurea*), with Walker's Low catmint (*Nepeta* 'Walker's Low') along the path behind. In the right midground at the path's edge, the *Echinacea* is repeated, with the catmint and meadow sage (*Salvia nemerosa*) behind. In the midground, to the right of the *Echinacea*, is Firedance bistort (*Persicaria amplexicaulis* 'Firedance').
Source: Photo courtesy of Piet Oudolf.

a pattern that gives cohesion to the whole scene. Plants like the *Persicaria* that are not part of the pattern because they are not repeated are disruptors that catch and hold the eye, adding variety and interest.

This planting illustrates the principle that regardless of climate, plant type or planting style, the plants within a designed composition need to be harmonious. As Piet has demonstrated here, they do this by their shared aesthetic qualities and by conveying suggestions and memories of similar landscapes (Figure 6.38).

Over the years, Piet has learned to use plants that are long-lived, that stay in place and that are compatible. This allows the Millennium Garden to be almost exactly as when it was planted (Stuart-Smith, 2013). While we might take this for granted, it is not common. Perhaps the biggest issue with meadow plantings that mix grasses and perennials is that the grasses will usually outcompete the forbs, so that within in as little as three years the wildflower meadow has become a hay field. Having both grasses and perennials that are long-lived but do not spread quickly provides clarity and longevity to the planting design.

Piet's early gardens, like Pensthorpe, featured block plantings. Later he used both block and matrix plantings and developed different ways of arranging plants using those techniques. In 2007, in Potter's Fields Park, Piet used matrix plantings to provide areas of simple interest within the broader composition (Figures 6.40 and 6.41).

The Lurie Garden

In the 1995 Droomparken (Dream Park) in Enköping, Sweden, and in the 2004 Lurie Garden in Chicago, Piet planted a linear block of *Salvias* as the

▶ Figure 6.39

Pensthorpe's Millennium Garden in winter: In the foreground are the skeletal remains of *Lythrum salicaria* with the russet spires of *Astilbe chinensis* var. *tacqetii* 'Purpurlanze' behind. In the centre of the view, dark pompoms of *Echinacea* seed heads are silhouetted against frost-covered grasses. The scene has a sense of mystery, as proceeding into the landscape will reveal something different, but related to the place you are in.
Source: Photo courtesy of Imogen Checketts.

▶ Figure 6.40

Matrix planting in Potter's Fields Park, London: *Salvia nemorosa* 'Rhapsody in Blue' is the focal plant set in a matrix of autumn moor grass (*Sesleria autumnalis*), with *Sedum* 'Sunkissed' in the foreground. The matrix planting is visually simple, as it has only two colours and textures, and the blades of grass compliment the spiky form of the *Salvia*. A matrix planting like this is a figure–ground. This planting illustrates the principle that the background needs to be uniform so that the figure can be isolated.
Source: Image courtesy of Adam Woodruff.

central element. In the Lurie Garden, he used four cultivars of meadow sage (*Salvia nemorosa*) ranging in colour from the light blue-purple of *S.* 'Rügen' to the deep violet of *S.* 'Mainacht' to create a river of *Salvia* running through the centre of the garden.[5] In the Droomparken and Lurie Garden, using different cultivars of the same plant creates a colour gradation that adds variety to what is essentially a large block planting. Conversely, without the complexity of their setting, the two Rivers of *Salvias* would not be nearly so arresting.

CHAPTER 6 **The elements of design**

◀ Figure 6.41

The clumps of *Salvia* create a pattern across the meadow of moor grass. The matrix planting provides a unified centre and adds an order that allows the surrounding frame of diverse perennials to be more complex without destroying the unity of the whole.
Source: Photo courtesy of Adam Woodruff.

Salvia 'Rugen' (light blue-purple) *Salvia* 'Blue Hill' (blue-purple) *Salvia* 'Wesuwe' (violet) *Salvia* 'May Night' (deep violet)

◀ Figure 6.42

By using four cultivars of the same plant, Piet has kept the form of the plant and the texture of both leaf and flower constant, but has varied colour. This is an analogous colour scheme (see Chapter 7) in which having lighter colours in the background and darker, more saturated colours in the foreground creates a sense of depth.
Source: Image courtesy of Yiwen Ruan.

In the central portion of the River, the blocks of *Salvia* are overlain with scattered clumps of prairie dropseed (*Sporobolus heterolepis*), red switch grass (*Panicum virgatum* 'Shenandoah') and little bluestem (*Schizachyrium scoparium* 'The Blues'); see Figure 6.44. The block planting of the *Salvias* has become a matrix for the grasses. This is a reversal of the usual matrix in which the primary plants are colourful perennials and the grasses are the ground or matrix plants. Matrix plantings have the visual strength of block plantings, but more complexity, because they combine the primary plant with the matrix plants.

By converting the block to a matrix, Piet is tying the central section of the river to adjacent areas by sharing common plants between them. This is a classic way to transition between different areas of a planting design. He

▶ Figure 6.43

This concept plan for the planting design of the Lurie Garden by Piet Oudolf (P.O.) and Kathryn Gustafson (K.G.) of the landscape architecture firm GGN: The central boardwalk is aligned with the Seam, a runnel of descending water that references the filling of the original Lake Michigan shoreline, far below this rooftop garden. On the east side of the Seam, the shadier, treed planting is known as the Dark Plate, while the more open herbaceous planting to the west is the Light Plate. In this concept, the River of *Salvia* is that broad purple arc that runs north to south in the light plate.
Source: Image courtesy of GGN Landscape Architects.

is also adding interest and structure. Not only does the centre of the River become more complex, it becomes a distinct centre to the River. A person walking the seam from north to south, or south to north, would experience an A (beginning), B (centre), A (repeat of beginning) sequence in the character in the River itself. So there are two patterns present in the Lurie Garden River of *Salvias*: The pattern of the four repeated *Salvias* and the A-B-A patterns created by intermingling plants from adjoining areas to create a centre in the River. Although these two patterns would be consciously observed by only a few, they add a reassuring order and interest.

The meadow

At the southern edge of the Lurie Garden, on both sides of the seam, lies a meadow of prairie dropseed (*Sporobolus heterolepis*) that is infilled with perennials, many of which are native to the American prairie. The *Sporobolus* is a native drought-tolerant grass with medium-green leaves that form arching 18-inch (0.48-metre) clumps beneath slender stems and tawny panicles rising to 36 inches (0.9 metres) (Figure 6.46). In the autumn, its foliage turns golden with tints of orange before changing to a pale bronze in winter. *Sporobolus* is a low-maintenance bunch grass that tolerates a wide range of soils, provides a long season of interest and maintains its form throughout the winter.

Large drifts, divided into sub-areas composed of *Echinacea purpurea* 'The Virgin' and *Eryngium yuccifolium* (labelled E+E) or *Dalea purpurea*

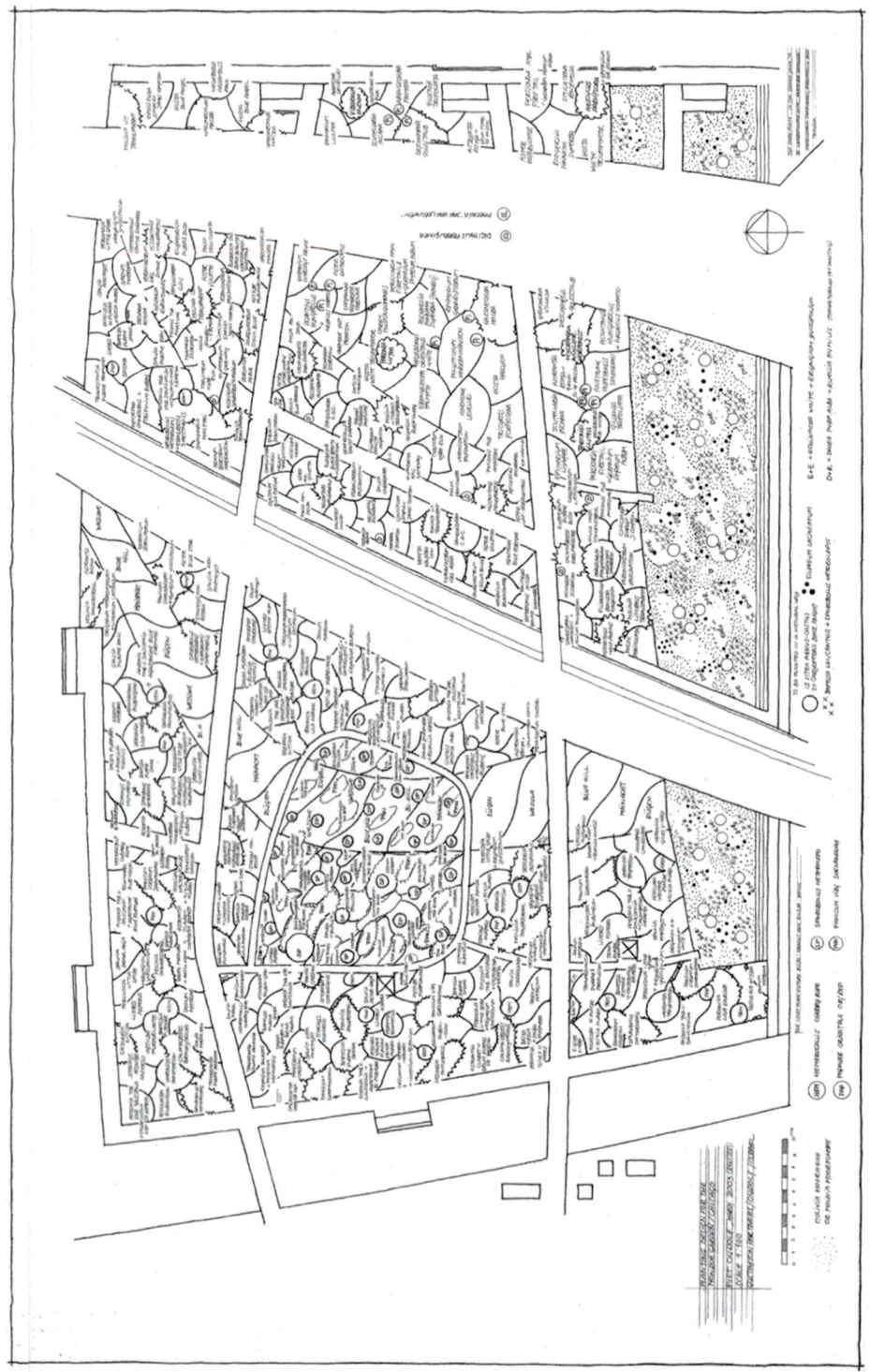

▲ Figure 6.44

The Planting Plan of the Lurie Garden. In the River of Salvia, notice that the blocks of S. 'Wesuwe', S. 'Blue Hill', S. 'Mainacht' and S. 'Rügen' are repeated in that order. This pattern occurs four times from north to south.

Source: Image courtesy of Piet Oudolf.

▲ Figure 6.45

A view of the River of *Salvia* in the Lurie Garden showing the repeated pattern of the different *Salvia* varieties. The background yews, *Taxus* x *media* 'Hicksii', provide an orderly frame to the complexity of the dark and light plates. This is another device that arranges the complex and the simple in a recognisable order.
Source: Photo courtesy of Piet Oudolf.

and *Ruellia humilis* (labelled D+R), are placed diagonally throughout the meadow, establishing repetition and pattern; see Figure 6.44. If no more plants had been added, this would be a type of matrix planting, with the grasses being the matrix plants and the drifts the primary plants. Instead, the large drifts and grasses are overlain with a separate pattern of smaller scatter plantings that sometimes fall within the grassy matrix and sometimes in the larger perennial drifts. In these plantings, *Baptisia leucantha* and *Silphium laciniatum* are used alone and *Vitex agnus-castus* is paired with *Caryopteris* 'Black Knight'. Because the smaller block plants are scattered over the matrix grasses and the large drifts, the drifts are not islands in a sea of *Sporobolus*. The smaller blocks stitch together the perennial drifts and the grassy matrix. So much complexity is added that the figure–ground relationship that occurs in a true matrix is lost. The result is a complex visual tapestry in which the order seen on the plan is hidden in a complex pattern of repeating, intermingled forms, colours and textures. Despite this complexity, the repetition of the plants and the association of a particular plant exclusively with its partner plant creates the patterns that humans so love to find.

In looking at Piet's plan for the meadow at the Lurie Garden, it appears as if the layer of smaller blocks was arranged independently, on a separate piece of tracing paper, and then located atop the first two layers of the matrix and larger drifts. This is indeed how Piet works, arranging one set of plants on one layer and another on a second or third layer. As he has explained, "the first layer consists of structural plants, followed by a matrix of grasses, and then a layer of accent and filler plants. Lay all the

CHAPTER 6 **The elements of design**   253

Sporobolus heterolepis

Echinacea purpurea 'The Virgin'

Eryngium Yuccifolium

Dalea purpurea

Ruellia humilis

Vitex agnus-castus

Caryopteris 'Black Knight'

Baptisia leucantha

Silphium laciniatum compass plant

▲ Figure 6.46

Lurie Garden meadow plants.
Source: Image courtesy of Yiwen Ruan.

▶ Figure 6.47

Intermingled planting conceived in layers.
Source: Image courtesy of Yiwen Ruan.

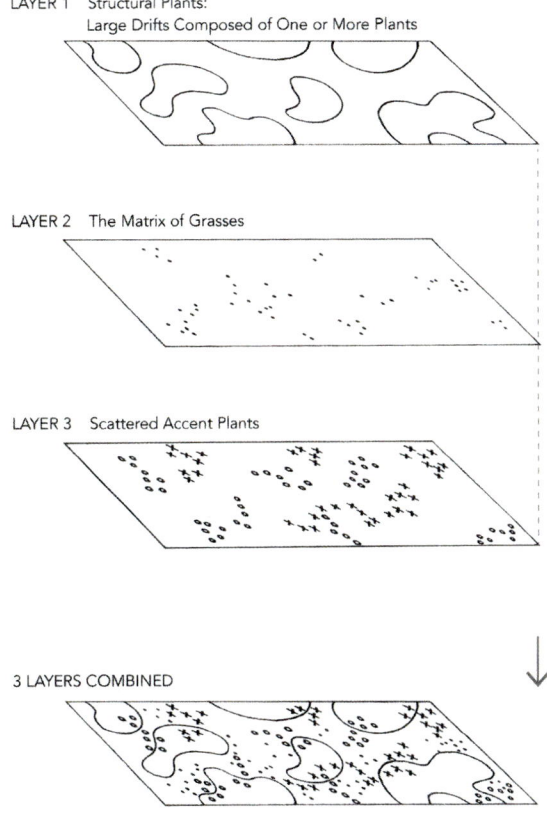

sheets together and I'll have the makings of a highly intermingled perennial planting design" (in Spencer, 2018) (Figure 6.47). The separate layers are then combined in a final planting plan with quantities per area, calculated using programs like Google Sketchup or Autocad (Kingsbury and Oudolf, 2016). Designing in separate layers, like this, can help the designer to envision and maintain control over very complex plantings, and the drawings of the separate layers can simplify setting out plants in the field. In both forest and meadow settings, biodiversity is increased if multiple layers of different heights are used. This is referred to as foliage height diversity or vertical stratification and is more likely to find its way into our plantings if we are thinking in layers.

Piet often uses a simpler planting in the centre of a designed area and more visually complex plantings as a frame to the centre. This provides a clear visual order that is easy to perceive and permits the use of greater complexity in the whole design. The centre can be a simple matrix, like Potter's Fields, or a variety of cultivars of the same species, like the Lurie Garden River of *Salvia*.

CHAPTER 6 **The elements of design**   255

The High Line

The High Line is a 1.45-mile (2.3-kilometre) linear park, constructed on an abandoned railway viaduct in Manhattan and operated by the NYC Department of Parks & Recreation and the Friends of the High Line. Since opening in 2009, it has become a major tourist destination, generated new investment in the surrounding neighbourhood and inspired similar adaptive reuse projects worldwide. It is a place of prospect refuge where pedestrians look out over ever-changing views of the city and the Hudson River from a calm oasis 30 feet (9 metres) above the bustle of the streets below (Field Operations, n.d.).

In 2004, American landscape architect James Corner, of the firm Field Operations, asked Piet to join in what became the winning proposal for the High Line. Their design, in collaboration with Diller Scofidio + Renfro, recalls the old freight rail line and the self-seeding plants that had colonised it when rail traffic ceased. After refurbishing the steel structure, more than a third of the old rails were replaced in their original position and are now embedded within walkways or plantings (Figures 6.48 and 6.52).

In a 2016 interview, Piet described his process for developing the planting for the High Line as a narrative or drama.

> For the High Line, we have a narrative … a story that is told by the architects. We enter in a woodland situation and that opens up to meadow and then continues into this water landscape or swamp landscape. We get the whole story from this sort of storybook and I translate that into plants. When I read a story of what I like, I get a picture in front of me and then for every part of the High Line I put together a sort of palette of plants; a sort of number of plants that could work in that character of what they have written down. It's like a stage play and we have this play and in it needs so many people and he plays that character and the other plays that character. That's how I put it together. I put them together in a palette and then I put them on paper but it's a whole process that is very complex because it's more that … I get the script and then translate that into what you see now.
> (Yoneda, 2016)

As long ago as the publication of *Droomplanten* in 1994, Piet articulated the idea that each plant has a personality that evokes a particular feeling. In the High Line, more than 350 varieties of woody plants, grasses, perennials, bulbs and vines are arranged in a series of different landscapes with names like Gansevoort Woodland, Chelsea Thicket, Meadow Walk and Wildflower Field. In this quote, Piet tells us that the plants in each landscape establish a distinct character for that section. As one walks the High Line, the different plant associations generate a series of experiences that, like a story or a play, can only be experienced temporally.

▲ Figure 6.48

The Northern Spur in April. The Pennsylvania sedge (*Carex pensylvanica*) (midground centre of the tracks) have recently been shorn and are starting to regrow. White Persian squill (*Scilla mischtschenkoana*), blue glory of the snow (*Chiondoxa sardensis*) and the brilliant red George Baker fumewort (*Corydalis solida* 'George Baker') are the earliest colour plants in the Northern Spur. These small bulbous plants appear in early spring and die back soon after. The burgundy plants in the left foreground are Dale's Strain American alumroot (*Heuchera Americana* 'Dale's Strain'). Against the back wall, the willow-leaved spice bush (*Lindera glauca* var. *salicifolia*) (since removed) is beginning to leaf out.
Source: Photo courtesy of Piet Oudolf.

The Northern Spur Preserve

The Northern Spur Preserve is a small branch of the High Line that terminates at a bricked-up wall where the trains once entered the Merchants Refrigerating Company House, a frozen food plant. The area is planted with some of the plants that colonised the High Line when it was abandoned, and is reminiscent of the character of the viaduct before it was repurposed as a linear park. The spur is viewed from above and has no public access. Maintenance access is also restricted, and shallow soils reduce available moisture and intensify soil temperature extremes. In designing the Northern Spur, Piet used predominantly native plants that could thrive in these harsh conditions.

The least interesting part of the year in many gardens is the period after perennials and grasses have been cut back and the emerging perennials do not yet provide structure. As Piet has demonstrated in the Northern Spur, small bulbs can be used to add colour and draw attention in early spring. In addition to those plants that he used in the Northern Spur (Figure 6.48), reticulate *Iris* (*Iris reticulata*), dwarf *Narcissus* like *Narcissus* 'Toto', common snowdrops (*Galanthus nivalis*), and species tulips like *Tulipa tarda* or *T. humilis* 'Alba Coerulea Oculata' are early blooming, low-maintenance bulbs that naturalise easily and that could be used more commonly in public landscapes.

In the Northern Spur, continuous interest and change begins in April with these small bulbs that die back after blooming and are soon hidden by the foliage of the later perennials. After the peak flowering times of spring and summer, the garden changes dramatically in autumn. It becomes a different garden. The goldenrods, asters and the autumnal

CHAPTER 6 **The elements of design**

257

▲ Figure 6.49

The Northern Spur in May. In the foreground, and scattered throughout, the lobed leaves of wild Geranium (*Geranium maculatum*) and Max Frei bloody cranesbill (*Geranium sanguineum* 'Max Frei') make a pattern against more finely textured plants like northern sea oats (*Chasmanthium latifolium*). Seen against this green backdrop are the white flowers of early blooming bulbs and perennials: Pheasant's eye daffodil (*Narcissus poeticus* var. *recurvus*), the eastern shooting star (*Dodecatheon meadia*) (white form) and eastern foam flower (*Tiarella cordifolia*).
Source: Photo courtesy of Piet Oudolf.

tints of Indian physic announce that winter is coming—but it is a long, slow turning, a savouring of the autumn that lingers into winter. Like scenes in a movie, as one image fades, another quite different scene emerges.

The Chelsea Thicket

Between 21st and 22nd Street, visitors encounter the Chelsea Thicket, a two-block-long forest of small trees and shrubs underplanted with perennials.

Bromelike sedge (*Carex bromoides*), bristle-leaf sedge (*C. eburnea*) and bunny blue sedge (*C. laxiculmis* 'Hobb') are used together in the Chelsea Thicket. These non-invasive, native evergreen groundcovers are long-lived, hardy and tolerate full sun to part shade. They will form a matrix to the thicket without crowding out other forest-floor plants and will be able to adapt to changing light conditions as the woody plants mature.

Compared to Piet's other work, like The Battery and the Lurie Garden, the High Line looks wilder, less ordered and more like the ruderal landscape it replaced. It is characterised by a greater interweaving of plants and a closer mimicry of plant associations and patterns found in nature. The overriding order of the High Line is provided by its sequence of diverse plant

▲ Figure 6.50

Autumn is the time of peak interest in the Northern Spur. In the midground, the yellow flowers of the bluestem goldenrod (*Solidago caesia*) are paired with mauve Michaelmas daisy (*Aster amellus*). In the foreground, the small white blossoms of flowering spurge (*Euphorbia corollata*) float in the air like sea spray, and the flat-topped clusters of American boneset (*Eupatorium perfoliatum*) go to seed. Indian physic (*Porteranthus stipulatus*) and Bowman's root (*Porteranthus trifoliatus*) are native American wildflowers that grew on the abandoned High Line. In May, their delicate white five-petalled blossoms attract bees and butterflies. Seen here in autumn, their leaves turn a bronzy red. In winter, they display persistent seed heads on reddish stems.
Source: Photo courtesy of Piet Oudolf.

communities. This allows for a more complex planting in which moments of delightful surprise follow one after the other, regardless of the season.

Planting for biodiversity

In designing the planting of the High Line, Piet used predominately native American plants in ecologically based plant associations. Because of the variety of blossom types and extended period of bloom, the High Line provides habitat for bees, butterflies, moths, other pollinating insects and birds. New York City is located on the Atlantic Flyway and is home to more that 200 different species of birds annually (Audubon Society, n.d.). The High Line provides habitat for a number of native bird species that are year-round residents—like peregrine falcon (*Falco peregrinus*), northern cardinal (*Cardinalis cardinalis*), mourning dove (*Zenaida macroura*) and northern mockingbird (*Mimus polyglottos*)—or that use the High Line for rest and foraging on migration, like the ruby-crowned kinglet (*Regulus calendula*), white-throated sparrow (*Zonotrichia albicollis*) and palm warbler (*Setophaga palmarum*) (High Line a, n.d.). Piet's planting of the High Line demonstrates that designing for aesthetics and experience can also support biological diversity. Such landscapes are multi-functional biophilic landscapes in which the presence of other life forms makes them inherently more attractive to humans.

CHAPTER 6 **The elements of design**

▲ Figure 6.51

The Northern Spur in winter is especially reminiscent of the landscape of the abandoned rail line. In the foreground left, the Pennsylvania sedge is still green and the fine seed heads of alumroot are held aloft on thin stems. In the foreground centre, the palmate leaves of wild *Geranium* display their autumn colour. On the right (foreground and midground), northern sea oats (*Chasmanthium latifolium*) provides winter structure. Source: Photo courtesy of Piet Oudolf.

Maintenance

Unlike traditional perennial plantings that are cut down in autumn, Piet's designs are intended to be left standing through the winter. As well as giving seasonal interest, overwintering plants provide cover and food for small birds and mammals and hibernating insects. However, the plants do need to be cut back in spring before new growth emerges, and this can foster soil health and subsequent plant growth. In March and April, the High Line staff direct more than 100 volunteers in the annual Spring Cutback. The cuttings are shredded and composted before being returned to the High Line plantings as mulch in a process that simulates the plant decomposition and nutrient cycling found in nature (High Line b, n.d.).

At the Lurie Garden, selected areas, such as those over the root zone of trees, are cut by hand. The rest of the garden is cut once a year, when the ground is frozen, using a ride-on brush cutter. The resulting mulch is left in place to suppress weeds, hold moisture and, when decayed, add organic matter and nutrients to the soil. This produces a healthy soil and a plant community that does not require frequent watering, additional fertiliser or chemical pest controls (Lurie Garden, n.d.).

In both the Lurie Garden and the High Line, plantings are given supplemental watering as needed and mowed or cut back in early spring. It might be possible in some perennial and grass plantings to eliminate

▲ Figure 6.52

Redbud trees (*Cercis canadensis*) (foreground, left of path) and flowering quince (*Chaenomeles speciosa* 'Toyo-Nishiki') (midground right of path) provide spring bloom in the Chelsea Thicket. On the ground plane, Balkan cranesbill (*Geranium macrorrhizum* 'Spessart') (left of path foreground), spring vetch (*Lathyrus vernus*) (reddish-purple beneath the redbud), yellow Pagoda dog's tooth violet (*Erythronium* 'Pagoda') (far left foreground), Blue Moon wild *Phlox* (*Phlox divaricata* 'Blue Moon') (left, centre of the tracks foreground) and white eastern foam flower (*Tiarella cordifolia*) (far left) bloom amidst low-growing sedges (*Carex* spp.) and barrenwort (*Epimedium* x *perralchicum* 'Fröhnleiten').
Source: Photo courtesy of Piet Oudolf.

supplemental watering altogether, but this would depend on the region, the plants used, the soil and other site conditions.

If left to evolve through biotic succession, some plants will become more numerous, while others decline or even drop out of the mix. Plants can be "edited" each year to restrict their spread. After a period of evolution, the whole meadow might be cultivated and replanted. From an ecosystem services perspective, these landscapes can conserve potable water, reduce fossil fuel emissions and provide pollinator and bird habitat. These benefits are not a given of naturalistic landscapes, but with intention and knowledge they can be incorporated.

Many public and private institutions are struggling to afford the maintenance of green lawns and traditional plantings. The Lurie Garden and the High Line demonstrate the possibility of having low-chemical, low-water, low-fossil-fuel and low-maintenance landscapes that attract the public and support regional biological diversity.

Conclusion

Over the years, as his knowledge and experience grew, Piet developed a number of different ways of positioning plants in the landscape. He can now use these methods in different areas within the overall design, combine them in new ways and he will, no doubt, continue to create innovative ways of arranging plants. His early works featured block and matrix plantings, but he now uses more intermingled plants, giving his work a "wilder" and more visually complex appearance. The clipped shrubs that played a major role in his earlier work have diminished and American prairie plants like *Panicum*, *Schizachyrium* and *Sporobolus*, which he first encountered in designing the Lurie Garden, are increasingly used.

Especially in Piet's later work, one cannot be in his landscapes without being put in mind of the archetype of the landscape he is representing. To be in the Lurie Garden in Chicago is to be transported in feeling to the oak savannah and prairie of the American Midwest. In the truest sense, Piet is a creative artist who perceives the world in a singularly personal way and is able to interpret and share his affective response with the public.

Piet Oudolf's principles and practices

Piet Oudolf has spoken and written about a number of principles and practices that are expressed in his work. I have summarised several of these below and added some of my own observations.

The purpose of planting design is to create a particular intended experience.

- Inspired by the feelings evoked in natural landscapes, Piet seeks to convey a particular emotional response in his designs. To him, every plant has a character that is inseparable from the landscape in which it originates. The feelings it evokes result from its appearance and its association with that landscape. Piet's plantings convey the impression of a particular landscape and a specific atmosphere that changes with the seasons.

Create an overall unity so that complexity can be added.

- Piet uses different devices to establish a perception of unity in his plantings. In several of his works we see a visually simple centre surrounded by more complex plantings. The Rivers of *Salvia* in Droomparken in Enköping and in the Lurie Garden in Chicago, the matrix planting in Potter's Fields, London, and the central drift of *Deschampia caespitosa* 'Goldschleier' at Leuvehoofd, Rotterdam, are examples of this technique. In the High Line, the sequence of landscape types creates the order of the overall design that allows more complexity within each section of the park.

To increase unity, combine plants of similar form, texture and colour.

- Much of the sense of unity in Piet's work comes from the use of compatible forms. Mounded grasses like *Helictotrichon sempervirens* and *Sesleria nitida* blend with Mediterranean subshrubs that have low, rounded forms, such as rock rose (*Helianthemum alpestre*) and lavender-cotton (*Santolina chamaecyparissus*). Tall grasses are combined with perennials that display their flowers on upright stems. For example, the forms of *Calamagrostis* x *acutiflora* 'Karl Foerster' and *Veronicastrum virginicum* harmonise perfectly, making the overall planting more unified (King and Oudolf, 1998). Piet also combines perennials having upright spires of flowers, such as *Salvia, Nepeta, Lysimachia clethroides* and *Persicaria amplexicaulis*. These same perennials often have many small fine-textured florets. While their leaf texture may vary, the plant forms and the texture of their flowers are similar. Often, he uses analogous colour schemes that most people find harmonious. Taken together, the colours, plant forms and flower textures serve to unify the composition, while the foliage textures and winter seed heads add complexity.

Plants that have grassy leaves, like day lilies *(Hemerocallis)*, Siberian *Iris* (*Iris siberica*), big blue lily turf (*Liriope muscari*) and sedges (*Carex* spp.) harmonise with the form and textures of grasses.

- Where varied site conditions demand a variety of different plants, combining plants that have similar forms and foliage textures is a useful tool for maintaining visual unity. This principle may be applied to any planting design and not just "grassy" landscapes.

Create designed plant associations by combining plants that come from similar habitats.

- Piet mixes plants from different parts of the world that share a common ecological niche. For this reason, the plants in his designed plant associations look like they belong together, transmit the impression of the same landscape type and have the same horticulture requirements.

Use plants that have four seasons of interest.

- Piet's biggest innovation has been designing for year-round interest with herbaceous plants. Perennials and grasses that have interesting seed heads and maintain their structure through the winter are major components of his designs. Perennials that have two or more seasons of interest are commonly used. Non-structural plants, like early bulbs, provide interest in that brief period between the cutting back of the herbaceous plants in late winter or early spring and the emergence of the new foliage and flowers of the structural plants.

Plant in layers.

- Another way that Piet limits complexity in his design is by conceiving his plantings in layers. For example, a planting of low sedges and groundcovers, taller perennials, and shrubs would be a three-layer planting. Piet typically limits himself to two or three layers so that the design does not become visually confusing (Stuart-Smith, 2013).

Intermingle wild-looking plants for a wild look.

- Piet's plantings suggest the wild, untended places of the countryside. This is largely due to the appearance of the plants themselves. Many of the plants have a greater proportion of foliage to blossom than traditional garden perennials. Their flowers are often single blossoms or clusters of small florets rather than large double blossoms, and their inflorescences have a variety of forms, which draw attention during the growing season and produce interesting seed heads in autumn and winter.
- The arrangement of the plants is critical to the natural look of Piet's plantings. Recent plantings are more like successional landscapes in appearance. To achieve this look, he arranges plants in separate layers, scattering plants throughout the matrix and among the drifts so that they intertwine rather than staying in clear drifts or blocks. In the Lurie Garden or his home garden of Hummelo, Piet allows the plants to self-sow and then follows up with an artistic "editing". This is a major change from traditional landscape maintenance that uses weeding, mowing and herbicides to freeze biotic succession and maintain each plant in its original location. Allowing self-sowing, in imitation of the natural process of biotic succession, achieves an intermingled look similar to that of natural landscapes.

Plant cespitose grasses.

- Grasses add continuity and interest. Their structure, texture, lightness and movement provide a year-round ambiance. Cespitose grasses are long-lived, low-maintenance plants that convey a sense of unity and naturalness. Their persistent seed heads add winter interest. When combined with long-lived clump-forming perennials, cespitose grasses create landscapes that stay in place or evolve slowly.

Apply the 70 per cent rule to meadow plantings.

- In meadow plantings, Piet recommends using about 70 per cent structural plants. That is, plants that maintain a good visual structure and interest for most of the year. The remaining 30 per cent is comprised of "filler plants" that offer colour and interest early in the season. A good example is any of the perennial *Geraniums*, which could provide pattern and colour as the other perennials are growing and then largely disappear amongst the later-flowering perennials.

In a matrix planting, use long-lived clump-forming plants to provide the ground for the figure of the primary plants.

- A matrix planting is a figure–ground pattern. The matrix plants provide a unified backdrop of texture and colour so that the primary plants stand out as a figure against the ground of the matrix plants. Therefore, matrix plants should be visually subdued plants that provide a solid year-round presence. It is also imperative that they be long-lived clump-forming plants that do not out-compete the primary plants. In Piet's matrix plantings, cespitose grasses are used most often as the matrix plants, but clump-forming perennials like *Epimedium* and *Tellima* are also appropriate (Kingsbury and Oudolf, 2016).
- There are no fixed rules for the proportion of matrix plants to primary plants, but there must be a clear setting of matrix plants around each primary plant or group of primary plants in the matrix so that the figure–ground effect is achieved.

Use repetition to create pattern.

- The larger the area being planted, the more difficult it is to get a sense of unity. Repeating individual plants or plant groupings creates a visible pattern and gives a sense of cohesion to the design (Kingsbury and Oudolf, 2016).

Create a feeling of increased depth and a dreamlike atmosphere.

- Piet uses two techniques to get a sense of depth and a dreamlike atmosphere in his plantings. The perception of depth is increased by placing stronger saturated colours in the foreground and muted tints of the same hue in the background. This is especially true of saturated reds, which advance more than other colours.
- In the same way, using coarser foliage in the foreground and very fine textured plants behind, or even just layering fine textures, one behind the other, into the background increases a sense of depth.
- A large part of the atmosphere that Piet achieves in his designs is due to his use of grasses. For example, the very fine seed heads *Molinia caerulea* 'Transparent' and *Sporobolus heterolepis* float in an almost transparent cloud above the grassy foliage and give a misty, dreamlike quality to the scene (see Figure 7.18).

Plant for biodiversity.

- Using a wide variety of flower forms and providing a long season of bloom are key principles in creating pollinator habitat. When perennial plants are left to overwinter, they provide winter cover and persistent seeds and fruits that are eaten by resident and migrating birds. Planting in layers also adds biodiversity.

Chapter 6 principles

In addition to the design principles and practices illustrated in the work of Piet Oudolf, others that are discussed in this chapter are summarised below.

- A variety of design elements can be used in any planting as long as a unified quality is maintained.
- More than one aesthetic element of any design needs to be sustained if a sense of unity is to prevail.
- The more elements of design that are fixed by the designer, the greater will be the sense of unity, order and harmony.
- All plantings should be balanced compositions, because unbalanced compositions appear arbitrary, unfinished and unstable.
- Landscape designers need to take care to design balanced views. The goal should be to compose and balance views that are seen most often or that have greater importance.
- Plant masses in a planting design should be balanced, either symmetrically or asymmetrically.
- Objects in space have suggested directional movement.
- If opposing directional movement forces are balanced, the place becomes stable and balanced. This is calming.
- If opposing forces are asymmetrically balanced, the resulting balance is usually imperfect and a suggested movement of objects in space remains. This is dynamic and draws people's attention.
- Larger, denser objects have more momentum and require greater oppositional force to be balanced.
- Objects with larger mass attract the eye more strongly than those with lesser mass.
- When two objects of unequal visual weight are placed together, they will appear unbalanced.
- If two plants are of the same variety, the larger plant will have the greater visual weight.
- Two or more smaller plants can be used to balance a larger plant.
- If two plants are of different types, the denser, darker and more compact plant will have greater visual weight for its size.
- The scalene triangle can be used to lay out plants in plan and elevation where a "natural" appearance and asymmetrical balance is desired.
- It is essential that a harmonious and unified plant palette be implemented if a restorative experience is intended.
- Visual unity can be achieved while using a great many plants, if those plants share similar forms, colours and textures.
- Organising plants into distinct areas that have repeating colours and textures and a limited number of contrasting textures increases visual unity and preference.
- When plants are arranged in groups, visual unity is supported.

- Plants will be perceived as groups when they are placed in proximity to each other, are placed similarly, when they are visually similar and when they have movement in the same direction.
- A strong figure–ground relationship, such as that created in a matrix planting, creates a focal point and focuses the viewer's attention.
- Using isolated plants that have exaggerated visual characteristics increases viewer pleasure.
- In any figure–ground composition, overall uniformity is required if the figure is to be clearly seen.
- Juxtaposition is one of the strongest triggers of attention available to the designer.
- Uniform textures promote simplicity and unity.
- Fine textures have been shown to increase preference.
- Repetition of plants, or plant groupings that have the same or similar aesthetic qualities, helps landscapes to appear unified.
- Sudden changes in the landscape may feel jarring or discordant. Visual gradation of form, texture and colour are used to make subtle and harmonious transitions that increase a sense of unity.
- Textural gradation is a simple and effective way to make gradual transitions in the landscape.
- People tend to perceive a line as having movement in a certain direction and will mentally or physically continue that movement in its current direction.
- The places where lines in the landscape converge are places where the eye is led to rest and where important elements should be placed.
- In a plant palette that is largely evergreen plants, between 30 and 40 per cent of the plants should be deciduous or herbaceous plants, selected for their uncluttered winter silhouette or pruned to achieve a clear line. These plants add balance and lightness to what would otherwise be a visually heavy planting.
- The line of a plant's shape expresses a vector of movement along the axis of the plant's mass.
- Objects in space, particularly vertical objects, draw us towards them
- Planting design should reinforce circulation by creating lines of continuation that visually reinforce the intended movement in the landscape.

Glossary

Asymmetrical balance: A form of balance in which elements on either side of an axis or dividing line are off centre, and the objects themselves are unequal in visual weight, but the whole visual array is balanced.

Balance: The sense created in the viewer that the visual weights or movements in a visual array are in equilibrium. It helps to create a sense that everything is "in its place" and increases the viewers' preference for what is seen.

Biotic or **ecological succession**: A sequence of plant communities that develop in the same area in a predictable sequence over a period of time.

Block planting: A planted area that is usually composed of a single species or cultivar. They may be straight-lined geometric or curvilinear in shape. In the Lurie Garden meadow, Piet Oudolf used blocks composed of two different perennials.

Coherence: One of four components of Stephen and Rachel Kaplan's preference matrix. It includes anything that allows the viewer to mentally organise the two-dimensional view into a number of coherent zones. A coherent scene has only a few distinct areas, repeating themes and textures, and limited contrasting textures.

Complexity: The measure of visual richness of a view, including different colours, textures, plants, materials, structures and topography.

Continuity: The principle of continuity states that people perceive a line as having movement and will visually or physically continue that line of movement. In landscape design, the principle of continuity is used to guide the viewer or the viewer's eye through the landscape to places of importance.

Density: Visual density is the perceived weight per unit of volume of an object. Visually dense objects have greater visual weight.

Drifts: This term was first used by Gertrude Jekyll to define her manner of planting perennial flower beds. Drifts are multiple plants of the same kind, arranged in long, narrow masses. When drift plantings are viewed obliquely, the effect of layering multiple plants one behind another makes the planting more naturalistic because it gives the sense that the plants are intermingled. When the colours of the drifts are similar in saturation and hue, optical mixing occurs at the edges.

Elements of design: Line, shape, form, mass, texture and colour comprise the elements of design. Every visual design employs some or all of these elements, as they are the essential building blocks of a visual composition.

Figure–ground: A property of perception. It refers to the human tendency to perceive objects as being distinct from a contrasting background. Any design element can be used to separate a figure from its ground, but colour is particularly effective.

Focal point: An element in the landscape that attracts attention because it contrasts aesthetically with its surroundings. Focal points draw attention and stimulate and support aesthetic experience while fostering wayfinding.

Forb: Any perennial that is not a grass.

Form: The form of any object is its three-dimensional shape.

Gestalt theory: A theory of perception developed by a group of German psychologists in the 1920s. It posits a process of perception in which stimuli are ordered so that a structured whole is perceived from individual parts.

Gradation: A form of transition in which change occurs by steps or degrees, from one condition to another.

Harmony: This occurs when things seem right or suitable together. In a harmonious planting design, the plants are in visual harmony because they are in some way similar or related. They share some common aesthetic quality, such as similar forms and textures, or they are related in some other way, such as by the use of grouping or an analogous colour scheme. Harmony in design supports unity and vice versa.

Juxtaposition: In design, the term *juxtaposition* refers to the combining of dissimilar elements so that their essential qualities are revealed more strongly.

Line: The continuous element linking points in space. Lines describe shapes or forms.

Mass: Visual mass is a measure of the ability of an object to draw the eye. Objects or groups of objects that occupy a larger proportion of the picture plane have greater visual mass than those that occupy less of the picture plane. The figure in a figure–ground has greater visual mass than the ground, and warm and saturated colours have greater visual mass than pastel and cool colours (see Chapter 7 for more discussion).

Massed planting: A style of planting associated with modernism in which sub-areas of the total design are filled with plants of the same type. It produces a simple visual array that is clearly not natural and that emphasises the characteristics of the chosen plants through repetition and the relative proportion of the visual array that each plant type occupies.

Matrix planting: A type of planting in which visually interesting so-called primary plants are inserted into a uniform mass of a single plant or a few plants. Matrix plantings create a figure–ground relationship that causes viewers to mentally engage the landscape.

Naturalise: The term *naturalise* refers to plants or animals that are able to become established and reproduce in an area in which they are not native.

Naturalistic: Derived from or imitative of nature.

Natural landscape or **environment**: A landscape that is largely unaltered by human activities. The term is also used to mean naturalistic, that is, in imitation of nature. Throughout this book I have used this term to describe a landscape that is high in natural content and in this chapter to mean a landscape whose design has been influenced by wild or ruderal landscapes, rather than by the traditions of cultural landscape design. (See also *Wild*.)

New Perennial Movement: Also known as the New Perennial Planting Movement, Dutch Wave Movement and New Wave Movement, the New Perennial Movement is epitomised by the work of Piet Oudolf. It uses a range of perennials and grasses to achieve a natural look with an emphasis on structural characteristics and four-season interest.

Order in design: The way in which elements of a design are arranged in relation to each other or a particular characteristic (Cambridge English Dictionary, n.d.). Establishing a visual order is a prerequisite to having people engage with the designs we create, so that they may be stimulated or satisfied. Establishing a visual hierarchy or balance, the use of repetition and transitions are some ways of establishing order in design.

Perception: The process of receiving and interpreting sensory stimulus. Human perception of the landscape involves quickly and unconsciously comprehending the content of a scene or view and assessing the possibilities for action in that landscape (Hadavi et al., 2015).

Perceptual process: A series of steps which people take when confronted with a visual array or other sensory stimulus. They mentally organise and interpret that stimulus and finally respond to that stimulus. A person's response to their perception includes their affective response or emotional experience.

Picture plane: See *Visual array*.

Ruderal landscape: Ruderal plants are those that colonise disturbed areas. A landscape that humans have disturbed and then abandoned will be filled with both native and non-native ruderal plants and is a ruderal landscape. Ruderal landscapes are the wild places of cities; vacant lots, highway verges and post-industrial sites.

Shape: The two-dimensional form of an object. For example, an upright narrow tree is said to have a fastigiate or columnar shape. The line of the silhouette of a plant describes the shape of the plant.

Simple structure: Simple structures may be created by design or be formed in a person's mind in the process of perception. They group information, elements and stimuli into blocks or groups as a way of organising and simplifying that which is seen.

Symmetrical balance: A form of balance in which the size, shape and visual weight of objects on opposite sides of an axis or dividing line are equal.

Texture: Visual texture is the visual impression of smoothness or roughness of the surface of an object. Plant texture is created by shadows cast by the foliage of the plant.

Unity: Visual unity is the quality in a work of art or design that causes it to be perceived as a whole. It is produced though the use of such things as hierarchy, repetition, harmony and balance and is the state in which all the parts of the design look as if they belong together and nothing is incongruous or out of place. Perceiving unity gives people pleasure, and unified designs are preferred.

Variety: See *Complexity*.

Visual array: That which is seen. It may be a two-dimensional view of the three-dimensional landscape or of a two-dimensional art poster.

Visual composition: A visual array that is not haphazard; its elements have been purposefully arranged with a particular intent, such as unity or harmony.

Visual weight: The idea that some objects are perceived as being heavier than others. Compact forms and darker colours increase visual weight. Visual weight is used in design to create balance, hierarchy and harmony.

Wild: The term *wild* refers to plants or animals that grow or live independently of people in natural conditions and with natural characteristics (Cambridge English Dictionary, n.d.). Practitioners of the New Perennial Movement seek to create a wild aesthetic in order to provoke an experiential response that is similar to what people experience in natural or ruderal landscapes.

Notes

1 Colour is so powerful and complex an element in design that it is the subject of the whole of Chapter 7.
2 While the availability of plant images and information on the internet is an important aid to modern designers, it cannot substitute for direct knowledge built up over a long period of time (and preferably by growing the plants used). However, since few designers could grow everything they would wish to use over the course of a career, continual self-education, combined with critical evaluation of one's own and others' completed projects, should be used to compensate for a lack of direct experience with particular plants.
3 *Heemparks* or home parks are a Dutch invention in which native plants are artistically composed to simulate the natural ecosystems of the broader landscape.
4 It is also referred to as the Dutch Wave, New Wave or New Perennial Planting Movement.
5 Meadow sage is commonly a hybrid between *Salvia nemorosa* and other perennial sages like *S. pratensis* and *S. amplexicaulis*. They may be listed as *Salvia nemorosa*, *S. sylvestris* and *S.* x *Superba*. Meadow sages are disease- and pest-resistant and tolerate a wide variety of soils, but require good drainage. Woodland sage and wood sage are also accepted common names. These sages are compact, upright plants that do not need staking. Throughout their long season of bloom, they support pollinators and hummingbirds and if spent flowers are removed will provide a second, and even third, set of blooms. In many areas they can be left standing all winter long and cut back just as new foliage appears in spring.

References

Arnheim, R. (1974). *Art and visual perception: A psychology of the creative eye. The new version.* Berkeley, CA: University of California Press.

Aronoff, J., Woike, B.A., & Hyman, L.M. (1992). Which are the stimuli in facial displays of anger and happiness? Configurational bases of emotion recognition. *Journal of Personality and Social Psychology,* 62(6), 1050.

Audubon Society. (n.d.). *New York City.* Accessed July 16, 2017 at www.nycaudubon.org/go-birding.

Bar, M., & Neta, M. (2006). Humans prefer curved visual objects. *Psychological Science,* 17(8), 645–648.

Barron, F., & Welsh, G.S. (1952). Artistic perception as a possible factor in personality style: Its measurement by a figure preference test. *Journal of Psychology,* 33(2), 199–203.

Bell, S. (2004). *Elements of visual design in the landscape.* London: Spon Press.

Bell, S. (2012). *Landscape: Pattern, perception and process.* New York: Routledge.

Cambridge English Dictionary. (n.d.). Accessed September 15, 2017 at http://dictionary.cambridge.org/dictionary/english/matrix.

Cárdenas, R.A., & Harris, L.J. (2006). Symmetrical decorations enhance the attractiveness of faces and abstract designs. *Evolution and Human Behavior,* 27(1), 1–18.

Davies, J. (2014). *Riveted: The science of why jokes make us laugh, movies make us cry, and religion makes us feel one with the universe.* New York: Palgrave Macmillan.

Eisenman, R., & Coffee, S. (1964). Aesthetic preferences of art students and mathematics students. *Journal of Psychology,* 58(2), 375–378.

Field Operations. (n.d.). Accessed September 28, 2017 at www.fieldoperations.net/project-details/project/High Line.html.

Hadavi, S., Kaplan, R., and Hunter, M.C.R. (2015). Environmental affordances: A practical approach for design of nearby outdoor settings in urban residential areas. *Landscape and Urban Planning,* 134, 19–32.

Hartlage, R., & Fischer, S. (2015) *The authentic garden: Naturalistic and contemporary landscape design.* New York: Monacelli Press.

Hawthorne, L. (2009). *Gardening with shape, line and texture: A plant design sourcebook.* Portland, OR: Timber Press.

High Line a. (n.d.). *The Friends of the High Line blog.* Accessed September 20, 2017 at www.thehighline.org/blog/tagged/birds.

High Line b. (n.d.). *The Friends of the High Line blog.* Accessed June 17, 2017 at www.thehighline.org/blog/2017/04/26/it-s-a-wrap-gardeners-volunteers-complete-spring-cutback.

Hightshoe, G.L. (1987). *Native trees, shrubs, and vines for urban and rural America: A planting design manual for environmental designers.* New York: John Wiley & Sons.

Hobhouse, P. (1985). *Colour in your garden.* London: Harper Collins.

Jekyll, G. (1908). *Colour in the flower garden.* London: Country Life Ltd.

Kaplan, R. (1984). Impact of urban nature: A theoretical analysis. *Urban Ecology,* 8(3), 189–197.

Kaplan, R., Kaplan, S., & Ryan, R. (1998). *With people in mind: Design and management of everyday nature.* Washington, DC: Island Press.

Kaplan, S. (1975). An informal model for the prediction of preference. In E.H. Zube, R.O. Brush, & J.G. Fabos (Eds.), *Landscape assessment: Values, perceptions, and resources* (pp. 92–101). Stroudsburg, PA: Dowden, Hutchinson, & Ross.

Kaplan, S. (1988). Perception and landscape: Conceptions and misconceptions. In J.L. Nasar (Ed.), *Environmental aesthetics: Theory, research, and application* (pp. 45–55). New York: Cambridge University Press. Accessed May 5, 2018 at www.fs.fed.us/psw/publications/documents/psw_gtr035/psw_gtr035_05_s-kaplan.pdf.

Kaplan, S., & Kaplan, R. (1982). *Cognition and environment* (pp. 88–98). New York: Praeger.

King, M., & Oudolf, P. (1998). *Gardening with grasses.* London: Frances Lincoln Ltd.

Kingsbury, N., & Oudolf, P. (2016). *Planting: A new perspective.* Portland, OR: Timber Press.

Kuck, L.E., (1984). *The world of the Japanese garden.* New York: Weatherhill.

Kuper, R. (2017). Evaluations of landscape preference, complexity, and coherence for designed digital landscape models. *Landscape and Urban Planning*, 157, 407–421.

Lurie Garden. (n.d.). *It's time to cut the garden down.* The Lurie Garden blog. Accessed September 27, 2017 at www.luriegarden.org/2016/02/20/its-time-to-cut-down-the-garden/.

Mallet, R. (2011). *Envisioning the garden: Line, scale, distance, form, color, and meaning.* New York: WW Norton & Company.

Masuno, S. (1994). *Kokoro: The Japanese garden as an expression of mind in Nitobe Memorial Garden.* International Symposium Proceedings, University of British Columbia (pp. 7–11).

McGrane, S. (2008). *A landscape in winter, dying heroically.* New York Times. Accessed September 10, 2017 at www.nytimes.com/2008/01/31/garden/31piet.html.

Oudolf, P. quoted in Spencer, T. (n.d.). *Bringing Hummelo home.* The New Perennialist: Explorations in Naturalistic Planting Design. Accessed November 28, 2017 at www.thenewperennialist.com/bringing-hummelo-home/.

Oudolf, P. (2015). Personal communication.

Oudolf, P., and Darke, R. (2017). *Gardens of the High Line: Elevating the nature of modern landscapes.* Portland, OR: Timber Press.

Oudolf, P., and Kingsbury, P. (2015). *Oudolf Hummelo: A journey through a plantsman's life.* New York: Monacelli Press.

Özdil, T., Pradhan, R., Munshi, R., & Khoshkar, A. (2017). 2017's LAF's CSI Program Landscape Performance Series: Wayne Ferguson Plaza. Arlington, TX: University of Texas. Accessed September 10, 2017 at https://landscapeperformance.org/sites/default/files/Wayne%20Ferguson%20Methodology_0.pdf.

Ramachandran, V.S. (2003). The artful brain. 2003 BBC Reith Lectures. Accessed May 15, 2017 at https://net.educause.edu/ir/library/pdf/ffp0511s.pdf.

Robinson, F.B. (1940). *Planting design.* New York: McGraw Hill.

Robinson, N. (2004). *The planting design handbook.* Aldershot: Ashgate Publishing.

Rodenas, M., Sancho-Royo, F., & González-Bernáldez, F. (1975). Structure of landscape preferences: A study based on large dams viewed in their landscape setting. *Landscape Planning*, 2, 159–178.

Spencer, T. (2018). *Bringing Hummelo home.* The New Perennialist: Explorations in Naturalistic Planting Design. Accessed May 15, 2018 at www.thenewperennialist.com/bringing-hummelo-home/.

Stuart-Smith, T. (2013). *Dutch master: The garden design genius of Piet Oudolf.* The Telegraph. Accessed June 17, 2017 at www.telegraph.co.uk/gardening/10036592/Dutch-master-the-garden-design-genius-of-Piet-Oudolf.html/.

Yoneda, Y. (2016). (Interview). *Walking the High Line with its garden designer Piet Oudolf.* Inhabit blog. Accessed September 20, 2017 at http://inhabitat.com/interview-walking-the-high-line-with-its-garden-designer-piet-oudolf/.

Suggested reading

Kaplan, R., Kaplan, S., & Ryan, R. (1998). *With people in mind: Design and management of everyday nature.* Washington, DC: Island Press.

Oudolf, P. & Gerritsen, H. (2000). *Dream plants for the natural garden.* Portland, OR: Timber Press.

Chapter 7

Colour

This chapter discusses:

- The attributes of colour
- Colour perception
- The history of colour theory
- Gertrude Jekyll's application of colour theory to planting design
- Colour preference
- Human emotional response to colour
- Developing colour schemes in planting design
- A summary of principles of using colour in planting design

The human response to colour

Humans are visual creatures who collect information about their environment primarily by using their eyes. Colour recognition allows people to separate an element from its surroundings and enhances information gathering. Researchers posit that colour recognition is an evolutionary adaptation that improved the ability of our hunter-gatherer ancestors to find food (Regan et al., 2001; Sumner and Mollon, 2003), but even when it no longer supports survival, colour continues to attract people's attention and influence their moods and emotions (Mahnke, 1996). Colour stimulates and soothes, creates patterns, provides a sense of knowing and supports exploration. Designers employ colour to create places that are distinct, even unique, and that respond to people's need for stimulation, information and restoration.

However, colour is a complex and unstable element. Colours in the landscape alter their appearance with changing light conditions. Two colours viewed together will appear differently than when viewed alone, and certain pairings will intensify each colour. Designers who are able to anticipate how colours will interact and affect people's emotional state can use colour to create a desired experience.

The attributes of colour

The three basic attributes of colour—hue, saturation, and value or brightness—determine the appearance of each particular colour. What we usually speak of as a colour is the *hue* or name of the colour, such as pink or orange. Hue is the essential aspect of the appearance of a colour. *Saturation* or chroma indicates the intensity of the colour. Saturated or high-chroma colours are seen as being stronger or more vivid than low-saturation colours (Valdez and Mehrabian, 1994). The *value* or brightness of a colour is a measure of the amount of black and white that has been added to the hue. Adding white to a colour increases its value, and adding black lowers it. A colour to which white has been added would be a high-value colour. If black or grey had been added to the original hue, the resulting colour would have a lower value. A *tint* is a hue that has been mixed with white. When we speak of light green or pale yellow, we are referring to hues that have been tinted, or tints. A very light tint is sometimes referred to as a pastel, so the terms tint, high-value colour or pastel all describe a saturated hue to which white has been added (Figure 7.0).

Mixing a hue with black produces a shade of that hue. Shading makes a hue appear muted but can also increase its visual strength, causing it to be perceived as more powerful (Kaya and Epps, 2004). Such colours, especially in the foliage of a planting scheme, can be used to anchor or give repose to the composition (Figure 7.1). When mixed with both white and black, that is, grey, the resultant colour is called a tone. A saturated vermillion red in our paint box, mixed with both white and black, could produce a red brick colour that would be a tone of red.

◀ Figure 7.0

The paler *Crocosmia* seen on the right foreground is a tint of orange and has a higher value than the more saturated orange *Crocosmia* behind.
Source: Photo by Patrick Mooney.

▲ Figure 7.1

This cardinal flower (*Lobelia* 'Queen Victoria') has a saturated red flower colour, while its maroon leaves and stems are a shade of red.
Source: Photo by Patrick Mooney.

Different hues may also vary in their *brilliance* (also called *luminosity* or luminance and brightness[1]). Brilliance is a measure of the light reflectance of the hue and results from the wavelength of the hue. Yellow is the nearest to white in wavelength and so has the highest brightness, while violet is the nearest to black and so is the least brilliant.

Colour perception

Colour is the perception we humans have of reflected light. Light that humans can see, or visible light, has wavelengths of between 740 and 380 nanometres (nm) in length.[2] Within this visible light spectrum, humans perceive different wavelengths of light as being different colours, and objects that reflect light of certain wavelengths will be seen as being the colour of that wavelength of light.

When we look at the world around us, light reflected to our eyes by objects in our environment passes through the cornea, anterior chamber and lens of the eye before hitting the retina—a thin membrane that covers the interior of the back of the eyeball (Figure 7.2). Light entering the retina passes through a layer of tissues and two layers of nerve cells before falling on a layer of light-sensitive receptor cells called rods and cones. Rods enable us to perceive size and shape and help us to see at night, but do not play a role in colour vision. At higher light levels, three different types of

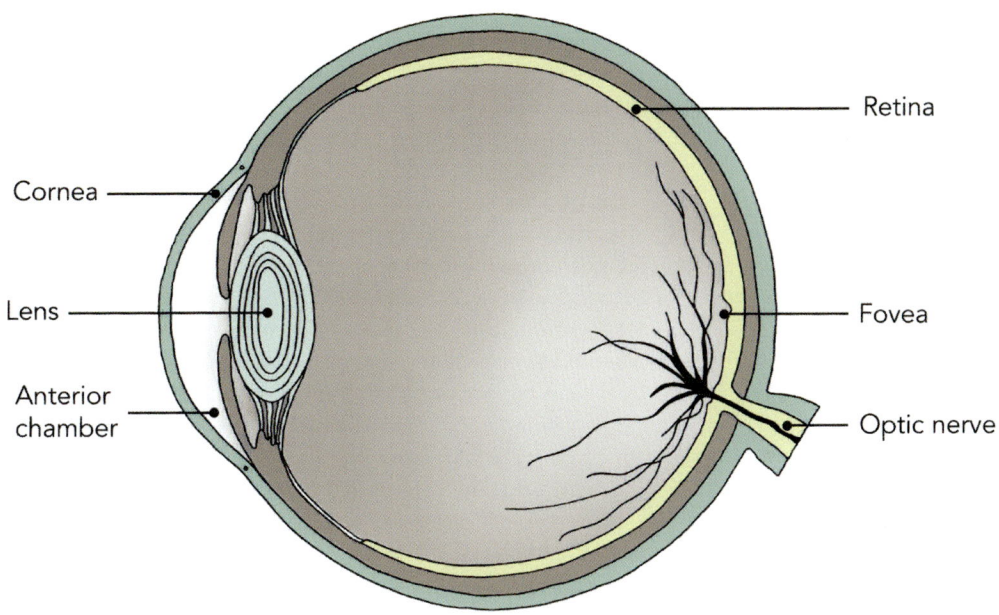

▲ Figure 7.2

The anatomy of the human eye.
Source: Image courtesy of Yiwen Ruan.

cones, that are sensitive to red, green or blue light, mediate the perception of colour by sending impulses via the optic nerve to the brain, where the impulses are processed as perceived colours. Although there is great variability in the number of red, green and blue receptors in individuals' eyes, most people see colour very similarly, suggesting that colour perception is not so much in the eye of the beholder as in their brain.

A brief history of colour

The ancient Greeks were the first to suggest that colour is not an absolute. Both Plato and Aristotle believed that light reflection was important to producing the sensation of colour. In the middle ages Galileo wrote:

> I think that tastes, odors, colors and so on are no more than mere names so far as the object in which we place them is concerned, and that they reside only in the consciousness … If the living creature were removed, all these qualities would be wiped away and annihilated.
> (Galileo, 1610, in Hilbert, 1987, p. 3)

It was Isaac Newton (1634–1727) who first set us on the road to understanding the physics of colour when he wrote "The Colors of all natural Bodies have no other origin that this, that they are variously qualified to reflect one sort of light in greater plenty than another" (Newton, 1671, p. 3084).

Newton discovered that light passing through a glass prism was bent, or refracted, into different-coloured bands of light. This effect happens because the glass of the prism slows each of the wavelengths within the light beam at a different rate, causing the light to be broken into separately coloured beams of light. He rightly hypothesised that different-coloured lights were associated with wavelengths of different speeds, with red light moving most quickly and therefore bending less sharply than violet light, which moved more slowly through the prism.[3] Newton was the first to refer to the colour "spectrum", which he divided into seven colours—red, orange, yellow, green, blue, indigo and violet—while recognising the existence of an infinite number of gradations between these colours and that colours not in the spectrum could be created by mixing the colours of the spectrum. Long-wavelength colours like red and yellow are commonly referred to as warm colours and shorter-wavelength colours like blue and violet as cool colours. Green, which lies between the warm and cool colours in the colour spectrum, is considered a neutral in garden colour schemes, because it is made by mixing warm yellow with cool blue (Wolfrom, 1992).

By bending the colour spectrum into a circle, Newton invented the colour circle or wheel, which has been used ever since to define colour relationships and develop colour schemes. Newton's discoveries led to the understanding that we see leaves as green because the chlorophyll that gives the leaves their colour absorbs the red, yellow and violet light

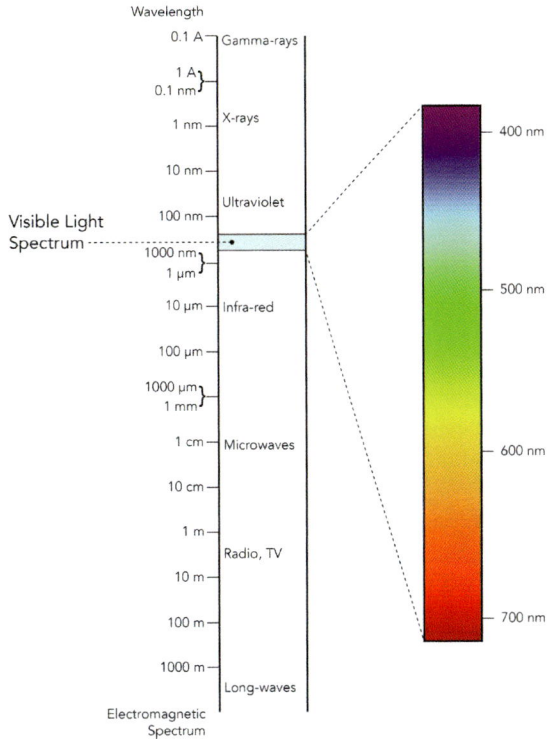

▶ Figure 7.3

Visible light within the electromagnetic spectrum. Source: Image courtesy of Yiwen Ruan.

wavelengths and reflects the wavelengths between 492 and 577 nm that our eyes and brains perceive to be green (Mahnke, 1996).

German author and statesman Johann Wolfgang von Goethe (1749–1832) is perhaps best known for his drama, *Faust*, but he was also a dedicated scientist who conducted his own experiments with light by varying the distance of the prism from the plane that caught the refracted light. In 1810, he published his *Zur Farbenlehre* or *The Theory of Colors*. In it, Goethe disputed Newton's findings and put forward his own theory that colour is a balance between light and dark. Goethe believed that darkness weakened by light produced the dark colours of blue, indigo and violet. These he referred to as "minus" colours that were associated with melancholy moods. Light mixed with darkness created red, red-orange and yellow, which he termed "plus" colours that were softly exciting and created an impression of warmth and gladness (Seamon, 1998).

Although some of Goethe's conclusions were incorrect, he made influential discoveries about how colours interact that have provided much of the basis for colour theory in art and design. Goethe found that if person looked at a high-chroma colour for a few minutes and then looked away to a neutral grey surface they would see an afterimage of a different colour. These afterimages result from the interplay of light being reflected or absorbed. The reflected light is the colour we see and the absorbed colours combine to create the afterimage. These two colours Goethe referred to as completing colours. The colour and its afterimage are in perfect harmony with each other and for this reason are today called complementary colours. Light pink is the afterimage of forest green and the afterimage of yellow is a light blue-violet (Wolfrom, 1992). When such colours are placed together, each colour appears to be intensified. Gordon Cullen described this phenomenon when he wrote:

> In a large landscape by Corot, I forget its name, a landscape of sombre greens, almost a monochrome; there is a small figure in red. It is probably the reddest thing I have ever seen.
>
> (Cullen, 1961, p. 12)

This intensification effect is now understood as one expression of what is known as the law of simultaneous contrast and Goethe's experiments with colour afterimage contributed to its discovery. Based on his observations of afterimages, Goethe developed a six-hued colour wheel in which the primary colours of red, blue and yellow alternate with the secondary colours—orange, violet and green—and each colour is placed opposite its completing colour (Figure 7.4).

Where Newton explained the cause of colour, Goethe observed and reported the effects of colours, including assigning them emotional effects. Goethe's contribution of the opposing-hue colour wheel and the principles of colour contrast and harmony are fundamental to modern colour theory and are widely used today.

◀ Figure 7.4

Goethe's colour wheel (after Briggs, 2013).
Source: Image courtesy of Yiwen Ruan.

The next influential figure in our understanding of colour was the French scientist and director of dyes for the world-renowned Gobelins tapestry works, Michel Eugène Chevreul (1786–1889), who further advanced colour theory based on his understanding of Goethe's completing colours. In attempting to resolve a complaint from the weavers that the black woolen yarns used to shade blue and violet in tapestries were weak in colour, Chevreul discovered that when colours are placed together, they alter each other in sometimes unintended ways. This led him to the discovery of his law of simultaneous contrasts, which states that "In the case where the eye sees at the same time two contiguous colours, they will appear as dissimilar as possible, both in their optical compositing and in the strength of their colour" (Chevreul, 1987, in Roque, 2011, p. 4). This occurs because the brain exaggerates the differences between colours in order to see them more distinctly, especially along the edge where two colours meet (Roque, 2011).

Chevreul's comprehensive study of the principles of colour interaction, *The Principles of Harmony and Contrast of Colors: and their Application to the Arts*, was published in France in 1839, with the first English translation following in 1854. In it, we learn that the law of simultaneous contrast is expressed differently in different colour combinations. For example, when light and dark colours are placed side by side, the lighter colour will appear lighter and the darker colour darker than when the same two colours are not juxtaposed. When two hues are placed together, we perceive them as if a small amount of the complementary colour of each had been added to the other. In the case of the red and green described by Cullen above, red and green are complementary colours. When the colours are seen together, the brain will tint the red with the complement of green, which is red, and the green will appear as if tinted with the complement of red, which is green; thus, the red becomes redder and the green becomes greener. The greater the relative amount of green in the scene, the greater will be the intensification of the red and vice versa. This same effect, then, will be found in any set of complementary colours when placed in proximity. "If the pair of juxtaposed colors is already complementary, they will simply appear intensified, and their degree of contrast will be exaggerated" (Hobhouse, 1985, p. 42).

In the case that Chevreul examined of black being mixed with violet, the black would appear as if a small amount of the yellow, the complement of violet, had been added, giving the black a weakened, greenish appearance. Chevreul also discovered that intense colours gave their hues to surrounding areas of grey or white. So that if a bright pink tree peony (*Paeonia suffruticosa* 'Leda') is planted above a grey-foliaged groundcover plant like snow-in-summer (*Cerastium tomemtosum*), the *Cerastium* will take on a pinkish tint. In the same way, any colour will influence a colour next to it, whether they are complements or not. A red flower bed placed next to a blue bed will impose its complementary colour of green on the blue bed, making it seem a little greenish, and the blue will add its complement of yellow to the red flower bed, making the red appear slightly orange-red (Capó-Aponte et al., 2009). Chevreul's treatise became so widely studied that it influenced the French Impressionist painters, modern colour theory and eventually the use of colour in garden design.

Gertrude Jekyll: Colour in the garden

In 1861, when the Central School of Design in Kensington first admitted women, an 18-year-old Gertrude Jekyll (1843–1932) enrolled to study painting. While there, she fell under the influence of some of the most important artists, designers and critics of the era. The school's principal, Richard Redgrave (1804–1888), taught the scientific principles of colour harmony as developed by Chevreul. William Morris (1834–1896), the great arts and crafts designer, lectured, as did John Ruskin (1819–1900), artist, author, critic and social thinker. Ruskin was a patron and proponent of the contemporary English painter J.M.W. Turner (1775–1851) and encouraged Jekyll to study Turner's work (Bisgrove, 2006). Turner had studied the English translation of Goethe's *Zur Farbenlehre*, and many of his paintings place Goethe's plus and minus colours in opposition to increase contrasts (Figure 7.8).

Through her studies at the Central School of Design, Jekyll developed an understanding of simultaneous contrast, colour transition and the use of colour to create dramatic effects. She considered herself an artist-gardener rather than a garden designer. The garden was her canvas and flowering plants her palette. In 1882, she purchased Munstead Wood, the 15-acre (6-hectare) site near Godalming in Surrey that was to be her home for the rest of her life. There, she integrated her artistic education and sensibility with a deep horticultural knowledge in her design of the grounds.

In 1908, Jekyll published *Colour in the Flower Garden* (later republished as *Colour Schemes for the Flower Garden*). In it she presented her principles of garden design, which she illustrated by describing the different areas of Munstead Wood. It is principally through this work that she established the herbaceous border as a serious artistic enterprise, introduced the knowledge of colour theory as developed by Chevreul into garden design, and continues until today to influence garden designers.

Munstead Wood contained ten acres of young woodland which Jekyll describes "editing" over the subsequent years. In the section below, she explains how she attempted to create unity within the different sections of the garden while establishing greater variety throughout the entire garden.

> I did not specially aim at variety, but, guided by the natural conditions of each region, tried to think out how best they might be fostered and perhaps a little bettered. The only way in which variety of aspect was deliberately chosen was in the way of thinning out the natural growths. It was a wood of seedling trees that had come up naturally after an old wood of Scotch Fir had been cut down, and it seemed well to clear away all but one, or in some cases two kinds of trees in the several regions. Even in this the intention was to secure simplicity rather than variety,

so that in moving about the ground there should be one thing at a time to see and enjoy. It is just this quality of singleness or simplicity of aim that I find wanting in gardens in general, where one may see quantities of the best plants grandly grown and yet no garden pictures.

(Jekyll, 1908, p. 8)

What evolved was a garden of woodland walks comprised of different areas, having distinct and harmonious colour schemes that bloomed in sequence, from early spring to early summer, with the open area of the main border blooming in July and August (Munstead Wood Website, n.d.).[4] Dark evergreens help to form the garden rooms and also provide the visual backdrop for the colourful flower displays within each compartment.

Like the Impressionist artists, Jekyll used complementary colours to accentuate each other but also imperceptibly blended colours together. This blending effect results, in part, from her use of overlapping linear patches of plants that she called "drifts" (Figure 7.5). The drifts juxtapose colour against colour and also serve to minimise the yellowing foliage of bulbs that, having flowered, are past their prime.

▼ Figure 7.5

In this plan view of the Hidden Garden at Munstead Wood, evergreen plants create the space and their dark green shades contrast with the drifts of high-value colours in front. Using masonry walls and dark evergreens to background colourful flowers has since become a common garden design practice. (This image has been redrawn from Jekyll's original black-and-white plan, and the colours of the evergreens and perennials she used have been added to show her colour harmonies and the use of overlapping drifts of similarly coloured flowers.)
Source: Image courtesy of Yiwen Ruan.

Code	Plantlist
aa	Asphodelus albus
ac	Asarum canadense
af	Athyrium filix-femina
ah	Asplenium scolopendrium
am	Arenaria montana
as	Anemone sylvestris
au	Achillea umbellata
av	Aquilegia vulgaris
ce	Camassia esculenta
co	Corydalis ochroleuca
ct	Cerastium tomentosum
cu	Cupressus macrocarpa
df	Dryopteris filix-mas
ep	Epimedium pinnatum
ge	Geranium ibericum
gi	Geranium incanum
go	Galium odoratum
hs	Hosta sieboldiana
ia	Ilex aquifolium
ic	Ilex crenata
if	Iris florentina
ig	Iris germanica
ir	Iris Cristata
is	Iberis Sempervirens
l	Lilium rubellum & Lilium szovitzianum & Lilium testaceum
mo	Myrrhis odorata
mp	Muscari plumosum
nr	Nepeta racemosa
os	Onoclea sensibilis
pb	Polygonatum biflorum
pc	Paeonia suffruticosa 'Comtesse de Tudor'
pd	Phlox divaricata
pl	Paradisea liliastrum
ps	Paeonia Suffruticosa 'Baronne d'Ales'
re	Rosa eglanteria
st	Sedum telephium
su	Saxifraga x urbium
tm	Taxus media
ug	Uvularia Grandiflora
vt	Viola tricolor var. hortensis

CHAPTER 7 Colour

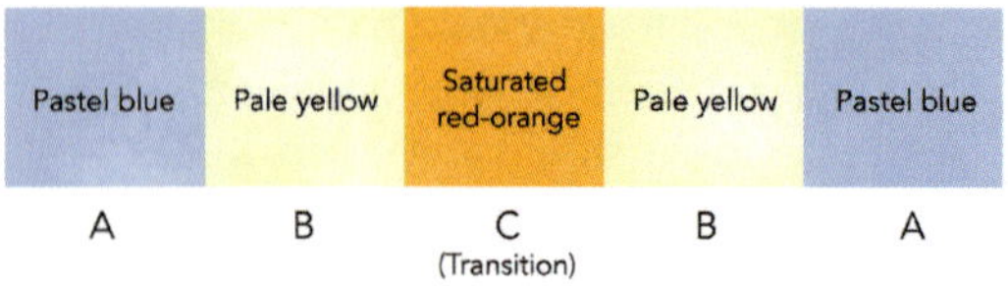

◀ **Figure 7.6**

The pale yellows (B) create a transition between the pastel blues and the saturated red-oranges in the centre of the border. The saturated warm colours in the centre act as a landmark and transition between the cooler colours at either end. This sequence of complementary colours makes all of the colours appear more vivid.
Source: Image courtesy of Yiwen Ruan.

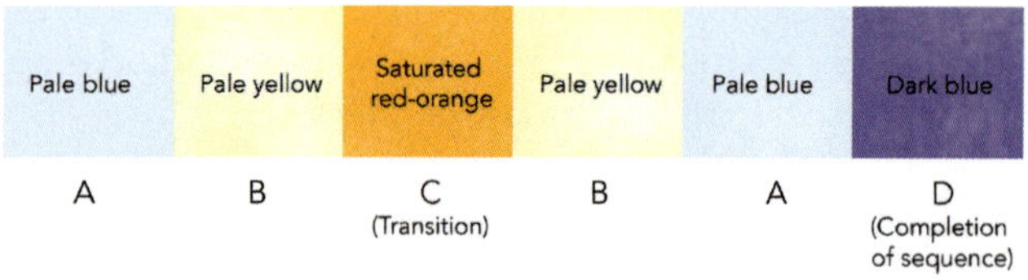

◀ **Figure 7.7**

The deeper-toned dark blue at the end of the border adds visual weight and brings the colour sequence to an emphatic close.
Source: Image courtesy of Yiwen Ruan.

Jekyll was aware of the principle of simultaneous contrast and used it with intention to make her colours more brilliant, writing:

> Standing for a few moments before the end-most region of grey and blue, and saturating the eye to its utmost capacity with these colours, it passes with extraordinary avidity to the succeeding yellows. These intermingle in a pleasant harmony with the reds and scarlets, blood-reds and clarets, and then lead again to yellows. Now the eye has again become saturated, this time with the rich colouring, and has therefore, by the law of complementary colour, acquired a strong appetite for the greys and purples. These therefore assume an appearance of brilliancy that they would not have had without the preparation provided by their recently received complementary colour.
>
> Jekyll, 1908, p. 52

As described above, a typical Jekyll border would begin with muted pastel colours at one end, then move on to the complementary colours, with, perhaps, an increase in saturation of those colours in the centre and then a return to the pastels at the other end of the border. This meant that the border had an A-B-C-B-A colour sequence or pattern whether one began their walk from one end of the border or the other (Figure 7.6). A variation on this theme would be the same scheme that finished with darker cool colours at one or both ends (Hobhouse, 1985) (Figure 7.7).

Bisgrove (2006) suggests that this use of greys and blues at one end of the border, moving to pastel pinks and yellows, to a strong chroma warm-coloured centre and then a return to blues and greys is a colour sequence

CHAPTER 7 **Colour**

▶ Figure 7.8

J.M.W. Turner's *The Burning of the Houses of Lords and Commons* shows the use of Goethe's minus colours of grey-blues on either side with fully saturated plus colours in the centre. This use of complementary colours to maximise contrast and intensity may have influenced Gertrude Jekyll.
Source: Public domain.

that Jekyll learned from Turner's use of colours in paintings like *The Burning of the Houses of Lords and Commons* (Figure 7.8).

Famed colour consultant Faber Birren provides a rationale for using this colour sequence.

> Just as warm colors are exciting and cool colors are tranquilizing, so is brightness stimulating and darkness relaxing. Change, variation, sequence are all vital in the use of color … For sedation, begin with cool colors, dim illumination, quiet environment. Blood pressure and pulse rate should drop. Follow gradually with warm color, brighter illumination, and moderate sound. End with gradual restoration of the first condition or exposure to pale yellow.
>
> (Birren, 1978, pp. 261–263)

Colour preference

For more than a century, researchers have studied colour preference and the psychology of colour (Hurlbert and Ling, 2012), yet for practical purposes the body of knowledge remains inconclusive and sometimes contradictory. Eysenck (1941) reviewed the published literature on colour preference. Because he found no cross-cultural differences, he proposed a universal preference ranking of colours from most to least liked, as follows: 1 blue, 2 red, 3 green, 4 violet, 5 orange and 6 yellow (Saito, 1996). A subsequent longitudinal study at the Oxford Brookes University School of Architecture (1970–2009) found that the order of colour preference among architecture students matched that reported by Eysenck in 1941 (Mikellides, 2012).

However, the researchers did find differences between men and women in the discernment of and preference for colours. For both genders, blue was the most popular hue and yellow the least preferred. The second most preferred colour for women was green, but red was the second most preferred colour for men. Males liked orange and yellow more than females, and females preferred pinks and lilacs more than men. Males had less marked colour preferences than women, and both men and women disliked yellow-green (Mikellides, 2012). Other researchers have found that women are better at distinguishing colours than men (Abramov, Gordon, Feldman and Chavarga, 2012a), but men are more sensitive to fine detail and movement (Abramov et al., 2012b). Despite these gender differences, there seems to be a cross-cultural preference for reds and blues, with blue being the most preferred hue and yellow-green the least preferred. However, this general finding is modified by the individual's age, experience and culture (Hurlbert and Ying, 2012).

Research in colour preference has generally involved subjects selecting colour chips on a neutral background in order of preference. However, the preferences found in such controlled, context-free research do not appear to transfer to the real world. For example, the order of colour preference found by Eysenck and other researchers does not apply to the facades of buildings (Janssens, 2001). While many studies support the finding that yellow is the least preferred colour, researchers report that pale yellows and white are the most preferred building colours (Küller, 1980), and, as we all know, yellow flowers and foliage are commonly used in landscape design.

Because early researchers did not control for saturation, brightness and hue, their results are questionable.[5] Smets (1982) found that highly saturated and brighter colours were preferred and that hue played almost no role in colour preference. More recently, researchers have found that, for objects in the real world, saturation levels and brightness affect preference more than hue. For example, people prefer room colours that correspond with their desired feeling when inhabiting the room and choose cool tints for calming effect (Manav, 2007; Palmer and Schloss, 2015).

The role of green

In real exterior environments, it would be almost impossible to experience a colour in isolation and, as we have seen, the experience of colour is mediated by its juxtaposition with other colours. In the landscape, coloured foliage and flowers are most often seen against a background of green. While the laws of simultaneous contrast tell us the effect of that juxtaposition on perceived hue, there is no consistent theory that predicts preference for colours when juxtaposed with green. However, there is reason to believe that colours seen in the context of green create positive feelings and associations. Green is generally associated with growth (Lichtenfeld, Elliot, Maier and Pekrun, 2012), feelings of calmness, happiness and relaxation, and nature (Saito, 1996). Researchers report that green has the highest number of positive emotional associations of any hue (Kaya and Epps, 2004) and that even a brief glimpse of the colour green enhances creative performance (Lichtenfeld et al., 2012). The biggest contributor to preference of a landscape scene is the amount of vegetation in the view (Arriaza, Cañas-Ortega, Cañas-Madueño and Ruiz-Aviles, 2004; R. Kaplan, 2007; Polat and Akay, 2015). Therefore, an emphasis on which colours people prefer is misplaced, and landscape designers need to be more concerned with the emotional effect of colours, their associations and their interaction in the real world (Schloss and Palmer, 2011).

Human emotional response to colour

Most people intuitively react to colour and understand that colour influences emotions. Goethe assigned lively and warming associations to the warm colours and a sense of melancholy to the cool colours. This intuitive understanding has been borne out by numerous research studies (Birren, 1978; Mahnke 1996).

Different colours affect our emotions and physiological responses differently. In art and design, it has been traditional to divide the colours into the categories of warm or cool. Long-wavelength colours, or red and yellow and any colours made by combining them, including their tints, tones and shades, are referred to as warm colours. The short-wavelength or cool colours have blue as their basis and include blue, violet and indigo. Warm colours are considered to be stimulating, especially in their most saturated form, while cool colours are thought to be soothing or calming, especially when tinted or toned. However, even cool colours when saturated can also be highly stimulating. A brilliant turquoise, for example, will attract our attention and can be more stimulating than a pastel yellow.

A number of studies have found that warm colours are arousing and cool colours relaxing (Wexner, 1954; Schaie, 1961; Wright and Rainwater, 1962). In a study that tested this hypothesis and also whether warm or cool colours were preferred, the researchers controlled for hue, saturation and brightness and asked subjects about their colour preferences over different periods of time throughout a day. They found not only that cool colours were calming and warm colours stimulating, but also that most people change their colour preference over the course of a day (Walters, Apter and Svebak, 1982). When subjects were in a state of playfulness, spontaneity or excitement, or seeking to be in that state, they preferred the high-arousal warm colours. When they were in a more serious or relaxed mood, or wishing to be in that mood, they chose the low-arousal cool colours. It appears that the preference for warm or cool colours indicates a preference for a different arousal state. The researchers labeled this oscillating colour preference *reversal theory*. Reversal theory states that people seek either a high-arousal or low-arousal state. At any point in time, a person will prefer one or the other of these arousal states but not the intermediate state, that is, neither relaxed nor stimulated, and their preference can change over periods of time as short as a few hours.

Note that reversal theory is congruous with the curiosity models discussed in Chapter 1. In what I have called the knowledge-seeking model, the reward for exploring the landscape is the removal of uncertainty and with it a change in emotional state from one of anxiety to one of clarity and the ability to relax. In the pleasure-seeking model, the reward for exploration is the replacement of boredom with aesthetic stimulus. In constructing his curiosity model, Litman (2005) recognised that people seek stimulus and arousal or clarity and relaxation. Reversal theory also recognises the preference for both high and low arousal states as fundamental to human behaviour.

Colour preference and arousal

Strongly preferred colours are associated with positive emotions and colours that are disliked with negative emotions. Colour preference is influenced not only by hue but also by tinting and shading. While the warm colours are generally seen as exciting and stimulating and cool colours as calming and relaxing (Mikellides, 2012), some researchers have concluded that people are stimulated by highly saturated hues, whether they be cool or warm (Sivik, 1974; Valdez and Mehrabian, 1994). Nevertheless, Simmons (2006) found that the most mood-lifting colours were saturated reds and yellows, while the most calming were blue and lilac tints. Tints of both warm and cool hues have been found to be have a calming effect, and light pink has such a tranquilising effect that it is used in prisons and military holding cells to calm the aggressive behaviours of inmates (Schauss, 1979).

In the real world, it seems that colour preference is based on the mood that people wish to achieve in a particular space and time. Neither warm nor cool colours, saturated nor tinted colours, should be seen as preferred in the landscape, as all will be preferred at different times. It seems that saturated colours are arousing, and saturated warm colours are perhaps more so, while tints of either warm or cool colours are calming. Understanding this, designers can adapt their colour schemes to support their overall intention.

People seek visually induced stimulation and relaxation and change their preferences over short periods of time. A landscape designer might choose to support these preferences by mixing tints with saturated colours and using complementary colours to make their colour compositions more vivid and arresting, thus producing both relaxation and arousal within a single composition, as illustrated in Figures 7.6 and 7.7, or they might seek to create a setting for a particular type of mood or experience throughout a particular landscape or in different sub-areas of that landscape.

Colour systems

Humans have attempted to communicate their understanding of colour relationships and provide guidance in the development of colour harmonies by creating colour order systems. Colour wheels, or systems, are similar to musical systems in that they prescribe harmonies and discords. Yet, just as in the musical systems, the arrangement of the notes or colours and the separations between them determine the harmony, dissonance and beauty of the final composition (Arnheim, 1965). Any mix of colours can be made to harmonise (Doyle, 2007), and all aspects of colour—hue, value, saturation, brilliance, distance between the colours, and the proportion and arrangement of each colour in the composition—can contribute to a sense of harmony. Different colour harmonies can engage, intrigue, calm, please, stimulate and evoke a particular mood or feeling (Mahnke, 1996; Walters et al., 1982).

Goethe's contribution of completing colours and the six-hued colour wheel—or the colour circle, as it is sometimes called—has had a lasting influence on art and design (Holtzschue, 2011). On the colour wheel, the hues are arranged in a circle in the same order of wavelength as they occur in nature. The colours that cannot be reduced into component colours, or what we call the primary colours of red, blue and yellow, are arranged in a triad. Equidistant between these are the secondary colours that can be produced by mixing any two primary colours: Orange, purple and green. These are the primary colours and their complements. On either side of the secondary colours are the hues that can be created by mixing a primary colour and its adjacent secondary colour, for example, yellow + orange = yellow-orange. These intermediate colours (yellow-orange, red-orange, red-violet, blue-violet, blue-green and yellow-green) are visually equidistant points between a primary and a secondary hue. The colour wheel or colour circle shown in Figure 7.9 has been developed to assist in understanding colour relationships like simultaneous contrast, and colour schemes derived from the relationships illustrated on the colour wheel are considered harmonious and thus to be preferred.

Colour harmonies

Harmony results from two or more things occurring together being perceived as complementary or pleasing. In architecture, design and music, the arrangement and proportions of the parts creates the overall sense of harmony. A colour harmony is the pleasing joining of two or more colours in a composition.

In Figure 7.9, we can see that the longer-wavelength or warm colours are located on the right side of the colour wheel and the cool colours are opposite. Although green is here treated as a cool colour, it can be used with both warm and cool colour schemes because it is a mixture of cool blue and warm yellow.

Most designers use colour intuitively to create a certain mood or visual effect. An understanding of colour harmonies can help to evaluate, refine and improve intuitively derived colour schemes and can suggest alternative colour compositions. However, there are so many variables acting simultaneously in creating colour harmonies that rigid adherence to rules of colour

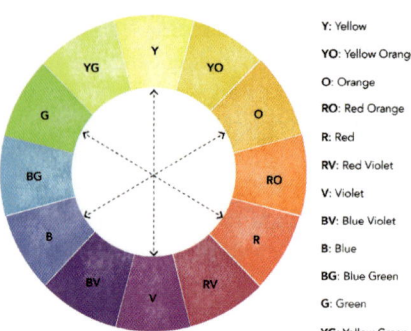

◀ Figure 7.9

The colour wheel.
Source: Image courtesy of Yiwen Ruan.

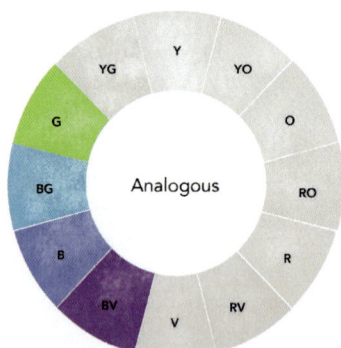

◀ Figure 7.10

The analogous colour scheme.
Source: Image courtesy of Yiwen Ruan.

composition can limit the designer's creative expression, range of considerations and experimentation. While colour systems can inform and suggest, the final arbitrator of the colour composition must be the informed artistic judgement of the designer. Some of the basic colour harmonies used by artists and designers are discussed below for the readers' consideration and thoughtful use.

The analogous colour scheme

Analogous colours are adjacent on the colour wheel and are bounded by a primary and secondary colour, such as blue, blue-green and green. Designers often employ expanded analogous colour schemes that are simply colours that are side by side on the colour wheel. To create such an expanded analogous colour scheme, select one hue that will dominate the picture plane. To this dominant colour, add three or more adjacent colours on either side of this colour on the colour wheel. If blue were the dominant colour chosen, a classic analogous colour scheme would consist of blue, blue-green and green. Adding blue-violet would produce an expanded analogous colour scheme. In this colour scheme, the colours that are furthest apart from each other on the colour wheel are green and blue-violet. Because these colours have blue in common, they will harmonise (Figure 7.10).

The harmony provided by analogous colour schemes was first discovered by Chevreul. He maintained that people found combinations of colours of the same or similar hues that differed in lightness to be most harmonious. There is some empirical evidence for this view. Research subjects thought that analogous colours went together more or were more harmonious than other colour combinations. Within all analogous colour schemes, they considered cool colour combinations to be most harmonious, and these harmonies were most preferred (Schloss and Palmer, 2011).

Complementary colour schemes

Complementary colours are found opposite each other on the colour wheel. The complement of each primary colour is the secondary colour comprised of the other two primary colours. The primary colour complements are red and green, yellow and violet, and blue and orange. When placed together, they maximise the vividness of each other. Even when tinted, toned or shaded, all colours retain their complementary relationships. All other opposing colours on the colour wheel are complementary, in that they make each other appear more intense, but to a lesser degree than the primary complementary pairings because all opposite colour pairs on the colour wheel, other than the primary complements, share at least one common hue. For example, red-orange and its complement, blue-green, both contain yellow.

When the primary complementary colours are most saturated, they maximise the vividness of each other and are often used in garden design with that intention. However, this effect can also be jarring. A highly saturated orange meeting a saturated pure blue can seem to vibrate at the edges and will be fatiguing to the eye. By tinting one or both colours, or by reducing the proportion of the picture plane occupied by the more saturated colour, such a combination can be made more harmonious.

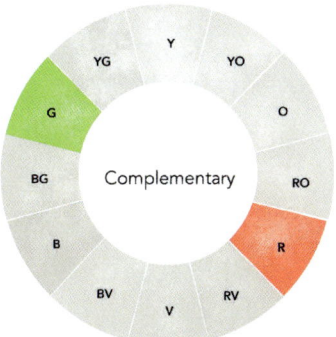

◀ Figure 7.11

The complementary colour scheme.
Source: Image courtesy of Yiwen Ruan.

The split complementary colour scheme

A harmonious colour scheme that is less stimulating than the primary complementary contrast can be achieved by employing a split complementary scheme. This scheme uses a primary colour and the intermediate colours on either side of its complement on the colour wheel. These colours are sometimes termed *near complements*, and, while attractive to the eye, they will be less contrastive and more subtle than a simple complementary scheme. For example, instead of pairing red and green, the designer could choose to combine red with blue-green and yellow-green (Figure 7.12). This might suggest a monochromatic red colour scheme using tints of red with a background of blue-green and yellow-green foliage. Another possibility would be to make use of a ubiquitous background of green foliage with varied tints of red-violet and red-orange foliage and flower colour.

The analogous complementary colour scheme

The analogous complementary colour scheme is a variation on the split complementary scheme that includes two complementary colours and the

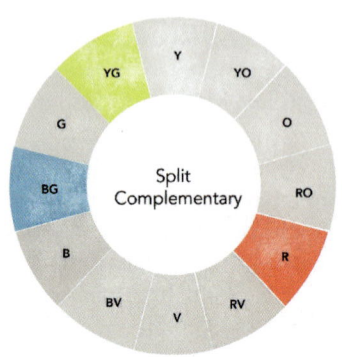

◀ Figure 7.12

The split complementary colour scheme.
Source: Image courtesy of Yiwen Ruan.

◀ Figure 7.13

The analogous complementary colour scheme.
Source: Image courtesy of Yiwen Ruan.

intermediate colours on either side of one of the colours (Figure 7.13). It provides the subtle harmony and smooth transition of colours of the analogous scheme while maintaining the strong simultaneous contrasts of the complementary scheme. In this type of colour scheme, the composition will appear to be more harmonious if the analogous hues dominate the picture plane and the complementary colour is used as an accent. The proportion and saturation of these complementary accents is up to the aesthetic judgement of the designer and is endlessly variable.

The monochromatic colour scheme

A monochromatic colour scheme is one that uses only a single hue. One reason that there are no true monochromatic colour schemes in planting design is that foliage or flower colours are always mixed with the ever-present green foliage. A second reason is that flower colours are rarely pure. The colour in most flowers comes from a group pigments called anthocyanins. These pigments may yield red, purple or blue flowers. Within some plants, the red hues of the anthocyanins are masked to produce a purple or blue flower colour. However, because this masking is imperfect, most red or pink flowers are tinged with blue and most blue flowers are tinged with red. Fewer than 10 per cent of all flowers are actually blue (Lee, 2010).

If we examine the famous red border at Hidcote Manor Garden in Gloucestershire (Figure 7.14), we will very quickly discern that these are not pure reds but a composition of reds, red-oranges and red-violets seen

▼ Figure 7.14

The Red Garden at Hidcote Manor. Source: Dave Catchpole | Flickr (used under the Creative Commons licence).

▲ Figure 7.15

A contemporary watercolour of a border designed by Gertrude Jekyll at Munstead Wood (Elgood and Jekyll, 1904). This "blue" border is actually an analogous scheme. Source: Public domain.

against a near-complementary green foliage. This is the analogous complementary colour scheme shown in Figure 7.13.

Similarly, in a violet colour scheme, the colours are likely to range from red-violet through violet to blue-violet. In a contemporary painting of a "blue" border at Munstead Wood (Figure 7.15), we can see tints of violet, red-violet and red but no true blues at all. Rather than being a monochromatic blue border, this is another example of an analogous scheme.

Although there are many other possible colour schemes, using the analogous and complementary colour schemes and their variations discussed here will enable a planting designer to develop a harmonious colour scheme that supports either restoration, stimulation or a sequence of both.

Figure–ground relationships

Part of Chevreul's law of simultaneous contrasts states that juxtaposing light and dark colours increases their contrasts. Researchers have found that these contrasts increase preference for the colour pairing. Light hues on dark backgrounds and dark or saturated colours on lighter backgrounds, and warmer colours on cooler backgrounds or vice versa are all preferred (Schloss and Palmer, 2011). In placing either warm, saturated hues or pale pastels against the cool dark green of yews and hollies, Jekyll was maximising the contrasts between the foreground flowers and their evergreen backdrop by simultaneously placing light against dark and warm against cool. In doing so she used Chevreul's principles of simultaneous contrast and her own creativity to create colour combinations that modern research has shown to be preferred.

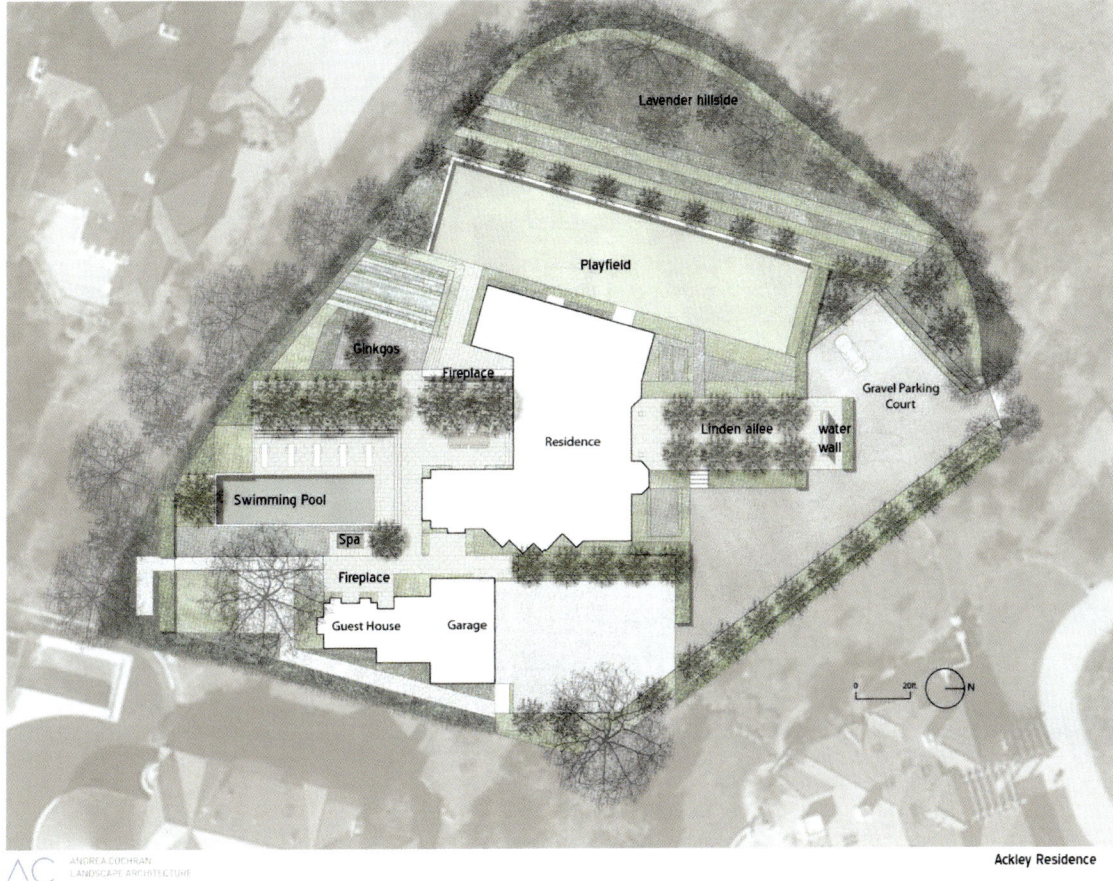

▲ Figure 7.16

Annotated plan of the Ackley Residence. The different areas of the garden are geometrically related to the axes of the residence. The beautifully proportioned entry court with its allée of lindens, the exterior living room adjacent to the fireplace wall in the back yard, the sunken swimming pool and plaza and the formal playfield are visual rhymes that connect house and landscape. Most visual patterns are created by repetitions of forms or colours that are seen at a glance. In the Ackley Residence, the repetition of forms and materials creates an overall pattern that appears sequentially as one moves through the garden.
Source: Courtesy of Andrea Cochran Landscape Architecture.

Case study: Andrea Cochran Landscape Architects

Ackley Residence, Atherton, California: Andrea Cochran Landscape Architecture (ACLA).
ACLA design team members: Andrea Cochran, Principal; Emily Rylander, Senior Associate (2011 Award of Merit, American Society of Landscape Architects).

ACLA's design for the Ackley Residence employs rectilinear forms, axial geometries, refined detailing and massed plantings to unite the home and landscape. Prior to the redesign, the lot, of slightly more than an acre, lacked the ordered connections between house and grounds, connected spaces and sense of mystery that characterise the firm's designs. It consisted of a large circular driveway on the north side of the house and open lawn on the other three sides.

▲ Figure 7.17

In the entry court that connects the residence and parking court, a water wall of charcoal-coloured stone creates a sense of mystery by breaking the line of sight. The sound of its gently falling water entices people through the court on arrival and departure. An allée of Littleleaf linden trees (*Tilia cordata* 'Green Spire') flanked by a double row of boxwood (*Buxus sempervirens*) reinforces the spatial definition of the court.
Source: Photo by Marion Brenner.

While incorporating a new pool, pool house and garage, the landscape architects recognised the need to resolve the irregular angles and forms of the house, and they responded by designing a number of garden rooms that extend the geometries and the adjacent uses of the house (Figure 7.16). Hardscape and plantings combine to reinforce the boundaries and geometries of the new outdoor spaces (Figure 7.17). The large lawn, which required copious amounts of water and served no useful purpose, was reduced to a smaller area for children's play.

The sloped site was graded into a series of terraces, with care to preserve the existing native oaks. Clearing overgrowth and installing an invisible deer fence opened views to the adjacent properties and the foothills of the Santa Cruz mountains, connecting the garden to the seasonal changes of the Californian landscape.

The fireplace wall, in the rear yard, separates adjacent areas that are set at different grades. On the east side, it encloses an outdoor living room that steps down to a sunken pool and plaza, which also acts as a water feature seen from the outdoor living room (Figure 7.18). A row of plane trees, which echoes the allée of lindens in the entry courtyard, connects the outdoor living room and sunken pool. On the west side of the wall, the fan-shaped Ginko Courtyard, off the study, provides a pivot between two different axes of the house (Figure 7.16). Each of these garden rooms provides a distinct view from the interior of the house: The alignment of the pool

▶ Figure 7.18

In the rear yard, the swimming pool doubles as a water feature that is seen from both the indoor and outdoor living rooms. The materials, the forms and the sound of the water in the sunken pool echo the entry court (Figure 7.17).
Source: Photo by Marion Brenner.

▶ Figure 7.19

The various shades of green foliage provide contrast and interest long after the massed lavender has finished blooming. The foliage of the plants establishes a cool analogous colour scheme of blue-green, green and yellow-green—the colour scheme that people consider most harmonious (Schloss and Palmer, 2011). Adding the blue-violet of the lavender flowers creates an expanded analogous scheme from which the true blue hue has been omitted (see Figure 7.9). The masses of lavender, contrasted with the yellow-green of the boxwood, are striking, but because the colours are cool analogous tints, the overall sense of tranquility remains.
Source: Photo by Marion Brenner.

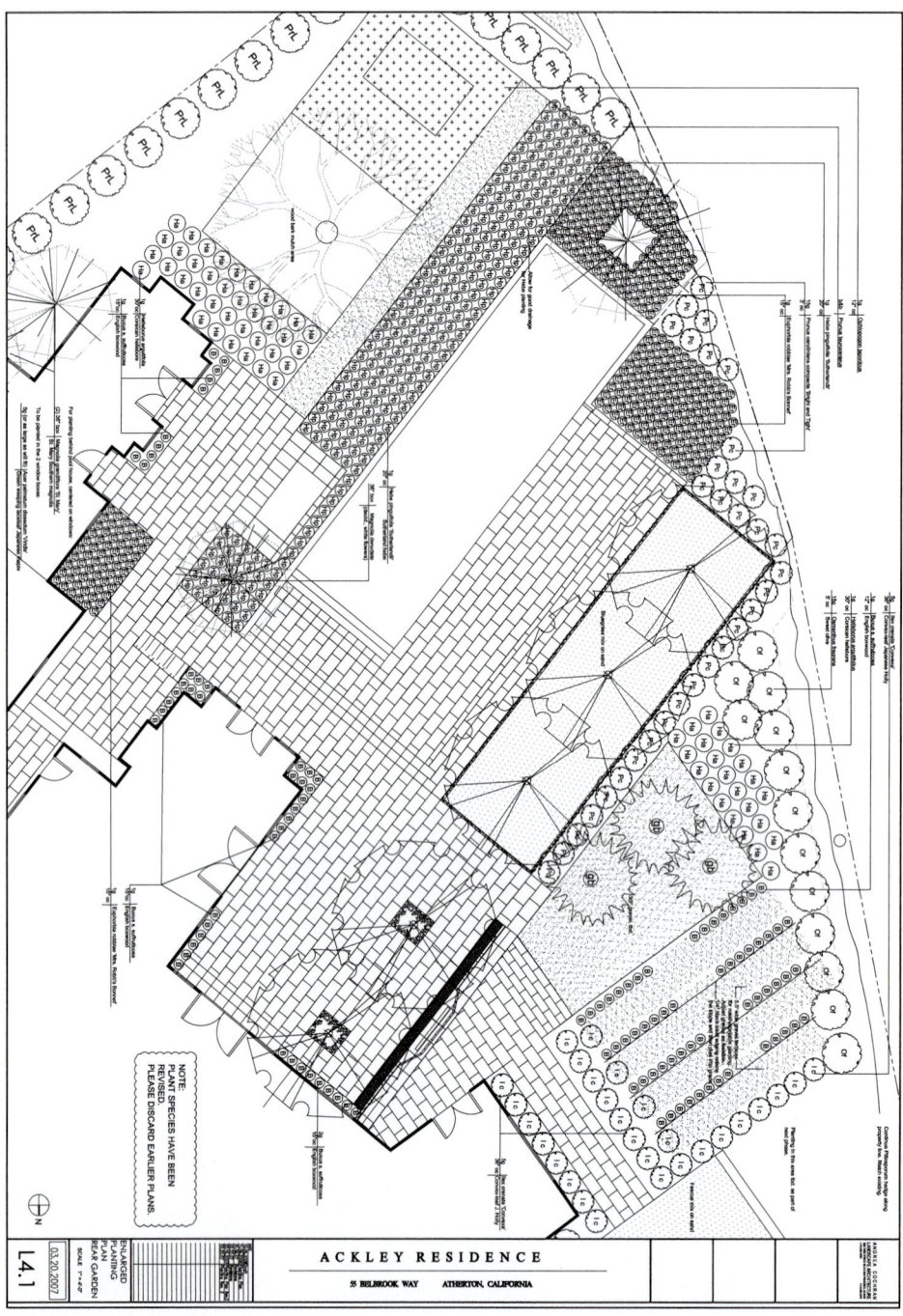

▲ Figure 7.20

Rear yard planting of the Ackley Residence. Much of the sense of unity in this design is due to the massed plantings of shrubs.
Source: Courtesy of Andrea Cochran Landscape Architecture.

TABLE 7.0 Ackley Residence, Atheron, California, plant list by sub-area

Garden Sub-area	Botanic Name	Common Name	Colour
Front Exterior	*Ilex* x *meserveae* 'Blue Maid'	Blue Maid meserve holly	Red fruit
	Ribes viburnifolium	Evergreen currant	Red flower and fruit
	Teucrium fruticans 'Compactum'	Germander	Grey foliage, blue-purple flower
	Euphorbia characias wulfenii	Mediterranean spurge	Blue-green foliage, chartreuse flower
	Ilex vomitoria 'Nana'	Dwarf yaupon holly	Yellow-green foliage changing to green, white flower, red fruit
Courtyard	*Prunus caroliniana* 'Bright and Tight'	Bright and Tight Carolina cherry laurel	Dark green foliage, white flower
	Anemone x *hybrida* 'Honorine Jobert'	Honorine Jobert Japanese *Anemone*	Green foliage, white flower
	Buxus sempervirens suffruticosa	Dwarf English boxwood	Yellow-green foliage
	Viburnum plicatum 'Watanabe'	Watanabe *Viburnum*	Yellow-green foliage, white flower
	Osmanthus fragrans	Tea olive	Green foliage, white flower
	Ribes sanguineum 'Inverness White'	White currant	Green foliage, white flower
	Ribes viburnifolium	Evergreen currant	Green foliage, red fruit and flower
	Olea europea 'Little Ollie'	Dwarf olive	Olive-green foliage
Front Entry	*Tilia cordata* 'Green Spire'	Green Spire littleleaf	Dark green foliage
	Hydrangea paniculata 'Limelight'	Limelight *Hydrangea*	Green foliage, chartreuse flower, matures to pink
	Euphorbia robbiae	Mrs Robb's Bonnet	Dark green foliage, chartreuse flower
	Ilex crenata	Japanese holly	Yellow-green to dark green foliage
	Ilex crenata 'Convexa'	Convex Japanese holly	Yellow-green to dark green foliage
	Buxus sempervirens	English boxwood	Yellow-green foliage

(continued)

TABLE 7.0 (Cont.)

Garden Sub-area	Botanic Name	Common Name	Colour
Hillsides	*Laurus nobilis* 'Saratoga' (standard tree)	Saratoga laurel	Dark green foliage, yellow flower
	Pittosporum tobira 'Wheeler's Dwarf'	Dwarf *Pittosporum*	Yellow-green to dark green foliage, white flower
	Trachelospermum asiaticum	Asiatic star jasmine	Green foliage, white flower
	Lavandula 'Provence'	Provence lavender	Grey-green foliage, blue-purple flower
	Crataegus 'Winter King'	Winter King hawthorn	White flowers, red fruit, pale grey bark
Backyard Pool Garden	*Ginkgo biloba* 'Autumn Gold'	Autumn Gold maidenhair tree	Gold fall colour
	Platanus x *acerifolia* 'Yarwood'	Yarwood plane tree	Yellow-brown fall colour, exfoliating bark
	Magnolia denudata	Yulan *Magnolia* tree	Green foliage, white flower
	Euphorbia robbiae	Mrs Robb's Bonnet	Dark green foliage, chartreuse flower
	Prunus caroliniana 'Bright and Tight'	Bright and Tight Carolina cherry laurel	Dark green foliage, white flower
	Hebe pinguifolia 'Sutherlandii'	Sutherland *Hebe*	Grey-green foliage, white flower
	Ophiopogon japonicus	Mondo grass	Dark green foliage, purple flower
	Helleborus foetidus	Bear's foot hellebore	Green foliage, pink or black flower
	Prunus laurocerasus	English laurel	Yellow-green foliage
Side at Garage	*Lagerstromeia* 'Natchez'	Acoma crape myrtle	Green foliage, white flower
	Nepeta x *fassenii* 'Snowflake'	Snowflake catmint	Grey-green foliage, white flower

Source: Andrea Cochran Landscape Architecture.

creates an axial view from the living room, an informal arrangement of the gingko trees is seen from the study and the children enjoy views of flower and fruit tree terraces from their play room (Andrea Cochran Landscape Architecture, n.d.).

The deliberately narrow plant selection provides a full palette of greens in which the grey-greens of *Hebe* and *Pittosporum*, the rich glossy greens of *Osmanthus* and *Hellebores* and the blue-green and chartreuse of *Euphorbia* are skillfully blended for gradation and interest. Massed plantings of these vivid greens contrast with paving and walls that were fabricated from the same muted grey stone. Within this structure of greens and greys, the seasonal colours of spring *Hellebores*, summer lavenders and *Hydrangeas* give way to the golden autumn tints of the *Gingko* trees and the rich red of hawthorn and holly fruits in winter (O'Keefe, 2014). The massed plantings provide blocks of colour that add a powerful visual energy but do not detract from the overall sense of serenity of the garden (Figures 7.19 and 7.20).

ACLA's design turned the architectural challenges of the site into opportunities to create calming, human-scale spaces that integrate house and site. Tranquil modernist spaces are imbued with a sense of mystery as the views, focal elements, and the sights and sounds of water lead people through the landscape. The design team has created a functional landscape that is highly engaging yet restful and harmonious.

Chapter 7 principles

Mix saturated warm colours with plenty of green.

- Having too many different colours in a composition is a common way to destroy the unity of the landscape composition. In a colour scheme that is intended to be calming, too many colours will over-stimulate. In a highly saturated colour scheme intended to stimulate, multiple colours will be arousing but ultimately visually fatiguing. Warm colours and green can be seen together without requiring the frequent refocusing that leads to visual fatigue (Murch, 1985). Since green commonly makes up the majority of the picture plane in a planting, this backdrop of greens, especially toned greens, lessens the stimulating effect of the warm colours. Using small points of warm, saturated colours against a mostly green backdrop will allow the colours to sing and stimulate without being visually tiring (Figure 7.21).

Let one or two hues dominate.

- However many colours are used in the planting design, no more than one or two hues should dominate. In the early stages of the design, it is wise to determine a specific colour scheme. Once a colour scheme is selected, a few plants will suggest themselves to the designer. This

◀ Figure 7.21

The use of saturated colour in Dan Pearson's gold-medal-winning and Best in Show for the 2015 Chelsea Garden Show, Laurent Perrier Chatsworth Garden. In this view, the red campions and yellow *Rhododendron lutea* blossoms are small points of saturated color in a sea of green foliage. The proportion of green to red and yellow increases simultaneous contrast, making the red especially vivid and tinting the yellow a golden color. These hues command our attention despite the fact that they are but a small proportion of the larger scene. Because warm colours can be seen with green without refocusing the eye, the effect is powerful without becoming visually fatiguing.
Source: Photo courtesy of The Frustrated Gardener.

immediately raises the question: What other plant would be suitable to use with these first plant choices? There will be many considerations other than colour in answering this question. The form and texture of the plant, its horticultural requirements, flowering time and seasonal appearance, and the mood or place that the planting is to evoke must all be taken into consideration. Suppose that two plants, Hidcote lavender (*Lavendula* 'Hidcote') and Russian sage (*Perovskia atriplicifolia*) have inserted themselves into the mind of the designer and are clamouring for inclusion in the proposed planting because they are drought tolerant, their bloom times overlap, they have similar textures, foliage and flower colour, and they provide winter interest. Setting aside considerations other than colour for the moment, the initial choice of these two plants might suggest a blue-violet colour scheme. This might be an analogous blue-violet–violet–red-violet scheme with grey foliage, a split analogous blue-violet–violet-red (pink)–pale-yellow scheme, or simply blue-violet with various greens and greys. After selecting a few other candidate plants, the designer should decide on a colour scheme and then proceed to find the plants to realise it.

Increasing the range of values in a composition without adding more hues increases the contrast and complexity in the scene and will arouse interest without becoming visually "busy". It is usually easy to add a paler or more saturated variety of the same or a different plant, if needed, to achieve the image in the mind's eye. This is an iterative process in which plants, and even the colour scheme, that were initially considered are often discarded by the time the planting design is finished.

Multiple colours will harmonise if they are similar in hue and saturation.

- While it's true that fewer hues will feel more unified and support landscape restoration, there can be no hard and fast rule as to what constitutes "too many colours" in a single composition. Where colours are similar in hue and saturation, a broader range of colours can be used because they will be seen to blend and harmonise (Wolfrom, 1992). Because people prefer colour schemes where the colours are similar in hue and saturation, each section of a planting plan should be similar in saturation (Hobhouse, 1985). Highly contrasting levels of saturation are more visually stimulating and must be mixed with less stimulating sections if visual overstimulation is to be avoided. If more hues are to be added to a colour scheme, using tints of these colours will make the landscape more restorative. The most harmonious analogous colour schemes are those in which the value intervals between the different hues are evenly spaced (Holtzschue, 2011). Such colour schemes can produce a good balance of interest and unity.

Harmonise colours by reducing the value of one of both of the colours, reducing the proportion of one colour to the other or separating them with green or white.

- Recall that when complementary colour combinations like yellow and violet are seen together, they may seem to vibrate, causing the eyes to refocus frequently. This effect is increased if the colours are more saturated, and it is ultimately visually tiring. Separating the complementary colours with another colour or white reduces this effect, as does the use of paler tints or tones of one or both complementary colours (Murch, 1985). This use of value to harmonise colour schemes is especially important in complementary colour schemes.

  It is not necessarily the case that the colour that occupies the largest proportion of the picture plane will be the dominant colour. When even small dollops of highly saturated colours are paired with larger areas of paler tints, the high-contrast saturated colours will draw attention and become the dominant colours of the scheme, while paler tints provide a gentle harmony with the dominant colour. When pairing complementary colours, the one which occupies the larger area of the picture plane or has the fuller saturation will become the dominant colour, and the second should be tinted and/or reduced in area to become a subordinate accent colour.

By reducing the value of the colours, reducing the proportion of the picture plane that they occupy, or separating them with dark-toned greens, grey foliage or white flowers, the colours can be balanced and harmonised.

Use luminosity values to balance colours.

- To achieve a balance between two colours in a composition, they should be apportioned within the picture plane according to their luminosity ratios (De Grandis, 1986). Goethe organised hues in terms of their luminous values as follows: White 10, yellow 9, orange 8, magenta 6, green 5, cyan blue 4, violet 3 and black 0. Since yellow and violet have a luminosity ratio of 9:3, the area of violet should be three times the area of yellow to balance the composition. If the paired colours were blue and orange, the brilliance ratio would be orange 8 to blue 4, or 2:1, and the amount of blue in the composition should be twice that of the orange to balance the composition. Since green and red both have a reflectance value of 6, equal amounts of each hue would balance a composition (Holtzschue, 2011).

    The ratios of two hues that is required for them to balance is predicated on the assumption that the two hues are equally saturated. If the two colours are not equally saturated, the ratio required for them to visually balance will not be the same. For example, in the case of a yellow/violet colour scheme, tinting the violet will increase its luminosity, resulting in less yellow being needed to balance the violet. Most designers do this intuitively. The addition of tinting, toning or saturation makes the ratios necessary to balance any two colours infinitely variable. While these ratios could be calculated by measuring light reflectance, designers and artists use their artistic judgement; nevertheless, it is useful to be aware of the principle of colour luminosity balance.

Use of colour to add depth to a composition.

- Objects in the distance are less distinct and appear bluer than near objects.[6] There are two colour illusions that mimic the visual effects of distance and that can be used to fool the eye into seeing a space as larger than it really is. First, some colours seem to advance while others appear to recede. Saturated oranges and reds will advance the most (see Figure 7.22), while grey-blues, blues, violets and toned greens appear to recede (De Grandis, 1986). By placing warm and more saturated colours nearer the viewer and paler or cooler tints in the background, the apparent depth of the scene will be increased. Additionally, when two colours that are similar in hue and value are seen together, the edges of the two colour masses become indistinct. This effect, known as optical

▲ Figure 7.22

Much of the work of Dutch landscape designer Piet Oudolf has an ethereal quality and sense of depth. Note the saturated red *Persicaria amplexicaulis* in the foreground and the paler, tinted reds in the background.
Source: Photo courtesy of Piet Oudolf.

mixing, occurs most often with hues that are tinted or toned, especially when the two hues are seen from an angle (Wolfrom, 1992). This blending of colours is one of the chief attractions of tinted analogous schemes. In Figure 7.15, the pale tints of violet and red-violet seen in this Gertrude Jekyll "blue border" blend at the edges of coloured flower masses, making the individual plants and colours less distinct.

Increasingly in the work of such artists as Piet Oudolf we get a sense of this particular effect. These landscapes employ Jekyll's technique of using similar hues and values to blend colours, thereby blurring edges to create a sense of distance and an almost an atmospheric effect of misty moodiness. Certainly, foggy mornings and coatings of hoarfrost enhance this sense, but these are merely ephemeral embellishments overlying what the designer has created.

A landscape designer who wished to add depth to a scene might use warm, saturated colours in the foreground and paler tints similar in value in the midground and background to create a sense of depth. The use of paler, cooler colours in the background would increase this impression of blurring and depth.[7]

Use colour to create focal points.

- Recall that when people first look at a scene they scan it for what is different, for what stands out (Tverksy, 2000). Focal points, or landmarks, are elements in the landscape that attract our attention because they stand out from their surroundings in some way. This differentiation from surroundings may be established by contrasting size, position, form and texture and is often a figure–ground relationship. However, because people are so sensitive to colour, focal points are easily established though the use of contrasting colours. Light colours seen against darker colours, saturated colours against toned colours, will attract our attention. The brighter and more saturated the colours and the greater the degree of contrast with the surroundings, the greater will be the attention given to the focal point.

In a designed landscape, focal points must draw attention to what is important, that is, to what supports our purposes. They can guide us to entries and exits, views, rest areas and other significant program elements. In so doing, focal points help people to form cognitive maps and to wayfind, providing a sense of knowing while also stimulating them aesthetically. In this way, focal points in the landscape are compatible because they support the basic human needs to be stimulated and to know. This combination of knowing where one is located and being able to find one's way allows the person in the landscape to relax, while the aesthetic appeal and order of the landscape provided by the focal point increase a person's enjoyment of the landscape.

A design may have more than one focal point. However, where multiple focal points are used, it is important that a hierarchy be established in accordance with the hierarchy of space or use within the design. For example, the main space of the design may contain the major focal point. Throughout the design, multiple focal points of greater or lesser importance attract attention, encourage exploration and support wayfinding. At the lowest level of the hierarchy, a small planting next to a path may act as a focal point and mark an entry point or change in direction (Figure 7.23). Conversely, if multiple focal points of equal weight are used throughout or are seen simultaneously within the same landscape composition, no clear sense of order or direction will be established, and the resulting ambiguity may cause people to choose not to spend time in the landscape.

- In landscape design, focal points seem most often to be created by the placement of an artifact in the landscape. In many instances, built focal points like pergolas and fountains are suitable for major focal points, but when the focal point is lower in the hierarchy, when it wants to draw attention to itself without competing with its surroundings or more prominent focal points, plants are a good choice, as their infinite variety allows the creation of tasteful and subtle contrasts at any level of hierarchy. These lower-level points of interest may change with the seasons or even the time of day.

Use light to emphasise focal plants.

- The effect of standing out from the background is heightened at the times of day when the plant is back-lit or side-lit by the sun. Grasses

▶ Figure 7.23

This small planting at Hidcote Manor is a focal point that stands out from its surroundings, attracts attention and stimulates viewers while marking a change in direction along a path.
Source: Dave Catchpole | Flickr (used under the Creative Commons licence).

▶ Figure 7.24

At Sissinghurst Garden, this copper planter filled with warm-coloured tulips stands out from a contrasting wall and surrounding dark evergreens, making a strong focal point in the landscape.
Source: Esther Westerveld | Flickr (used under the Creative Commons licence, photo cropped).

are especially luminous when lit in this way, as are plants with saturated flower or foliage colour. This increased emphasis can be easily achieved by placing the focal plant so that it will be between the viewer and the sun when the sun is at a low angle (Figure 7.25).

◀ Figure 7.25

Mexican feather grass (*Nassella tenuissima*) and Columbia lily (*Lilium columbianum*) glow in the evening sun. These plant focal points are temporarily enhanced each day by the setting sun. Source: Photo by Patrick Mooney.

Use colour to create transitions.

- Recall that transitions are places where aesthetics, function and/or character change. Transitions modulate change in the landscape, making the users' experience feel seamless and natural rather than fragmented and unexpected. Like the spaces in a landscape, transitions should be hierarchical. Where major change occurs, transitions will be major and may require more space. Where minor change occurs, the transitions can be small, requiring little space.

  Transitions are created by providing a neutral zone that blends with the adjoining landscape rooms while using the properties of neither, or by creating an in-between space that borrows some of the aesthetic characteristics of the two adjoining sub-areas. While they can be generated by using all the aesthetic properties of landscape—materials, spatial enclosure, light, form, texture and colour—let us, for the moment, consider only the use of colour. A change from one landscape space of saturated turquoise, orange and yellow blossoms to one of pale oranges and blues could not go unnoticed. To make such a change feel less abrupt, a transition is needed. One common response is to provide a small space between the two highly coloured spaces that is all green. Such a transition space will blend with the foliage of either room and clash with none of the adjoining colours while being its own distinct space (Figures 7.26 and 7.27). This neutral transition is the easiest and most common transition used in landscape design. A similar transition would be to provide a room of green foliage and white or a pale floral colour as a transition between the two rooms, or even between two plants.

A more complex way to create a visible order between the two colours is by transitioning between them with colours that are a mixture of the two and are evenly stepped in terms of their saturation. Consider, for

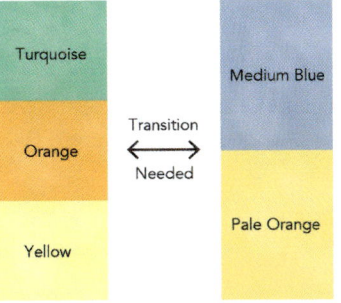 

▶ Figure 7.26

Neutral, restorative green vegetation is commonly used to make a transition between different-coloured outdoor spaces.
Source: Image courtesy of Yiwen Ruan.

▶ Figure 7.27

This simple green passage provides a transition between adjoining spaces.
Source: Esther Westerveld | Flickr (used under the Creative Commons licence, photo cropped).

CHAPTER 7 **Colour**

309

▲ Figure 7.28

This diagram illustrates the principle of transitioning between colours in even steps.
Source: Image courtesy of Yiwen Ruan.

example, a pale orange and a saturated maroon: A transition between these, or any other two colours, can be achieved by placing a series of evenly spaced tints of the two between them (Figure 7.28).

A lack of transition can be used to create a sudden and dramatic change in the landscape experience. When making such colour transitions, the magnitude of the change in the landscape should be reflected in the degree of colour change (Hobhouse, 1985).

Provide sequential seasonal colour interest.

- Even in cold climates, it is important that the designed landscape provide four seasons of interest to help connect people to place and mark the passage of the year.

  At Munstead Wood, Gertrude Jekyll had different garden rooms for different seasons as well as for different colour schemes. In winter, the evergreen hollies, ilexes, yews and woodlands maintained structure and interest. Today it is more frequently the case that a single landscape area must maintain four-season interest. One response is to create plantings that have something in bloom most of the year. However, this approach can result in too little colour or seasonal interest at any time of year.

  In the traditional Japanese garden, the response has been to design for periods of very strong colour at different seasons of the year and a peaceful, green garden in the interim periods. In winter, the garden is a quiet tapestry of reflective sheets of water, of rocks and gravel, and of evergreen pines and broad-leaved evergreen shrubs and groundcovers, glistening in the rain. In spring it awakens with a profusion of pale pink-and-white flowering cherry and azalea blossoms. It then becomes a green garden until the Japanese irises bloom in summer, after which it once again rests until the autumn foliage of the Japanese maples and flowering cherries blaze against the dark evergreens that enclose the garden. This waiting between periods of colour makes the flowering period that much more anticipated and celebrated, as seen in the *Hanami* or flower-viewing celebrations that

▶ Figure 7.29

Many grasses and perennials can provide winter interest. Here, the tawny, late-summer colour of the Mexican feather grass (*Nassella tenuissima*) provides a background to the hot pink of the purple coneflower (*Echinacea purpurea* 'Kim's Knee High') and dried seed heads of meadow sage (*Salvia nemerosa* 'Caradonna'). In winter, the dark seed heads of the coneflower and meadow sage will stand out against the lighter blonde feather grass. Source: Photo by Patrick Mooney.

take place each spring in Japan. It is better to design for sequential periods of colour than to have a weak smattering of colour throughout much of the year.

In a garden that relies on strong seasonal interest followed by periods of green, the foliage carries much of the structure and interest of the garden in the periods between showy foliage and flowers. In such gardens, it is important that the designer be attuned to the various shades of green in plants and the winter colour of grasses and perennials that can provide interest and contrast when nothing is in bloom. Form and texture also have very important roles to play providing interest in the green garden (see Alexander's Crown by ACLA, Chapter 6).

- Another response to having year-round interest in the garden is making coloured foliage the dominant colour interest in the garden. At the extreme, the picture plane becomes dominated by golden, purple and variegated foliage. In such a landscape the sense of rest and restoration provided by green foliage is lost. For this reason, colourful foliage compositions must be used with restraint. In the red border at Hidcote Manor (Figure 7.14), the toned plum-coloured foliage is used in a balanced way with red and red-orange flowers and green foliage. Similarly, pots of highly stimulating coloured foliage and flowers seen against the background of a cool green lawn or hedge can be attractive focal points in the landscape.

- A mixed planting that combines trees and shrubs, perennials, grasses, flowering groundcovers, bulbs and even climbers and annuals to maximise four-season colour interest is another very workable way to provide sequential interest. Small trees, evergreen shrubs and ornamental grasses or persistent perennials provide visual interest and spatial structure throughout the year. Their contribution to the mixed border may be as a background hedge or the repetition of evergreen or grey-foliaged shrubs and sub-shrubs, such as the Mexican orange blossom (*Choisya ternata*) and the sweet box (*Sarcococca*), with lavender (*Lavendula*) and daisy bush (*Brachyglottis greyi*) and with taller ornamental grasses like Chinese silvergrass (*Miscanthus sinensis*) or Scottish tufted hair grass (*Deschampsia cespitosa* 'Schottland').

Within the structure created by woody plants and persistent grasses and perennials, it is quite possible to have two or more distinct colour periods. For example, the spring palette might be comprised of yellow Mediterranean spurge (*Euphorbia characias* subsp. *wulfenii*), Lady's Mantle (*Alchemilla mollis*), white gold *Spiraea* (*Spiraea japonica* 'White Gold') and the dwarf white *Narcissus* (*Narcissus* 'W.P. Milner' under white Mount Fuji flowering cherry (*Prunus serrulata* 'Shirotae'). Some portion of the ground can be covered with prostrate groundcovers like creeping *Phlox* (*Phlox subulata*), Whitley's *Veronica* (*Veronica whitleyi*) or the pale-blue-flowered *Lithodora diffusa* 'Baby Blue'. Under-planting with small bulbs like the white Grecian windflower (*Anemone blanda* 'White Splendour'), the early bulbous *Iris* (*Iris reticulata*) or Glory of the Snow (*Chionodoxa luciliae*) increases early spring interest. These small plants will die back almost imperceptibly. For taller bulbs, like full-sized daffodils, the foliage must be left to yellow and die in order to feed the bulb so that it will naturalise and produce flowers in following years. It is common practice to hide the dying foliage with a plant that grows up later, in front of the early blooming bulb. *Narcissus* is often paired with the later-flowering daylilies, *Hemerocallis*. Late summer and autumn blooming Japanese *Anemones* like *Anemone x hybrida* 'Honorine Jobert' can also be used.

When the pastel spring flowers have finished, a second sequence of warmer analogous colours of red hot poker (*Kniphofia*), montbretia (*Crocosmia*), butterfly plant (*Asclepias tuberosa*), red valerian (*Centranthus ruber*) and long-blooming roses (*Rosa* spp.) can combine with cooler-coloured plants like catmint (*Nepeta*) and blue beard (*Caryopteris*) to provide floral interest from summer into early autumn.

Like the herbaceous border, the mixed border should be planted in repetitive drifts or blocks, and the number of plants of one variety placed together should be dictated by the size of the mass of the plant that the designer wishes and the time allowed for the plants to fill in. Once again, the form, textures and colours of the foliage are most important to achieving a balance of harmony and contrast.

Glossary

Brilliance: See *Luminosity*.

Colour: The perception that people have of reflected light. Different wavelengths of visible light are perceived as being different colours. The appearance of the colour is influenced by its hue, saturation and value.

Colour circle: See *Colour wheel*.

Colour harmony: The impression created when two or more colours seen together are considered to coordinate, or go together, creating a pleasing overall impression.

Colour scheme: A harmonious arrangement of colours.

Colour wheel: An organising diagram in which the hues of the visible light spectrum are arranged in a circle in order of their wavelength, from longest to shortest, and each colour is positioned opposite its complementary colour. It is used to maintain a visual image of possible colour schemes.

Completing colour: See *Complementary colour*.

Complementary colour: Visible light contains all visible colours. Any object absorbs some wavelengths (colours) and reflects the wavelengths of the remaining (the possible colours). For example, a red object reflects red and absorbs yellow and blue wavelengths. The complementary colour of any other colour is the mix of all wavelengths of light that are absorbed when that colour is seen.

Cool colour: Blue is the basic hue from which the cool colours of blue, violet and indigo are derived. Cool colours are shorter in wavelength than warm colours and are sometimes referred to as short-wavelength colours.

Drifts: This term was first used by Gertrude Jekyll to define her manner of planting perennial flower beds. Drifts are multiple plants of the same kind, arranged in long, narrow masses. When drift plantings are viewed obliquely, the effect of layering multiple plants one behind another make the planting more naturalistic because it gives the sense that the plants are intermingled. When the colours of the drifts are similar in saturation and hue, optical mixing occurs at the edges.

Focal point: An element in the landscape that attracts attention because it contrasts aesthetically with its surroundings. Focal points draw attention, stimulate and support aesthetic experience while fostering wayfinding.

Hue: That characteristic by which we can distinguish a colour from other colours, such as blue versus yellow. It is determined by the dominant wavelength of the colour.

Landmark: See *Focal point*.

Law of simultaneous contrast: "In the case where the eye sees at the same time two contiguous colours, they will appear as dissimilar as possible, both in their optical compositing and in the strength of their colour" (Michel Eugène Chevreul, 1987). This principle covers all the possible ways in which two or more colours being seen together will alter their appearance. For example, dark colours seen against light colours will seem darker and vice versa; a cool colour surrounded by a yet cooler colour will appear warmer; two colours seen together will appears as if each is mixed with the complementary colour of the other; saturated colours will add their hue to adjacent light colours; and complementary colours will intensify each other.

Lightness: See *Value*.

Luminosity: A measure of the light reflectance of a hue which results from the wavelength of the hue. Yellow is the nearest to white in wavelength and so has the highest luminosity, while violet is the nearest to black in wavelength and so has the lowest luminosity.

Optical mixing: Two or more colours that are positioned next to each other will appear to mix so that a colour that is not actually present can appear to be so. For example, if red and blue are placed side by side, purple may appear at the junction of the two colours. This effect helps to unify the colours. Colours that are similar in hue and value, especially when tinted and toned, blend to such a degree that the colour edge can be lost and the mass of the flower drift can become indistinct.

Reversal theory: A theory of colour preference which states that people prefer warm colours when they are in a playful or excited state, or wish they were, and that they prefer cool or toned and tinted colours when they are in a resting, low-arousal mood, or wish to be. The theory further states that the preference for these high- or low-arousal states varies within the period of a day, and that either the high- or low-arousal states are preferred at all times but not an intermediate state.

Saturation: A measure of the colour intensity of a colour. A fully saturated colour would be a pure colour containing no black or white.

Shade: A colour to which black has been added.

Tint: A colour to which white has been added. It appears lighter than a saturated colour.

Tone: A colour to which some mixture of both black and white has been added.

Transitions: Places where aesthetics, function and/or character change. Their purpose is to modulate change in the landscape so that the users' experience feels seamless and natural rather than fragmented and unexpected.

Value: The darkness or lightness of a colour. A high-value colour is light and has a lot of white in it. A low-value colour is seen as dark because it has black mixed with it. Mid-value colours contain a mixture of both white and black.

Visible light spectrum: Light that people can see. On the electromagnetic spectrum, the visible light spectrum lies between ultraviolet and infra-red light.

Warm colours: Red and yellow and any colour derived from mixing these colours, such as orange and red-orange, are referred to as warm colours. These colours are also termed long-wavelength colours because they have the longest wavelength of any colours in the visible light spectrum.

Notes

1. The reader will note that the term *brightness* is used for both value, or the amount of black or white in a colour, and for its brilliance, or the luminosity that results from its wavelength. These are quite separate concepts. To make the distinction I will use the terms tint, shade or tone to refer to the value of a hue and brilliance or luminosity to refer to the inherent light reflectance of a hue.
2. A nanometre is about one billionth of a metre.
3. The colours of visible light, listed from longest to shortest in wavelength, are red (780 to 622 nm), orange (622 to 597 nm), yellow (597 to 577 nm), green (577 to 492 nm), blue (492 to 455 nm) and violet (455 to 390 nm) (Figure 7.3). Colours like magenta and purple are not found in the visible light spectrum, as they are only formed through the mixing of separate wavelengths of light.
4. Research has shown that a small number of coherent areas, that is, areas having a similarity of plant species or function, encourage exploration because they make a place easier to understand (R. Kaplan et al., 1998). From the above quote, it seems that Gertrude Jekyll intuitively understood this in 1908.
5. Further research is needed until more commonality in conclusions is found. Until then, readers of the scientific literature will need to use their own judgement in assessing the validity of the reported results (Mikellides, 2012). I have reported here what appear to me to be the most well-founded research results on colour preference and response.
6. This bluing effect of distance occurs because blue light is scattered by molecules in the Earth's atmosphere.
7. The previous chapter discussed the use of texture to enhance the perception of depth. Here, the ways in which colour can be used to enhance a sense of depth are discussed separately. A planting designer could employ these devices together to achieve maximum effect.

References

Abramov, I., Gordon, J., Feldman, O., & Chavarga, A. (2012a). Sex and vision II: Color appearance of monochromatic lights. *Biology of Sex Differences*, 3(1), 2.

Abramov, I., Gordon, J., Feldman, O., & Chavarga, A. (2012b). Sex and vision I: Spatio-temporal resolution. *Biology of Sex Differences*, 3(1), 20.

Andrea Cochran Landscape Architecture. (n.d.). *Ackley Garden description*. Personal correspondence, March 28, 2018. Unpublished.

Arnheim, R. (1965). *Art and visual perception: A psychology of the creative eye*. Oakland, CA: University of California Press.

Arriaza, M., Cañas-Ortega, J.F., Cañas-Madueño, J.A., & Ruiz-Aviles, P. (2004). Assessing the visual quality of rural landscapes. *Landscape and Urban Planning*, 69(1), 115–125.

Birren, F. (1978). *Color psychology and color therapy: A factual study of the influence of color on human life*. Secaucus, NJ: Citadel Press.

Bisgrove, R. (2006). The colour of creation: Gertrude Jekyll and the art of flowers. *Journal of Experimental Botany*, 64(18), 5783–5789.

Briggs, D. (2013). *The dimensions of color*. Accessed July 30, 2019 at www.huevaluechroma.com.

Capó-Aponte, J., Temme, L., Task, H., Pinkus, A., Kalich, M., Pantle, A., & Rash, C. (2009). Visual perception and cognitive performance. In C.E. Rash, M.B. Russo, T.R. Letowski, & E.T. Schmeisser (Eds.), *Helmet-mounted displays: Sensation, perception and cognitive issues* (pp. 335–390). Fort Rucker, AL: US Army Aeromedical Research Laboratory.

Chevreul, M.E., (1987) *The principles of harmony and contrast of colours and their application to the arts*. West Chester, PA: Schiffer Publishing Ltd.

Cullen, G. (1961). *The concise townscape*. London: Architectural Press.

De Grandis, L. (1986). *Theory and use of color*. New York: Abrams.

Doyle, M.E. (2007). *Color drawing* (3rd ed.). New York: Van Nostrand Reinhold Company.

Elgood, G., & Jekyll, G. (1904). *Some English gardens* (2nd ed.). London: Longmans & Green.

Eysenck, H.J. (1941). A critical and experimental study of colour preferences. *The American Journal of Psychology*, 54(3), 385–394.

Hilbert, D.R. (1987). *Color and color perception: A study in anthropocentric realism*. Stanford, CA: Stanford University: Center for the Study of Language and Information.CSLI, Stanford.

Hobhouse, P. (1985). *Color in your garden*. Boston, MA: Little, Brown.

Holtzschue, L. (2011). *Understanding color: An introduction for designers*. Hoboken, NJ: John Wiley & Sons.

Hurlbert, A., & Ling, Y. (2012). Understanding colour perception and preference. In J. Best (Ed.), *Colour design: Theories and applications* (pp. 129–157). Duxford: Woodhead Publishing.

Janssens, J. (2001). Facade colors, not just a matter of personal taste: Psychological account of preferences for exterior building colors. *Nordic Journal of Architectural Research*, 14(2), 17–21.

Jekyll, G. (1908). *Colour in the flower garden*. London: Country Life Ltd.

Kaplan, R. (2007). Employees' reactions to nearby nature at their workplace: The wild and the tame. *Landscape and Urban Planning*, 82(1), 17–24.

Kaplan, R., Kaplan, S., & Ryan, R. (1998). *With people in mind: Design and management of everyday nature*. Washington, DC: Island Press.

Kaya, N., & Epps, H.H. (2004). Color-emotion associations: Past experience and personal preference. In J.L. Caivano and H.P. Struck (Eds.), *AIC 2004 Color and paints: Proceedings of the interim meeting of the International Color Association* (Vol. 5) (pp. 31–34). Porto Alegre: Associacão Brasileira da Cor.

Küller, R. (1980). Architecture and emotions. In B. Mikellides (Ed.), *Architecture for people: Explorations in a new humane environment* (pp. 87–100). London: Studio Vista.

Lee, D. (2010). *Nature's palette: The science of plant color*. Chicago, IL: University of Chicago Press.

Lichtenfeld, S., Elliot, A.J., Maier, M.A., & Pekrun, R. (2012). Fertile green: Green facilitates creative performance. *Personality and Social Psychology Bulletin*, 38(6), 784–797.

Litman, J. (2005). Curiosity and the pleasures of learning: Wanting and liking new information. *Cognition & Emotion*, 19(6), 793–814.

Mahnke, F. (1996). *Color, environment, and human response*. Detroit, MI: Van Nostrand Reinhold.

Manav, B. (2007). Color-emotion associations and color preferences: A case study for residences. *Color Research & Application*, 32(2), 144–150.

Mikellides, B. (2012). Colour psychology: The emotional effects of colour perception. In J. Best (Ed.), *Colour design: Theories and applications* (pp. 105–128). Duxford: Woodhead Publishing.

Munstead Wood. (n.d.). Accessed June 9, 2016 at www.munsteadwood.org.uk.

Murch, G.M. (1985, June). Colour graphics: Blessing or ballyhoo? In *Computer graphics forum* (Vol. 4, No. 2) (pp. 127–135). Oxford, UK: Blackwell Publishing Ltd.

Newton, I. (1671). *A Letter of Mr. Isaac Newton, Professor of the Mathematicks in the University of Cambridge; containing his new theory about light and colors: Sent by the author to the publisher from Cambridge, febr. 6. 1671/72; in order to be communicated to the Royal Society*. Philosophical transactions (1665–1678), 3075–3087. Accessed June 10, 2016 at www.jstor.org/stable/101125?seq=1#page_scan_tab_contents.

O'Keefe, L. (2014, May). Andrea Cochran coaxes the grounds of an Atherton property into a sublime formal garden. San Francisco Cottages and Gardens. Accessed August 28, 2018 at www.cottages-gardens.com/San-Francisco-Cottages-Gardens/May-2014/Andrea-Cochran-2014-Cooper-Hewitt-Design-Award-for-Landscape-Architecture-Atherton-Formal-Garden/.

Palmer, S.E., & Schloss, K.B. (2015). *Color preference*. Accessed June 10, 2015 at https://scholar.google.ca/scholar?hl=en&q=One+of+the+most+fascinating+aspects+of+the+perception+of+colors+is+that+people+have+relatively+strong+preferences%2C+liking+certain+colors+and+color+combinations+much+more+than+others.+++Below+we+will+discuss+what+is+known+about+human+color+preferences%2C+not+&btnG=&as_sdt=1%2C5&as_sdtp=.

Polat, A.T., & Akay, A. (2015). Relationships between the visual preferences of urban recreation area users and various landscape design elements. *Urban Forestry & Urban Greening*, 14(3), 573–582.

Regan, B.C., Julliot, C., Simmen, B., Vienot, F., Charles–Dominique, P., & Mollon, J.D. (2001). Fruits, foliage and the evolution of primate colour vision. *Philosophical Transactions of the Royal Society B: Biological Sciences*, 356(1407), 229–283.

Roque, G. (2011). Chevreul's colour theory and its consequences for artists. *The Colour Group* (Great Britain). Accessed September 5, 2015 at www.colour.org.uk/%5C/Chevreuls%20Law%20F1%20web%20good.pdf.

Saito, M. (1996). Comparative studies on color preference in Japan and other Asian regions, with special emphasis on the preference for white. *Color Research & Application*, 21(1), 35–49.

Schaie, K.W. (1961). A Q-sort study of color-mood association. *Journal of Projective Techniques*, 25(3), 341–346.

Schauss, A.G. (1979). Tranquilizing effect of color reduces aggressive behavior and potential violence. *Journal of Orthomolecular Psychiatry*, 8(4), 218–221.

Schloss, K.B., & Palmer, S.E. (2011). Aesthetic response to color combinations: Preference, harmony, and similarity. *Attention, Perception, & Psychophysics*, 73(2), 551–571.

Seamon, D. (1998). *Goethe, nature and phenomenology: An introduction in Goethe's way of science: A phenomenology of nature* (pp. 1–14). Albany, NY: SUNY Press. Accessed June 9, 2016 at www.sunypress.edu/pdf/53817.pdf.

Simmons, D.R. (2006). The association of colors with emotions: A systematic approach. *Journal of Vision*, 6(6), 251–251.

Sivik, L. (1974). *Color meaning and perceptual color dimensions: A study of color samples*. Gothenburg: Gothenburg University, Department of Psychology.

Smets, G. (1982). A tool for measuring relative effects of hue, brightness and saturation on color pleasantness. *Perceptual and Motor Skills*, 55(3f), 1159–1164.

Sumner, P., & Mollon, J.D. (2003). Colors of primate pelage and skin: Objective assessment of conspicuousness. *American Journal of Primatology*, 59(2), 67–91.

Tverksy, B. (2000). Levels and structure of spatial knowledge. In R. Kitchin & S. Freundschuh (Eds.), *Cognitive mapping: Past, present, and future* (Vol. 4) (pp. 24–43). London: Routledge.

Valdez, P., & Mehrabian, A. (1994). Effects of color on emotions. *Journal of Experimental Psychology: General*, 123(4), 394.

Walters, J., Apter, M.J., & Svebak, S. (1982). Color preference, arousal, and the theory of psychological reversals. *Motivation and Emotion*, 6(3), 193–215.

Wexner, L.B. (1954). The degree to which colors (hues) are associated with mood-tones. *Journal of Applied Psychology*, 38(6), 432.

Wolfrom, J. (1992). *The magical effects of color*. Lafayette, CA: C&T Publishing Inc.

Wright, B., & Rainwater, L. (1962). The meanings of color. *Journal of General Psychology*, 67(1), 89–99.

Additional reading

Hobhouse, P. (1985). *Color in your garden*. Boston, MA: Little, Brown.

Jekyll, G. (1908). *Colour in the flower garden*. Country Life Ltd.

Schloss, K.B., & Palmer, S.E. (2011). Aesthetic response to color combinations: Preference, harmony, and similarity. *Attention, Perception, & Psychophysics*, 73(2), 551–571.

Index

Note: Page references in **bold** refer to glossary entries.

acequias 116, 118, **145**
adsorption 75, **89**
affordance 11–13, 16, 17 19, 20, **25**, 41, 53
Alexander's Crown, Andrea Cochran Landscape Architecture 217–219
Appleton, Jay 10, 11, 23
aquifers 113, 118, 125, **145**
architectural plant forms 195–202
arroyos 117, 123, **145**
asymmetrical balance 42, 225, 226, 231, 235, **267**
attention restoration theory 33–35, 38, **61**

balance 42, 224–235, 266
barriers 199, **208**
being away 38–40, 45, 48, 56–57, 59, **61**, 119, 120
biodiversity 100, 103–105, 128–130, **145–146**, 217, 255, 259, 265
biological oxygen demand 126, **146**
biomass 104, 129, **146**
biome 85, **89**, 143
biophilia 9, 10, **26**, 120
bioproductivity 129, **146**
bioswales 104, 126, 128, 145, **146**
biotic succession 227, 261, 264, **268**
block planting 236, 240, 242, 248–250, **268**
borrowed view 176–177, **208**
bosque 171, 181, 184, 185, 201, 202, **208**
brilliance *see* luminosity
Bryant Park, Hanna Olin 201–202, 216

canopy 170, 195–197, 202, 204, **208**
carbon nitrogen ratio 76, **89**
cation exchange capacity 75, 78, **89**
Charlie Mountain Ranch, Design Workshop Inc. 134–139, 190–192
Children's Garden, Andrea Cochran Landscape Architecture 55–56
cloister garden 5
cognitive map 13, 18, **26**, 49–54, **61**, 173

Cochran, Andrea 164–165
coherence 14, 15, 16, 23, 25, **26**, 56, 60, 224, **268**
colour 265–267, 275–282; harmony 280–281, 289–291, 303; scheme 278, 282, 289, 290–294; wheel 280, 289, **312**; *see also* complementary colours; completing colours; cool colours; warm colours
compatibility 38, 42, 49, 57, 59, **61**, 122; compatible landscapes 42, 49, **61**
complementary colours 280, 281, 283–285, 288, 291, 292–294, 303, **313**
completing colours 281, 298, **313**
complexity 14–16, 22–26, 51, 56, 120, 215, 236, 247, 249, 250, 253, 262, 263, **268**, 303
continuity 6, 181, 207, 218, 233–235, 265, **268**
cool colours 278, 284, 287, 288, 289, 291, **313**
cubist space 162–163, 172, **208**
curiosity models 18–20, **26**; curiosity-driven curiosity models 18–20, 23, **26**, 54, 288

defensible space 159–160, **208**
density 214, 215, 226, 231, 232, **268**
design process 94, 135, **146**, 164
design program 94, 95, 98, 105, 112, 144–146, 156, 165, 166, 170, 173, 195, 202, 204, 216
Design Workshop Inc. 134–135
designed landscape **26**
directed attention 32–35, 38, 39, 42, **61**
districts 50, 51, **61**
drifts 106, 168, 169, 190, 191, 236, 240, 247, 253, 264, **268**, 283, 312, **313**
duration 33, 35, 37, 58, **61**
Dutch Wave Movement *see* New Perennial Movement

ecological infrastructure 95, 96, 98, 99, **146**
ecological restoration **89**, 131–139, 145, **146**

ecological succession *see* biotic succession
ecosystems 89; ecosystem services 95, 96, 98, 100, 102–105, 123–124, 129, 130, 144, 145, **146**, 237, 261
edges 51, 53, **62**, 120
Egyptian gardens 1–2
elements of design 213–215, 222, 266–268
environmental gradients 86, 87, **89**, 131, 132, **146**
exploration 11, 13–17, 19, 22, **26**, 35, 36, 40, 41, 42, 48, 49, 51, 59, 60, 144, 160, 163, 288, 306, 315
extent 38, 40–42, 43, 46, 48, 56–57, 59, **62**, 119, 120, 121, 176, 194, 198, 201, 222

fascination 38–39, 48, 56–58, **62**, 119–120, 122
field capacity 78, **89**
figure–ground 220–221, 223, 249, **268**
filtered view 199, **209**
focal points 196, 198, 203, 204, 216, 218, 219, 221, 222, 267, **268**, 305–308, 311, **313**
forbs 248, **268**
form 170, **209**, 213–214, 216–219
formation *see* biome
framed view 50 180, **209**
frequency 33, 37, 58, **62**

genius loci 183, **209**
Gestalt theory 165, 215–216, 233, **269**
gradation 221, 222, 224, 249, 267, **269**, 301
Grecian landscapes 2
Green Acre Park, Sasaki, Dawson & Demay 181–188
green infrastructure *see* ecological infrastructure
green roofs 112, 126, 128–129, **147**, 155
greenness 37
groundcovers 114, 129, 180, 198, **209**

habitat 12, 96, 98, 100–112, 114, 124, 125, 126, 128, 129–136, 138, 145, **147**, 247, 259, 261, 263, 265
harmony 169, 208, 218, 221–222, 266, **269**, 280, 289–294, 303
Hartlage, Richard 202
hazard 10–11, **26**
hierarchy 120, 122, 169, 174, 181, 194, 195, 219, **209**, 270, 306

The High Line, Field Operations and Piet Oudolf 256–261
hue 276, 277, **313**
human-scale space 157, 170, 171, 194, 195, 202, 204, 208, **209**, 301
humus 76, 78, **90**
hunter-gatherers 9, 10, 52, 53

information processing model 2–14, 20, 23, 24, 26
interflow **90**
intimate scale spaces 171, 194, **209**
invasive plants 103, 115, 124–125, 134, 145, **147**
involuntary attention 32, 33, 38, 39, **62**
involvement 13–15, 17–18, **27**, 36–38, 51, 58–59, 156, 161

juxtaposition 184, 223, 235, 267, 269

Kaplan, Steven and Rachel 11–12
knowledge seeking model 11–12, 18, 19, 20, **27**, 54, 213, 288

landmark 12, 50, 51, 52, 53, 60, **62**, 122, 159, 173–176, 181, 212, 217
landscape **27**, **90**; landscape character 40, 138, 174, 175, 177, 182, 184, 204, **209**
law of simultaneous contrast 286, 280, 281, 282, 284, 286, **314**
legibility 14, 16, 17, 21, 23, 24, 26, **27**, 41, 48, 51, 53, 60, 121, 122, 136, 216
lightness *see* value
line 213, 214, 223, 224, 233–234, 236, 267, **269**
luminosity 277, 304, **314**
Lurie Garden, Gustafson Guthrie Nichol Ltd. and Piet Oudolf 248–255, 260

macronutrients 72–75, **90**
maintenance 260
Masuno, Shunmyo 44
mass 213, 214, 217, 218, 224–235, 266, 267, **269**
massed planting 98, 170, 188, 190, 191, 216, 234, 236, **269**, 295, 297, 301
matrix 173–174, 182, 188, **209**
matrix planting 242, 248, 249, 250, 253, 255, 258, 262, 264, 265, 267, **269**
micronutrients 75, **90**
Millennium Garden, Pensthorpe, Piet Oudolf 248–249
Minghu Wetland Park, Turenscape 98–101
Mountsier Estate, Land Morphology 202–203

monumental scale 171, 172, 194, 209
mulch 80, 82–83, 88, **90**, 115, 166, 168, 260
mystery 14, 17, 18, 21, 23, 24, **27**, 47, 48, 119, 162, 163, 175, 176, 180, 192, 200, 201, 249, 295, 296, 301

native plants 45, **90**, 111, 114–115, 127, 144, 188, 191, 257
natural **27**; natural content **27**; natural landscapes 12, 23, 24, **27**, 42, 57, 87, 105, 119, 121, 122, 182–192, 244, 245, 247, 262, 264
naturalisation 168, 257, **269**, 312
naturalistic landscapes 112, 143, 185, 240, 243, 261, **269**
negative space 157, 160, 161, 162, 173, 201, 208, **209**
New Perennial Movement 243, **270**, 271
New Wave Movement *see* New Perennial Movement
nodes 50, 51, 60, **62**, 98

Olmsted, Frederick Law 7
optical mixing 304–305, 313, **314**
optimal arousal model 19, 27
order 215, 222, 224, 225, 233, 236, 247, 250, 251, 253, 255, 267, **270**
Oudolf Piet 242–248, 261–265

paradise garden 1–5, 8
parent material 67, 68, 69, 70, 73, **90**
parks 3, 6, 7, 8, 96, 105, 107, 112, 201, 202
patches 106, 107, 108, 111, 173, **209**
paths 5, 13, 17, 18, 41, 49, 51, 60, 62, 174–179, 208, **209**
pattern 15, 21, 22, 23, 25, 47, 53–56, 60–61, **62**, 247–248, 250, 251, 265, 284, 295
peat 81–82, **90**
perception **27**, 215, 216, 219, 247, **270**
permanent wilting point 78, 79, **90**
Persian gardens 3, 4
pH 70–72, 73, 75, 76, 81, 83–84, 88, **90**
picture plane 14, 15, 16, **270**
places 172–173, **210**
plant association 85, 86, 87, **90**, 103, 131, 134, 144, 204, 246, 263
plant community 68, 85–88, **90**
plant hardiness 85–86, **90**; plant hardiness zone 85–86, **91**
pleasure-seeking model *see* optimal arousal model
pollinator habitat 105–112

positive space 157–159, 160–161, 195, 196–197, 202–203, **210**
Potter's Field, Piet Oudolf 249–250
preference 12–18, 23; preference matrix 14–15
primary productivity 104, 129
prospect 10, 11, 24, **28**; prospect refuge theory 10, 11
psycho-evolutionary perspective 8, 9

Quarry House, Design Workshop Inc. 187–189

rain gardens 126–128
Redekop, Melody 105
refuge 10, 11, 24, **28**
regionally appropriate plants 115, 144, 145, **147**
restoration 32, 33
restorationists 131, 132, **147**
restorative environments *see* restorative landscapes
restorative landscapes 32–66, 45, 48–49, 56–57, 59, **62**
reversal theory 287, 288, **314**
Roman villa 2–3
romantic gardens 5–6
romanticism 6, 7, **28**
route *see* paths
ruderal landscape 258, **270**
runoff *see* stormwater runoff

Samukawa Shrine, Japan Landscape Consultants Ltd. 45–49
saturation 276, 284, 286, 303–304, 309, **314**
scale 170–172
screens 195, 198, 199, 204, 205, **210**
scrim 195, 198, 199, 200, 201–202, 204, 205, **210**
sequential experience 20–23
sequential view 174, 175, 176, 179, **210**
shade 276, 277, **314**
shakkei *see* borrowed view
shape 213, 214, 223, 230, 267, **270**
simple structures 165, 215, 216, 220, **270**
Snake River Residence, Design Workshop Inc. 183–186
soft fascination 38, 39, 62
soil 67–70, **91**
soil aggregates 78, 80, **91**
soil colour 76
soil horizons 68, 69, **91**
soil profile 68–70, **91**

.ture 76–78, **91**
...ies/habitat models 131–132, **147**
...ormwater 98, 105, 117, 118, 123, 125, 126, **147**
stormwater runoff 113, 117, 123, 125, 126, **147**
Stone Edge Farm, Andrea Cochran Landscape Architecture 165–170
Stravinsky, Igor 20, 21
stress recovery theory 32, 33, 34, 35, **63**
subdivided view 179, 180, **210**
supra-human scale see monumental scale
symmetrical balance 224, 225, 226, **270**

Ten Eyck, Christine 116
texture 15, 25, 47, 56, 167, 168, 169, 198, 214, 215, 216–219, 221, 222, 246, 247, 263, 265, 267, **270**
tint 276, 286, 287, 288, 303, 304, 305, 310, **314**
tone 276, 284, 287, 301, 303, 304, 305, 311, **314**
topdressing 80, 83, 88, **91**
transitions 53, 157, 177, 181–192, 204, 205, 206, **210**, 222, 250, 284, 309, 310
tree density 199, 201

Ulrich, Roger 33, 34
understanding 13, 14, **28**
unity 144, 168, 169, 170, 215, 216–219, 220, 221–222, 236, 246–247, 250, 262–267, **270–271**, 282, 298, 301

University of Texas at El Paso (UTEP) Campus Transformation Project, Ten Eyck Landscape Architects Inc. 116–124
urban heat island 114, 128, **147**

value 276, 283, 303–305, **315**
variety 215, 217, 248, 249, 268
visible light spectrum 277, 279, **315**
visual array see picture plane
visual composition 215, 225, 226, 271
visual penetrability 195, 199, 201, 208, **210**
visual weight 214, 224, 225, 226, 229–231, 232, 266, **271**, 284
voluntary attention see directed attention

warm colours 278, 284, 287–288, 289, 301, **315**
watershed 118, 125, 126, 128, **147**
wayfinding 13, 32, 49–52, 53, 59, 60, **63**, 122, 181, 306
Wayne Ferguson Plaza, Design Workshop Inc. 237–241
wild 98, **271**
wild planting 143, 185, 191, 243–247, 257–259, 264
wildflower meadow 111–112, 129, 184–185, 190, 240, 248, 251–255
wildflowers 111–112, 129, 184, 185, 190
wildlife 101, 118, 120, 128, 131, 135, 136, 247
wildness 185, 260

Yu, Kongjian 95–98